365 Yummy Mixer Recipes

(365 Yummy Mixer Recipes - Volume 1)

Mary Traylor

Copyright: Published in the United States by Mary Traylor/ © MARY TRAYLOR

Published on December, 02 2020

All rights reserved. No part of this publication may be reproduced, stored in retrieval system, copied in any form or by any means, electronic, mechanical, photocopying, recording or otherwise transmitted without written permission from the publisher. Please do not participate in or encourage piracy of this material in any way. You must not circulate this book in any format. MARY TRAYLOR does not control or direct users' actions and is not responsible for the information or content shared, harm and/or actions of the book readers.

In accordance with the U.S. Copyright Act of 1976, the scanning, uploading and electronic sharing of any part of this book without the permission of the publisher constitute unlawful piracy and theft of the author's intellectual property. If you would like to use material from the book (other than just simply for reviewing the book), prior permission must be obtained by contacting the author at publishing@crumblerecipes.com

Thank you for your support of the author's rights.

Content

365 AWESOME MIXER RECIPES..............8

1. Aligot Gratin 8
2. Almond Butter Crisps 8
3. Almond Cakes... 9
4. Almond Praline Semifreddo With Grappa Poached Apricots 10
5. Almond Plum Buckle 10
6. Alphabet Cookies 11
7. Anise Sesame Cookies 12
8. Anise Scented Fig And Date Swirls 13
9. Anzacs 13
10. Apple And Blackberry Meringue Souffles 14
11. Apricot Butter Cookies 14
12. Apricot Linzertorte With Quark Whipped Cream 15
13. Apricot Souffles With Vanilla Rum Crème Anglaise 16
14. Asian Potato Latkes 17
15. Bacon Banana Cookies 17
16. Baked Coconut (Cocada De Forno) 18
17. Baked Yams With Cinnamon Chili Butter 18
18. Bakewell Tart 19
19. Banana Chocolate Walnut Cake 20
20. Banana Rum Cream Pie 20
21. Banana Walnut Upside Down Cakes ... 21
22. Banoffee Pie 22
23. Bittersweet Chocolate Irish Whiskey Cake 22
24. Bittersweet Chocolate Soufflé 23
25. Black Bottom Pie................................... 24
26. Black Pepper Biscotti........................... 25
27. Black Sesame Pear Tea Cake............... 25
28. Blinis With Tapioca Caviar, Candied Fruits, Toasted Pecans, And Crème Fraîche 26
29. Blueberry Coffee Cake 27
30. Blueberry Lemon Pound Cake 28
31. Blueberry Pie With Cornmeal Crust And Lemon Cream 28
32. Bobbie Mills's Cinnamon Cake 29
33. Braided Egg Bread 30
34. Brioche 30
35. Brown Butter Almond Torte With Sour Cherry Sauce 31
36. Brown Sugar Buttercream 32
37. Brown Sugar–Ginger Cream Cake 33
38. Brownie Bottom Lemon Cheesecake .. 33
39. Burnt Orange Panna Cotta 34
40. Butter Cake 35
41. Butter Nut Blondies 35
42. Buttermilk Cookies 36
43. Buttermilk Panna Cotta With Berries And Vanilla Sabayon 36
44. Butterscotch Pecan Thins 37
45. Café Au Lait Puddings......................... 38
46. Cape Brandy Tart With Brandy Sauce 38
47. Cappuccino Cheesecake...................... 39
48. Cappuccino Chocolate Layer Cake 40
49. Caramel Macadamia Nut Crunch 40
50. Caramel Nut Tart.................................. 41
51. Caramelized Winter Fruit Custards ... 42
52. Cardamom Butter Squares 43
53. Cardamom Crescents 44
54. Cashew Cookies 44
55. Cheddar And Chive Yorkshire Pudding 45
56. Cheesecake.. 45
57. Cheesecake Mousse With Rum Poached Plums... 46
58. Cherries In The Snow 46
59. Cherry Almond Shortbread Cookies.. 47
60. Cherry Double Chocolate Cookies..... 48
61. Cherry Chocolate Chip Oatmeal Cookies 48
62. Cherry Cornmeal Upside Down Cake 49
63. Chestnut Cheesecake............................ 50
64. Chewy Ginger Cookies 51
65. Chicken Sausage................................... 51
66. Chocolate Cake With Caramel Coconut Almond Filling 52
67. Chocolate Cake With Chocolate Orange Frosting... 53
68. Chocolate Caramel Frozen Parfaits.... 54
69. Chocolate Chip Cookies 54
70. Chocolate Chip Crunch Cookies 55
71. Chocolate Chip Zucchini Cupcakes ... 55
72. Chocolate Chip Peanut Butter Cookies 56
73. Chocolate Chipotle Shortbread........... 57
74. Chocolate Cinnamon Cream Pie 57
75. Chocolate Cupped Cakes With Coffee And Chicory.. 58
76. Chocolate Gelato.................................. 59
77. Chocolate Hazelnut Cake With Praline

Chocolate Crunch 59
78. Chocolate Hazelnut Cakes 61
79. Chocolate Hazelnut Crinkle Cookies 61
80. Chocolate Hazelnut Praline Torte With Frangelico Whipped Cream 62
81. Chocolate Mint Mousse 63
82. Chocolate Orange Cheesecake With Orange Tangerine Glaze 63
83. Chocolate Peppermint Bark Cookies 64
84. Chocolate Puddings With Orange Whipped Cream 65
85. Chocolate Raspberry Icebox Cake 66
86. Chocolate Sheet Cake With Sour Cream Frosting 66
87. Chocolate Souffles 67
88. Chocolate Souffles With Creamy Caramel Sauce 67
89. Chocolate Soufflé 68
90. Chocolate Spoonful Cake 68
91. Chocolate Banana Tarts 69
92. Chocolate Cherry Tart 70
93. Chocolate Chocolate Chip Cookie And Strawberry Gelato Sandwiches 71
94. Chocolate Orange Carrot Cake 71
95. Chocolate Orange Decadence 72
96. Chocolate Orange Fruitcake With Pecans 73
97. Chocolate Peanut Butter Terrine With Sugared Peanuts 74
98. Chocolate Whiskey Truffles Souffles With Caramel Sauce 75
99. Cinnamon Caramel Bread Puddings 77
100. Citrus Pound Cake 77
101. Citrus Sponge Cake With Strawberries 78
102. Classic Coconut Cake 79
103. Classic White Cake Layers 80
104. Coconut Angel Food Cake 80
105. Coconut Cream Pie 81
106. Coconut Cupcakes With White Chocolate Frosting 81
107. Coconut Flans 82
108. Coconut Pineapple Cake 83
109. Coconut And Macadamia Nut Banana Bread 84
110. Coconut Chocolate Chip Cupcakes 85
111. Coconut Macadamia Crescents 86
112. Coconut Peach Layer Cake 86
113. Coeurs À La Crème With Blackberries 87

114. Coffee Granita With Cardamom Whipped Cream 88
115. Corn Bread 88
116. Cornbread Muffins With Maple Butter 88
117. Cornmeal Blini With Tomato Corn Salsa .89
118. Cornmeal Cake With Sweet Rosemary Syrup And Blackberries 89
119. Cornmeal Cookies 90
120. Cornmeal Pound Cake With Rosemary Syrup, Poached Pears, And Candied Rosemary .91
121. Cranberry Oat Bars 91
122. Cream Cheese Flan 92
123. Cream Cheese – Yukon Gold Whipped Potatoes 93
124. Currant Scones 93
125. Currant And Spice Oatmeal Cookies 94
126. Custard Gelato 94
127. Damson Tartlets 95
128. Dark Chocolate Wedding Cake With Chocolate Orange Ganache And Orange Buttercream 96
129. Date & Blue Cheese Ball 98
130. Devil's Food Cake With Chocolate Spiderweb 98
131. Devil's Food Cake With Peppermint Frosting 99
132. Double Chocolate Layer Cake 100
133. Double Chocolate Brownies 101
134. Dried Tart Cherry And Almond Muffins 102
135. Dutch Sugar Cookies 103
136. Easy Cranberry & Apple Cake 103
137. Egg Sponge 104
138. Espresso Ganache Tartlets 104
139. Fig And Fennel Bread 105
140. Figgy Scones 106
141. Flaxseed, Fig, And Walnut Crackers 106
142. Flourless Chocolate Cake With Coffee Liqueur 107
143. Fougasse 108
144. Four Layer Pumpkin Cake With Orange Cream Cheese Frosting 108
145. Frozen Almond Cappuccino Dacquoise 109
146. Frozen Lemon Cream Meringue Cake ... 110
147. Frozen Meyer Lemon Cream With Blackberry Sauce 111
148. Frozen White Chocolate And Raspberry Mousse Torte 112

149. Fudgy Chocolate Chunk Brownies With Walnuts 112
150. Fudgy Meringue Cookies 113
151. German Lebkuchen Cake With White Chocolate Frosting 114
152. Gilded Sesame Cookies 115
153. Ginger Cake 115
154. Ginger Cream 116
155. Ginger Honey Cookies 116
156. Ginger Whipped Cream 117
157. Gingerbread Bars 117
158. Gingerbread Christmas Pudding With Orange Hard Sauce 118
159. Gingerbread Puddings With Candied Apples 119
160. Gingered Peach Pavlovas 120
161. Glazed Chocolate Cake With Sprinkles .. 121
162. Glowing Jack O' Lantern Cookies 122
163. Golden Eggs 122
164. Golden Onion Pie 123
165. Grapefruit Pie 124
166. Grapes With Kir Sabayon 124
167. Greek Honey And Anise Twists (Koulourakia) 125
168. Green Curry Chicken 125
169. Green Tea Cheesecake With Raspberries And Raspberry Mint Tisane 126
170. Grilled Flatbreads 127
171. Ham Mousse With Hollandaise 128
172. Hazelnut Crunch Cake With Honeyed Kumquats 128
173. Hazelnut And Chocolate Pithiviers 130
174. Homemade Butter And Buttermilk 130
175. Honey, Date, And Pecan Tart 131
176. Honey Glazed Bunny Rolls 132
177. Honey Orange Madeleines 132
178. Hot Milk Cakes With Strawberries And Cream 133
179. Hurry Up Black Bean Dip 134
180. Ice Cream Cone Cake 134
181. Iced Lemon Cookies 136
182. Inside Out Carrot Cake Cookies 137
183. Jack Stein's Mashed Potatoes 137
184. Key Lime Cheesecake With Tropical Dried Fruit Chutney 138
185. Key Lime Coconut Cake 138
186. Key Lime Mousse 139
187. Kouign Amann 140
188. Lavender Honey And Yogurt Pie 141
189. Lemon Aioli 142
190. Lemon Butter Cookies 142
191. Lemon Buttermilk Chess Tartlets 143
192. Lemon Cheesecake Squares With Fresh Berries 143
193. Lemon Crisps 144
194. Lemon Crostata 144
195. Lemon Layer Cake 145
196. Lemon Snow Pudding With Basil Custard Sauce 146
197. Lemon Souffles With Boysenberries 147
198. Lemon Thyme Madeleines With Lemon Vodka Syrup 147
199. Lemon Glazed Butter Cake 148
200. Lemon Lattice White Chocolate Cake 149
201. Lemon Raspberry Cupcakes 150
202. Lillet Marshmallows 150
203. Lime And Lemon Friands 151
204. Limoncello Tiramisu (Tiramisu Al Limoncello) 152
205. Little Lemony Ricotta Cheesecake 153
206. Low Fat Banana Bread 153
207. Mace Cake 154
208. Madeleines With Lavender Honey 154
209. Maida Heatter's Chocolate Cookies With Gin Soaked Raisins 155
210. Maida's Skinny Whipped Cream 155
211. Majestic And Moist New Year's Honey Cake 156
212. Maple Crunch Layer Cake 157
213. Maple Walnut Coffeecake 158
214. Maple And Chocolate Chip Shortbread . 159
215. Maple Glazed Sour Cream Doughnuts With Sugared Walnut Streusel 159
216. Mascerated Berries With Vanilla Cream . 161
217. Mashed Potatoes With Black Olives 161
218. Maytag Blue Cheese Souffles With Black Corinth Grapes And Muscat Grape Reduction 162
219. Mexican Chocolate Icebox Cake 163
220. Mexican Chocolate Cherry Rounds 163
221. Meyer Lemon Budino 164
222. Meyer Lemon Shortcakes With Meyer Curd And Mixed Citrus 164
223. Meyer Lemon Soufflé 165
224. Mi Tierra Biscochitos 166

225. Mile High Chocolate Cake With Vanilla Buttercream 167
226. Milk Chocolate Mousse 168
227. Milk Chocolate Mousse With Port Ganache And Whipped Crème Fraîche 169
228. Milk Chocolate Soufflés With Nougat Whip 169
229. Mincemeat Soufflé 170
230. Mini Chocolate Sandwich Cookies 170
231. Mini Crab Cakes 171
232. Mint Brownies 172
233. Minted Blueberries With Lemon Cream . 173
234. Mixed Fruit Pavlovas 173
235. Mocha Rum Cake 174
236. Mocha And Raspberry Trifle 174
237. Mocha Chip Cookies 175
238. Molasses Crinkles 176
239. Moscato Zabaglione With Cornmeal Cookies 176
240. Nectarine Cake Squares 177
241. Nectarine Golden Cake 178
242. New York Style Crumb Cake 178
243. Old Fashioned Chocolate Chip Cookies . 179
244. Onion Fennel Flatbread 179
245. Orange Angel Food Cake With Caramel Sauce And Tropical Fruit Compote 180
246. Orange Chocolate Chip Cupcakes With Chocolate Frosting 181
247. Orange Soufflé 182
248. Orange Tapioca Pudding 182
249. Orange Almond Cake With Chocolate Icing 183
250. Orange Almond Cream Cake 184
251. Panettone With Candied Fruit 185
252. Paskha Cheese 186
253. Pavlova With A Passionfruit Curd 187
254. Pb&j Crumble Bars 187
255. Peach Ice Cream Pie With Amaretti Cookie Crust 188
256. Peach Sabayon With Balsamic Peaches ... 189
257. Peach And Mascarpone Cheesecake With Balsamic Syrup 189
258. Peaches Under Meringue 190
259. Peanut Butter Cupcakes 190
260. Peanut Butter Pie 191
261. Peanut Butter Swirl Brownies 191
262. Peanut Butter Tart With Caramel Peanut Glaze 192
263. Peanut Butter And Chocolate Chunk Brownies 193
264. Peanut Dacquoise With Peanut Butter Mousse 193
265. Pecan Caramel Cheesecake 195
266. Pecan Praline Trellis 195
267. Pecan Sandies For My Mom 196
268. Pecan Spice Layer Cake With Cream Cheese Frosting 197
269. Peppermint Meringue Cake With Chocolate Buttercream 198
270. Peppermint Patties 200
271. Peppermint Profiteroles With Chocolate Sauce 200
272. Pie Crust 201
273. Pierogies 201
274. Pineapple Apricot Upside Down Cake ... 202
275. Pineapple Upside Down Cake With Dried Cherries 203
276. Pistachio Buttercream Frosting 203
277. Pistachio Ice Cream 204
278. Plain Bagels 204
279. Plain Genoise 205
280. Plum Hazelnut Torte 205
281. Plum Küchen 206
282. Polish Rugelach 207
283. Pomegranate Sheet Cake With Lime Glaze 208
284. Poppy Seed Sweet Bread 208
285. Potato Ghosts 209
286. Prune Souffles 210
287. Pumpkin Bread Pudding 211
288. Pumpkin Muffins 211
289. Quick Pear Napoleans 212
290. Raspberry Fool 212
291. Raspberry And Peach Parfait Cake 213
292. Raspberry Yogurt Cake 214
293. Red Velvet Cake With Raspberries And Blueberries 214
294. Rhubarb Fool 215
295. Rhubarb Sponge Pudding 216
296. Rhubarb Gingersnap Parfaits 216
297. Rich Chocolate Cake With Salty Dulce De Leche & Hazelnut Brittle 217
298. Ricotta Pancakes With Brown Sugar Cherry Sauce 218

299. Ricotta And Cherry Strudel 219
300. Roasted Pear And Amaretto Trifle 220
301. Roquefort Dip With Apple, Endive, And Celery Hearts 221
302. Royal Icing 222
303. Salvadorian "Quesadilla" Cake 222
304. Savory Mascarpone Cheesecake With Sun Dried Tomato Pesto 223
305. Scrambled Egg Pasta 224
306. Sefrou Apricot (Galettes Sucrees) 224
307. Self Stomped Thick White Noodles 225
308. Semolina Pudding With Fresh Berries 226
309. Sesame Citrus Crackers 227
310. Smoked Trout Soufflé In A Phyllo Crust 227
311. Soft Chocolate Cookies With Grapefruit And Star Anise 228
312. Sour Cream Chocolate Cake 229
313. Sour Cream Chocolate Chip Cake 229
314. Sour Cream Layer Cake With Pecan Brittle 230
315. Sour Cream Raisin Pie 231
316. Spiced Cranberry Bundt Cake 232
317. Spiced Crumble Cake With Chocolate Frosting 233
318. Spiced Pumpkin Layer Cake With Cream Cheese Frosting 234
319. Spiced Snowflakes 235
320. Spinach Soufflé With Shallots And Smoked Gouda Cheese 235
321. Spinach Parmesan Soufflés 236
322. Stained Glass Lemon Cookies 236
323. Sticky Toffee Banana Pudding 237
324. Strawberry Cream Puffs With Strawberry Sauce 238
325. Sugar Cookies 239
326. Sugarplum Orange And Apricot Earl Grey Jam Tarts 239
327. Super Quick Mocha Yule Log 240
328. Sweet Breakfast Bread 241
329. Sweet Lemon Thyme Crisps 241
330. Swiss Sandwich Cookies (spitzbuben) 242
331. Tangerine Semifreddo With Salted Almond Brittle 242
332. Tea Cake Sandwich Cookies 244
333. The Ultimate Valentine Cake 245
334. Three Berry Butter Cake 246
335. Tomato Focaccia 247
336. Triple Chocolate Biscotti 248
337. Triple Ginger Layer Cake 249
338. Tropical Lime Torte With Mango Compote 250
339. Trout Dale Oatmeal Raisin Cookies 250
340. Turkish Water Borek (Suborgei) 251
341. Two Layer Cake 252
342. Ultimate Mud Pie 253
343. Upside Down Pear Chocolate Cake 254
344. Valrhona Chocolate Cherry Cake 255
345. Vanilla Buttercream 255
346. Vanilla Crumb 256
347. Vanilla Ice Cream And Ginger Molasses Cookie Sandwiches 256
348. Vanilla Whipped Buttercream 257
349. Virginia Eggnog 258
350. Walnut Cake With Sauteed Pears And Cinnamon Cream 258
351. Walnut Cigarette Cookies 259
352. Walnut And Almond Cake With Orange Pomegranate Compote 260
353. Walnut Date Torte 261
354. Warm Lemon Chiboust With Lemon Thyme Infused Milk Chocolate Velouté 261
355. Warm Sour Apple And Buttermilk Torte 263
356. Whipped Parsnips With Roasted Garlic . 263
357. White Chocolate Tartlets With Strawberries And Bananas 263
358. White Chocolate And Lemon Wedding Cake 264
359. Winter Raspberry Souffles 267
360. World Peace Cookies 268
361. Yellow Cake 268
362. Yogurt Cake With Currant Raspberry Sauce 269
363. Zeppole 270
364. Zucchini Ginger Cupcakes 270
365. Zucchini Pecan Cake With Cream Cheese Frosting 271

INDEX 273
CONCLUSION 277

365 Awesome Mixer Recipes

***

1. Aligot Gratin

Serving: Serves 6 | Prep: | Cook: |Ready in:

Ingredients

- 1 3/4 pounds russet (baking) potatoes
- 3 tablespoons unsalted butter, softened
- 4 garlic cloves, minced
- 3/4 cup milk
- 1 pound fresh mozzarella cheese, chopped fine
- 2/3 cup chilled heavy cream
- 2 tablespoons drained bottled horseradish

Direction

- Cover potatoes by 2-in. salted water in a big saucepan; simmer for 50 minutes till very tender. Drain potatoes. Put potatoes in pan; heat on low heat till dry, shaking pan. Cool till they can get handled.
- Peel potatoes. Through ricer/medium food mill's disk, force into pan. Add milk, garlic and butter; cook on medium low heat for 2 minutes till heated through and fluffy, constantly beating using wooden spoon.
- Add pepper and salt to taste and mozzarella; cook till it makes long elastic strands when you lift spoon and cheese melts.
- Divide aligot to 6 1-cup buttered shallow gratin dishes/1 buttered 6-cup gratin dish. At this point, you can prep it maximum of 1 day ahead, covered, chilled. Before proceeding, bring it to room temperature.
- Preheat a broiler.
- Beat cream using an electric mixer till soft peaks form in a bowl; beat in salt to taste and horseradish. Spread horseradish cream on aligot; broil for 1 minute till golden 4-in. from heat.

Nutrition Information

- Calories: 508
- Fiber: 3 g(12%)
- Total Carbohydrate: 28 g(9%)
- Cholesterol: 122 mg(41%)
- Protein: 21 g(42%)
- Total Fat: 35 g(54%)
- Saturated Fat: 22 g(111%)
- Sodium: 590 mg(25%)

2. Almond Butter Crisps

Serving: Makes about 11 dozen cookies | Prep: | Cook: |Ready in:

Ingredients

- 2 2/3 cups blanched almonds (about 3/4 pound)
- 1/2 cup sugar
- 1/4 teaspoon salt
- 1 1/2 teaspoons almond extract
- 1/2 prepared Basic Butter Cookie Dough at room temperature
- 2 egg whites, beaten lightly

Direction

- Halve 1 cup almonds; put aside.
- Grind sugar, salt and almonds till fine in a food processor. Beat almond extract and almond mixture into basic dough just till well combined in a standing electric mixer's bowl; pat dough into rectangle. Chill dough for a minimum of 1 hour – overnight, wrapped in wax paper.

- Preheat an oven to 350°F.
- Roll out each dough piece to 12x9-in., slightly thicker than 1/8-in. thick, rectangle between 2 wax paper sheets, using 1/3 dough at 1 time; cut dough to 1 1/2-2-in. almond shapes/other desired shapes. Put cookies on baking sheets, 1/2-in. apart. Freeze/chill uncut dough on the baking sheet till firm if dough is too soft to manage.
- Lightly brush egg whites on cookies; press reserved almond half in middle of every cookie lightly.
- In batches, bake cookies for 10 minutes till pale golden in center of oven; cool on racks. You can keep cookies for a maximum of 6 weeks frozen in airtight containers, between wax paper layers.

Nutrition Information

- Calories: 21
- Total Fat: 1 g(2%)
- Saturated Fat: 0 g(1%)
- Sodium: 11 mg(0%)
- Fiber: 0 g(1%)
- Total Carbohydrate: 2 g(1%)
- Protein: 1 g(1%)

3. Almond Cakes

Serving: Makes 12 individual cakes | Prep: 15mins | Cook: 35mins | Ready in:

Ingredients

- 3 tablespoons unsalted butter, softened, plus 1/2 tablespoon, melted
- 3 tablespoons all-purpose flour plus additional for dusting molds
- 1/8 teaspoon salt
- 1/4 cup granulated sugar
- 2 tablespoons almond paste (not marzipan; 1 ounce)
- 1/4 teaspoon pure vanilla extract
- 1 large egg
- Confectioners sugar for dusting
- 12 (1/8-cup) barquette molds or a mini-muffin pan with 12 (1/8-cup) muffin cups

Direction

- In upper oven third, put oven rack; preheat the oven to 400°F. Brush melted butter on molds. Dust with flour lightly; knock extra flour out.
- Mix salt and 3 tbsp. flour in a small bowl.
- Beat granulated sugar and softened butter with an electric mixer on high speed till fluffy and pale in a bowl. Beat in vanilla and almond paste till well combined; beat in egg till combined. Lower speed to low. Add flour mixture; stir just till combined.
- Divide batter to muffin cups/molds, evenly spread; transfer to baking sheet. If using muffin pan, not necessary.
- Bake cakes for 15 minutes till edges are golden and just firm. Turn cakes onto racks; fully cool for 5 minutes. Flip cakes right side up; before serving, dust confectioners' sugar on tops.
- You can make the cakes 1 day ahead; fully cooled, uncovered. Keep at room temperature in airtight container.

Nutrition Information

- Calories: 242
- Fiber: 2 g(7%)
- Total Carbohydrate: 31 g(10%)
- Cholesterol: 47 mg(16%)
- Protein: 5 g(10%)
- Total Fat: 11 g(17%)
- Saturated Fat: 4 g(18%)
- Sodium: 273 mg(11%)

4. Almond Praline Semifreddo With Grappa Poached Apricots

Serving: Makes 4 servings | Prep: 1.25hours | Cook: 7hours | Ready in:

Ingredients

- 1/3 cup plus 1/4 cup sugar, divided
- 1/3 cup sliced almonds with skin (1 ounce), toasted and cooled
- 2 large eggs
- 1/8 teaspoon pure almond extract
- 1 1/2 cups chilled heavy cream
- 1 cup water
- 2/3 cup sugar
- 1 (3-inch) strip lemon zest
- 1/2 cup grappa
- 8 firm-ripe apricots (1 1/2 to 1 3/4 pounds), halved and pitted
- 1 tablespoon fresh lemon juice

Direction

- Semifreddo: line plastic wrap on 8 1/2 x 4 1/2-in. lightly oiled loaf pan; on all sides, leave 2-in. overhang. Oil baking sheet lightly.
- Cook 1/3 cup of sugar in a small dry heavy skillet on medium heat till it starts to melt, undisturbed. Cook till deep golden caramel, occasionally mixing with a fork.
- Mix in almonds to coat; scrape onto baking sheet and cool. Break to pieces. Pulse till praline is ground finely, not to a paste, in a food processor.
- Beat pinch salt, leftover 1/4 cup sugar and eggs in 2-qt. metal bowl above pot with simmering water with handheld electric mixer on high speed for 8 minutes till very thick and tripled in volume. Take off heat; beat for 5 minutes till it cools to room temperature. Mix in extract.
- Beat cream till it holds stiff peaks with cleaned beaters. Fold 1/3 whipped cream to lighten into egg mixture; fold in all but 1 tbsp. praline and leftover cream thoroughly yet gently. Keep 1 tbsp. praline as garnish. Put into loaf pan; freeze for minimum of 6 hours till firm, covered.
- Poach apricots: Simmer zest, sugar and water in 12-in. heavy skillet, mixing till sugar dissolves. Simmer for 5 minutes. Add grappa; simmer. Toss lemon juice and apricots; put in grappa syrup, cut sides down. Simmer for 5 minutes. Flip apricots; simmer for 1-3 minutes till just tender.
- Put apricots in 1 layer in a 13x9-in. dish with a slotted spoon. Boil syrup in skillet for 3 minutes till reduced to 1/2 cup; put on apricots and cool it to room temperature.
- Uncover semifreddo; invert onto chilled platter using the plastic wrap to pull it from the mold. Sprinkle top with reserved praline. Crosswise slice semifreddo; serve with syrup and apricots.
- You can make semifreddo 3 days ahead, kept, well wrapped, frozen.
- You can make apricots with syrup 2 days ahead, chilled.
- Eggs aren't fully cooked in this recipe.

Nutrition Information

- Calories: 778
- Saturated Fat: 22 g(108%)
- Sodium: 75 mg(3%)
- Fiber: 4 g(18%)
- Total Carbohydrate: 86 g(29%)
- Cholesterol: 215 mg(72%)
- Protein: 9 g(18%)
- Total Fat: 40 g(61%)

5. Almond Plum Buckle

Serving: Makes 8 servings | Prep: | Cook: |Ready in:

Ingredients

- Nonstick vegetable oil spray
- 1/2 cup whole almonds (about 2 1/2 ounces)
- 1 1/2 cups all purpose flour

- 1 teaspoon baking powder
- 1/4 teaspoon fine sea salt
- 1 cup (2 sticks) unsalted butter, room temperature
- 1 cup plus 4 teaspoons sugar
- 2 large eggs
- 1 teaspoon vanilla extract
- 1/2 teaspoon almond extract
- 1 1/4 pounds plums (about 8 medium), halved, pitted, cut into 1/2-inch-thick slices
- 3/4 teaspoon ground cinnamon

Direction

- In the middle of oven, put rack; preheat it to 350°F. Spray nonstick spray on 9-in. diameter cake pan that has 2-in. high sides. Line parchment paper round on bottom of the pan.
- Grind almonds finely in a processor; put in a medium bowl. Whisk in salt, baking powder and flour. Beat butter till fluffy with an electric mixer in big bowl. Add 1 cup of sugar; beat till blended well. One by one, add eggs; beat well after each addition. Beat in almond and vanilla extract then the flour mixture till incorporated.
- Put batter in a prepped pan; evenly spread and smooth top using spatula. Press plum slices gently into batter, flesh side down, in spoke pattern around middle of cake and outer rim, placing near each other. Mix 4 teaspoons sugar and cinnamon in a small bowl; sprinkle on plums.
- Bake cake for 50 minutes till inserted tester in the middle exits clean; cool cake for 20 minutes in a pan on a rack. Run a small knife between pan and cake's sides to loosen. Onto platter, invert cake; remove parchment paper. Put another platter on top of the cake; firmly hold both platters together using both hands. Invert cake with plum side up; fully cool cake. Cut into wedges.

Nutrition Information

- Calories: 519
- Saturated Fat: 16 g(78%)
- Sodium: 140 mg(6%)
- Fiber: 3 g(11%)
- Total Carbohydrate: 56 g(19%)
- Cholesterol: 108 mg(36%)
- Protein: 7 g(13%)
- Total Fat: 31 g(48%)

6. Alphabet Cookies

Serving: Makes 3 to 5 dozen cookies (depending on size of cookie cutters) | Prep: 1.5hours | Cook: 4hours | Ready in:

Ingredients

- 2 1/2 cups all-purpose flour
- 3/4 teaspoon salt
- 1 1/2 sticks (3/4 cup) unsalted butter, softened
- 3/4 cup sugar
- 1 large egg
- 1 teaspoon vanilla
- Decorating icing
- Various food colorings *
- Special equipment: 2- to 3-inch alphabet cookie cutters**; several sealable plastic bags (not pleated)

Direction

- Whisk salt and flour in small bowl.
- Use electric mixer on medium high speed to beat sugar and butter for 6 minutes by handheld/3 minutes in stand mixer (best with paddle attachment) till fluffy and pale in a big bowl; beat in vanilla and egg. Lower speed to low. Add flour mixture; mix just till combined.
- Shape dough to 2 balls; flatten each to 6-in. disk. Chill disks for 1 hour till firm, wrapped in plastic wrap.
- In center position, put oven rack; preheat the oven to 350°F.
- Roll 1 dough piece out to 1/4-in. thick 8 1/2-in. round using well-floured rolling pin on well-floured surface; keep leftover dough chilled. Rewrap in plastic then chill till firm if dough is too soft to roll. Cut as many cookies

as you can from dough out using cutters; put on 2 ungreased big baking sheets, 1-in. apart.
- 1 sheet at 1 time, bake cookies for 10-12 minutes till edges are golden. Put on racks using metal spatula; fully cool.
- Gather scraps; chill for 10-15 minutes till dough firms to reroll. With leftover scraps and dough, make more cookies in same way on cooled baking sheets; reroll only once.
- For every color, you can create 7, put 1/4 cup icing into another small bowl; tint using food coloring. To make 1/4-in. opening, snip 1 corner off of every plastic bag; put each color icing into bag, pressing extra air out. Firmly twist each bag above icing; pipe decoratively/spread colored icing on cookies. Fully dry icing before storing cookies; 1 hour, varies on humidity.
- You can chill dough for 3 days.
- With or without icing, you can make cookies 1 week ahead, layers between parchment/wax paper sheets, in airtight container in room temperature.

7. Anise Sesame Cookies

Serving: Makes about 3 dozen | Prep: 30mins | Cook: 4hours | Ready in:

Ingredients

- 1 tablespoon whole anise seeds
- 2 tablespoons boiling-hot water
- 2 cups all-purpose flour
- 1/8 teaspoon baking soda
- 1/2 teaspoon salt
- 1 1/2 sticks (3/4 cup) unsalted butter, softened
- 2/3 cup sugar
- 2 large eggs
- 1/4 cup sesame seeds, lightly toasted
- a 2 1/2-inch fluted round cookie cutter

Direction

- Soak anise seeds for 15 minutes in boiling-hot water till most of water gets absorbed.
- Whisk salt, baking soda and flour in a bowl.
- Beat sugar and butter using an electric mixer on medium-high speed for 4 minutes if using handheld or 2 minutes if using a stand mixer (best when fitted with paddle attachment), till fluffy and pale in a big bowl. Beat in anise seeds with leftover soaking liquid and 1 egg till combined. Lower speed to low; mix in flour mixture just till combined.
- Divide dough to 4 balls; flatten each to 4-in. disk. Chill disks for 3 minutes till firm, wrapped in plastic wrap.
- In lower and upper thirds of oven, position oven racks; preheat the oven to 350°F.
- Roll 1 dough piece out to 7-in. round (little less than 1/4-in. thick) with well-floured rolling pin on well-floured surface as oven preheats; keep leftover dough chilled. Chill on baking sheet till firm if dough gets too soft to get rolled out. Use a cutter to cut as many cookies out as possible from dough; put onto 2 ungreased big baking sheets, 1-in. apart. Beat 1 tbsp. water and leftover egg to make an egg wash in a small bowl. Lightly brush egg wash on each cookie; sprinkle some sesame seeds over.
- Bake cookies for a total of 10-12 minutes till bottoms are golden, switching sheets position halfway through baking. Put onto racks using a metal spatula; fully cool.
- Gather scraps; chill till firm enough to reroll. With leftover scraps, dough (reroll only once), and sesame seeds, you can make more cookies; bake on the cooled sheets.
- Cookies keep for 1 week at room temperature in an airtight container, layered between parchment/wax paper sheets.

Nutrition Information

- Calories: 258
- Protein: 4 g(8%)
- Total Fat: 14 g(22%)
- Saturated Fat: 8 g(40%)

- Sodium: 129 mg(5%)
- Fiber: 1 g(4%)
- Total Carbohydrate: 29 g(10%)
- Cholesterol: 62 mg(21%)

8. Anise Scented Fig And Date Swirls

Serving: Makes about 36 cookies | Prep: | Cook: | Ready in:

Ingredients

- 1 cup firmly packed dried figs (as soft as possible)
- 1 cup firmly packed pitted dates
- 1/3 cup water
- 1/2 cup plus 2 tablespoons granulated refined sugar
- 1 3/4 cups all-purpose flour
- 1 tablespoon ground anise seeds
- 1/4 teaspoon baking powder
- 1/4 teaspoon baking soda
- 1/4 teaspoon salt
- 1 stick (1/2 cup) unsalted butter, softened
- 4 ounces cream cheese
- 1 teaspoon vanilla extract
- 1 large egg yolk
- 1/4 cup granulated raw sugar (turbinado or Demerara)

Direction

- Puree dates and figs with 2 tablespoons of refined sugar and water in a blender. Beat together salt, baking soda, baking powder, anise and flour in a bowl. Use an electric mixer to whisk together the remaining half cup of refined sugar, cream cheese and butter in another bowl until fluffy and light. Add flour mixture, yolk and vanilla; beat until a dough forms. Shape dough into a disk. Wrap the dough in wax paper and chill for 1 hour until it reaches enough firmness to handle.
- On a lightly floured sheet of wax paper, roll out dough into a 13x10-inch rectangle, about 1/3 inch thick, using a floured rolling pin. Drop fig mixture by spoonfuls onto dough; gently spread a layer evenly over dough. Roll dough in jelly-roll style into a 13-inch log, starting with a long side, using wax paper as a guide. Turn log over in raw sugar to coat. Wrap in wax paper and chill log until firm or for 4 hours.
- (When the dough has been shaped into a log, you can keep it in the fridge for 1 week or the freezer for 1 month. Thaw the frozen dough in the fridge until sliceable, about 4 hours. You can keep the baked cookies for 4 days in airtight containers at room temperature.)
- Set the oven to 350° F and start preheating; lightly butter two baking sheets.
- Cut log into 1/3-inch-thick rounds and place about 2 inches apart on baking sheets. In the middle of the oven, bake cookies in batches for about 13 minutes until pale golden; place on racks to cool. You can keep the baked cookies for 4 days in airtight containers at room temperature.

Nutrition Information

- Calories: 97
- Saturated Fat: 2 g(11%)
- Sodium: 40 mg(2%)
- Fiber: 1 g(3%)
- Total Carbohydrate: 15 g(5%)
- Cholesterol: 15 mg(5%)
- Protein: 1 g(2%)
- Total Fat: 4 g(6%)

9. Anzacs

Serving: Makes 48 cookies | Prep: | Cook: | Ready in:

Ingredients

- 1 1/2 cups rolled oats

- 1 cup plus 1 tbsp whole-wheat flour
- 2/3 cup Sucanat organic sugar (found at health food stores)
- 1 1/4 cups sweet shredded coconut (comes in a bag)
- 3/4 cup soybean margarine (found at health food stores)
- 3 tbsp maple syrup
- 1 tsp baking soda

Direction

- Preheat an oven to 300°F. Mix coconut, sugar, flour and oats in medium-sized mixing bowl. Melt syrup and margarine in a small saucepan. Boil 3 tbsp. water in another small pan. Add baking soda; mix. Mix dissolved baking soda into syrup mixture; add into dry ingredients. Shape small balls; put on baking sheet, 2-in. apart. Bake till golden brown, for 15 minutes.

10. Apple And Blackberry Meringue Souffles

Serving: Serves 2 generously | Prep: | Cook: | Ready in:

Ingredients

- 2 cups coarsely grated peeled Golden Delicious apples (about 2)
- 1/2 cup firmly packed light brown sugar
- 1 teaspoon cinnamon
- 2 tablespoons brandy
- 2 large egg whites
- 3/4 cup picked-over fresh blackberries, quartered
- 1 tablespoon confectioners' sugar for sprinkling

Direction

- Preheat an oven to 450°F. Lightly butter 2 4-in. diameter, 1 1/2-in. high 1-cup ramekins.
- Simmer brandy, cinnamon, brown sugar and apples in heavy saucepan for 10 minutes, occasionally mixing, covered.
- Beat whites till they hold stiff peaks using electric mixer in a bowl; beat in blackberries and hot apple mixture just till combined.
- Put mixture in ramekins, mounding it in middles. Around sides, run a knife, freeing it to help rising. Bake soufflés on baking sheet for 8 minutes in center of oven till golden brown and puffed. Sprinkle confectioners' sugar while still warm.
- Immediately serve.

Nutrition Information

- Calories: 358
- Protein: 5 g(10%)
- Total Fat: 1 g(1%)
- Saturated Fat: 0 g(0%)
- Sodium: 73 mg(3%)
- Fiber: 6 g(25%)
- Total Carbohydrate: 79 g(26%)

11. Apricot Butter Cookies

Serving: Makes about 32 cookies | Prep: | Cook: | Ready in:

Ingredients

- 3/4 cup (about 1/4 pound) dried apricots
- 3/4 cup granulated sugar
- 1 tablespoon dark rum
- 2 1/2 cups all-purpose flour
- 1 teaspoon double-acting baking powder
- 2 sticks (1 cup) unsalted butter, softened
- 1/4 cup firmly packed brown sugar
- 1 teaspoon vanilla
- 1 large egg
- 1 cup confectioners' sugar
- 2 teaspoons fresh lemon juice

Direction

- Mix 2/3 cup of water, 1/4 cup of the granulated sugar, and apricots together in a small saucepan, simmer the mixture until there is half of the mixture left, about 15-18 minutes, and add the rum. Let the mixture cool down slightly and put in a blender to purée.
- Combine a pinch of salt, baking powder, and flour in a bowl. Whisk brown sugar, the rest 1/2 cup granulated sugar, and butter together with an electric mixer in a big bowl until the mixture is fluffy and light, whisk in egg and vanilla, and whisk until well blended. Add the flour mixture and whisk the dough until it's just blended. Shape the dough into a log, refrigerate for 1 hour, and split into 8 portions.
- Working with 1 piece of dough at a time, , on a sheet of plastic wrap shape it into 8-inch ropes, wrap around the ropes with the plastic wrap to keep the dough from sticking, and tap the rope into an 8x1 1/2-inch rectangle on 2 cookie sheet. Use your finger to make a canal down the middle of each rectangle and spread in the canal with the apricot purée. Put the rectangles in the center of a 350°F preheated oven and bake in 2 batches until the edges are golden, about 18-20 minutes. Move them to the rack and let them cool down. For a thick and pourable icing, combine enough water, lemon juice, and confectioners' sugar in a small bowl. Sprinkle over the rectangles diagonally with 1-inch strips of icing. You can keep the cookie in an airtight container for 1 week.

Nutrition Information

- Calories: 138
- Fiber: 1 g(2%)
- Total Carbohydrate: 20 g(7%)
- Cholesterol: 21 mg(7%)
- Protein: 1 g(3%)
- Total Fat: 6 g(9%)
- Saturated Fat: 4 g(19%)
- Sodium: 16 mg(1%)

12. Apricot Linzertorte With Quark Whipped Cream

Serving: Makes 10 to 12 servings | Prep: | Cook: |Ready in:

Ingredients

- 2 cups blanched hazelnuts, toasted , cooled (about 10 ounces)
- 1 1/4 cups all purpose flour, divided
- 2 teaspoons unsweetened cocoa powder
- 1 teaspoon ground cinnamon
- 3/4 teaspoon salt
- 1/4 teaspoon (generous) ground cloves
- 14 tablespoons (1 3/4 sticks) unsalted butter, room temperature
- 1 1/4 cups sugar
- 1 large egg
- 1 large egg yolk
- 2 teaspoons finely grated orange peel
- 1 cup apricot preserves
- 2/3 cup chilled heavy whipping cream
- 1/3 cup whole-milk quark* or Greek-style yogurt
- Powdered sugar

Direction

- Preheat an oven to 375°F. Coat a 10-inch springform pan with butter. Then process 1/4 cup flour and nuts in a processor until the nuts are finely ground. Place in a medium bowl. Whisk in cloves, 3/4 teaspoon salt, cinnamon, cocoa powder and one cup of flour. Beat 1 1/4 cups sugar and 14 tablespoons of butter with an electric mixer in a large bowl. Then beat in egg, followed by egg yolk and orange peel. Slowly mix in the dry ingredients. Ladle 1 1/2 cups of batter into a pastry bag that is fitted with 3/8-inch plain round tip. Pour the remaining batter in the pan.
- Bake the torte bottom for about 35 minutes until turned golden. Let to cool for 10 minutes in the pan on rack. Maintain the oven temperature.

- Pipe the border around the edge of torte bottom with some of the batter in pastry bag. Evenly spread the preserves atop torte bottom. Then pipe the remaining batter atop preserves in lattice pattern, about 5 to 6 strips in every direction. Bake for about 40 minutes until the preserves are bubbling and lattice is firm to touch. Let to cool completely. You can make three days ahead and then keep in airtight container at room temperature.
- Beat the cream in a bowl until peaks are formed. Then beat in quark. Sprinkle powdered sugar over torte. You can serve together with quark whipped cream.

13. Apricot Souffles With Vanilla Rum Crème Anglaise

Serving: Serves 6 | Prep: | Cook: | Ready in:

Ingredients

- 6 ounces dried apricots (about 1 1/2 cups)
- 1 1/2 cups water
- 3/4 cup sugar plus additional for coating ramekins
- 1 tablespoon fresh lemon juice
- 1 tablespoon dark rum if desired
- 1/2 teaspoon vanilla extract
- 5 large egg whites
- 1/4 teaspoon cream of tartar
- Accompaniment:
- 2 cups half-and-half
- 1/2 vanilla bean, split lengthwise
- 5 large egg yolks
- 1/4 cup sugar
- 1 tablespoon dark rum, or to taste

Direction

- Apricot soufflé: Simmer 1/2 cup sugar, water and apricots for 20 minutes in a heavy saucepan, covered. Put hot mixture in a food processor; puree till very smooth. Through a fine sieve, force puree into bowl; mix in pinch salt, vanilla, rum and lemon juice. Fully cool puree. You can make puree 2 days ahead, covered, chilled. Before proceeding, bring to room temperature. Put puree into a big bowl.
- Preheat an oven to 350°F. Butter 7-oz. 3 1/2x1 3/4-in. ramekins generously. Coat in extra sugar; knock extra out.
- Beat pinch of salt and whites using electric mixer till foamy in another big bowl; beat in the cream of tartar. Beat whites till it holds soft peaks. Little by little, beat in leftover 1/4 cup sugar; beat meringue till it holds stiff peaks. Whisk 1/4 meringue to lighten into puree; thoroughly yet gently fold in leftover meringue. Put batter in ramekins; bake soufflés on baking sheet in center of oven till just set in middle, golden brown and puffed for 20-25 minutes.
- Take ramekins from oven; pull open middle of each soufflé using 2 forks. In each opening, put some crème anglaise; immediately serve.
- Vanilla rum crème anglaise: Boil vanilla bean and half and half in a heavy small saucepan; take off heat. Using a knife, scrape seeds from bean into half and half; if desired, keep pod for another time.
- Whisk pinch of salt, sugar and yolks in a bowl; in a stream, whisk in the hot half and half. Put custard in pan; cook on medium low heat till thick and candy thermometer reads 170°F, constantly mixing with a wooden spoon; don't boil. Through a fine sieve, put sauce into a bowl; cool, occasionally mixing. Mix in run; chill sauce for a minimum of 2 hours – maximum of 2 days till very cold, covered. Creates 2 1/4 cups.

Nutrition Information

- Calories: 386
- Saturated Fat: 7 g(36%)
- Sodium: 92 mg(4%)
- Fiber: 2 g(10%)
- Total Carbohydrate: 58 g(19%)
- Cholesterol: 184 mg(61%)
- Protein: 9 g(17%)

- Total Fat: 13 g(20%)

14. Asian Potato Latkes

Serving: Makes about 65 pancakes | Prep: | Cook: | Ready in:

Ingredients

- 4 large all-purpose potatoes (about 2 1/2 pounds), peeled
- 1/2 cup fresh cilantro, finely chopped (about 1 small bunch)
- 1/4 cup fresh ginger, finely chopped (1 ounce, about a 2-inch piece)
- 2 cups dry Italian breadcrumbs, plus additional, if needed
- 1 cup heavy cream
- 1 teaspoon unsalted butter

Direction

- Grate potatoes coarsely in a food processor with coarse grating disk/hand grater. To eliminate as much moisture as you can, squeeze between several paper towel thicknesses.
- Put potatoes in an electric mixer's bowl. Add ginger and cilantro; use a spoon to toss. Mix in butter, cream and breadcrumbs; season with pepper and salt.
- Beat mixture to blend for 2 minutes on low speed using paddle attachment. Beat in more breadcrumbs if it looks too wet to make into balls, few tsp. at a time, till you get desired consistency; rest for 30 minutes, uncovered.
- Heat a big nonstick skillet without any oil on medium high heat. Shape mixture to 1-in. balls using a tablespoon. Put 6-8 balls into skillet; cook for 2-3 minutes till bottoms are golden brown, gently pressing with spatula to flatten. Flip pancakes; cook for 2-3 minutes longer till cooked through and golden brown, pressing occasionally.
- In same manner, use leftover batter to create more pancakes; serve warm.
- Scrape ginger with a teaspoon's edge to easy peel the ginger.

Nutrition Information

- Calories: 37
- Saturated Fat: 1 g(5%)
- Sodium: 27 mg(1%)
- Fiber: 0 g(2%)
- Total Carbohydrate: 5 g(2%)
- Cholesterol: 5 mg(2%)
- Protein: 1 g(2%)
- Total Fat: 2 g(2%)

15. Bacon Banana Cookies

Serving: Yields 30 cookies | Prep: | Cook: | Ready in:

Ingredients

- 2 1/2 cups sifted all-purpose flour
- 2 teaspoons baking powder
- 1/4 teaspoon baking soda
- 1 1/2 teaspoons ground cinnamon
- 1/4 teaspoon kosher salt
- 1/2 cup (1 stick) unsalted butter
- 1 1/4 cups sugar
- 2 large eggs
- 1 teaspoon vanilla extract
- 4 bananas, mashed (about 1 1/3 cups)
- 1/2 pound bacon, cooked crisp, chopped

Direction

- Preheat oven to 400°F. Use a parchment paper to line the baking sheet. Set aside.
- Sift together the salt, 1/2 teaspoon of cinnamon, baking soda, baking powder, and flour in a large mixing bowl.
- In a medium mixing bowl, cream together 1 cup of sugar and butter using a hand mixer. Beat the eggs in one at a time until they are

completely mixed in. Add and beat in the vanilla. Pour the butter mixture to the flour mixture. Add and mix the mashed bananas one at a time, beating well after each addition. Fold in the bacon.
- Mix together the leftover cinnamon and 1/4 cup of sugar.
- In heaping tablespoons, put the dough on the baking sheet with 1 inch spacing between the doughs. Generously sprinkle with cinnamon-sugar and bake for 10 to 12 minutes until slightly brown. Let the cookies cool completely before putting in an air-tight container. Consume in 5-7 days.
- For rock-hard bananas, ripen them immediately by placing the peeled bananas on a parchment-lined baking sheet. Bake them in the oven on 400°F for 10 minutes until soft.
- Try adding 4 slices of cooked and chopped bacon into the batter next time you make banana bread.

Nutrition Information

- Calories: 140
- Total Carbohydrate: 18 g(6%)
- Cholesterol: 26 mg(9%)
- Protein: 3 g(5%)
- Total Fat: 7 g(10%)
- Saturated Fat: 3 g(15%)
- Sodium: 102 mg(4%)
- Fiber: 1 g(2%)

16. Baked Coconut (Cocada De Forno)

Serving: Makes 4 to 6 servings | Prep: | Cook: |Ready in:

Ingredients

- 8 tablespoons (1 stick) unsalted butter, at room temperature
- 1/2 cup sugar
- 3 whole eggs
- 1/3 cup coconut milk
- 1/3 cup sweetened condensed milk
- 1 tablespoon Malibu rum
- 1 1/2 cups unsweetened grated coconut
- 2 tablespoons all-purpose flour, sifted
- 1 24-ounce baking dish

Direction

- Preheat an oven to 350°F; use some spray to grease a baking dish lightly.
- Mix sugar and butter for 5 minutes at medium speed till creamy and light in an electric mixer's bowl with paddle attachment. One by one, add eggs; mix. After each addition, scrape bowl's sides.
- Add Malibu, coconut milk and sweetened condensed milk; mix on medium speed for 1 minute till batter is blended well. Add coconut; mix till all gets incorporated yet looks grainy.
- Use a rubber spatula to fold in flour; spread batter in prepped baking dish. You may keep in, covered with plastic wrap, in the fridge 2 days ahead.
- Bake in oven for 20 minutes till edges set, top looks golden brown and center is slightly jiggly. Remove from oven; rest for 10 minutes.
- Serve this with lemon sorbet scoop.

17. Baked Yams With Cinnamon Chili Butter

Serving: Makes 6 servings | Prep: | Cook: |Ready in:

Ingredients

- 1/2 cup (1 stick) unsalted butter, room temperature
- 1 tablespoon plus 2 teaspoons New Mexico chili powder*
- 1 tablespoon ground cinnamon
- 1/2 teaspoon salt
- 1/8 teaspoon cayenne pepper
- 6 yams (red-skinned sweet potatoes)

Direction

- Beat initial 5 ingredients using electric mixer till fluffy in medium bowl. You can make it 3 days ahead, refrigerated, covered. Before using, bring to room temperature.
- Preheat an oven to 400°F. Line foil on big baking sheet. On sheet, put yams; bake for 1 hour 10 minutes till tender. Lengthwise slit each yam; put 1 tbsp. butter in each. Serve with leftover butter separately.
- Use even amount of the regular mild chili powder if you can't find pure chili powder.

Nutrition Information

- Calories: 299
- Saturated Fat: 10 g(49%)
- Sodium: 272 mg(11%)
- Fiber: 7 g(27%)
- Total Carbohydrate: 38 g(13%)
- Cholesterol: 41 mg(14%)
- Protein: 3 g(5%)
- Total Fat: 16 g(24%)

18. Bakewell Tart

Serving: Makes 8 servings | Prep: | Cook: | Ready in:

Ingredients

- 4 cups all-purpose flour
- 1/8 teaspoon fine sea salt
- 1 pound (4 sticks) unsalted butter
- 1 large egg white
- 1/2 cup huckleberry jam or jam of choice, such as blackberry or strawberry
- 4 large eggs
- 3/4 cup (1 1/2 sticks, or 12 tablespoons) unsalted butter
- 3/4 cup sugar
- 1/2 cup all-purpose flour
- an 8-inch deep-dish pie plate, parchment paper, pie weights or dried beans, and a pastry brush

Direction

- Puff pastry: Sift salt and flour in a big bowl; mix in 1 cup water using a knife till dough clumps together and comes together yet is still string. As needed, mix in more water, you might use 1 3/4 cups total, till dough brings itself to ball-like shape and is smooth.
- Turn dough onto lightly floured surface; roll to 1/2-in. thick long rectangle using a rolling pin. Put all butter in middle of dough so butter divides dough rectangle in half, 2 sticks over 2 sticks. Fold 1 long dough end on butter; fold other long end over, similar to folding a business letter. In plastic wrap, wrap dough; refrigerate dough for 10 minutes. Put dough on lightly floured surface; roll to 1/2-in. thick, long rectangle. Fold 1 long dough end toward center; fold other long end over. Wrap dough in plastic wrap; refrigerate for 10 minutes then repeat step again so dough gets rolled, folded and refrigerated 3 times. You can make puff pastry ahead, refrigerated for up to 3 days, wrapped in double plastic wrap layer/frozen for up to 3 months.
- Put rack into center of oven; preheat it to 325°F. Butter the deep-dish 8-in. pie plate.
- Roll puff pastry to 12-in. diameter, 1/4-in. thick circle on lightly floured surface. Fit dough in prepped pie plate; remove extra dough. Keep excess for another use. Crimp edge of tart using a fork (optional). Prick sides and bottom of tart shell all over using a fork; chill for 15 minutes.
- Line parchment paper on a tart shell; fill with dried beans/pie weights. Bake for 15 minutes till pale golden along edge and pastry is set. Remove beans/weights and parchment paper; brush egg white on sides and bottom of tart shell gently. Cook for 5 more minutes. Take tart from oven; evenly spread jam across bottom. Put aside; cool.

- Filling; Beat sugar and butter for 2 minutes till pale in color, fluffy and light in a stand mixer's bowl with paddle attachment. One by one, add eggs, beating well after every addition for 2 minutes, scraping bowl down as needed. Fold in flour gently using a spatula. Put batter onto jam in cooled tart shell; smooth top and bake for 40-45 minutes till tart is set and golden. Put tart on rack; cool. Serve in room temperature/warm.

Nutrition Information

- Calories: 963
- Sodium: 104 mg(4%)
- Fiber: 3 g(10%)
- Total Carbohydrate: 76 g(25%)
- Cholesterol: 261 mg(87%)
- Protein: 12 g(24%)
- Total Fat: 69 g(106%)
- Saturated Fat: 42 g(208%)

19. Banana Chocolate Walnut Cake

Serving: Makes 8 servings | Prep: 30mins | Cook: 2.5hours | Ready in:

Ingredients

- 2 1/4 cups all-purpose flour
- 1 teaspoon baking soda
- 1/2 teaspoon salt
- 1 stick unsalted butter, softened, plus 2 tablespoons, melted and cooled
- 1 cup sugar, divided
- 2 large eggs
- 1 1/4 cups mashed very ripe bananas (about 3 medium)
- 2/3 cup plain whole-milk yogurt
- 1 teaspoon pure vanilla extract
- 1 (3 1/2- to 4-ounce) bar 70%-cacao bittersweet chocolate, coarsely chopped
- 1 cup walnuts (3 ounces), toasted, cooled, and coarsely chopped
- 1/2 teaspoon cinnamon

Direction

- Preheat an oven with rack in center to 375°F; butter 9-in. square cake pan.
- Mix salt, baking soda and flour together.
- Beat 3/4 cup sugar and 1 stick softened butter using an electric mixer on medium speed till fluffy and pale in a medium bowl. One by one, beat in eggs till blended. Beat in vanilla, yogurt, and bananas; it'll look curdled.
- Add flour mixture with mixer on low speed; mix just till incorporated.
- Toss leftover 1/4 cup sugar, melted butter, cinnamon, nuts and chocolate in small bowl. Spread 1/2 banana batter into cake pan; sprinkle with 1/2 chocolate mixture. Evenly spread leftover batter on filling; sprinkle top with leftover chocolate mixture.
- Bake for 35-40 minutes till inserted wooden pick in middle of cake exits clean and cake is golden; cool cake for 30 minutes in pan on rack. Turn onto rack; fully cool, right side up.
- You can make cake 2 days ahead; keep at room temperature in an airtight container.

Nutrition Information

- Calories: 548
- Saturated Fat: 13 g(65%)
- Sodium: 335 mg(14%)
- Fiber: 3 g(14%)
- Total Carbohydrate: 71 g(24%)
- Cholesterol: 87 mg(29%)
- Protein: 9 g(17%)
- Total Fat: 28 g(42%)

20. Banana Rum Cream Pie

Serving: Makes 8 servings | Prep: 35mins | Cook: 1hours | Ready in:

Ingredients

- 1 1/4 cups graham cracker crumbs from 9 (4 3/4 - by 2 1/4-inch) crackers
- 5 tablespoons unsalted butter, melted
- 1 teaspoon curry powder (preferably Madras)
- 1/4 teaspoon cinnamon
- 1/2 cup packed dark brown sugar
- 8 ounces cream cheese, softened
- 1 teaspoon finely grated fresh lemon zest
- 1 cup chilled heavy cream
- 4 teaspoons dark rum
- 4 firm-ripe bananas
- a 9-inch pie plate

Direction

- In center position, put oven rack; preheat an oven to 350°F.
- Mix 2 tbsp. brown sugar, cinnamon, curry powder, butter and crumbs with a fork till well combined in a bowl; keep 1 tbsp. crumb mixture as garnish. Evenly press leftover crumb mixture up side and on bottom of pie plate; bake it for 10 minutes. Fully cool for 20 minutes in pie plate on rack.
- Beat leftover 6 tbsp. brown sugar, zest and cream cheese using electric mixer on high speed for 1 minute till fluffy and light in a bowl.
- Beat rum and cream using cleaned beaters on medium speed till it holds soft peaks in another bowl; mix 1/3 whipped cream gently to lighten into cream cheese mixture. Gently yet thoroughly fold in leftover whipped cream.
- Slice bananas thinly; evenly put on crust's bottom. Spread all cream filling on bananas; sprinkle the reserved crumb mixture over. Chill pie for 20 minutes, loosely covered.

Nutrition Information

- Calories: 430
- Protein: 4 g(8%)
- Total Fat: 30 g(45%)
- Saturated Fat: 17 g(86%)
- Sodium: 181 mg(8%)
- Fiber: 2 g(9%)
- Total Carbohydrate: 39 g(13%)
- Cholesterol: 91 mg(30%)

21. Banana Walnut Upside Down Cakes

Serving: Serves 2 | Prep: | Cook: | Ready in:

Ingredients

- 3 tablespoons unsalted butter, softened
- 2 tablespoons firmly packed brown sugar
- 2 tablespoons lightly toasted chopped walnuts
- 1 banana
- 1/4 cup all-purpose flour
- 1/4 teaspoon baking powder
- 1/8 teaspoon ground cardamom
- 3 tablespoons granulated sugar
- 1 large egg
- 1/4 teaspoon vanilla

Direction

- Preheat an oven to 350°F.
- Melt 2 tbsp. butter in a small saucepan; divide to 2 1-cup ramekins. Sprinkle walnuts and brown sugar on butter. Cut banana to 1/4-in. thick slices; put on walnuts, overlapping, lightly pressing to fit.
- Whisk pinch salt, cardamom, baking powder and flour in a small bowl. Beat granulated sugar and 1 tbsp. butter using an electric mixer till well combined in a bowl. Beat in vanilla and egg till combined; beat in flour mixture just till batter is combined. Divide batter to ramekins; bake on baking sheet in center of oven for 25 minutes till tester exits clean. Around ramekin's edges, run a sharp knife; invert cakes onto plates.

Nutrition Information

- Calories: 470

- Cholesterol: 139 mg(46%)
- Protein: 7 g(13%)
- Total Fat: 25 g(38%)
- Saturated Fat: 12 g(61%)
- Sodium: 88 mg(4%)
- Fiber: 2 g(10%)
- Total Carbohydrate: 59 g(20%)

22. Banoffee Pie

Serving: 8 | Prep: | Cook: 35mins | Ready in:

Ingredients

- Crust
- 1 cup graham cracker crumbs (see Tip)
- 3 tablespoons butter, melted
- Filling
- 1 14-ounce can nonfat sweetened condensed milk
- Pinch of salt
- 4 medium ripe but firm bananas, sliced, divided
- ½ cup heavy cream
- 1 teaspoon vanilla extract

Direction

- Crust: Preheat an oven to 350°F. Use cooking spray to coat 9-in. tart pan that has a removable bottom.
- Blend butter and graham cracker crumbs with your fingers till well combined in a medium bowl; press mixture halfway up sides and bottom of prepped pan. Bake for 10 minutes till lightly brown; cool on wire rack.
- Filling: Put oven temperature to 425°; boil kettle with water.
- Put condensed milk into ceramic/glass pie pan; mix in salt. Cover pan with foil tightly; put in big roasting pan. Put 1-in. boiling water into roasting pan carefully; put into oven. Bake for 1 3/4 hours till condensed milk is caramel in color, sticky and thick. Halfway through, check; if water level is low, add boiling water.
- Keep 2 tbsp. condensed milk toffee in small bowl. Dollop leftover toffee onto crust, it'll be a bit lumpy and sticky, while warm; spread to cover bottom gently. Cover; refrigerate pie and reserved toffee for 1 hour till chilled. Loosely cover after 1 hour then refrigerate for up to 1 day if making ahead.
- Take pie from fridge; put 3 sliced bananas on toffee.
- Beat cream using an electric mixer at medium speed till soft peaks form in a bowl. Add vanilla; beat till stiff. Spread whipped cream on pie; leave 1-in. border around edge. Use leftover banana to garnish. Mix 1 tsp. water into reserved toffee till smooth; drizzle on pie. Before cutting, remove pan sides. Immediately serve.

Nutrition Information

- Calories: 338 calories;
- Fiber: 2
- Total Carbohydrate: 54
- Sugar: 41
- Protein: 6
- Total Fat: 11
- Saturated Fat: 6
- Sodium: 133
- Cholesterol: 38

23. Bittersweet Chocolate Irish Whiskey Cake

Serving: Makes 8 to 10 servings | Prep: | Cook: | Ready in:

Ingredients

- 1/2 cup plus 2 tablespoons Irish whiskey
- 6 ounces bittersweet (70% cocoa) chocolate (such as Scharffen Berger or Lindt), chopped
- 2 teaspoons instant espresso powder dissolved in 6 tablespoons hot water

- 1/3 cup blanched almonds (about 2 ounces), lightly toasted
- 6 tablespoons all purpose flour, divided
- 3/4 cup (1 1/2 sticks) unsalted butter, room temperature, divided
- 7 tablespoons vanilla sugar, divided
- 3 large eggs, separated
- Pinch of fine sea salt
- 2 ounces semisweet chocolate, chopped

Direction

- Put rack in middle of oven; preheat to 350°F. Butter then flour 8-in. diameter springform pan.
- In small saucepan, boil 1/2 cup whiskey for 2 minutes till reduces to 1/4 cup. Mix 1/4 cup boiled whiskey, espresso powder mixture and bittersweet chocolate in small metal bowl. Put bowl above saucepan with simmering water; mix till smooth. Take bowl from above water. Grind 2 tbsp. flour and almonds finely in processor.
- Beat 6 tbsp. vanilla sugar and 1/2 cup butter using electric mixer till fluffy in medium bowl. One by one, beat in egg yolks; beat in sea salt. Fold in the chocolate mixture; fold in ground almond mixture. Beat egg whites using dry clean beaters till soft peaks form in another bowl. Add 1 tbsp. vanilla sugar slowly; beat till stiff peaks form. Alternately with leftover 4 tbsp. flour, fold whites into batter in 3 batches. Put batter in prepped pan.
- Bake cake for 40 minutes till inserted tester in middle exits clean; cool for 30 minutes in pan on rack. Remove pan sides; fully cool cake.
- Mix leftover 2 tbsp. whiskey and semisweet chocolate till smooth in a small metal bowl above saucepan with simmering water; take bowl from above water. 1 small piece at 1 time, put leftover 1/4 cup butter in chocolate mixture, whisking till each piece melts prior to adding next. Put bowl above bigger bowl with ice water. Beat icing using electric mixer for 1 minute till thickens to spreadable consistency; spread icing on sides and top of cake. You can make it 8 hours ahead. Use cake dome to cover; stand in room temperature.

Nutrition Information

- Calories: 465
- Cholesterol: 116 mg(39%)
- Protein: 6 g(12%)
- Total Fat: 31 g(48%)
- Saturated Fat: 17 g(84%)
- Sodium: 70 mg(3%)
- Fiber: 3 g(10%)
- Total Carbohydrate: 35 g(12%)

24. Bittersweet Chocolate Soufflé

Serving: Serves 8 | Prep: | Cook: | Ready in:

Ingredients

- 1/3 cup granulated sugar plus additional for coating soufflé dish
- 3 tablespoons all-purpose flour
- 3 large egg yolks
- 1 1/2 cups milk
- 2 teaspoons vanilla extract
- 6 ounces fine-quality bittersweet chocolate (not unsweetened), chopped fine
- 6 large egg whites
- 1/4 teaspoon salt
- confectioner's sugar
- Accompaniment: lightly sweetened whipped cream

Direction

- Preheat an oven to 375°F. Butter the 6-cup soufflé dish. Use extra granulated sugar to coat; knock excess sugar out. Butter then sugar 6-in. wide wax paper/foil doubled piece long enough to fit around the dish. With the collar extending 2-in. above the rim, fit prepped dish.

- Whisk 1 tbsp. granulated sugar and flour in a bowl. Whisk 1/4 cup milk and egg yolks in a small bowl. Add to flour mixture and whisk till smooth.
- Heat leftover 1 1/4 cups milk till it reaches a boil in a heavy saucepan on high heat; in a slow stream, whisk into yolk mixture. Put mixture in pan; cook on medium heat till it boils, whisking. At a bare simmer, cook mixture for 2 minutes till very thick, constantly whisking; take off heat. Whisk in chocolate and vanilla till custard in smooth; put custard into a big bowl.
- Beat salt and egg whites using an electric mixer till they hold soft peaks in another bowl. In a slow stream, beat in leftover sugar, beating till meringue holds stiff peaks. Mix 1/4 meringue to lighten into custard; gently yet thoroughly beat in leftover meringue. Put mixture in prepped dish. At this point, you can make soufflé 1 day ahead, covered with paper towel then plastic wrap, chilled. Don't let paper towel touch souffle's surface. In preheated oven, put cold soufflé; bake soufflé in center of oven till set in center and firm for 30-35 minutes.
- Remove collar carefully from soufflé dish; sift confectioners' sugar on soufflé. Serve whipped cream with soufflé immediately.

Nutrition Information

- Calories: 214
- Saturated Fat: 5 g(26%)
- Sodium: 139 mg(6%)
- Fiber: 1 g(5%)
- Total Carbohydrate: 28 g(9%)
- Cholesterol: 74 mg(25%)
- Protein: 6 g(13%)
- Total Fat: 10 g(15%)

25. Black Bottom Pie

Serving: Makes 8 servings | Prep: | Cook: | Ready in:

Ingredients

- 6 ounces gingersnap cookies (about 24)
- 3 tablespoons unsalted butter, melted
- 1 tablespoon heavy cream
- 1 envelope unflavored gelatin powder
- 1 1/2 cups whole milk
- 1/2 cup heavy cream
- 4 large egg yolks
- 1/2 cup sugar
- 2 tablespoons dark rum
- 1 tablespoon cornstarch
- 1 teaspoon vanilla extract
- 1/4 teaspoon kosher salt
- 1/4 cup mascarpone
- 5 ounces semisweet or bittersweet chocolate, finely chopped
- 1/4 cup hot espresso or strong coffee
- 1 cup chilled heavy cream
- 3 tablespoons powdered sugar
- 1 tablespoon dark rum
- 1/2 teaspoon vanilla extract
- Natural unsweetened cocoa powder
- Grated semisweet or bittersweet chocolate
- Toasted sliced almonds
- A 9"-diameter glass or ceramic pie dish

Direction

- Gingersnap crust: Preheat an oven to 350°F. Pulse the cookies till finely ground in food processor. Drizzle in cream and butter; pulse till blended well. Put in prepped dish; pack crumbs up sides and on bottom of dish using sides and bottom of measuring cup; bake for 12-15 minutes till crust is set. Fully cool on a wire rack; put aside.
- Custard: Sprinkle gelatin over 2 tbsp. water in a small bowl; stand for 10 minutes till gelatin softens. Heat cream and milk in a big saucepan on medium heat till it just reaches a simmer.
- In medium bowl, whisk egg yolks with next 5 ingredients; whisk egg mixture slowly into milk mixture then whisk in gelatin. Constantly whisk for 5 minutes on medium low heat till thick.

- Take vanilla custard off heat; mix in mascarpone. In medium bowl, put 1 cup custard; add chocolate. Mix till smooth and melted; mix in espresso. Put chocolate custard in crust; smooth top. Chill pie for 30 minutes till set; stand vanilla custard in room temperature.
- Slowly pour leftover vanilla custard on chilled chocolate layer to not disturb chocolate layer then smooth top; chill for 1 hour till set/keep covered for maximum of 1 day.
- Assembly: Beat sugar and cream using electric mixer on medium low speed till cream starts to thicken in a medium bowl. Add vanilla and rum; put speed on high. Beat till stiff peaks form. Spread custard with whipped cream; dust cocoa powder. Garnish using almonds and grated chocolate. You can make it 4 hours ahead and chill, uncovered.

26. Black Pepper Biscotti

Serving: 48 | Prep: | Cook: 30mins | Ready in:

Ingredients

- 2 cups all-purpose flour
- 2 teaspoons coarsely ground pepper
- 1 teaspoon baking powder
- ½ teaspoon baking soda
- ½ teaspoon salt
- 1½ tablespoons butter, softened
- ¼ cup sugar
- 2 large eggs
- 2 large egg whites
- 1 cup finely chopped dried figs, chopped

Direction

- Preheat the oven to 350°F. Combine salt, baking soda, baking powder, pepper and flour. Whisk sugar and butter together. One at a time, beat in egg whites and eggs; mix well till the butter is distributed. Mix in the dry ingredients till almost smooth. Add in figs and stir.
- On a floured surface, shape the dough into two 14-in.-long logs with 1 1/2 in. thick. Transfer the logs onto a prepped baking sheets and flatten the logs to 1/2 in. high by pressing on the top. Bake for 18-23 minutes till firm to the touch. Place the logs on a rack and let cool. Lower the temperature of the oven to 300°.
- Cut diagonally to divide the logs into slices with 1/2 in. thick. Let the slices stand upright on the baking sheet and bake for half an hour. Allow to cool.

Nutrition Information

- Calories: 38 calories;
- Saturated Fat: 0
- Sodium: 55
- Cholesterol: 9
- Total Carbohydrate: 7
- Total Fat: 1
- Fiber: 0
- Sugar: 3
- Protein: 1

27. Black Sesame Pear Tea Cake

Serving: Makes 10-12 servings | Prep: | Cook: | Ready in:

Ingredients

- 1/2 cup (1 stick) unsalted butter, room temperature, plus more
- 1 1/2 cups plus 2 tablespoons all-purpose flour
- 1 cup almond flour or almond meal
- 2 teaspoon baking powder
- 1/2 teaspoon baking soda
- 1/2 teaspoon kosher salt
- 2 tablespoons plus 1/2 cup black sesame seeds
- 1 1/3 cups plus 2 tablespoons sugar
- 1 large egg
- 1 large egg yolk

- 3/4 cup buttermilk
- 1 (medium) firm but ripe Bosc pear, peeled, cored, cut into 1/4" cubes
- Ingredient info: Almond flour is sold at some supermarkets and at natural foods stores. Black sesame seeds are available at some supermarkets and at Asian markets.

Direction

- Preheat an oven to 325°F. Butter 6 4x2x2-in. metal/paper loaf pans or 1 9x5x3-in. pan. Whisk 2 tbsp. sesame seeds, 1 1/2 cups flour and next 4 ingredients in a medium bowl. Grind leftover 1/2 cup sesame seeds for 2 minutes to make a thick paste in spice mill.
- Beat 1 1/3 cups sugar and 1/2 cup butter using an electric mixer for 2-3 minutes till well combined in big bowl. Add sesame paste; beat for 1-2 minutes till blended, scraping bowl's sides down occasionally. Add egg yolk and egg; beat for 3-4 minutes till fluffy and pale. In 3 additions, beat in flour alternating with the buttermilk in 2 additions on low speed, starting and ending with the dry ingredients. Toss leftover 2 tbsp. flour and pear in small bowl then fold into batter.
- Put batter in prepped pan; smooth top. Sprinkle leftover 2 tbsp. sugar.
- Bake for 45-55 minutes for the small loaves, 1 hour 40 minutes for big loaf till inserted tester in middle exits clean; cool in pans on the wire rack.

Nutrition Information

- Calories: 418
- Cholesterol: 62 mg(21%)
- Protein: 8 g(16%)
- Total Fat: 21 g(32%)
- Saturated Fat: 7 g(36%)
- Sodium: 276 mg(11%)
- Fiber: 3 g(13%)
- Total Carbohydrate: 53 g(18%)

28. Blinis With Tapioca Caviar, Candied Fruits, Toasted Pecans, And Crème Fraîche

Serving: Makes 8 servings | Prep: | Cook: | Ready in:

Ingredients

- 3 quarts water
- 1/2 cup small pearl tapioca*
- 1 cup whipping cream
- 1 3-inch piece vanilla bean, split lengthwise
- 3 large egg yolks (reserve whites for blinis)
- 1/3 cup sugar
- Pinch of salt
- 1/2 pound Yukon Gold potatoes, peeled, cut into 1/2-inch cubes (about 1 1/2 cups)
- 1/2 pound parsnips, peeled, cut into 1/2-inch cubes (about 1 1/2 cups)
- 1/4 cup whole milk
- 1/4 cup all purpose flour
- 3 large eggs
- 2 tablespoons sugar
- 1 teaspoon salt
- 3 large egg whites (reserved from tapioca)
- Vegetable oil
- 1 cup candied red cherries, halved
- 1 cup candied or dried apricots (about 8 ounces), cut in half horizontally, then sliced crosswise into 1/4-inch-wide strips
- 1 cup pecans, toasted, coarsely broken
- 1 cup crème fraîche
- 1/2 cup honey
- 1/4 cup ground cinnamon
- *Available at some supermarkets and specialty foods stores, and at Asian markets.

Direction

- Tapioca: Boil 3-qt. water in big saucepan. Add tapioca; boil, occasionally mixing, for 16 minutes till tapioca is clear. Drain; under cold water, rinse till cool. Put tapioca into a medium bowl.
- Into heavy small saucepan, put cream. From vanilla bean, scrape in seeds; add bean. Simmer. Whisk salt, sugar and egg yolks for 1

minute in medium bowl. Whisk hot cream mixture slowly into yolks. Put it into saucepan; mix on medium heat for 5 minutes till it is thick to coat back of a spoon. Don't boil. Put custard in medium metal bowl. Put bowl above bowl of ice water; mix till custard cools. Mix 3/4 cup of custard into the tapioca. You can make it 1 day ahead. Cover; separately chill leftover custard and tapioca. Mix all leftover custard into tapioca so it loosens before proceeding.

- Blinis: Cook parsnips and potatoes in different medium saucepans with boiling salted water for 15 minutes till very tender. Drain veggies well; put into sieve above medium bowl. Through sieve, force parsnips and potatoes into bowl; mix in milk. In 3 additions, whisk in flour. One by one, add eggs, whisking after each addition to blend. Whisk salt and sugar into batter. Beat egg whites using electric mixer till stiff yet not dry. Fold the egg whites into the batter.
- Line foil on rimmed baking sheet. Heat griddle on medium heat; brush using oil. Drop rounded tablespoonfuls of batter onto griddle in batches, spreading to make 2 1/2-3-in. rounds. Cook for 2 1/2 minutes per side till brown. Put onto sheet. You can make it 1 day ahead. Cool; tightly cover with foil. Chill. Rewarm for 7 minutes in 350°F oven, uncovered.
- Divide tapioca to 8 small bowls. On each of the 8 plates, put 1 bowl. Divide warm blinis to plates. Put toasted pecans, candied apricot slices and dried cherry halves on plates. Put dollop of honey and crème fraiche then small ground cinnamon mound onto plates.

Nutrition Information

- Calories: 642
- Total Fat: 36 g(56%)
- Saturated Fat: 12 g(59%)
- Sodium: 427 mg(18%)
- Fiber: 8 g(32%)
- Total Carbohydrate: 76 g(25%)

- Cholesterol: 187 mg(62%)
- Protein: 10 g(20%)

29. Blueberry Coffee Cake

Serving: Serves 12 | Prep: | Cook: | Ready in:

Ingredients

- 2 1/3 cups all purpose flour
- 3/4 cup (1 1/2 sticks) unsalted butter, room temperature
- 1 cup flaked sweetened coconut
- 1/2 cup (packed) golden brown sugar
- 1 teaspoon ground cinnamon
- 2 1/2 teaspoons baking powder
- 1/2 teaspoon salt
- 1 cup sugar
- 2 large eggs
- 1 cup milk
- 1 12-ounce package frozen blueberries, unthawed, or 2 1/2 cups fresh

Direction

- Mix cinnamon, brown sugar, coconut, 1/4 cup butter and 1/3 cup flour till crumbly and moist in a medium bowl; put aside the topping.
- Preheat an oven to 375°F. Butter then flour the 13x9x2-in. baking pan. Sift salt, baking powder and leftover 2 cups flour into a small bowl. Beat leftover 1/2 cup butter with an electric mixer till fluffy in a big bowl. Add 1 cup sugar slowly; beat till blended well. One by one, add eggs; beat to blend after every addition. Alternately with milk, stir the dry ingredients into batter in 3 additions each and fold in the blueberries.
- Put the cake batter in prepped baking pan; evenly sprinkle topping on batter. Bake cake for 40 minutes till topping is golden brown and inserted tester in the middle exits clean; slightly cool the cake. Serve at room temperature/warm.

Nutrition Information

- Calories: 364
- Saturated Fat: 11 g(54%)
- Sodium: 200 mg(8%)
- Fiber: 2 g(9%)
- Total Carbohydrate: 51 g(17%)
- Cholesterol: 64 mg(21%)
- Protein: 5 g(10%)
- Total Fat: 16 g(25%)

30. Blueberry Lemon Pound Cake

Serving: One 10-inch bundt cake | Prep: | Cook: | Ready in:

Ingredients

- 1/3 cup milk
- 6 large eggs
- 1 1/2 tablespoons vanilla extract
- 2 2/3 cups all-purpose flour
- 1 teaspoon double-acting baking powder
- 1 1/4 teaspoons salt
- 3 sticks (1 1/2 cups) unsalted butter, softened
- 1/2 cup granulated sugar
- 3/4 cup firmly packed light brown sugar
- 1/4 cup freshly grated lemon zest
- 3 cups picked over blueberries, tossed with 1 1/2 tablespoons flour
- 1/3 cup fresh lemon juice
- 1/2 cup granulated sugar

Direction

- Cake: Whisk vanilla, eggs and milk in a small bowl. Sift salt, baking powder and flour into a bowl. Cream granulated sugar, zest, brown sugar and butter using an electric mixer till it is fluffy and light in big bowl. Alternately with egg mixture, add flour mixture, starting then finishing with flour mixture; beat batter till just combined after each addition. Fold in 1 1/2 cups blueberries. Put 1/3 batter into 10-in. 3-qt. greased then floured Bundt pan, evenly spreading. Sprinkle 1/2 cup leftover blueberries over; put leftover batter in pan, evenly spreading. Sprinkle leftover blueberries over; bake cake till tester exits clean and golden for 1 hour-1 hour 10 minutes in center of preheated 350°F oven.
- Remove cake from oven; immediately poke all over using wooden skewer. Brush 1/2 syrup. Cool cake for 10 minutes in pan on rack. Invert onto rack; poke all over using skewer. Brush leftover syrup on cake.
- As cake bakes, make syrup; Boil sugar and lemon juice in a small saucepan, mixing till sugar dissolves. Take off heat.

Nutrition Information

- Calories: 5875
- Saturated Fat: 186 g(932%)
- Sodium: 3832 mg(160%)
- Fiber: 22 g(90%)
- Total Carbohydrate: 700 g(233%)
- Cholesterol: 1856 mg(619%)
- Protein: 82 g(163%)
- Total Fat: 312 g(481%)

31. Blueberry Pie With Cornmeal Crust And Lemon Cream

Serving: Makes 8 servings | Prep: | Cook: | Ready in:

Ingredients

- 2 1/2 cups all purpose flour
- 1/4 cup cornmeal (preferably stone-ground, medium grind)
- 3 tablespoons sugar
- 3/4 teaspoon salt
- 1/2 cup plus 6 tablespoons (1 3/4 sticks total) chilled unsalted butter, cut into 1/2-inch cubes
- 1/4 cup nonhydrogenated solid vegetable shortening, frozen, cut into 1/2-inch pieces

- 4 tablespoons (or more) ice water
- 5 cups fresh blueberries (about 27 ounces)
- 3/4 cup sugar
- 1/4 cup cornstarch
- 1 tablespoon fresh lemon juice
- 1 tablespoon water
- Milk (for brushing)
- 1 1/2 tablespoons raw sugar*
- Lemon Cream

Direction

- Crust: Blend salt, sugar, cornmeal and flour in processor. Add shortening and butter; blend till it looks like coarse meal with on/off turns. Add 4 tbsp. ice water; blend till moist clumps start to form. If dough is dry, add extra ice water by teaspoonfuls. Gather dough to ball. Halve dough; flatten each half to disk. Separately wrap disks in plastic; chill for a minimum of 1 hour. You can make it 1 day ahead, kept chilled. Before rolling out, soften dough in room temperature for 10 minutes.
- Filling: Toss 1 tbsp. water, lemon juice, cornstarch, sugar and blueberries to blend in big bowl; stand for 30 minutes till juices start to form in room temperature.
- Preheat an oven to 400°F. In bottom of oven, put rimmed baking sheet. Roll 1 dough disk out to 12-in. round between 2 generously floured parchment paper sheets. Peel top parchment sheet off; invert dough in 9-in. diameter glass pie dish. Peel 2nd parchment sheet off carefully. Press dough in pie dish carefully; as needed, press cracker together to seal. Leave dough overhang. Put filling in pie crust.
- Roll 2nd dough disk out to 12-in. round between 2 generously floured parchment paper sheets; peel top parchment sheet off. Evenly and carefully invert dough on filling; peel 2nd parchment sheet off. Trim both crust's overhang to 1-in. Fold the overhang under; to seal, press. Decoratively crimp edges. Cut 5 2-in. long slits on pie's top crust to let steam escape while baking. Brush milk lightly on top crust, not edges. Sprinkle raw sugar.
- Bake pie for 15 minutes. Lower oven temperature to 350°F; bake for 1 hour 15 minutes till filling thickly bubbles through slits and crust is golden brown; fully cool pie on rack. Cut to wedges; serve with lemon cream.

32. Bobbie Mills's Cinnamon Cake

Serving: | Prep: | Cook: | Ready in:

Ingredients

- 2 cups sifted cake flour (not self-rising)
- 2 teaspoons baking powder
- 4 teaspoons cinnamon
- 2/3 cup vegetable shortening, softened
- 1 1/3 cups sugar
- 2/3 cup milk
- 3 large eggs
- an 8-ounce package cream cheese, softened
- 1 stick (1/2 cup) unsalted butter, softened
- 3 3/4 cups confectioners' sugar
- 1 teaspoon freshly grated lemon zest
- 1 teaspoon fresh lemon juice

Direction

- Cake layers: Preheat an oven to 350°F. Butter then flour 2 round 8-in. cake pans; knock out extra flour.
- Whisk cinnamon, baking powder and flour in a bowl. Using an electric mixer, beat sugar and shortening till fluffy and light in another bowl. Beat in milk. One by one, beat in eggs; beat well after each. Add flour mixture; beat till smooth. Divide batter to pans; smooth tops. Bake in center of oven till tester exits clean for 30 minutes; cool layers for 10 minutes in pans on the rack. Invert onto rack; fully cool.
- Frosting: Beat butter and cream cheese till smooth using electric mixer in a bowl. Beat in confectioners' sugar slowly; beat in juice and lemon zest.

- Assemble cake, spreading the frosting between layers then on side and on top.

Nutrition Information

- Calories: 346
- Fiber: 1 g(2%)
- Total Carbohydrate: 48 g(16%)
- Cholesterol: 53 mg(18%)
- Protein: 3 g(6%)
- Total Fat: 16 g(25%)
- Saturated Fat: 7 g(36%)
- Sodium: 94 mg(4%)

33. Braided Egg Bread

Serving: 60 | Prep: 30mins | Cook: 55mins | Ready in:

Ingredients

- 2 (.25 ounce) packages active dry yeast
- 1/2 cup warm water (110 degrees F/45 degrees C)
- 2 cups hot milk
- 1/2 cup white sugar
- 1/2 cup butter
- 2 teaspoons salt
- 1/2 cup water
- 5 eggs
- 11 cups all-purpose flour
- 1 egg
- 2 tablespoons sesame seeds

Direction

- Proof 1/2 cup warm water and yeast in a large mixing bowl.
- Mix 1/2 cup water, salt, butter, sugar, and hot milk in a medium bowl. Let the mixture cool to 110 degrees.
- Place 5 eggs in a small bowl and lightly beat, then place into cooled milk mixture. Transfer milk mixture to yeast mixture. Whisk in 2 cups flour until smooth. Gradually add the rest of the flour until it forms a stiff dough. Place on a floured board and knead for 10 minutes (5 minutes with a bread hook). Transfer to a large plastic or glass bowl that is lightly greased. Flip the dough over to grease both sides. Cover and allow it to rise in a warm, dark place for about 60 minutes until twice size.
- Smash down, cover, and allow it to rise again for about 30 minutes until doubled.
- Smash again, and form into three parts. Turn each part into a 20-inch roll. Braid rolls on a large cookie sheet that is greased. Cover and allow it to rise until twice size.
- Lightly whisk the rest of the egg and brush loaf. Dust with sesame seeds. Place in the preheated oven and bake for about 55 minutes at 350°F (175°C) until nicely browned. You can make it into two regular sized loaves. Lower baking time slightly.

Nutrition Information

- Calories: 117 calories;
- Sodium: 99
- Total Carbohydrate: 19.7
- Cholesterol: 23
- Protein: 3.4
- Total Fat: 2.6

34. Brioche

Serving: 16 | Prep: 40mins | Cook: 30mins | Ready in:

Ingredients

- 1 tablespoon active dry yeast
- 1/3 cup warm water (110 degrees F)
- 3 1/2 cups all-purpose flour
- 1 tablespoon white sugar
- 1 teaspoon salt
- 4 eggs
- 1 cup butter, softened
- 1 egg yolk
- 1 teaspoon cold water

Direction

- Melt yeast in warm water in a small bowl; stand for 10 minutes till creamy.
- Mix salt, sugar and flour in a big bowl. Create a well in middle of the bowl; mix in yeast mixture and eggs; beat well till dough pulls together. Turn out on lightly floured surface; knead for 8 minutes till supple and smooth.
- Flatten dough; spread it using 1/3 butter then knead well. Repeat two times to incorporate leftover butter. Rest dough between additions of butter for a few minutes, this can take around 20 minutes or longer. Oil a big bowl lightly. Put dough into bowl; turn to coat in oil. Cover using plastic wrap; rise for 1 hour in a warm place till doubled in volume.
- Deflate dough; cover in plastic wrap. Refrigerate it for 6 hours – overnight to make it more workable.
- Preheat an oven to 200°C/400°F. Grease 2 9x5-inch loaf pans lightly. Beat 1 teaspoon water and egg yolk for glaze.
- Turn dough on lightly floured surface. Divide dough to 2 even pieces; shape to loaves. Put into prepped pans. Use greased plastic wrap to cover; rise for 1 hour till doubled in volume.
- Brush egg wash on rolls/loaves; in preheated oven, bake till deep golden brown. Begin checking loaves for doneness 25 minutes after and at 10 minutes for rolls. Cool loaves for 10 minutes in pans. Transfer to wire racks; fully cool.

Nutrition Information

- Calories: 228 calories;
- Total Fat: 13.3
- Sodium: 246
- Total Carbohydrate: 22.1
- Cholesterol: 90
- Protein: 5

35. Brown Butter Almond Torte With Sour Cherry Sauce

Serving: | Prep: | Cook: | Ready in:

Ingredients

- 1 stick (1/2 cup) unsalted butter
- 1 teaspoon vanilla
- 1 cup blanched whole almonds (about 4 ounces)
- 1/2 cup all-purpose flour
- 1 cup sugar
- 3/4 teaspoon salt
- 6 large egg whites
- 1/3 cup sliced almonds
- 3 cups sour cherries (about 1 1/2 pounds)
- 1/2 cup sugar
- 1/2 cup water
- 1 teaspoon cornstarch mixed with 1 tablespoon water

Direction

- Torte: Melt and heat butter till golden brown with a nutlike fragrance in a small saucepan on medium low heat; pan's bottom with be covered in brown specks. Cool the butter to warm; mix in vanilla.
- Preheat an oven to 375°F. Butter then flour 9-in. round cake pan; knock extra flour out.
- Finely grind 1/2 tsp. salt, 2/3 cup sugar, flour and whole almonds in a food processor.
- Beat leftover 1/4 tsp. salt and whites using an electric mixer till they hold soft peaks in a big bowl. Slowly add leftover 1/3 cup sugar; beat till meringue holds stiff peaks. Thoroughly yet gently fold in nut mixture then gently yet thoroughly fold in butter; it'll deflate. Spread in pan.
- Evenly sprinkle sliced almonds over batter; bake torte in center of oven till tester exits clean and starts to pull away from pan's sides for 35-40 minutes.
- Cool torte for 15 minutes in pan on rack; invert onto rack. Turn torte right side up; fully cool.

- You can make torte 1 day ahead; keep in room temperature in airtight container.
- Serve sauce with cake.
- Sauce: Pit cherries above a heavy saucepan. Boil water, sugar and cherries in a pan. Mix cornstarch mixture; add to sauce, mixing. Simmer sauce for 2 minutes; cool to room temperature. You can make sauce 2 days ahead, covered, chilled. Before serving, bring it to room temperature. Creates 3 cups.

Nutrition Information

- Calories: 292
- Total Fat: 14 g(21%)
- Saturated Fat: 5 g(27%)
- Sodium: 176 mg(7%)
- Fiber: 3 g(10%)
- Total Carbohydrate: 39 g(13%)
- Cholesterol: 20 mg(7%)
- Protein: 6 g(11%)

36. Brown Sugar Buttercream

Serving: Makes about 3 1/2 cups | Prep: 15mins | Cook: 25mins | Ready in:

Ingredients

- 3 large egg whites at room temperature
- 3/4 teaspoon salt
- 1 cup packed dark brown sugar
- 1/2 cup water
- 1/2 teaspoon fresh lemon juice
- 3 sticks (1 1/2 cups) unsalted butter, cut into pieces and softened
- 2 teaspoons vanilla
- a candy thermometer

Direction

- Mix salt and egg whites in a big bowl.
- Boil water and brown sugar in a heavy small saucepan on medium high heat, washing down pan's sides with pastry brushed dipped into water. Beat whites using electric mixer on medium high speed till frothy when sugar syrup boils. Add lemon juice; beat on medium speed till whites hold soft peaks. Don't beat again till sugar syrup is done.
- Meanwhile, place candy thermometer in sugar syrup; boil till syrup reads 238-242°F. Take off heat right away; put into 1-cup heatproof glass measure. In a thin stream, put hot syrup down bowl's side slowly into egg whites, constantly beating on high speed. Beat meringue for 6 minutes till meringue is cool to touch, scraping bowl down with rubber spatula. Be sure meringue is fully cool before continuing.
- 1 piece at 1 time, add butter slowly with mixer on medium speed, beating well after every addition till incorporated. Chill bowl's bottom briefly in a big bowl with ice water for several seconds before beating in leftover butter if buttercream looks soup after adding some butter and meringue is too warm. Beat till buttercream is smooth; might look curdled at first, but it'll come back together before you finish beating. Add vanilla; beat for 1 minute.
- You can make buttercream 1 week ahead, covered, chilled, or frozen for 1 month. Bring, don't use a microwave, to room temperature; before using, beat with electric mixer.

Nutrition Information

- Calories: 281
- Fiber: 0 g(0%)
- Total Carbohydrate: 18 g(6%)
- Cholesterol: 61 mg(20%)
- Protein: 1 g(2%)
- Total Fat: 23 g(36%)
- Saturated Fat: 15 g(73%)
- Sodium: 154 mg(6%)

37. Brown Sugar–Ginger Cream Cake

Serving: Serves 8 | Prep: | Cook: | Ready in:

Ingredients

- 3/4 cup all-purpose flour
- 3/4 cup cake flour
- 1 1/2 teaspoons baking powder
- 1/4 teaspoon salt
- 2 eggs, at room temperature
- 1 cup heavy cream
- 1 cup maple sugar, dark muscovado, or organic dark brown sugar
- 1 1/2 teaspoons ground ginger
- 1/8 teaspoon freshly ground pepper
- 1 teaspoon vanilla extract

Direction

- Prepare a loaf pan or an 8-inch springform pan by buttering and flouring. If loaf pan is used, line the ends and bottom with a parchment paper. Set oven to 350°F; preheat.
- In a large bowl, mix baking powder, salt, and flours; whisk together. Create a well at the center.
- Whisk eggs until foamy using an electric mixer with whisk attachment, then add the sugar, flavorings, and cream. Continue whisking until mixture resembles soft whipped cream. (The cream will not thicken if you're using maple sugar, but it still works on the cake). Transfer mixture into the middle of the flour mixture and beat all together until well blended and lumps free. Transfer batter into the pan and spread evenly.
- For 50 to 60 minutes, bake until a tester for cake comes out clean. Set aside to cool, for 15 minutes. Take out the rim or invert the cake out from the pan. Peel off paper. Let cool; slice and serve.

38. Brownie Bottom Lemon Cheesecake

Serving: Makes 10 to 12 servings | Prep: | Cook: | Ready in:

Ingredients

- Nonstick vegetable oil spray
- 6 tablespoons all purpose flour
- 1 1/2 teaspoons unsweetened cocoa powder
- 1/8 teaspoon salt
- 3 ounces bittersweet chocolate (54% to 60% cacao), chopped
- 1/4 cup (1/2 stick) unsalted butter
- 3/4 cup sugar
- 1/4 cup (packed) golden brown sugar
- 1 large egg
- 1/2 teaspoon vanilla extract
- 5 8-ounce packages cream cheese, room temperature
- 1 3/4 cups sugar
- 2 tablespoons all purpose flour
- 1 tablespoon finely grated lemon peel
- 4 teaspoons fresh lemon juice
- 5 large eggs
- 2 large egg yolks
- 1/2 cup sour cream
- 1/4 cup heavy whipping cream
- 1 cup sour cream
- Bittersweet chocolate curls or shavings
- 1 lemon, halved lengthwise, thinly sliced crosswise
- 9-inch-diameter springform pan with 2 3/4-inch- to 3-inch-high sides
- Offset spatula

Direction

- Crust: Preheat an oven to 350°F. Spray nonstick spray inside 9-in. diameter springform pan that has 2 3/4-3-in. high sides. Whisk salt, cocoa and flour in small bowl; put aside. Mix butter and chocolate in metal medium bowl; put bowl above saucepan of simmering water. Mix till smooth and melted; take bowl from above water. Put both sugars in chocolate mixture; whisk till blended. Cool for 10 minutes till it is barely lukewarm. Whisk vanilla and egg into chocolate mixture then fold flour mixture into the chocolate mixture; evenly spread brownie batter on bottom of prepped pan.

- Bake brownie crust for 20 minutes till inserted tester in middle exits with some of the moist crumbs attached and top looks slightly cracker. Put pan on rack; cool crust for 30 minutes to room temperature. Maintain the oven temperature.
- Filling: On rimmed baking sheet, put pan with cooled crust. Beat cream cheese using electric mixer till smooth in a big bowl. Add lemon juice, lemon peel, flour and sugar; beat till smooth. One by one, add yolks and egg; beat till just incorporated after every addition. Beat in whipping cream and 1/2 cup sour cream. Put filling on brownie crust in pan and smooth top.
- Bake cake for 1 hour 20 minutes till set around edges, light golden, puffed and middle slightly moves when pan is shaken gently. From oven, remove cake; maintain the oven temperature.
- Topping: In dollops, put 1 cup sour cream over cake's top; evenly spread with offset spatula on top. Put cake in oven; bake for 5 minutes. Around cake's sides, run small sharp knife to loosen. Put pan with the cake directly in the fridge; chill overnight, uncovered. Cake might sink in middle. You can make it 2 days ahead, kept chilled.
- From cake, remove pan sides. Between crust and pan bottom, run thin sharp knife to loosen. Put cake on platter using 2 metal spatulas for aid. Use lemon slices and chocolate curls to garnish cake's top edge.

39. Burnt Orange Panna Cotta

Serving: Makes 6 servings | Prep: 30mins | Cook: 9hours | Ready in:

Ingredients

- 1 1/2 teaspoons unflavored gelatin
- 2 tablespoons whole milk
- 1/4 cup confectioners sugar
- 1/8 teaspoon salt
- 1 1/2 cups heavy cream
- 1/4 cup granulated sugar
- 2 1/2 teaspoons finely grated fresh orange zest
- 1/4 cup fresh orange juice
- 3/4 cup sour cream
- 2 navel oranges
- Special equipment: 6 (1/2-cup) metal molds

Direction

- Sprinkle gelatin on milk in small bowl; stand to soften for 1 minute.
- Whisk 1 cup heavy cream, salt and confectioners' sugar.
- Cook granulated sugar till it starts to melt in small dry heavy saucepan on medium heat, undisturbed; cook till sugar melts into golden caramel, occasionally mixing with fork. Mix in 1 1/2 tsp. zest; cook for 30-60 seconds till zest is fragrant and toasted, mixing. Mix cream mixture. Add to caramel carefully; it'll harden and steam. Cook on medium low heat till caramel dissolves, mixing.
- Mix in leftover 1 tsp. zest and gelatin mixture till gelatin dissolves; mix in orange juice. Stand till just cooled to room temperature. Put through fine sieve in medium bowl.
- Use electric mixer to beat leftover 1/2 cup heavy cream to soft peaks. Whisk sour cream till smooth in another bowl. Into sour cream, fold whipped cream; fold into caramel till well combined.
- Put into molds; chill for 8 hours till firm.
- In hot water, dip molds for 2-3 seconds; run thin knife around mold's edges to release panna cotta then invert onto dessert plates. Stand for 20 minutes at room temperature.
- Remove white pith and peel from oranges using a sharp knife as panna cotta stands. Cut sections free from the membranes holding oranges above bowl to catch juices. From

membranes, squeeze juice into bowl; chop orange sections coarsely.
- Put orange juice and pieces on desserts before serving.

Nutrition Information

- Calories: 346
- Total Carbohydrate: 23 g(8%)
- Cholesterol: 97 mg(32%)
- Protein: 3 g(6%)
- Total Fat: 28 g(43%)
- Saturated Fat: 17 g(86%)
- Sodium: 89 mg(4%)
- Fiber: 1 g(5%)

40. Butter Cake

Serving: 12 | Prep: 25mins | Cook: 30mins | Ready in:

Ingredients

- 1 1/2 cups all-purpose flour
- 1/2 teaspoon salt
- 2 teaspoons baking powder
- 1/2 cup butter, room temperature
- 1 cup white sugar
- 2 eggs, room temperature
- 1 teaspoon vanilla extract
- 3/4 cup milk, room temperature

Direction

- Preheat an oven to 175°C/350°F; grease 8-in. square baking pan lightly. Line wax paper/parchment paper on bottom or lightly dust with flour.
- Sift baking powder, salt and flour together.
- Beat white sugar and butter till light in color and fluffy. Add eggs slowly, beating well after each addition; mix in vanilla. Add sifted dry ingredients into creamed mixture alternately with milk; mix just till blended. Pour batter in prepped pan.
- Bake for 30 minutes at 175°C/350°F till cake springs back when touched lightly; cool for 10 minutes in pan. Invert onto wire rack; fully cool.

Nutrition Information

- Calories: 210 calories;
- Sodium: 251
- Total Carbohydrate: 29.6
- Cholesterol: 53
- Protein: 3.2
- Total Fat: 9

41. Butter Nut Blondies

Serving: Makes 2 dozen (2-inch) squares | Prep: | Cook: | Ready in:

Ingredients

- One half cup (1 stick, 4 ounces) unsalted butter
- 2 cups (15 ounces) packed dark brown sugar
- 3 large eggs
- 1 tablespoon vinegar, preferably apple cider vinegar
- 1 teaspoon vanilla extract
- 1/4 teaspoon butter-rum, butterscotch or butter-pecan flavor (optional but delicious)
- 1 teaspoon baking powder
- 1 teaspoon salt
- 1 1/2 cups (6 ounces) traditional whole wheat flour
- 1 1/2 (5 5/8 ounces) chopped pecans or walnuts

Direction

- Preheat an oven to 350°F. Grease 9x13-in. pan lightly. Melt butter in a saucepan on low heat/microwave-safe bowl; remove from heat. Add sugar; mix till blended well. Transfer mixture into a mixing bowl; cool to lukewarm.

- One by one, add eggs; beat well after each addition. Beat in salt, baking powder, flavor (optional), vanilla and vinegar; mix in nuts and flour. Spread batter in prepped pan.
- Bake blondies for 26-28 minutes till top looks shiny. Don't overbake; bake till a sharp knife's tip poked into very middle shows sticky crumbs, yet not wet batter, and edges begin to pull away from pan's sides. Remove from oven; run knife all around pan's edges. This keeps blondies fat as they cool by letting edges settle in pan along with the center. Before cutting, fully cool. Wait 24 hours prior to cutting into squares if you like squares with very smooth texture. Waiting will give the bran in the whole wheat time to soften up.

42. Buttermilk Cookies

Serving: 36 | Prep: 20mins | Cook: 6mins |Ready in:

Ingredients

- 1 cup shortening
- 2 cups white sugar
- 4 eggs
- 4 cups all-purpose flour
- 4 teaspoons baking powder
- 2 teaspoons baking soda
- 1 teaspoon salt
- 1 cup buttermilk
- 4 teaspoons vanilla extract

Direction

- Preheat an oven to 220 °C or 425 °F. Oil cookie sheets.
- Cream together the sugar and shortening in a big bowl. Whisk in eggs, one by one, then mix in vanilla. Into the creamed mixture, mix the salt, baking soda, baking powder and flour, mix alternately with buttermilk. Onto the prepped cookie sheets, drop by rounded spoonfuls.
- In the prepped oven, allow to bake for 6 to 8 minutes. On baking sheet, let the cookies cool for 5 minutes prior to taking to a wire rack to cool fully.

Nutrition Information

- Calories: 157 calories;
- Total Carbohydrate: 22.3
- Cholesterol: 24
- Protein: 2.4
- Total Fat: 6.4
- Sodium: 204

43. Buttermilk Panna Cotta With Berries And Vanilla Sabayon

Serving: Makes 4 servings | Prep: | Cook: |Ready in:

Ingredients

- 3/4 teaspoon powdered unflavored gelatin (1/4-ounce envelope)
- 1/2 cup heavy cream
- 1/4 cup sugar
- 1 vanilla bean, split lengthwise
- 1 cup well-shaken buttermilk
- 1/2 cup heavy cream
- 3 large egg yolks
- 2 tablespoons sugar
- 2 tablespoons sweet dessert wine, such as sauterne
- 1 tablespoon orange liqueur such as Grand Marnier
- 1/2 cup mixed fresh berries such as blackberries, blueberries, and raspberries
- 1/4 cup fresh strawberries, hulled and quartered
- 4 (4- to 6-ounce) ramekins, kitchen blowtorch (optional)

Direction

- For panna cotta: Sprinkle gelatin over 3 tbsp. of water in a small bowl. Allow to stand for 1 minute to soften the gelatin.
- Whisk sugar and cream together over moderate heat in a heavy medium saucepan. Scrape in vanilla bean's seeds and place in bean. Heat for 2 minutes while whisking occasionally to dissolve the sugar. Take away from the heat then whisk in buttermilk and gelatin. Through a fine-mesh sieve, strain the mixture into a medium nonreactive bowl and remove the vanilla bean. Use plastic wrap to cover the surface and allow to rest for 15 minutes at room temperature.
- Place the mixture into ramekins then store for at least 8 hours or overnight in the fridge till set.
- For sabayon: Use a whisk or an electric mixer to beat cream in a medium bowl till it forms stiff peaks. Use a whisk or an electric mixer to whisk egg yolks and sugar together in a large nonreactive metal bowl for 1 minute till pale yellow and light. Place the bowl over a saucepan filled with barely simmering water then whisk in wine. Cook and stir constantly for 5 minutes till thick and it reads 140°F on an instant-read thermometer, be careful not to allow the mixture to steam.
- Take the bowl out of the saucepan then keep whisking for 2-3 minutes till cool. Fold in orange liqueur then whipped cream gently.
- For assembly and serving: Cut around the edge on the inside of each ramekin using a thin sharp knife till loosen. Dip 1 ramekin's bottom into a bowl filled with very warm water for 6 seconds. Set a dessert plate on top of the ramekin, upside-down and invert, gently lift off the ramekin to let the panna cottas settle on the plate. Do the same to unmold the leftover panna cottas.
- Place berries on top and around each panna cotta then place over the berries with sabayon. Lightly brown sabayon with kitchen blowtorch (if preferred) and serve at once.

Nutrition Information

- Calories: 385
- Fiber: 1 g(3%)
- Total Carbohydrate: 28 g(9%)
- Cholesterol: 222 mg(74%)
- Protein: 7 g(14%)
- Total Fat: 26 g(40%)
- Saturated Fat: 15 g(76%)
- Sodium: 150 mg(6%)

44. Butterscotch Pecan Thins

Serving: Makes about 48 cookies | Prep: | Cook: | Ready in:

Ingredients

- 1 1/2 sticks (3/4 cup) unsalted butter, softened
- 1 cup firmly packed light brown sugar
- 1 large egg
- 1 1/2 teaspoons vanilla extract
- 1 1/2 cups all-purpose flour
- 3/4 teaspoon double-acting baking powder
- 1/2 teaspoon salt
- about 48 pecan halves

Direction

- Cream brown sugar with butter using an electric mixer till fluffy and light in a bowl; beat in vanilla and egg. Sift salt, baking powder and flour into bowl; beat dough till firm to handle. Halve dough; shape each half to 6-in. log on wax paper piece, using wax paper for a guide. Chill logs for at least 4 hours – overnight, wrapped in wax paper.
- Preheat an oven to 350°F. Use a sharp knife to cut logs to 1/4-in. thick slices; put onto lightly buttered baking sheets, 3-in. apart. Onto each cookie, press a pecan half. In batches, bake cookies till golden for 10-12 minutes in center of oven; cool for 1 minute on baking sheets. Put cookies on racks; fully cool.

Nutrition Information

- Calories: 69
- Fiber: 0 g(1%)
- Total Carbohydrate: 8 g(3%)
- Cholesterol: 12 mg(4%)
- Protein: 1 g(1%)
- Total Fat: 4 g(6%)
- Saturated Fat: 2 g(10%)
- Sodium: 33 mg(1%)

45. Café Au Lait Puddings

Serving: Makes 4 servings | Prep: 15mins | Cook: 45mins | Ready in:

Ingredients

- 2 cups whole milk
- 3 tablespoons instant coffee granules
- 2 tablespoons plus 2 teaspoon cornstarch
- 1/4 cup plus 2 tablespoon sugar, divided
- 1/2 cup heavy cream
- 1/4 teaspoon pure vanilla extract
- Cinnamon for sprinkling
- Equipment: 4 (4-to 5-ounces) cups or ramekins

Direction

- Whisk small pinch salt, 1/4 cup sugar, cornstarch, coffee granules and milk in medium heavy saucepan; boil on medium heat, occasionally mixing. Boil for 1 minute, constantly mixing. Put in a metal bowl in ice bath; cool for 10 minutes, mixing often. Put into ramekins/cups; chill for 20 minutes, uncovered.
- Use an electric mixer to beat leftover 2 tbsp. sugar, vanilla and cream till soft peaks form; put whipped cream on puddings. Lightly dust cream with cinnamon.

Nutrition Information

- Calories: 280
- Saturated Fat: 9 g(46%)

- Sodium: 65 mg(3%)
- Fiber: 0 g(1%)
- Total Carbohydrate: 32 g(11%)
- Cholesterol: 53 mg(18%)
- Protein: 5 g(10%)
- Total Fat: 15 g(23%)

46. Cape Brandy Tart With Brandy Sauce

Serving: Makes 6 servings | Prep: | Cook: | Ready in:

Ingredients

- 1 cup pitted, chopped dates
- 1 teaspoon baking soda
- 2 1/2 tablespoons unsalted butter or margarine, softened
- 1 cup superfine sugar
- 1 large egg
- 1 1/2 cups flour
- Pinch of salt
- 3 teaspoons baking powder
- 1/2 cup pecans or walnuts, chopped
- Brandy sauce
- 1 to 2 cups whipped cream, for topping
- 1/2 cup sugar
- 1/2 tablespoon unsalted butter
- 1/2 teaspoon vanilla extract
- 1/4 cup brandy (or rum)

Direction

- For the tart, set the oven to 350°F for preheating.
- In a small bowl, put the dates and drizzle with 1 cup of boiling water. Add the baking soda to the bowl. Allow the dates to stand for 10 minutes until soft.
- Combine the sugar and butter in a bowl of an electric mixer with beaters attached to it. Beat the mixture until creamy. Whisk in egg. Sift in baking powder, flour, and salt. Add the date

mixture with water and the pecans. Stir the mixture well.
- Use a parchment paper to line the buttered or lightly oiled 9-inches aluminum pie plate (you can also use the 9-inches springform pan). Spread the date and nut mixture into the prepared pie plate. Let it bake for 45 minutes until the inserted toothpick in the center comes out dry. Remove it from the pie plate, discarding the parchment paper. Let it cool slightly. Cut it into wedges and pour the whipped cream and Brandy Sauce on top.
- For the brandy sauce, mix 1/4 cup of cold water and sugar in a saucepan that is set over medium-high. Bring the mixture to a boil. Boil for 5 minutes while stirring often until the sugar has dissolved. Remove it from the heat and mix in vanilla and butter. Pour in the brandy.
- Note: If you prepare the tart in advance, allow it to cool first to room temperature. Transfer it in a plastic freezer bag, expelling any excess air before sealing the bag. You can store it inside the freezer for up to 1 month. Reheat the tart inside the 250°F oven for 45 minutes until warm.

Nutrition Information

- Calories: 588
- Total Fat: 16 g(25%)
- Saturated Fat: 7 g(33%)
- Sodium: 407 mg(17%)
- Fiber: 4 g(17%)
- Total Carbohydrate: 104 g(35%)
- Cholesterol: 58 mg(19%)
- Protein: 6 g(13%)

47. Cappuccino Cheesecake

Serving: Makes 12 servings | Prep: | Cook: |Ready in:

Ingredients

- 8 whole graham crackers, crushed
- 5 tablespoons melted unsalted butter
- 1 1/2 cups sugar
- 1/2 cup whipping cream
- 4 teaspoons instant espresso powder or coffee powder
- 1 1/2 teaspoons vanilla extract
- 4 8-ounce packages cream cheese, room temperature
- 4 large eggs
- 2 tablespoons all purpose flour
- 1 cup (6 ounces) semisweet chocolate chips
- Chocolate curls (optional)

Direction

- Preheat an oven to 350°F. In medium bowl, mix 1/4 cup sugar, butter and crackers; press on bottom, not the sides, of 9-in. diameter springform pan that has 2 3/4-in. high sides. Bake the crust for 10 minutes; cool. Maintain the oven temperature.
- Mix vanilla, espresso powder and cream in small bowl; put aside. Beat cream cheese till smooth using electric mixer in big bowl; beat in leftover 1 1/4 cups sugar slowly then eggs, one by one. Beat in flour. Mix espresso mixture till powder is dissolved; beat into the cream cheese mixture. Mix in chocolate chips. Put batter on crust; bake cake for 1 hour 5 minutes till middle is just set and edges start to crack and are puffed. Cool for 30 minutes on rack; chill cake for 6 hours till cold, uncovered. Cover; keep for a minimum of 1 to a maximum of 2 days, chilled.
- To loosen, cut around cake; release pan sides. If desired, top with curls.

Nutrition Information

- Calories: 565
- Sodium: 348 mg(15%)
- Fiber: 1 g(5%)
- Total Carbohydrate: 46 g(15%)
- Cholesterol: 169 mg(56%)
- Protein: 8 g(16%)

- Total Fat: 41 g(62%)
- Saturated Fat: 23 g(114%)

48. Cappuccino Chocolate Layer Cake

Serving: Makes 12 servings | Prep: | Cook: | Ready in:

Ingredients

- 6 tablespoons water
- 3 tablespoons sugar
- 1 tablespoon instant coffee powder
- 4 ounces unsweetened chocolate, chopped
- 2 cups all purpose flour
- 1 1/2 teaspoons baking powder
- 1 teaspoon ground cinnamon
- 1/4 teaspoon salt
- 2 teaspoons instant coffee powder
- 1 1/2 cups whole milk
- 2 cups sugar
- 1/2 cup (1 stick) unsalted butter, room temperature
- 2 large eggs
- 2 teaspoons vanilla extract
- Fudge Frosting

Direction

- Preparation of coffee syrup: In a small saucepan, mix together all the ingredients. On low heat, stir until coffee and sugar dissolves. Set aside to cool. (Can be done 2 days in advance. Put in chiller)
- Preparation of cake: Set oven at 350°F and place rack at the middle; preheat. Prepare two 9-in diameter cake pans with a height of 2 inches; butter pans and using a waxed paper, line the bottom of each pan and butter the paper. Dust with flour. On top of the double boiler set over simmering water, stir in the chocolate until melted. Take out from the top of the water.
- In a medium bowl, sift baking powder, cinnamon, salt, and flour. In a separate medium bowl, add in coffee powder into the milk; stir. In a large bowl of an electric mixer, whisk butter and sugar until well incorporated. Add in eggs one by one. Combine in melted vanilla and chocolate and pour in the dry ingredients alternately with the milk mixture in 3 additions. Distribute into the pans.
- For about 35 minutes, bake the cakes until tester inserted at the middle comes out clean. For 10 minutes, cool the cakes in pans onto the racks. Slice around the side of pans and invert cakes onto the racks. Let completely cool. Remove the paper.
- Slice the cake horizontally in half. Place 1 layer of cake, cut side up, to the platter using the bottom part of the tart pan. Add 2 tablespoons of syrup and brush into the layer of cake. Add 3/4 cup of the frosting and spread over the cake layer. Do the layering twice, with 1 layer of cake, 2 tablespoons of the syrup and 3/4 cup of the frosting per layer. Top with the fourth layer of the cake, cut side down. Add the rest of the frosting; spread. (Can be done 1day in advance. Set aside at room temperature with cover)

Nutrition Information

- Calories: 380
- Total Carbohydrate: 57 g(19%)
- Cholesterol: 55 mg(18%)
- Protein: 6 g(11%)
- Total Fat: 15 g(22%)
- Saturated Fat: 9 g(44%)
- Sodium: 123 mg(5%)
- Fiber: 2 g(9%)

49. Caramel Macadamia Nut Crunch

Serving: Makes 20 cookies | Prep: | Cook: | Ready in:

Ingredients

- 1 cup sugar
- 1 cup heavy cream
- 1 pound macadamia pieces, or whole nuts, roughly chopped
- 1 chilled log of butter shortbread cookie dough

Direction

- Heat an oven to 325 degrees F. Oil one baking sheet, desirably with rim.
- Mix half cup water and sugar in a medium-size saucepan. Heat on moderate heat for 3 minutes, till mixture starts to come to a simmer. Put on pan cover and keep on simmering, letting steam from the cooking mixture to wash down the pan sides. Uncover and keep simmering for 7 to 8 minutes till mixture becomes golden. Take off from stove immediately, and, add cream cautiously in a steady, slow stream in pan to prevent mixture from bubbling over; avid mixing. Set pot back to stove, turn the heat to low, and slowly mix mixture with wooden spoon, till cream incorporates fully.
- Turn the caramel into a heat-proof, medium-size bowl, put in nuts, and mix to cover nuts equally. Pour the mixture into baking sheet, scattering it smoothly, and bake 12 to 15 minutes, till dark brown. Let brittle cool down to room temperature and, in food processor, by hand or a cleaver, coarsely chop mixture.
- Slice log making 20 rounds measuring half-inch, force 1 cut side of every round to brittle, and place rounds on a parchment-covered or nonstick cookie sheet(s), spacing 2-inch apart on every side.
- Bake for 15 to 20 minutes till golden brown in color. Take cookies using spatula and transfer onto a wire rack to cool.

---

50. Caramel Nut Tart

Serving: Makes 8 servings | Prep: | Cook: | Ready in:

Ingredients

- 10 tablespoons (1 1/4 sticks) unsalted butter, room temperature
- 1/4 cup powdered sugar
- 1/4 teaspoon salt
- 1 large egg, separated
- 1 tablespoon heavy whipping cream
- 1 1/2 cups all purpose flour
- 1 cup sugar
- 1/4 cup water
- 1/4 cup orange juice
- 1/2 cup heavy whipping cream
- 2 tablespoons (1/4 stick) unsalted butter
- 1 tablespoon honey
- 2 teaspoons finely grated orange peel
- 1 teaspoon vanilla extract
- 1/4 teaspoon salt
- 1/2 cup roasted unsalted cashews (about 2 1/2 ounces)
- 1/2 cup pine nuts (about 2 1/2 ounces), lightly toasted
- 1/2 cup walnut pieces (about 2 1/2 ounces), lightly toasted

Direction

- Crust: Beat salt, powdered sugar and butter using electric mixer to blend in medium bowl. Add cream and egg yolks; beat till smooth. Add flour; beat till dough comes together. Turn out dough on lightly floured surface; briefly knead to combine. Bring dough to ball; flatten to disk. In plastic, wrap; freeze for 15 minutes till firm.
- Roll dough to 12-in. round on lightly floured surface; put in 9-in. diameter tart pan that has removable bottom. Fit dough into pan gently; trim all overhang but 1/2-in. Fold in overhang, making double-thick sides. Use fork to pierce crust's bottom all over; freeze for 30 minutes.
- Preheat an oven to 350°F. Line foil on crust; fill with pie weights/dried beans. Bake for 20 minutes till sides set. Remove beans and foil; bake crust for 20 minutes till golden. If crust bubbles, press with fork's back.

- Meanwhile, whisk the egg white till foamy and thick in small bowl.
- Lightly brush some beaten egg white on hot crust. Put on rack; cool. Maintain the oven temperature.
- Filling: Mix 1/4 cup water and sugar in medium heavy saucepan on low heat till sugar is dissolved. Put heat on medium high; boil, brushing pan's sides down using wet pastry brush. Cook for 9 minutes till syrup is deep amber, occasionally swirling pan; take off heat. Add juice then cream; whisk till smooth on low heat. Whisk in salt, vanilla, orange peel, honey and butter; mix in walnuts, pine nuts and cashews.
- Put filling in crust; bake for 22 minutes till filling is thickly bubbling all over. On rack, fully cool tart. You can make it 1 day ahead. Use foil to cover; keep in room temperature.
- Cut the tart to wedges; serve.

Nutrition Information

- Calories: 657
- Saturated Fat: 20 g(102%)
- Sodium: 170 mg(7%)
- Fiber: 2 g(8%)
- Total Carbohydrate: 56 g(19%)
- Cholesterol: 117 mg(39%)
- Protein: 8 g(17%)
- Total Fat: 47 g(72%)

51. Caramelized Winter Fruit Custards

Serving: Makes 8 servings | Prep: | Cook: | Ready in:

Ingredients

- 1 cup cake flour
- 3/4 teaspoon baking powder
- 1/2 teaspoon ground cinnamon
- 1/4 teaspoon ground nutmeg
- 1/8 teaspoon ground cloves
- 1/8 teaspoon fine sea salt
- 6 tablespoons lukewarm water
- 1 teaspoon vanilla extract
- 1/2 cup (packed) golden brown sugar
- 1/4 cup (1/2 stick) unsalted butter, room temperature
- 2 large egg whites, room temperature
- 2 tablespoons sugar
- 6 tablespoons (3/4 stick) unsalted butter
- 3/4 cup sugar
- 2 large Granny Smith apples (about 1 pound), peeled, quartered, cored, cut into 1/3-inch-thick slices
- 2 small Bosc pears (12 to 14 ounces total), peeled, quartered, cored, cut into 1/3-inch-thick slices
- 1 cup fresh or frozen cranberries
- 2 cups half and half
- 1/2 cup sugar
- 4 large egg yolks
- 1/4 teaspoon fine sea salt
- 1 tablespoon cornstarch
- 1 tablespoon unsalted butter
- 6 tablespoons apple brandy (such as applejack or Calvados) or poire Williams (clear pear brandy), divided

Direction

- For Spiced chiffon muffins: Preheat an oven to 350°F and lightly butter then flour 9 standard 1/3-cup muffin cups. Sift flour with following 5 ingredients into medium bowl twice. Mix vanilla and 6 tbsp. lukewarm water in small bowl. Beat butter and brown sugar using electric mixer till fluffy and light in big bowl. Add flour mixture in 3 additions alternately with the water in 2 additions, beating batter till blended after every addition.
- Beat egg whites using electric mixer fitted with clean dry batters till soft peaks form in medium bowl. Add 2 tbsp. sugar slowly; beat till glossy, firm peaks form. Fold 1/3 whites into the batter to lighten; fold in leftover whites. Spoon 1/4 cup batter in every prepped muffin cup.

- Bake muffins for 17 minutes till inserted tester in middle exits clean; cool muffins for at least 20 minutes in pan on rack. Remove muffins from pan; fully cool on rack. You can make it 1 day ahead. Put muffins on muffin pan; cover. Keep at room temperature.
- For Caramelized winter fruit: In big nonstick skillet, melt butter on medium heat. Sprinkle sugar on butter in skillet; in 1 layer (if possible), put pear slices and apple slices atop sugar. Increase heat on medium high; cook, without stirring for 8 minutes till fruit's bottom is golden, pressing out to single layer while fruit cooks and reduces in volume. Flip fruit over in skillet; cook for 5 minutes till golden. Add cranberries; cook for 2 minutes till juices in skillet is reduced by half.
- For Custard: In big heavy saucepan, heat half and half till bubbles form at pan's edge and heated through on medium heat. In medium bowl, whisk sea salt, egg yolks and sugar; whisk in cornstarch.
- Add hot half and half slowly into yolk mixture; whisk till blended. Return custard in same saucepan; mix on medium heat for 2-3 minutes till custard thickens and boils. Whisk in butter; whisk in 2 tbsp. brandy. Remove from heat.
- Brush leftover 4 tbsp. brandy several times on tops of muffins till absorbed. In each of the 8 dessert glasses/cups/bowls, put 1 muffin; divide caramelized fruits among bowls. Spoon warm custard on fruit and muffins in bowl, about 1/3 cup for each. Chill for at least 30 minutes. You can make it 2 hours ahead, kept chilled, covered. About 20 minutes before serving, allow it to stand at room temperature.

52. Cardamom Butter Squares

Serving: Makes about 6 dozen | Prep: 35mins | Cook: 5.5hours | Ready in:

Ingredients

- 3 cups all-purpose flour
- 1 teaspoon baking powder
- 3/4 teaspoon salt
- 1 1/2 teaspoons ground cardamom
- 1/2 teaspoon ground cinnamon
- 1/4 teaspoon ground allspice
- 2 sticks (1 cup) unsalted butter, softened
- 1 1/4 cups granulated sugar
- 2 large eggs
- 1 teaspoon vanilla
- 1 teaspoon instant-espresso powder
- 1 teaspoon vanilla
- 1 1/2 to 2 tablespoons milk
- 1 cup confectioners sugar
- 3 oz fine-quality bittersweet chocolate (not unsweetened), melted
- 2 small heavy-duty sealable plastic bags (for icing; not pleated)

Direction

- Cookies: Whisk allspice, cinnamon, cardamom, salt, baking powder and flour in a bowl.
- Beat sugar and butter using an electric mixer on medium high speed, 4 minutes for handheld, 2 minutes for stand mixer (best with paddle attachment), till fluffy and pale; beat in vanilla and eggs. Lower speed to low; mix in flour mixture just till combined.
- Shape dough, each on its own plastic wrap sheet, to 2 12-in., 1 1/2-in. diameter logs; roll, press then square off log sides using your hands and plastic wrap. Chill logs for 1 hour till slightly firm on baking sheet; smooth logs suing flat side of ruler and plastic wrap to get straight sides. Chill logs for 1 hour till firm on baking sheet.
- In lower and upper thirds of oven, put oven racks; preheat the oven to 350°F.
- Cut scant 1/4-in. thick slices with a knife from a log to fill 2 big ungreased baking sheets, 1-in. apart; chill leftover dough while wrapped in plastic wrap.
- Bake the cookies for 10-12 minutes total till edges are golden, switching sheet positions halfway through baking; cool for 3 minutes on

sheets. Put onto racks; fully cool. With leftover dough, create more cookies on cooled baking sheets.
- Icing cookies: Whisk 1 1/2 tbsp. milk, vanilla and espresso powder till espresso powder melts. Add confectioners' sugar with enough extra milk to create pourable yet thick icing. Put into sealable bag; snip 1/8-in. off bottom corner.
- Put melted chocolate into separate sealable bag; snip 1/8-in. off bottom corner.
- Pipe some chocolate and espresso icing on each cookie; stand on racks for 2 hours till icing sets.
- You can chill dough logs for 5 days/frozen for 1 month wrapped in double plastic layer; before slicing, thaw in fridge. Cookies, without or with icing, keep for 1 week in room temperature in airtight container, layered between parchment/wax paper sheets.

53. Cardamom Crescents

Serving: Makes about 50 | Prep: | Cook: | Ready in:

Ingredients

- 2 1/2 cups all-purpose flour
- 3/4 teaspoon ground cardamom
- 1/2 teaspoon ground cinnamon
- 1/2 teaspoon kosher salt
- 1 1/2 cups powdered sugar, divided
- 1 cup pecans
- 1 cup (2 sticks) unsalted butter, room temperature
- 1 tablespoon vanilla extract

Direction

- Place racks in bottom and top thirds of the oven; heat the oven to 350°F. Line parchment paper on 2 baking sheets. In a medium size bowl, whip the initial 4 ingredients. Use a food processor to mix pecans and half cup of sugar; pulse to form a coarse meal. In medium bowl, whip vanilla and butter for 2 to 3 minutes with electric mixer till creamy. Put in the nut mixture; whip to incorporate. Put in the dry ingredients; mix thoroughly, dough will moisten yet remain crumbly. Turn onto a work counter; knead approximately 4 turns, to create a ball.
- Scoop out a rounded tablespoon dough; shape to make ball, then roll to a log, 1 1/2-inch length. Slowly curve to make crescent shape, pressing ends to patch, cookies might crack a bit. Redo with the rest of the dough, with approximately an-inch intervals on prepped sheets.
- Bake for 12 to 15 minutes, rotate sheets midway through, till undersides turn golden. In one wide, shallow bowl, sift leftover one cup of powdered sugar. Roll the still warm cookies softly in powdered sugar till coated, doing it in batches of approximately eight cookies each. Turn onto wire rack to cool down. Dust or roll powdered sugar on cooled cookies. May be done 5 days in advance. Keep at room temperature, airtight.

Nutrition Information

- Calories: 84
- Saturated Fat: 2 g(12%)
- Sodium: 20 mg(1%)
- Fiber: 0 g(2%)
- Total Carbohydrate: 9 g(3%)
- Cholesterol: 10 mg(3%)
- Protein: 1 g(2%)
- Total Fat: 5 g(8%)

54. Cashew Cookies

Serving: 36 | Prep: 10mins | Cook: 15mins | Ready in:

Ingredients

- 1/2 cup butter, softened
- 1 cup brown sugar

- 1 egg
- 1/3 cup sour cream
- 1 teaspoon vanilla extract
- 2 cups all-purpose flour
- 3/4 teaspoon baking powder
- 3/4 teaspoon baking soda
- 1/4 teaspoon salt
- 1 3/4 cups chopped cashews
- 1/2 cup butter
- 3 tablespoons heavy whipping cream
- 2 cups confectioners' sugar
- 1 teaspoon vanilla extract

Direction

- Preheat the oven to 175°C or 350°F. Grease the cookie sheets.
- Cream together the sugar and half cup butter in a big bowl till fluffy and light. Put the egg, beating thoroughly, then mix in the 1 teaspoon vanilla and sour cream. Put together the salt, baking soda, baking powder and flour; slowly mix into the creamed mixture. Fold cashew pieces in. Onto the prepped cookie sheets, drop by rounded spoonfuls.
- In the prepped oven, bake for 12 to 15 minutes. Let cookies cool down on baking sheet for 5 minutes prior taking to a wire rack to fully cool.
- For the frosting, in a saucepan over medium heat, liquefy half cup butter. Cook till butter becomes light brown in color, keep from burning. Take off heat and mix in the cream. Slowly beat in the confectioners' sugar and a teaspoon vanilla till smooth. Scatter onto cooled cookies.

Nutrition Information

- Calories: 162 calories;
- Total Carbohydrate: 18.3
- Cholesterol: 21
- Protein: 2.1
- Total Fat: 9.3
- Sodium: 136

55. Cheddar And Chive Yorkshire Pudding

Serving: Makes 10 | Prep: | Cook: | Ready in:

Ingredients

- 8 tablespoons melted roast beef fat reserved from rib roast pan drippings or 8 tablespoons (1 stick) unsalted butter, melted, divided
- 6 large eggs
- 2 cups whole milk
- 2 cups all purpose flour
- 1 teaspoon salt
- 1/2 cup (packed) finely grated sharp cheddar cheese
- 1/3 cup (generous) chopped fresh chives

Direction

- Put rack in middle of oven; preheat it to 450°F. In oven, put big rimmed baking sheet. Use 2 tbsp. butter/fat to brush 10 ramekins/3/4-cup glass baking dishes.
- Whisk eggs in big bowl to blend. Add milk; whisk till blended well. Whisk salt and flour to blend in medium bowl. Whisk leftover 6 tbsp. fat/butter and flour mixture into egg mixture slowly till blended well. Some small lumps will be left. Whisk in chives and cheese; divide batter, 1/2 cup batter to each, to baking dishes.
- Put baking dishes onto hot baking sheet in the oven; bake for 25 minutes till it starts to brown and Yorkshire puddings are puffed. Lower oven temperature to 350°F; bake for 20 minutes till pudding are crisp around sides, puffed and brown. Put Yorkshire puddings on plates; immediately serve.

56. Cheesecake

Serving: 12 | Prep: | Cook: | Ready in:

Ingredients

- 3 (8 ounce) packages cream cheese
- 1 cup white sugar
- 1/4 teaspoon almond extract
- 1/4 teaspoon salt
- 5 eggs
- 1 cup sour cream
- 2 tablespoons white sugar
- 1/4 teaspoon vanilla extract

Direction

- Preheat an oven to 165°C/325°F. Beat salt, eggs, almond extract, 1 cup sugar and cream cheese till smooth in a big bowl; put into deep-dish greased pie plate.
- Bake for 45-50 minutes at 165°C/325°F; remove from oven. Cool it for 20 minutes.
- Topping: Mix 1/4 tsp. vanilla extract, 2 tbsp. sugar and sour cream till smooth; evenly spread on top of baked cheesecake. Bake to set the top at 165°C/325°F for 10 minutes.
- Cool; before serving, refrigerate for a few hours.

Nutrition Information

- Calories: 339 calories;
- Cholesterol: 148
- Protein: 7.5
- Total Fat: 25.6
- Sodium: 254
- Total Carbohydrate: 21.2

57. Cheesecake Mousse With Rum Poached Plums

Serving: Serves 2 | Prep: | Cook: | Ready in:

Ingredients

- 1 cup water
- 1/3 cup granulated sugar
- 2 tablespoons dark rum
- 2 plums
- 1/2 cup whipped cream cheese (about 3 ounces)
- 3 tablespoons confectioners' sugar
- 1/2 teaspoon vanilla
- 1/2 cup well-chilled heavy cream

Direction

- Prep a bowl with cold water and ice. Simmer rum, granulated sugar and 1 cup water in a small saucepan for 10 minutes, occasionally mixing. Pit plums. Slice every plum to 12 wedges. Simmer plums for 2-3 minutes till tender. Put plum mixture into bowl. Put into bowl with ice water. Allow plum mixture to stand till chilled, occasionally mixing.
- Whisk a pinch of salt, vanilla, confectioners' sugar and cream cheese in a bowl till smooth. Beat heavy cream in another bowl till it holds soft peaks. Whisk into the cream cheese mixture. Between 2 goblets, distribute mixture then chill for 15 minutes, covered. Serve mousse with plums on top with some syrup.

Nutrition Information

- Calories: 556
- Protein: 3 g(6%)
- Total Fat: 32 g(49%)
- Saturated Fat: 20 g(98%)
- Sodium: 32 mg(1%)
- Fiber: 1 g(4%)
- Total Carbohydrate: 60 g(20%)
- Cholesterol: 114 mg(38%)

58. Cherries In The Snow

Serving: makes 6 servings | Prep: 15mins | Cook: 1.25hours | Ready in:

Ingredients

- Vegetable oil for greasing baking dish

- 2 1/4 teaspoons unflavored gelatin (from a 1/4-oz envelope)
- 1/2 cup cold water
- 1 cup 1% or skim milk
- 1/3 cup sugar
- 1/4 teaspoon almond extract
- 1/3 cup dried cherries (2 ounces)
- 1 tablespoon sugar
- 1 cup Ruby Port

Direction

- For Almond snow gelatin: Use vegetable oil to oil 8-in. square glass baking dish lightly; use a paper towel to wipe out excess.
- Sprinkle gelatin on water to soften for 1 minute in a big heatproof bowl.
- Boil sugar and milk in 1-qt. saucepan, mixing till sugar dissolves; remove from heat. Mix into gelatin mixture then add almond extract; briskly whisk for 5 minutes till milk is foamy.
- Pour into baking dish; freeze to set the foam for 15 minutes. Chill for at least 45 minutes till firm in fridge, uncovered.
- For Cherries in Port: Simmer Port, sugar and cherries in cleaned 1-qt. heavy saucepan for 10 minutes till reduced to 1/2 cup, uncovered. Put pan in a bowl with cold water and ice; chill for 15 minutes till syrupy in the fridge.
- To assemble desserts: Cut gelatin to 1-in. squares using a knife dipped into hot water. Use a spatula to remove squares from dish; divide to 6 chilled plates, frothy sides up. Spoon cherries in port on squares.
- You can chill the gelatin for up to 2 days. (Cover after 45 minutes.)
- You can chill cherries in port, without bowl of ice water, for up to 1 week, covered.

59. Cherry Almond Shortbread Cookies

Serving: Makes about 24 | Prep: | Cook: | Ready in:

Ingredients

- 24 dried tart cherries (about 1 1/2 ounces)
- 1/3 cup crème de cassis (black-currant liqueur)
- 1/2 cup raw almonds with skins, divided
- 1/2 cup all purpose flour
- 1/2 cup whole wheat flour
- 1/2 teaspoon salt
- 1/2 cup (1 stick) unsalted butter, room temperature
- 1/2 cup powdered sugar, sifted
- 1 large egg, lightly beaten

Direction

- In small bowl, soak cherries in cassis for a minimum of 4 hours – overnight. Drain then pat dry.
- Grind 3 tbsp. almonds till finely ground in mini processor; chop leftover almonds finely.
- Whisk salt, whole wheat flour and all-purpose flour in medium bowl. Beat sugar and butter using electric mixer for 2 minutes till creamy in big bowl. Add ground almonds; beat for 1 minute till well blended. Beat in flour mixture to just blend on low speed.
- Scrape out dough on waxed paper/parchment sheet; shape dough to 8 1/2x1 3/4-in. log using paper as aid. Brush egg all over dough but ends; scatter the chopped almonds on plastic wrap sheet. Roll logs to coat in almonds; wrap in plastic wrap. Chill for a minimum of 2 hours. You can make dough 2 days ahead, kept refrigerated. Cover; chill berries.
- Preheat an oven to 350°F. Stand dough for 10 minutes in room temperature. Unwrap dough; cut to 3/8-in. thick slices. Put cookies on big ungreased baking sheet, 1-in. apart. In middle of each cookie, put 1 cherry.
- Bake for 10 minutes. Into cookies, press cherries; cookies will be soft. In oven, rotate baking sheet; bake for 18 minutes till slightly puffed and cookies are lightly golden. Cool cookies for 5 minutes on sheet on rack. Put cookies on rack; fully cool. You can make

cookies 2 days ahead; keep in room temperature, airtight.

Nutrition Information

- Calories: 94
- Protein: 2 g(3%)
- Total Fat: 6 g(9%)
- Saturated Fat: 3 g(13%)
- Sodium: 52 mg(2%)
- Fiber: 1 g(3%)
- Total Carbohydrate: 9 g(3%)
- Cholesterol: 18 mg(6%)

60. Cherry Double Chocolate Cookies

Serving: Makes about 2 dozen cookies | Prep: 25mins | Cook: 1.25hours | Ready in:

Ingredients

- 1 1/4 cups all-purpose flour
- 3/4 cup unsweetened Dutch-process cocoa powder
- 3/4 teaspoon baking soda
- Scant 1/2 teaspoon salt
- 1 1/2 sticks unsalted butter, softened
- 1 1/2 cups packed light brown sugar
- 2 large eggs
- 3 1/2 oz fine-quality milk chocolate, cut into 1/2-inch chunks
- 1 cup pecans, toasted and coarsely chopped
- 1 cup dried sour cherries

Direction

- Preheat an oven with racks in lower and upper thirds to 375°F.
- Whisk salt, baking soda, cocoa powder and flour in a small bowl.
- Beat brown sugar and butter using electric mixer on medium high speed till fluffy and pale. One by one, add eggs; beat till well combined. Lower speed to low. Add flour mixture; mix just till combined. Add cherries, pecans and chocolate chunks; mix just till incorporated.
- Drop 2 level tbsp. dough per cookie on 2 ungreased big baking sheets, 2-in. apart. Slightly flatten cookies with dampened fingers.
- Bake for 12-14 minutes till set and puffed, switching sheets positions halfway through baking. Put cookies on rack; cool.
- Cookies keep for 5 days in cool room temperature in airtight containers.

Nutrition Information

- Calories: 193
- Saturated Fat: 5 g(25%)
- Sodium: 102 mg(4%)
- Fiber: 2 g(7%)
- Total Carbohydrate: 24 g(8%)
- Cholesterol: 32 mg(11%)
- Protein: 3 g(5%)
- Total Fat: 11 g(17%)

61. Cherry Chocolate Chip Oatmeal Cookies

Serving: Makes 2 dozen | Prep: | Cook: | Ready in:

Ingredients

- 1 cup all purpose flour
- 1/2 teaspoon baking soda
- 1/4 teaspoon salt
- 1/2 cup plus 2 tablespoons (1 1/4 sticks) unsalted butter, room temperature
- 1/2 cup sugar
- 1/2 cup (packed) dark brown sugar
- 1 large egg
- 1 teaspoon vanilla extract
- 1/2 teaspoon almond extract
- 1 cup old-fashioned oats
- 1 1/2 cups semisweet chocolate chips

- 1 cup dried tart cherries
- 1/2 cup slivered almonds, toasted

Direction

- Put racks in top third and middle of oven; preheat it to 325°F. Line parchment paper on 2 big baking sheets. Sift flour, salt, and baking soda into medium bowl. Beat brown sugar, sugar and butter in a large bowl using electric mixer till well blended; mix in both extracts and egg. Beat in flour mixture; stir in oats, and then almonds, cherries and chocolate chips.
- By rounded tablespoonfuls, drop dough on baking sheets, 2-in. apart. Bake cookies for 12 minutes. Switch and rotate baking sheets; bake cookies for 6 minutes till golden. On baking sheets, cool them. As they cool, they will become firm. (You can make it 1 week ahead; keep at room temperature, airtight.)

Nutrition Information

- Calories: 297
- Saturated Fat: 8 g(39%)
- Sodium: 87 mg(4%)
- Fiber: 2 g(9%)
- Total Carbohydrate: 42 g(14%)
- Cholesterol: 31 mg(10%)
- Protein: 3 g(7%)
- Total Fat: 15 g(22%)

62. Cherry Cornmeal Upside Down Cake

Serving: 10 servings | Prep: | Cook: | Ready in:

Ingredients

- 3/4 cup (1 1/2 sticks) unsalted butter, room temperature, divided
- 1/4 cup (packed) dark brown sugar
- 2 teaspoons balsamic vinegar
- 3 cups whole pitted fresh Bing cherries or other dark sweet cherries (about 21 ounces whole unpitted cherries)
- 1 1/4 cups all purpose flour
- 1/4 cup yellow cornmeal (preferably stone-ground medium grind)
- 2 teaspoons baking powder
- 1/4 teaspoon salt
- 1 cup sugar
- 2 large eggs, separated
- 3/4 teaspoon vanilla extract
- 1/2 cup whole milk
- 1/4 teaspoon cream of tartar

Direction

- In middle of oven, put rack; preheat it to 350°F. Mix vinegar, brown sugar and 1/4 cup butter in 10-11-in. ovenproof skillet that has 2-in. high sides. Stir for 2 minutes on medium heat till sugar and butter melt. Upper heat on high then add cherries; boil. Take off heat.
- Whisk salt, baking powder, cornmeal and flour to blend in medium bowl. Beat 1/2 cup butter using electric mixer in big bowl. Add sugar; beat for 3 minutes till fluffy and pale; beat in vanilla and egg yolks. Alternately with milk, add flour mixture in 2 additions each; beat till just blended, scraping bowl's sides down occasionally. Beat egg whites using dry clean beaters till foamy in another medium bowl. Add cream of tartar; beat till whites are stiff yet not dry. Fold 1/4 whites to slightly lighten into batter using rubber spatula. In 3 additions, fold in leftover whites; batter will get thick. Put batter on cherries in skillet; evenly spread to cover cherries with offset spatula.
- Bake cake for 45 minutes till inserted tester in middle exits clean and top is golden brown; cool for 5 minutes in skillet on rack. To loosen, run spatula around cake's edges; put big serving platter on skillet, upside down. Firmly hold skillet and platter together using oven mitts/pot holders; invert. Leave skillet on cake for 5 minutes; remove skillet. Rearrange cherries that got dislodged if needed. Cool

cake for 45 minutes. Cut cake to wedges; serve at room temperature/slightly warm.

Nutrition Information

- Calories: 367
- Protein: 4 g(8%)
- Total Fat: 15 g(24%)
- Saturated Fat: 9 g(47%)
- Sodium: 157 mg(7%)
- Fiber: 2 g(7%)
- Total Carbohydrate: 55 g(18%)
- Cholesterol: 75 mg(25%)

63. Chestnut Cheesecake

Serving: Makes 8 servings | Prep: | Cook: | Ready in:

Ingredients

- 4 ounces (2 cups) Graham cracker crumbs
- 1/2 stick butter
- 1 heaped tablespoon sweetened chestnut purée
- 2 cups cream cheese
- 3/4 cup superfine sugar
- 3 eggs
- 3 egg yolks
- 3/4 cup sour cream
- 1 teaspoon lime juice
- 1 teaspoon vanilla extract
- 1–2 tablespoons rum
- 1 cup sweetened chestnut purée
- 1/3 cup water
- 1/4 cup rum
- 1 tablespoon sweetened chestnut purée
- 1/4 cup superfine sugar
- 1 tablespoon butter

Direction

- Preheat an oven to 350°F. Put kettle on boil.
- For the Base: Process heaped tablespoon of chestnut puree, butter and crackers till like fine crumbs; press mixture on bottom of 9-in. springform pan. Put in fridge while making filling.
- Beat cream cheese till smooth; add sugar. Add egg yolks and eggs; beating them in one by one till incorporated into sugar and cream cheese. Pour in rum, vanilla extract, lime juice and sour cream; beat till creamy and smooth. Fold in sweetened chestnut puree; smooth cream cheese with some grainy streaks of chestnuts is just fine if you want to make a fully amalgamated mixture.
- Line a good plastic wrap wrapping on outside of springform pan with crumb base so whole of sides and bottoms are enveloped in plastic; repeat with aluminum foil, covering the plastic wrap layer to make very watertight casing. Stand springform pan in roasting pan, thus covered; add chestnut filling. Once done, add water from recently boiled kettle into roasting pan to reach 1-in. up pan's sides. (Plastic wrap will move it up and down a little.) Put into oven for 1 hour to cook.
- Cheesecake should have hit of wobble underneath and just set on top when ready; it'll cook as it cools. Remove cheesecake from roasting pan; remove plastic wrap and foil. Cool cheesecake on rack. Before unmolding and leaving out to reach room temperature, refrigerate it first overnight; before eating, you have to unmold it a long time before serving then let it sit on the serving plate for 20-30 minutes in the fridge before serving. Serve it when they already sat down to lunch or dinner.
- You can make syrup ahead; don't pour over till serving.
- Melt all syrup ingredients in a saucepan; boil for 10 minutes. Cool to room temperature/warmish, then use it to crisscross the top of the cheesecake.

Nutrition Information

- Calories: 560
- Fiber: 0 g(2%)

- Total Carbohydrate: 47 g(16%)
- Cholesterol: 209 mg(70%)
- Protein: 8 g(16%)
- Total Fat: 36 g(55%)
- Saturated Fat: 19 g(97%)
- Sodium: 314 mg(13%)

64. Chewy Ginger Cookies

Serving: 20 | Prep: 15mins | Cook: 10mins | Ready in:

Ingredients

- 2 cups sifted all-purpose flour
- 4 teaspoons ground ginger
- 2 teaspoons baking soda
- 2 teaspoons ground cinnamon
- 1/2 teaspoon salt
- 1/4 teaspoon ground allspice
- 1 cup white sugar
- 3/4 cup butter, softened
- 1 egg
- 1/4 cup dark molasses
- 1/3 cup chopped crystallized ginger (optional)

Direction

- Set the oven to 350°F (175°C) and start preheating.
- In a mixing bowl, sift together allspice, salt, cinnamon, baking soda, ground ginger and flour; stir.
- In a large bowl, beat together butter and sugar with an electric mixer until creamy and smooth. Beat in molasses and egg. Gradually stir the flour mixture into butter mixture until just coming together into a batter. Fold crystallized ginger through the batter gently.
- Use your hands to roll rounded teaspoon-sized amounts of dough into small balls. Arrange balls 2 inches apart on ungreased baking sheets.
- Bake in preheated oven for about 10 minutes until the upper surfaces are slightly cracked and rounded. Allow to cool for 1 minute on baking sheets, transfer to a wire rack and sit until completely cooled.

Nutrition Information

- Calories: 168 calories;
- Cholesterol: 28
- Protein: 1.7
- Total Fat: 7.3
- Sodium: 239
- Total Carbohydrate: 24.4

65. Chicken Sausage

Serving: Makes about 2 pounds/900 grams sausage | Prep: | Cook: | Ready in:

Ingredients

- 1 1/2 pound/675 grams chicken thigh meat, diced and thoroughly chilled
- 225 grams schmaltz, frozen (or a scant cup if you don't have a scale, but shame on you)
- 1 tablespoon/10-12 grams kosher salt
- 3/4 cup roughly chopped fresh sage
- 2 large garlic cloves, finely minced
- 2 tablespoons finely chopped ginger
- 1 teaspoon freshly ground pepper
- 1/2 cup/120 milliliters dry white wine, chilled

Direction

- Mix all ingredients except for the wine in a big bowl; freeze for 20-30 minutes. Measure wine; put into freezer. Freeze grinder attachment if you're using the metal one and your mixing bowl. Prep your grinder. Take chicken mixture out from freezer; grind through medium/small die into freezing-cold mixing bowl. Put meat back into freezer for 10 minutes; set up the stand mixer.
- Take sausage mixture out from freezer; mix for 60 seconds with paddle attachment at medium high, adding very cold white wine while doing so. Paddling helps to bind the sausage

well and distributes the seasonings rather than crumbling. In order to be sure that the seasoning is right, fry small sausage portion, refrigerating mixing bowl while cooking test piece; taste test piece. Add more salt, ginger, sage or pepper if needed then repaddle it. Repeat till you get your preferred seasoning amount.
- In plastic wrap, wrap sausage in a shape of 7.5-cm/2 1/2-in. diameter cylinder; in plastic bag, put wrapped sausage. Keeps for 1 week in the fridge/frozen for 3 months. (It gets unpleasant freezer odors/freezer burn the longer you freeze the meat. Label bag with the date to avoid leaving it for too long.)

Nutrition Information

- Calories: 278
- Cholesterol: 52 mg(17%)
- Protein: 13 g(26%)
- Total Fat: 22 g(35%)
- Saturated Fat: 7 g(36%)
- Sodium: 222 mg(9%)
- Fiber: 3 g(13%)
- Total Carbohydrate: 6 g(2%)

66. Chocolate Cake With Caramel Coconut Almond Filling

Serving: Serves 12 | Prep: | Cook: |Ready in:

Ingredients

- 4 ounces unsweetened chocolate, chopped
- 1 cup water
- 1 tablespoon instant espresso powder or coffee powder
- 2 1/4 cups (packed) dark brown sugar
- 1 cup (2 sticks) unsalted butter, room temperature
- 3 large eggs
- 1 teaspoon vanilla extract
- 2 cups cake flour
- 2 teaspoons baking soda
- 1 teaspoon baking powder
- 1/2 teaspoon salt
- 1 cup sour cream
- 1 cup sugar
- 1/4 cup water
- 1 cup whipping cream
- 1 cup sweetened flaked coconut (about 2 1/2 ounces), toasted
- 1 cup thinly sliced almonds (about 4 ounces), toasted
- 1/2 cup (1 stick) unsalted butter
- 3 ounces unsweetened chocolate, chopped
- 1/2 teaspoon vanilla extract
- 2 cups powdered sugar, sifted
- 1/2 cup sour cream
- 2 cups sliced almonds (about 8 ounces), toasted

Direction

- Cake: Preheat an oven to 350°F. Butter the 3 9-in. diameter cake pans that have 1 1/2-in. high sides; line waxed paper on bottoms. Butter waxed paper. Mix espresso powder, 1 cup water and chocolate in small heavy saucepan on low heat till smooth and chocolate melts; take off heat. Fully cool, occasionally mixing.
- Beat butter and brown sugar using electric mixer till fluffy and light in big bowl. One by one, add eggs; beat well after each. Add vanilla and chocolate mixture; beat till blended. Sift salt, baking powder, baking soda and flour into medium bowl. Alternately with the sour cream in 3 batches, put dry ingredients into butter mixture, starting with dry ingredients, beating well after every addition.
- Evenly divide batter into prepped pans; bake cakes for 30 minutes till inserted tester in middle exits clean. Cool cakes for 10 minutes in pans on racks. Cut around pan's sides to loosen cakes using small knife. Turn cakes onto racks. Remove the waxed paper; fully cool.
- Filling: Mix 1/4 cup water and sugar in medium heavy saucepan. Mix on low heat till

sugar melts. Upper heat to high; boil without mixing for 10 minutes till syrup is deep amber, occasionally swirling, brushing pan's sides down with wet pastry brush. Take off heat. Add cream carefully; it'll vigorously bubble. Put pan on medium low heat; mix for 5 minutes till caramel bits melt. Mix in 1 cup almonds and coconut; cool filling for 45 minutes till thick enough to spread, occasionally mixing.

- Frosting: Melt chocolate and butter in small heavy saucepan on low heat, mixing till smooth; put into big bowl. Mix in vanilla; whisk in 1/4 cup sour cream and 1 cup powdered sugar. Whisk in sour cream and leftover powdered sugar.
- On platter, put 1 cake layer; evenly spread 1/2 filling on top. Leave 1/2-in. border. Put 2nd cake layer over. Spread leftover filling; leave 1/2-in. border. Put leftover cake layer over; spread frosting on top and sides of cake. Onto cake's sides, press 2 cups of sliced almonds. Decoratively swirl frosting over cake using pastry spatula. You can make it 1 day ahead. Use cake dome to cover; keep in room temperature.

Nutrition Information

- Calories: 1003
- Saturated Fat: 30 g(151%)
- Sodium: 413 mg(17%)
- Fiber: 7 g(29%)
- Total Carbohydrate: 107 g(36%)
- Cholesterol: 145 mg(48%)
- Protein: 13 g(27%)
- Total Fat: 61 g(93%)

67. Chocolate Cake With Chocolate Orange Frosting

Serving: Makes 12 servings | Prep: | Cook: |Ready in:

Ingredients

- Nonstick vegetable oil spray
- 1 cup all purpose flour
- 1 cup sugar
- 1/2 cup whole wheat pastry flour*
- 6 tablespoons unsweetened cocoa powder
- 1 teaspoon baking soda
- 1/2 teaspoon salt
- 3/4 cup water
- 1/3 cup vegetable oil
- 1/4 cup frozen orange juice concentrate, thawed
- 1 teaspoon vanilla extract
- 1 teaspoon distilled white vinegar
- 8 ounces bittersweet chocolate (donot exceed 61% cacao), chopped
- 6 tablespoons (3/4 stick) vegan "butter" (such as Earth Balance) or margarine, room temperature
- 1 cup powdered sugar
- 3 tablespoons frozen orange juice concentrate, thawed, divided
- 1/2 teaspoon vanilla extract
- Large pinch of salt
- 1/4 cup light agave nectar**

Direction

- Cake: Preheat an oven to 350°F. Spray nonstick spray on 9-in. diameter cake pan that has 2-in. high sides. Sift salt, baking soda, cocoa powder, whole wheat flour, sugar and all-purpose flour into big bowl. Add vinegar, vanilla, juice concentrate, oil and 3/4 cup water; whisk to blend. Put batter in prepped pan.
- Bake cake for 35 minutes till inserted tester in middle exits clean; cool cake in pan on the rack. Cut around pan sides carefully; turn cake out onto the serving platter.
- Frosting: In medium metal bowl, put chopped bittersweet chocolate. Put bowl above saucepan with barely simmering water; constantly mix till chocolate is smooth and melted. Put bowl on work surface carefully; cool melted chocolate down to room

temperature for 15-20 minutes, occasionally mixing.
- Beat "butter" till smooth using electric mixer in big bowl. Add salt, vanilla, 1 tbsp. juice concentrate and powdered sugar; beat till smooth. Add 2 tbsp. juice concentrate; beat till blended. Beat in the agave nectar; beat in chocolate. Stand for 10 minutes. Frost sides and top of cake. You can make cake maximum of 8 hours ahead; cover using cake dome. Keep in room temperature.

68. Chocolate Caramel Frozen Parfaits

Serving: Makes 8 servings | Prep: 1hours | Cook: 13.5hours | Ready in:

Ingredients

- 1/2 cup whole milk
- 1 1/2 cups chilled heavy cream
- 3 tablespoons water
- 3/4 cup sugar
- 8 large egg yolks
- 7 oz fine-quality bittersweet chocolate (not unsweetened), melted and cooled
- 1/2 teaspoon vanilla
- Accompaniments: hot fudge sauce ; unsweetened whipped cream; fresh raspberries
- an instant-read thermometer; a standing electric mixer; 8 (8- to 9-oz) paper cups

Direction

- Boil 1/2 cup cream and milk in a heavy small saucepan; remove from heat. Keep warm, covered.
- Boil 1/2 cup sugar and water in another heavy small saucepan, washing down sugar crystals on pan's sides with pastry brush dipped into cold water, mixing till sugar melts; boil syrup without mixing till it is deep golden caramel, swirling pan gently. Remove from heat. Add warm cream mixture slowly; it'll vigorously steam and caramel will be hard. Cook on low heat till caramel melts, whisking.
- Whisk a pinch of salt, leftover 1/4 cup sugar and yolks in metal bowl. In a slow stream, add hot caramel mixture, whisking. Transfer custard in saucepan; cook custard till thermometer reads 170°F and thick on moderately low heat, mixing; don't boil.
- Through fine-mesh sieve, pour custard into a standing mixer's bowl; beat for 10 minutes on high speed till pale, thick and fully cool. Beat in vanilla and melted chocolate.
- Whisk leftover cup cream till it holds stiff peaks in another bowl; whisk about 1/4 cream into chocolate mixture to lighten. Gently fold in leftover cream yet thoroughly; divide to paper cups, smoothing tops. Use foil to cover each cup; freeze parfaits for at least 12 hours.
- To Serve: Tear off every paper cup carefully; invert parfaits onto the plates.
- You can freeze parfaits for up to 3 days.

69. Chocolate Chip Cookies

Serving: 30 | Prep: | Cook: 30mins | Ready in:

Ingredients

- 1 cup all-purpose flour
- ½ teaspoon baking soda
- ½ teaspoon salt
- 2 tablespoons unsalted butter
- 2 ounces reduced-fat cream cheese, (Neufchâtel) (¼ cup)
- 6 tablespoons packed light brown sugar
- 6 tablespoons granulated sugar
- 1 large egg
- 1 large egg white
- 1 teaspoon vanilla extract
- ½ cup semisweet chocolate chips, coarsely chopped, or mini chocolate chips

Direction

- Preheat the oven to 375 degrees F. Coat two baking sheets with cooking spray or line with parchment paper.
- In a medium bowl, mix together flour, salt and baking soda and reserve. Over low heat, melt butter in a small saucepan. Cook while swirling the pan for 30 to 60 seconds until butter turns nutty brown. Transfer to a large mixing bowl. Add granulated sugar, cream cheese and brown sugar. Use an electric mixer on low speed to beat until the resulting mixture is smooth.
- Add vanilla, egg, and egg white and beat until incorporated well. Add chocolate chips and reserved flour mixture and mix with a wooden spoon just until combined. (Batter should be runny.)
- Transfer the batter by dropping rounded tablespoonfuls onto the prepared baking sheets, two inches apart. Bake for 12 to 15 minutes, one sheet at a time, until golden. Place cookies onto racks and leave them to cool.

Nutrition Information

- Calories: 62 calories;
- Sodium: 71
- Cholesterol: 9
- Sugar: 7
- Protein: 1
- Total Fat: 2
- Saturated Fat: 1
- Total Carbohydrate: 10
- Fiber: 0

70. Chocolate Chip Crunch Cookies

Serving: Makes about 16 cookies | Prep: | Cook: |Ready in:

Ingredients

- 1/2 stick (1/4 cup) unsalted butter, softened
- 1/3 cup firmly packed light brown sugar
- 1 large egg yolk plus 2 teaspoons water, or 1 large egg white
- 1/2 cup all-purpose flour
- 1/4 teaspoon double-acting baking powder
- 1/4 teaspoon salt
- 1/4 teaspoon vanilla extract
- 1 cup semisweet chocolate chips
- 1/2 cup toasted rice cereal

Direction

- Preheat an oven to 375°F. Cream brown sugar and butter till fluffy and light in bowl using an electric mixer; beat in egg white/egg yolk mixture. Add vanilla, salt, baking powder and flour, mixing till dough is well blended. Mix in cereal and chips; put level tablespoons of dough on lightly greased baking sheet, 2-in. apart. Bake cookies for 8-10 minutes till golden in center of oven. Put cookies on rack with spatula; cool.

Nutrition Information

- Calories: 115
- Total Fat: 6 g(10%)
- Saturated Fat: 4 g(19%)
- Sodium: 47 mg(2%)
- Fiber: 1 g(3%)
- Total Carbohydrate: 15 g(5%)
- Cholesterol: 19 mg(6%)
- Protein: 1 g(2%)

71. Chocolate Chip Zucchini Cupcakes

Serving: Makes 12 cupcakes | Prep: 15mins | Cook: 1.5hours |Ready in:

Ingredients

- 1 1/2 cups all-purpose flour

- 2 tablespoons unsweetened Dutch-process cocoa powder
- 1/2 teaspoon cinnamon
- 1/2 teaspoon baking soda
- 1/4 teaspoon baking powder
- 1/4 teaspoon salt
- 3/4 cup plus 2 tablespoon sugar
- 1/2 cup vegetable oil
- 1 large egg
- 1/2 teaspoon pure vanilla extract
- 1/2 pound zucchini, coarsely grated (1 cup)
- 1 (6-ounces) package semisweet chocolate chips
- Equipment: a muffin pan with 12 (1/2-cup) cups with paper liners

Direction

- Preheat an oven with rack in center to 350°F.
- Whisk salt, baking powder, baking soda, cinnamon, cocoa and flour. Beat vanilla, egg, oil and sugar using electric mixer for 2-3 minutes till creamy and thick in a big bowl. Mix in flour mixture till incorporated on low speed. Mix in chocolate chips and zucchini; divide to lined muffin cups. Bake for 30-35 minutes till tops spring back when pressed lightly; cool for 5 minutes in pan. Turn out; fully cool.

Nutrition Information

- Calories: 275
- Total Carbohydrate: 37 g(12%)
- Cholesterol: 16 mg(5%)
- Protein: 3 g(6%)
- Total Fat: 14 g(22%)
- Saturated Fat: 3 g(17%)
- Sodium: 117 mg(5%)
- Fiber: 2 g(7%)

72. Chocolate Chip Peanut Butter Cookies

Serving: Makes about 2 1/2 dozen | Prep: 30mins | Cook: 1hours15mins | Ready in:

Ingredients

- 1 1/2 cups all purpose flour
- 1/2 teaspoon baking powder
- 1/2 teaspoon salt
- 2/3 cup natural no-stir crunchy (or chunky) peanut butter
- 1/2 cup (1 stick) unsalted butter, room temperature
- 1/3 cup plus 1/4 cup sugar
- 1/3 cup (packed) golden brown sugar
- 1 large egg
- 1 teaspoon vanilla extract
- 1/2 cup bittersweet or semisweet chocolate chips
- 1 2.1-ounce Butterfinger candy bar, chopped (scant 1/2 cup)

Direction

- Put 1 rack into each of bottom and top third of oven; preheat it to 375°F. Line parchment paper on 2 baking sheets. Whisk salt, baking powder and flour to blend in medium bowl. Beat brown sugar, 1/3 cup sugar, butter and peanut butter using electric mixer till smooth in big bowl; beat in vanilla extract, egg then flour mixture. It'll look crumbly. Mix in chopped Butterfinger candy and bittersweet chocolate chips.
- Put leftover 1/4 cup sugar into small bowl. Roll dough between palms to make balls, 1 1/2 tbsp. dough for every cookie. Roll balls in sugar; put on prepped baking sheets, 1-in. apart. Press cookies to 1/3-in. thick rounds using bottom of measuring cup/glass.
- Bake cookies for 15-16 minutes till edges are golden brown; reverse sheets to evenly bake halfway through baking time. Put parchment paper with cookies on rack; cool.

73. Chocolate Chipotle Shortbread

Serving: Makes 16 cookies | Prep: 10mins | Cook: 1.25hours | Ready in:

Ingredients

- 1 cup all-purpose flour
- 1/4 cup unsweetened cocoa powder
- 1/2 teaspoon chipotle chile powder
- 1/2 teaspoon cinnamon
- 1/8 teaspoon salt
- 1 stick unsalted butter, softened
- 1/3 cup superfine granulated sugar

Direction

- Preheat an oven with rack in center to 350°F.
- Whisk salt, cinnamon, chile powder, cocoa powder and flour in a bowl.
- Beat sugar and butter using electric mixer on medium speed till fluffy and pale; mix in flour mixture till well blended on low speed. Halve dough; pat out to 2 7-in. 1/4-in. thick rounds. Put rounds on ungreased baking sheet, 2-in. apart. Cut each round to 8 wedges; don't separate wedges. Use fork to prick all over.
- Bake for 16-18 minutes till dry to touch. While hot, recut shortbread; cool on sheet. It crisps as it cools.
- Shortbread keeps for 1 week in room temperature in airtight container.

Nutrition Information

- Calories: 99
- Protein: 1 g(2%)
- Total Fat: 6 g(9%)
- Saturated Fat: 4 g(19%)
- Sodium: 22 mg(1%)
- Fiber: 1 g(3%)
- Total Carbohydrate: 11 g(4%)
- Cholesterol: 15 mg(5%)

74. Chocolate Cinnamon Cream Pie

Serving: Makes 8 servings | Prep: 30mins | Cook: 3.5hours | Ready in:

Ingredients

- 5 tablespoons unsalted butter, melted
- 1 1/2 cups cinnamon graham cracker crumbs (from about twelve 5-by 2 1/2-inch crackers)
- 2 tablespoons sugar
- 1/8 teaspoon salt
- 6 ounces fine-quality bittersweet chocolate (no more than 60% cacao if marked)
- 2 tablespoons cornstarch
- 1/3 cup packed light brown sugar, divided
- 2 whole large eggs
- 2 large egg yolks
- 2 cups whole milk
- 1/2 cup heavy cream
- 1/8 teaspoon salt
- 1/2 stick unsalted butter, cut into tablespoons
- 1 teaspoon pure vanilla extract
- 1 1/2 cups chilled heavy cream
- 5 tablespoons confectioners sugar
- 1/2 teaspoon cinnamon
- 1 (3-to 4-inch-thick) chunk bittersweet chocolate

Direction

- Crust: Preheat an oven with rack in center to 350°F.
- Mix all crust ingredients; press up side and on bottom of 9-in. pie plate. Bake for 12-15 minutes till set; cool.
- Filling: In a big bowl, melt chocolate.
- Mix 2 tbsp. brown sugar and cornstarch in a small bowl.
- Whisk yolks and whole eggs in another bowl; whisk in the cornstarch mixture.
- Mix leftover brown sugar, salt, cream and milk till it just boils in heavy medium saucepan on medium heat; put 1/2 milk mixture in a slow stream into egg mixture, whisking. Put egg mixture into leftover milk mixture. Boil on

medium low heat, constantly whisking; boil for 1 minute, whisking. Take off heat; whisk in vanilla and butter. Through fine-mesh sieve, strain into melted chocolate; whisk to mix.
- Put hot filling in crust; chill for 3 hours till filling is cold, surface covered in parchment.
- Whipped cream: Use an electric mixer to beat cinnamon, confectioners' sugar and cream till it holds stiff peaks in a big bowl; put on chilled filling.
- Chocolate curls: Microwave chocolate in 10-sec intervals on low power/hold in your hands till surface slightly softens. Peel big chocolate curls onto paper towel using vegetable peeler, Y-shaped is best. Rewarm chocolate just till surface softens if curls don't easily form or are too brittle.
- Sprinkle curls over pie.
- You can bake crust 2 days ahead, kept in room temperature, covered with foil loosely when cool.
- You can chill pie for up to 1 day, loosely covered in plastic wrap when cold.

Nutrition Information

- Calories: 638
- Saturated Fat: 28 g(140%)
- Sodium: 222 mg(9%)
- Fiber: 2 g(8%)
- Total Carbohydrate: 50 g(17%)
- Cholesterol: 218 mg(73%)
- Protein: 8 g(15%)
- Total Fat: 48 g(73%)

75. Chocolate Cupped Cakes With Coffee And Chicory

Serving: Serves 6 | Prep: | Cook: |Ready in:

Ingredients

- 2 cups plus 2 tablespoons sugar
- 1/4 cup light brown sugar
- 1/2 cup Dutch-processed cocoa powder
- 3 tablespoons unsalted butter, at room temperature
- 1 1/4 cups heavy cream
- 1 teaspoon vanilla extract
- 2 1/2 cups all-purpose flour
- 1 tablespoon instant espresso powder
- 2 teaspoons baking powder
- 1/2 teaspoon salt
- 1 cup brewed New Orleans–style chicory coffee

Direction

- Heat an oven to 350°F. Spray nonstick cooking spray on insides of 6 6-oz. ramekins/6 big oven-safe coffee cups; put onto rimmed baking sheet.
- Cocoa sprinkle: Whisk 2 tbsp. cocoa powder, light brown sugar and 1/4 cup sugar till most brown sugar lumps break up in a small bowl; put aside.
- Blend leftover sugar and butter on medium speed for 2 minutes till sugar resembles wet sand using a stand mixer/big bowl if using hand mixer. Lower speed to low; add vanilla and cream. Mix till blended well, scraping bowl's sides as needed with a rubber spatula.
- Whisk salt, baking powder, espresso powder and leftover cocoa powder in a big bowl; add to butter mixture. Mix at low speed till stiff dough comes together. Put speed on medium; beat for 15 seconds.
- Divide batter to coffee cups; fill each to 1/2 full. Press batter into cup using back of a spoon. Put 2 tbsp. reserved cocoa sprinkle over each; put 2 1/2 tbsp. coffee on cocoa. Bake for 55-60 minutes till dry on top with no obvious wet spots and each cake's top is crust; cool for a minimum of 20 minutes. Serve.
- Make ahead: Best eaten within several hours of baking while warm. Heat it up in a microwave before serving if you have leftovers over the following day.
- You can use leftover cocoa sprinkle to mix in iced coffee with some condensed milk or over scoop of ice cream. You can make this in 9-in.

square baking dish if you don't have oven-safe coffee cups, just bake it for 5-10 more minutes.

Nutrition Information

- Calories: 728
- Saturated Fat: 16 g(79%)
- Sodium: 340 mg(14%)
- Fiber: 4 g(14%)
- Total Carbohydrate: 123 g(41%)
- Cholesterol: 83 mg(28%)
- Protein: 8 g(16%)
- Total Fat: 26 g(39%)

76. Chocolate Gelato

Serving: Makes about 1 quart | Prep: | Cook: | Ready in:

Ingredients

- 2 ounces fine-quality bittersweet chocolate (not unsweetened)
- 2 1/4 cups whole milk
- 1/3 cup heavy cream
- 3/4 cup minus 2 tablespoons superfine granulated sugar
- 1 cup unsweetened cocoa powder
- 4 large egg yolks

Direction

- Chop chocolate coarsely. Put 1/2 sugar, cream and milk to a simmer in 2-qt. heavy saucepan, mixing till sugar melts. Take off heat; add chocolate and cocoa powder, till mixture is smooth and chocolate melts.
- Prep big bow with cold water and ice. Beat leftover sugar and yolks in bowl using an electric mixer till pale and thick. In a slow stream, add hot chocolate mixture, whisking; put in saucepan. Cook custard on medium low heat, constantly mixing, till a thermometer reads 170°F, don't boil. Through sieve, put custard into metal bowl that's set in cold water and ice; cool. Chill custard till cold, covered.
- In ice cream maker, freeze custard. Put in airtight container; put in freezer for 1-3 hours to harden.

Nutrition Information

- Calories: 167
- Saturated Fat: 7 g(33%)
- Sodium: 40 mg(2%)
- Fiber: 4 g(18%)
- Total Carbohydrate: 16 g(5%)
- Cholesterol: 113 mg(38%)
- Protein: 6 g(12%)
- Total Fat: 12 g(18%)

77. Chocolate Hazelnut Cake With Praline Chocolate Crunch

Serving: Makes 10 to 12 servings | Prep: | Cook: | Ready in:

Ingredients

- 1 1/2 cups sugar
- 1 1/2 cups blanched hazelnuts, toasted
- 1 teaspoon hazelnut or vegetable oil
- 4 ounces dark chocolate (do not exceed 72% cacao), chopped
- 4 ounces high-quality milk chocolate (such as Lindt or Scharffen Berger), chopped
- 1/4 teaspoon kosher salt
- 1 3/4 cups puffed rice cereal or crushed cornflakes
- Unsalted butter (for parchment paper)
- 1 cup all-purpose flour
- 1 cup natural unsweetened cocoa powder
- 8 large eggs
- 1 cup sugar, divided
- 2 tablespoons corn syrup
- 1/2 cup brandy or orange liqueur
- 1/2 cup heavy cream

- 1/2 cup hazelnut butter (or ground roasted hazelnuts)
- Pinch of kosher salt
- 3/4 cup (1 1/2 sticks) unsalted butter, room temperature
- 3 1/2 ounces dark chocolate (do not exceed 72% cacao), chopped
- 1 cup hazelnut praline paste (reserved from praline chocolate crunch)
- 5 tablespoons unsalted butter, room temperature, cubed
- 1 3/4 cups chilled heavy cream, divided
- Chocolate Glazeepi:recipelink
- 1/4 cup roasted hazelnuts

Direction

- Praline chocolate crunch: Line parchment paper on 2 rimmed baking sheets. Mix 1/3 cup water and sugar till sugar dissolves in small saucepan on medium low heat. Increase heat; cook without mixing, swirling pan occasionally, brushing sides down with wet pastry brush, for 7-8 minutes till amber is color. Mix in hazelnuts; put on 1 prepped sheet, separating nuts. Cool.
- Put candied nuts into food processor. Add the hazelnut oil; puree till smooth to create praline paste.
- Mix 3 tbsp. praline paste and both chocolates in medium metal bowl; keep leftover paste for the praline mousse layer. Put bowl above saucepan of simmering water; mix till it is smooth and chocolate melts. Take off heat; mix in salt then the cereal. Spread it out to 1/8-in. thick thin layer on 2nd prepped baking sheet; chill for 30 minutes till set. You can make it 1 day ahead. Cover; keep chilled. Cover; chill leftover praline paste.
- Cake: Preheat an oven to 375°F. Line parchment paper on 17x11x1-in. sheet pan; butter paper. Sift cocoa powder and flour into medium bowl; put aside. Separate 4 eggs; put whites into medium bowl and yolks into big bowl. Beat 1/2 cup sugar and yolks using electric mixer at medium speed for 3 minutes till light yellow and thick. One by one, beat in the 4 whole eggs; blend well between the additions.
- Beat leftover 1/2 cup sugar, corn syrup and egg whites using dry, clean beaters for 2 minutes till frothy and slightly thick. Put egg-white mixture in egg-yolk mixture; beat to blend. Add the flour-cocoa powder mixture; to just blend, fold. Evenly spread out on prepped baking sheet.
- Bake for 15 minutes till inserted tester in middle of cake exits clean; fully cool. Invert cake onto big baking sheet/cutting board; peel parchment off. Brush brandy all over cake. You can make it 1 day ahead; keep at room temperature, airtight.
- Nut ganache: Boil cream in small saucepan. Puree salt, hazelnut butter and hot cream in food processor; cool to room temperature. 1 tbsp. at a time, add butter as machine runs, pureeing between additions till smooth. You can make it 1 day ahead. Cover; chill. Before using, bring to room temperature.
- Praline mousse: Mix butter, praline paste and chocolate in medium bowl. Boil 3/4 cup cream in small saucepan; put on chocolate mixture. Stand for 1 minute; mix till smooth and melted. Beat leftover 1 cup chilled cream till soft peaks form. Into chocolate mixture, fold whipped cream. You can make it 1 day ahead. Cover; chill.
- Assemble: Spread nut ganache on cake; chill in freezer for 15 minutes till set. Spread mousse on ganache; chill in freezer for 15 minutes till set. Crosswise cut cake to thirds; stack the layers over each other. Trim the edges; spread chocolate glaze on sides and top of cake. Freeze for 1 hour till set. Put in fridge; chill overnight. You can make it 2 days ahead. Use foil to tent; keep chilled.
- Stand cake 30 minutes before serving at room temperature. Break praline chocolate crunch up to big shards; put over top of the cake. Garnish using roasted hazelnuts.

Nutrition Information

- Calories: 1263
- Sodium: 160 mg(7%)
- Fiber: 9 g(35%)
- Total Carbohydrate: 112 g(37%)
- Cholesterol: 310 mg(103%)
- Protein: 16 g(32%)
- Total Fat: 88 g(136%)
- Saturated Fat: 45 g(224%)

78. Chocolate Hazelnut Cakes

Serving: Makes 12 servings | Prep: | Cook: | Ready in:

Ingredients

- 8 ounces bittersweet chocolate
- 2 ounces unsweetened chocolate
- 4 ounces toasted hazelnuts
- 3 tablespoons confectioner's sugar
- 1/4 cup premium-quality Dutch-process cocoa powder
- 3/4 cup (1 1/2 sticks) unsalted butter, softened
- 3/4 cup plus 5 tablespoons granulated sugar
- 1/3 cup unsweetened hazelnut paste (available at specialty stores)
- 6 eggs, separated
- 2 teaspoons strong brewed espresso, cooled completely
- 2 teaspoons Frangelico (hazelnut liqueur)
- 2 teaspoons pure vanilla extract

Direction

- Preheat an oven to 325°F. Spray nonstick cooking spray on 1 9-in. springform pan/12 3-in. cake molds lightly; put aside.
- Use water to fill bottom of double boiler 1/3 full; simmer on medium low heat. Put a stainless-steel medium bowl above water; melt chocolates together, constantly mixing. Put aside when melted; cool.
- Pulse confectioners' sugar, cocoa and hazelnuts to make sand-like, fine mixture in a food processor's bowl.
- Beat 3/4 cup granulated sugar and butter in an electric mixer till fluffy and very light; beat in hazelnut paste, scraping bowl's sides down with a spatula. One by one, beat in egg yolks; beat in vanilla extract, Frangelico, espresso then melted chocolate. Fold in nut mixture.
- Beat egg whites using whip attachment till foamy in another mixing bowl. Add leftover 5 tbsp. sugar slowly, beating tills soft peaks form. Fold egg whites gently into cake batter using rubber spatula. Put prepped molds onto greased baking sheet; evenly divide batter to them.
- Bake cakes, 45-50 minutes for springform pan, 14 minutes for cake molds, till they slightly crack and puff. Remove from oven; cool in molds on wire rack. Remove molds gently when cakes are nearly fully cool. Chill till firm in the fridge. Keep cakes in an airtight container for 1 week, refrigerated.

Nutrition Information

- Calories: 422
- Cholesterol: 111 mg(37%)
- Protein: 7 g(13%)
- Total Fat: 30 g(46%)
- Saturated Fat: 14 g(68%)
- Sodium: 36 mg(2%)
- Fiber: 4 g(15%)
- Total Carbohydrate: 37 g(12%)

79. Chocolate Hazelnut Crinkle Cookies

Serving: Makes about 7 dozen cookies | Prep: 30mins | Cook: 4hours | Ready in:

Ingredients

- 2/3 cup hazelnuts
- 2 tablespoons granulated sugar
- 6 oz fine-quality bittersweet

- chocolate (no more than 60% cacao if marked), finely chopped
- 2 3/4 cups all-purpose flour
- 2 tablespoons unsweetened cocoa powder
- 2 teaspoons baking powder
- 3/4 teaspoon salt
- 1 stick (1/2 cup) unsalted butter, softened
- 1 1/2 cups packed light brown sugar
- 2 large eggs
- 1/4 cup whole milk
- 1 teaspoon pure vanilla extract
- 3/4 cup confectioners sugar
- Parchment paper

Direction

- Dough: In center position, put oven rack; preheat the oven to 350°F.
- Toast hazelnuts for 10 minutes till nuts are pale golden and skins split in shallow baking pan in the oven. Remove from oven; turn off oven. Wrap hazelnuts in kitchen towel; rub to remove loose skins. Fully cool nuts. Pulse granulated sugar and nuts till finely chopped in a food processor.
- Melt chocolate in metal bowl above saucepan with barely simmering water/on top of double boiler, mixing till smooth. Take bowl off heat; put aside.
- Whisk salt, baking powder, cocoa powder and flour in a bowl.
- Beat brown sugar and butter using electric mixer on medium high speed for 3 minutes till creamy in another bowl. One by one, add eggs; beat well after each. Beat in melted chocolate till combined. Add vanilla and milk; beat to incorporate. Lower speed to low. Add flour mixture; stir just till combined. Mix in nut mixture. Use plastic wrap to cover bowl; chill dough for 2-3 hours till firm.
- Shape and bake cookies: In lower and upper thirds of oven, put oven racks; preheat the oven to 350°F. Line parchment paper on 2 big baking sheets.
- Into a bowl, sift confectioners' sugar. Halve dough; chill, wrapped in plastic wrap, 1 half. Roll leftover half to 1-in. balls; as rolled, put onto wax paper sheet. 3-4 at 1 time, roll balls in confectioners' sugar to generously coat; put on lined baking sheets, 2-in. apart.
- Bake for 12-18 minutes total, switching sheets position halfway through baking, till cracked and puffed and edges feel dry yet centers are slightly soft. Put cookies on racks, still on parchment; fully cool.
- Roll leftover dough to balls as first batch bakes. Line fresh parchment on cooled cookie sheets. Coat balls in confectioners' sugar; bake the same way.
- Cookies keep for 5 days in room temperature in an airtight container, layered between wax paper/parchment sheets.

80. Chocolate Hazelnut Praline Torte With Frangelico Whipped Cream

Serving: Makes 1 torte | Prep: | Cook: | Ready in:

Ingredients

- 1 recipeHazelnut Praline
- 3 ounces fine-quality bittersweet chocolate (not unsweetened), chopped coarse
- 3/4 stick (6 tablespoons) unsalted butter, softened
- 1 teaspoon salt
- 1/2 cup sugar
- 4 large eggs, separated
- 1 teaspoon vanilla extract
- 1 cup well-chilled heavy cream
- 2 tablespoons Frangelico (hazelnut-flavored liqueur)

Direction

- Preheat an oven to 350°F. Butter the 8 1/2-in., 2-in. deep springform pan/other cake pan with the same dimensions; line wax paper round on bottom. Butter paper. Use flour to dust pan; knock excess flour out.

- Pulse praline till ground fine in a food processor; keep 1/4 cup ground praline. Put leftover praline into a bowl. Pulse chocolate till finely ground in a food processor; add to bowl with praline.
- Cream 1/4 cup sugar, salt and butter using an electric mixer till fluffy and light in a bowl. One by one, beat in yolks; beat well after each. Then beat in the vanilla. Mix in praline chocolate mixture; it'll be very thick.
- Beat whites using cleaned beaters till foamy in another bowl. In a stream, add leftover 1/4 cup sugar and pinch salt, beating till meringue holds stiff peaks. Fold 1/3 meringue to lighten into yolk mixture; gently yet thoroughly fold in leftover meringue. Put batter in pan; smooth top.
- Bake torte in center of oven till it starts to pull away from pan's sides for 45-55 minutes. In pan on rack, cool torte; it'll slightly fall and sets as it cooks. Remove from pan. You can make it 1 day ahead, covered, chilled. Before serving, bring to room temperature.
- Beat cream with an electric mixer in a bowl just until soft peaks hold. Mix in 1/2 reserved praline and Frangelico.
- Put whipped cream on torte; sprinkle leftover reserved praline. Immediately serve.

81. Chocolate Mint Mousse

Serving: Makes 4 servings | Prep: 15mins | Cook: 1.75hours | Ready in:

Ingredients

- 1 1/3 cups chilled heavy cream
- 5 oz fine-quality bittersweet chocolate (no more than 60% cacao if marked), finely chopped
- 1/2 teaspoon pure peppermint extract
- 1/2 cup coarsely crushed peppermint hard candies (2 oz)

Direction

- Over low heat, heat in a 1-quart saucepan the 1/3 cup of cream until hot. Add in chocolate and a pinch of salt then whisk until smooth. Prepare bowl and place mixture. Allow cooling at room temperature for about 30 minutes while occasionally stirring.
- In a separate bowl, set an electric mixer at medium speed and whisk the rest of the cream with extract until it holds soft peaks. Pour in cooled chocolate mixture and whisk until mousse holds stiff peaks. Add 1/4 cup of candy; fold. Scoop into 4 stemmed glasses and sprinkle with the rest of 1/4 cup candy. Place in the chiller for about 1 hour until cold.

Nutrition Information

- Calories: 410
- Protein: 9 g(17%)
- Total Fat: 34 g(53%)
- Saturated Fat: 21 g(106%)
- Sodium: 43 mg(2%)
- Fiber: 13 g(52%)
- Total Carbohydrate: 37 g(12%)
- Cholesterol: 109 mg(36%)

82. Chocolate Orange Cheesecake With Orange Tangerine Glaze

Serving: Serves 8 | Prep: | Cook: | Ready in:

Ingredients

- about 30 chocolate wafers, ground fine in a blender or food processor (1 3/4 cups)
- 1/2 stick (1/4 cup) unsalted butter, melted
- 1 1/2 pounds cream cheese, softened
- 1 1/4 cups sugar
- 1 cup sour cream at room temperature
- 2 tablespoons freshly grated orange zest (from about 4 navel oranges)
- 1/4 cup plus 2 tablespoons fresh orange juice
- 2 tablespoons Grand Marnier or other orange-flavored liqueur

- 1/2 teaspoon salt
- 1/4 cup all-purpose flour
- 4 large whole eggs
- 1 large egg yolk
- 3/4 cup orange and tangerine marmalade* (about 7 1/2 ounces)
- *available at some specialty food shops.

Direction

- For Crust: Mix butter and wafer crumbs till well combined in a small bowl; pat crumb mixture 1-in. up the side and on bottom of 9-in. springform pan. Chill crust for 30 minutes.
- For Filling: Preheat an oven to 300°F.
- Beat cream cheese till fluffy and light using an electric mixer in a bowl; slowly beat in sugar till well combined. Beat in flour, salt, liqueur, orange juice, zest and sour cream. Beat in yolk and whole egg, one at a time; beat well after each addition.
- Wrap side and bottom of springform pan, one at a time, using three 14x12-in. foil pieces, putting every piece in a different position to make sure that the foil is at least 1 1/2-in. up the side all around. In big baking dish, put pan; pour filling into the crust. Put dish in center of oven; slowly add water with a measuring cup to reach 1/4-in. up springform pan's side. Don't let water get in the foil. Cooling in water bath avoids the cheesecake surface from getting cracks.
- Bake cheesecake till edges are set yet center slightly trembles, for 1 hour 15 minutes; turn off oven. Allow cheesecake to stand for 1 hour; it sets while standing. Carefully take dish from oven. Put cheesecake in pan onto a rack; fully cool. Remove foil; chill cheesecake for 6 hours – overnight, loosely covered.
- For Glaze: Melt marmalade on medium heat in a small saucepan, mixing; cool to warm.
- Remove springform pan's sides; evenly spread marmalade over cheesecake. Chill cheesecake for 2 hours; glaze softens if served in room temperature.

Nutrition Information

- Calories: 610
- Total Fat: 44 g(67%)
- Saturated Fat: 24 g(122%)
- Sodium: 508 mg(21%)
- Fiber: 1 g(3%)
- Total Carbohydrate: 46 g(15%)
- Cholesterol: 240 mg(80%)
- Protein: 10 g(20%)

83. Chocolate Peppermint Bark Cookies

Serving: Makes about 36 | Prep: | Cook: | Ready in:

Ingredients

- Nonstick vegetable oil spray
- 2 cups all purpose flour
- 1/4 teaspoon salt
- 1 cup (2 sticks) unsalted butter, room temperature
- 1 cup sugar
- 1 teaspoon vanilla extract
- 1 large egg yolk
- 6 ounces bittersweet or semisweet chocolate, chopped
- 1/2 cup finely chopped red-and-whitestriped hard peppermint candies or candy canes (about 3 ounces)
- 2 ounces high-quality white chocolate (such as Lindt or Perugina)

Direction

- Preheat an oven to 350°F; spray nonstick spray on 13x9x2-in. metal baking pan. Line long 9-in. wide parchment paper strip on bottom of pan; leave overhang over both pan's short sides. Whisk salt and flour in medium bowl. Beat butter using electric mixer for 2 minutes till creamy in big bowl; beat in sugar slowly. Beat till fluffy and light for 3 minutes, occasionally stopping to scrape bowl's sides down. Beat in

vanilla; beat in egg yolk. Add flour mixture slowly; beat to just blend on low speed.
- By tablespoonfuls, drop dough in prepped baking pan, evenly spacing; press dough to make even layer on bottom of pan using moistened fingertips. Use fork to pierce dough all over.
- Bake cookie base for 30 minutes till edges start to come away from pan's sides, slightly puffed and light golden brown. Put pan on rack; sprinkle bittersweet chocolate immediately. Sprinkle bittersweet chocolate immediately. Stand for 3 minutes till chocolate softens. Spread bittersweet chocolate in thin even layer on top of cookie using small offset spatula; sprinkle chopped peppermint candies immediately.
- Mix white chocolate till smooth and melted in medium metal bowl above saucepan of simmering water; discard from over water. Drizzle white chocolate using fork all over cookies. Chill for 30 minutes till white chocolate sets.
- Lift cookie from pan using paper overhang for aid; put onto work surface. Cut cookie to irregular pieces using big knife. You can make it 1 week ahead; keep in airtight containers between wax paper/parchment paper layers in airtight containers.
- Variation: Sprinkle chopped peanut brittle/peanut butter cups with melted dark chocolate instead of peppermint candies.

84. Chocolate Puddings With Orange Whipped Cream

Serving: Makes 6 servings | Prep: 25mins | Cook: 3hours25mins | Ready in:

Ingredients

- 1/2 cup plus 3 tablespoons sugar, divided
- 2 tablespoons cornstarch
- 2 1/2 cups whole milk, divided
- 2 large egg yolks
- 1 1/2 cups bittersweet chocolate chips (do not exceed 61% cacao) or semisweet chocolate chips
- 2 tablespoons (1/4 stick) unsalted butter
- 1/4 teaspoon vanilla extract
- 3/4 cup chilled whipping cream
- 1 tablespoon Grand Marnier or other orange liqueur
- 1/4 teaspoon finely grated orange peel
- Test-kitchen tip: If you don't have orange liqueur on hand, skip the orange peel and use another liqueur. Kahlúa or amaretto would work well in this recipe.

Direction

- In a medium saucepan, whip cornstarch, quarter teaspoon of salt and half cup plus two tablespoons of sugar to incorporate. Put in egg yolks and half cup of milk; mix till smooth. Mix in the leftover 2 cups of milk. Boil mixture on moderately-high heat, whisk continuously. Boil for a minute, whisk continuously. Take pan off heat; put in butter and chocolate chips. Mix pudding till smooth and melted. Mix in vanilla.
- Evenly distribute pudding between six wineglasses or dessert cups. Put plastic wrap right on the top of each to cover pudding fully. Refrigerate for no less than 3 hours, till cold. DO AHEAD: may be done up to one day in advance. Keep in refrigerator.
- In a medium bowl, whip leftover 1 tablespoon of sugar, orange peel, Grand Marnier and whipping cream with electric mixer to form peaks. DO AHEAD: may be done 2 hours in advance. Refrigerate with cover.
- Remove puddings cover. Scoop whipped cream dollop on top of each to serve.

Nutrition Information

- Calories: 311
- Protein: 5 g(10%)
- Total Fat: 18 g(28%)
- Saturated Fat: 11 g(53%)
- Sodium: 58 mg(2%)

- Fiber: 0 g(0%)
- Total Carbohydrate: 32 g(11%)
- Cholesterol: 115 mg(38%)

85. Chocolate Raspberry Icebox Cake

Serving: Makes 1 serving | Prep: | Cook: |Ready in:

Ingredients

- 1/3 cup chilled heavy cream
- 1/2 teaspoon sugar
- 1/8 teaspoon vanilla
- 5 chocolate wafers such as Nabisco Famous
- 1/3 cup fresh raspberries
- grated bittersweet chocolate (not unsweetened)

Direction

- Beat vanilla, sugar and cream using an electric mixer just till it holds stiff peaks in a deep, small bowl.
- Onto each of the 4 wafers, spread 1 heaping tsp. cream; side by side, as near as possible, put enough raspberries to make an even layer onto 1 cream-topped wafer. On a plate, stack 2 cream-topped wafers, cream sides up; put berry wafer on top. Spread another 1 tsp. cream on berries carefully. Put last cream wafer over; cover with leftover plain wafer. Use leftover cream to frost sides and top of cake. Use an inverted bowl to cover; chill for 4 hours.
- Serve leftover berries with cake.
- You can chill cake for 1 day.

86. Chocolate Sheet Cake With Sour Cream Frosting

Serving: Makes 20 servings | Prep: | Cook: |Ready in:

Ingredients

- 2 cups all purpose flour
- 1 cup sweetened instant chocolate drink mix (such as NesQuik)
- 1 teaspoon baking soda
- 1 teaspoon baking powder
- 1/2 teaspoon salt
- 1 cup (2 sticks) unsalted butter, room temperature
- 1 1/2 cups (packed) golden brown sugar
- 3 large eggs
- 1 1/2 cups sour cream
- 3 cups semisweet chocolate chips (about 18 ounces)
- 1/2 cup almonds, toasted, chopped

Direction

- Preheat an oven to 350°F. Butter then flour 13x9x2-in. metal baking pan. Whisk initial 5 ingredients to blend in medium bowl. Beat butter till fluffy in big bowl; add sugar slowly, beating till blended well. One by one, beat in eggs. Alternately with the 3/4 cup sour cream in 3 batches, beat in the flour mixture in 4 batches; fold in almonds and 1 1/2 cups chocolate chips. In prepped pan, spread; bake for 45 minutes till inserted tester in middle exits clean. Put on rack; cool the cake. Meanwhile, mix 1 1/2 cups chocolate chips and leftover 3/4 cup sour cream in a medium heavy saucepan on very low heat till frosting is smooth and chocolate melts. Don't boil. Spread frosting on cake in pan; stand for a minimum of 1 hour till frosting sets.

Nutrition Information

- Calories: 418
- Saturated Fat: 14 g(71%)
- Sodium: 168 mg(7%)
- Fiber: 3 g(11%)
- Total Carbohydrate: 49 g(16%)
- Cholesterol: 61 mg(20%)
- Protein: 5 g(10%)
- Total Fat: 25 g(39%)

87. Chocolate Souffles

Serving: Makes 6 servings | Prep: | Cook: |Ready in:

Ingredients

- 1 tablespoon unsalted butter, softened
- 10 1/2 ounces (10 squares) extra-bittersweet chocolate
- 1 1/3 cups whole milk
- 1 tablespoon cornstarch
- 3 large egg yolks, room temperature, lightly beaten
- 6 large egg whites, room temperature
- 1/3 cup sugar; more for soufflé ramekins

Direction

- Heat an oven to 400°. Butter then flour 6 6-oz. soufflé ramekins. Put on rimmed baking sheet; put aside.
- Melt chocolate till smooth in double boiler above medium heat. Take off heat; keep warm.
- Mix cornstarch and milk well to blend with a wooden spoon in a heavy-bottom medium saucepan; boil on medium heat till thick, continuously mixing.
- Take off heat; mix in warm melted chocolate. Slightly cool. Put in lightly beaten egg yolks; mix till combined well.
- Whip egg whites at medium speed till foamy in a heavy-duty mixer's bowl. Add sugar slowly; put speed on high. Whip for 3 minutes till stiff and shiny peaks form.
- Lighten chocolate mixture with 1/3 beaten egg whites using a whisk; mix till combined well. Fold in leftover egg whites till just incorporated using a big rubber spatula.
- Put mixture in prepped soufflé ramekins; should reach ramekin's top. Put filled soufflé ramekins onto rimmed baking sheet in oven; bake for 12-15 minutes till risen. Immediately serve.

Nutrition Information

- Calories: 381
- Protein: 9 g(18%)
- Total Fat: 21 g(32%)
- Saturated Fat: 12 g(59%)
- Sodium: 88 mg(4%)
- Fiber: 3 g(12%)
- Total Carbohydrate: 47 g(16%)
- Cholesterol: 103 mg(34%)

88. Chocolate Souffles With Creamy Caramel Sauce

Serving: Serves 6 | Prep: | Cook: |Ready in:

Ingredients

- 1/4 cup sugar plus additional for coating ramekins
- 8 ounces fine-quality bittersweet chocolate (not unsweetened)
- 3/4 stick (6 tablespoons) unsalted butter
- 2 tablespoons heavy cream
- 4 large egg yolks
- 7 large egg whites
- 1/4 teaspoon cream of tartar
- Accompaniment: creamy caramel sauce

Direction

- Butter 6 4x2-in./1-cup ramekins. Coat using sugar; knock out extra sugar.
- Chop chocolate finely. Melt butter on low heat in a small saucepan. Add cream; boil. Take off heat. Add chocolate, mixing till smooth. Put mixture into a big bowl; mix in yolks.
- Beat cream of tartar, pinch salt and whites to stiff peaks using an electric mixer in another big bowl. Add 1/4 cup sugar slowly, beating just till combined. To lighten, mix 1/4 whites into the chocolate mixture; gently yet thoroughly fold in leftover whites.
- Divide soufflé mixture to ramekins; use knife to smooth tops. Run a knife's tip around

soufflé's edges to aid rising. At this point, you can make soufflés maximum of 1 day ahead, chilled, wrapped in plastic wrap loosely.
- Preheat an oven to 375°F.
- On lower third of oven, bake soufflés on baking sheet for 20 minutes till surfaces are cracked and puffed.
- Put sauce on soufflés; immediately serve.

Nutrition Information

- Calories: 390
- Total Fat: 28 g(43%)
- Saturated Fat: 16 g(81%)
- Sodium: 77 mg(3%)
- Fiber: 2 g(9%)
- Total Carbohydrate: 33 g(11%)
- Cholesterol: 160 mg(53%)
- Protein: 8 g(16%)

89. Chocolate Soufflé

Serving: Makes 8 servings | Prep: | Cook: | Ready in:

Ingredients

- 3/4 cup butter
- 1/2 cup flour
- 1/2 cup milk
- 1 cup sugar
- 2 egg yolks
- 3 1/2 ounces bittersweet chocolate, melted
- 1 tablespoon cocoa powder
- 5 egg whites

Direction

- Cook flour and butter in a saucepan until mixture forms a sandy roux. Prepare another pan, add sugar and milk, allow to boil. Pour milk mixture into the roux and cook until it forms a smooth paste. Let slightly cool before adding in egg yolks; beat. Stir in melted cocoa and chocolate. Beat egg whites until glossy, stiff peaks. Quickly, fold it into the base. Prepare buttered and sugared individual-sized ramekins with a dimension of about 1/2 inch from the top, then transfer the mixture into it. For 20 minutes, bake at 375°F. Dust with powdered sugar (or freshly whipped cream) then serve.

Nutrition Information

- Calories: 368
- Saturated Fat: 14 g(69%)
- Sodium: 40 mg(2%)
- Fiber: 1 g(5%)
- Total Carbohydrate: 40 g(13%)
- Cholesterol: 84 mg(28%)
- Protein: 4 g(9%)
- Total Fat: 23 g(35%)

90. Chocolate Spoonful Cake

Serving: Makes 1 cake | Prep: | Cook: | Ready in:

Ingredients

- 3 ounces semisweet chocolate, chopped
- 1 1/2 sticks (3/4 cup) unsalted butter, softened
- 1 1/2 cups granulated sugar
- 1/2 cup firmly packed light brown sugar
- 1 3/4 cups sour cream
- 1 1/2 teaspoons vanilla extract
- 3 large eggs
- 2 cups all-purpose flour
- 1/2 cup unsweetened cocoa powder (not Dutch-process)
- 1 teaspoon baking soda
- 1/2 teaspoon salt
- 3 ounces semisweet chocolate, chopped
- 2 cups sour cream
- 1 cup heavy cream
- 1 cup confectioners' sugar
- 1 teaspoon vanilla extract
- 3 ounces semisweet chocolate, chopped
- 2 tablespoons unsalted butter

- 1 cup semisweet chocolate chips and 1/2 cup semiseet chocolate shavings, shaved with a vegetable peeler from a bar of chocolate, for coating side of cake
- 1/2 cup semisweet chocolate shavings

Direction

- For cake layers: Prepare the oven by preheating to 375 degrees F. Prepare buttered and floured two round cake pans (9x2-inch), tapping out excess flour.
- Set a metal bowl or a double boiler over a pan with barely simmering water then put in chocolate to melt, whisking until smooth and cool.
- Use an electric mixer to whisk sugars and butter in a large bowl until fluffy and light. Whisk in vanilla and sour cream until blended. Put in 1 egg at a time, whisking well with after each addition.
- Combine salt, baking soda, cocoa powder, and flour in a bowl then slowly add to the sour cream mixture, whisking just until blended. Whisk in chocolate until batter is just blended and split up between pans.
- Place layers in the center of the oven and bake for about 30 minutes until a tester comes out clean. Cool layers for 10 minutes in pans on the rack and reverse onto racks to cool fully.
- For the filling/frosting: Put the chocolate in a metal bowl or a double boiler set over a pan with barely simmering water until melted, whisking until smooth and place at room temperature to cool. Use an electric mixer to whisk vanilla, confectioner's sugar, heavy cream, and sour cream in a large bowl until thickened. Whisk in chocolate until blended.
- For the glaze: Melt butter and chocolate in a metal bowl or a double boiler set over a pan with barely simmering water, whisking until smooth then cool.
- To assemble the cake: Horizontally halve cake layers using a long serrated knife. On a cake plate, pile layers, put 1 cup of filling/frosting between each layer and spread. Use the rest of the filling/frosting to spread the side of the cake.
- Drop glaze on top of the cake, spread just to cover the top and use chocolate shavings and chips to coat the side, pressing them in lightly.

Nutrition Information

- Calories: 9711
- Saturated Fat: 356 g(1780%)
- Sodium: 3281 mg(137%)
- Fiber: 55 g(219%)
- Total Carbohydrate: 1112 g(371%)
- Cholesterol: 1760 mg(587%)
- Protein: 101 g(202%)
- Total Fat: 597 g(918%)

91. Chocolate Banana Tarts

Serving: Makes 4 servings | Prep: | Cook: |Ready in:

Ingredients

- 4 tablespoons butter, softened
- 2 tablespoons sugar
- 1/8 teaspoon salt
- 1 large egg
- 3/4 cup all-purpose flour, plus extra for rolling crust
- 4 fluted 3-inch tart pans
- 4 tablespoons uncooked rice or dried beans
- 3 tablespoon heavy cream
- 1 teaspoon vanilla extract
- 1/2 teaspoon granulated sugar
- 1 medium banana, halved crosswise
- 3 tablespoon chocolate chips, melted
- 2 teaspoon packed brown sugar

Direction

- Crust: in a bowl, mix sugar, salt and butter. Whip egg in, then the flour, quarter cup at one time, to get a dough that's shaggy, it gathers together loosely, however not pliable or smooth. Sprinkle flour on a surface, turn the dough onto surface and, knead one or two times using slightly floured fingers to make a gooey dough. Encase with plastic wrap; chill for not less than 40 minutes. Split dough in 1/2; put 1/2 aside for Raspberry Marzipan Tarts or wrap well and freeze for other use. Heat the oven to 350°F. Split the leftover dough into quarters and, force a piece using a slightly floured fingertips to every of the 4 fluted tart pans, 3-inch in size, pressing dough up the sides smoothly. Patch dough on hole to seal it up in case dough tears on base. Use a fork to puncture pastry all over bottom a few times. Slowly force one small foil square to every pastry shell, avoid pressing it down hard, and put a tablespoon of dried beans or uncooked rice on each to avoid pastry from puffing up. Put on one baking sheet; bake for ten minutes. Take the rice and foil off pastry shells; throw. Put crust back to oven. Cook for 9 minutes longer, till golden. Cool fully.

- Filling: whip vanilla, granulated sugar and cream till firm. Whip in 1/2 of banana, mashed thoroughly, then fold chocolate in. Distribute filling between crusts; chill for an hour. Evenly spread brown sugar over base of a nonstick, small pan, then cut leftover banana half to pan. Heat over low. Once slices of banana begin to sizzle, mix till coated in sugar. Turn banana slices over once they turn clear around edges. Cook till slices caramelized on each side and turn browned. Put 3 slices of banana on every tart to serve.

92. Chocolate Cherry Tart

Serving: Makes 10 to 12 servings | Prep: | Cook: | Ready in:

Ingredients

- 1/2 cup water
- 1/2 cup sugar
- 1 cup (packed) dried Bing (sweet) cherries
- 1/3 cup kirsch (clear cherry brandy)
- 1 cup (2 sticks) unsalted butter, room temperature
- 1/2 cup sugar
- 1 large egg
- 1 teaspoon vanilla extract
- 2 cups all purpose flour
- 5 tablespoons unsweetened cocoa powder
- 1/2 teaspoon salt
- 3 large eggs
- 1/3 cup dark corn syrup
- 1/4 cup (1/2 stick) unsalted butter, melted
- 1 teaspoon vanilla extract
- 1/2 teaspoon (scant) salt
- 1/2 cup sugar
- 6 ounces bittersweet (not unsweetened) or semisweet chocolate, chopped
- Powdered sugar
- Unsweetened cocoa powder

Direction

- Fruit: Mix sugar and 1/2 cup water till syrup boils and sugar is dissolved in medium heavy saucepan on medium heat. Add cherries; take off heat. Cool for 30 minutes. Stir in kirsch; cover. Refrigerate for 1 day.
- Crust: Beat butter using electric mixer till fluffy in big bowl. Add sugar; beat till smooth. Beat in vanilla and egg. Sift salt, cocoa and flour on top; beat to blend. Press dough with moistened fingertips up sides and on bottom of 11-in. diameter tart pan that has removable bottom; cover. Chill for a minimum of 1 hour – maximum of 1 day.
- Filling: Preheat an oven to 350°F. Drain the cherries; keep cherry syrup. In crust, sprinkle cherries. Mix salt, vanilla, butter, corn syrup and eggs in big bowl. Add 1/4 cup sherry syrup and sugar; beat to blend. Stir in chocolate; put filling in crust.
- Bake tart for 1 hour till set in center; cool for 30 minutes on rack. You can make it 1 day ahead; cover. Keep in room temperature. From pan, release tart. Dust cocoa and powdered sugar; serve at room temperature/warm.

Nutrition Information

- Calories: 594
- Fiber: 3 g(12%)
- Total Carbohydrate: 74 g(25%)
- Cholesterol: 135 mg(45%)
- Protein: 7 g(13%)
- Total Fat: 31 g(47%)
- Saturated Fat: 18 g(92%)
- Sodium: 285 mg(12%)

93. Chocolate Chocolate Chip Cookie And Strawberry Gelato Sandwiches

Serving: Makes about 12 sandwiches | Prep: | Cook: | Ready in:

Ingredients

- 2 1/4 cups all purpose flour
- 1/2 cup natural unsweetened cocoa powder
- 1 teaspoon baking soda
- 1/2 teaspoon salt
- 1 cup (2 sticks) unsalted butter, room temperature
- 1 cup (packed) dark brown sugar
- 1/2 cup sugar
- 2 large eggs
- 1 teaspoon vanilla extract
- 1/2 teaspoon almond extract
- 2 cups semisweet chocolate chips
- Fresh Strawberry Gelato, slightly softened

Direction

- Preheat an oven to 375°F; line parchment on 2 big rimmed baking sheets. Sift initial 4 ingredients into bowl. Beat butter using electric mixer till fluffy in big bowl. Beat in both sugars; one by one, beat in eggs. Beat in extracts; beat in flour mixture. Fold in the chocolate chips. By heaping tablespoonfuls, drop batter on prepped sheets, with mounds 2-3-in. apart. Flatten mounds to 3/4-in. thick using moist fingertips.
- Bake cookies for 5 minutes. Reverse the sheets; bake for 5 minutes till soft to touch yet cookies look dry and are puffed. Fully cool. Freeze for 15 minutes on sheets.
- On 1 cookie's flat side, put 1/3 cup gelato; put 2nd cookie, flat side down, on top. Press together. Wrap; freeze. Repeat with leftover cookies and gelato. DO AHEAD: keep for maximum of 48 hours, frozen.

Nutrition Information

- Calories: 483
- Total Carbohydrate: 65 g(22%)
- Cholesterol: 72 mg(24%)
- Protein: 6 g(11%)
- Total Fat: 26 g(39%)
- Saturated Fat: 15 g(77%)
- Sodium: 225 mg(9%)
- Fiber: 4 g(15%)

94. Chocolate Orange Carrot Cake

Serving: Serves 8 to 10 | Prep: | Cook: | Ready in:

Ingredients

- Nonstick vegetable oil spray
- 1 1/2 cups vegetable oil
- 4 large eggs
- 2 1/2 cups all purpose flour
- 2 1/4 cups sugar
- 2/3 cup unsweetened cocoa powder
- 2 teaspoons baking soda
- 1 teaspoon salt
- 2 cups finely shredded peeled carrots (about 10 ounces)
- 1 cup (packed) sweetened flaked coconut
- 1 1/2 teaspoons grated orange peel
- 1 11-ounce can mandarin oranges, drained, cut into 1/2-inch pieces

- 2 1/2 cups semisweet chocolate chips (about 15 ounces)
- 1 cup (2 sticks) unsalted nondairy (pareve) margarine, room temperature
- 1/3 cup powdered sugar
- 1/4 cup frozen orange juice concentrate, thawed
- Additional canned mandarin orange segments, drained, patted very dry

Direction

- Cake: Preheat an oven to 350°F. Spray nonstick spray on 2 9-in. diameter cake pans that have 2-in. high sides. Beat eggs and 1 1/2 cups oil using electric mixer for 2 minutes till thick and well blended in big bowl. Add salt, baking soda, cocoa powder, sugar and flour; beat to blend on low speed. Increase speed; beat for 1 minute. It'll be very thick. Mix in orange peel, coconut, carrots then orange pieces. Divide the batter to prepped pans.
- Bake cakes for 40 minutes till inserted tester in middle exits clean; cool cakes for 10 minutes in pan. Turn onto racks; fully cool.
- Frosting: Mix chocolate chips till smooth and melted in medium heavy saucepan on very low heat; take off heat. Cool to lukewarm. Put 1/3 cup chocolate in small bowl; keep for decoration. Beat sugar and margarine till fluffy in medium bowl; beat in orange juice concentrate and leftover melted chocolate.
- On platter, put 1 cake layer; spread 2/3 cup frosting. Put 2nd cake layer over; spread leftover frosting on sides and top of cake. Put extra orange segments around cake's top edge. Rewarm 1/3 cup of reserved chocolate if needed to pourable consistency; drizzle chocolate on orange segments. You can make it 1 day ahead. Use a cake dome to cover; refrigerate.

Nutrition Information

- Calories: 1397
- Cholesterol: 93 mg(31%)
- Protein: 12 g(24%)
- Total Fat: 92 g(142%)
- Saturated Fat: 21 g(105%)
- Sodium: 826 mg(34%)
- Fiber: 10 g(39%)
- Total Carbohydrate: 146 g(49%)

95. Chocolate Orange Decadence

Serving: Serves 12 | Prep: | Cook: | Ready in:

Ingredients

- 2 medium oranges
- 1 1/3 cups sugar
- 1/4 cup orange marmalade
- 3/4 cup (1 1/2 sticks) unsalted butter, room temperature
- 1 teaspoon vanilla extract
- 4 large eggs, room temperature
- 2 1/2 cups cake flour
- 1/2 teaspoon baking powder
- 1/4 teaspoon baking soda
- 3/4 cup orange juice
- 2 1/2 cups whipping cream
- 9 tablespoons unsalted butter
- 30 ounces bittersweet (not unsweetened) or semisweet chocolate, chopped
- 7 tablespoons Grand Marnier or orange juice
- 3 tablespoons thawed frozen orange juice concentrate
- 2 tablespoons minced orange peel
- 6 tablespoons orange marmalade
- 6 tablespoons Grand Marnier or orange juice
- 3 1/2 1/2-pint baskets of raspberries (or 5 1/4 cups frozen unsweetened raspberries, thawed, drained
- Mint sprigs

Direction

- To make cake: Preheat the oven to 350°F. Butter 2 cake pans with 9 in. diameter and 1 1/2-in.-high sides. Line waxed paper on the bottoms of the pan. Use a vegetable peeler to discard strips of peel from the orange. In a processor, chop the peel coarsely and stop occasionally to scrap down the bowl's sides. Blend in 1/3 cup of sugar to mince the peel. Place in marmalade and puree. In a large bowl, cream vanilla and pureed mixture with cream butter using an electric mixer till fluffy and light. Add in the leftover 1 cup of sugar and beat. Add 1 egg at a time, beat well after each addition. In a small bowl, sift the dry ingredients then mix into the batter, alternating with orange juice.

- Place the batter into prepped pans. Bake cakes for 38 minutes till a tester comes out clean after being inserted in the middle and the tops turn golden. Let cakes cool for 10 minutes on racks. Loosen cakes by using a sharp knife to run around sides of the pan. Turn out and place the cakes onto racks to cool. Discard the paper.
- To make chocolate ganache: In a heavy large saucepan, bring butter and cream to a simmer. Lower to low heat. Stir in chopped chocolate till melted. Add in the leftover ingredients and mix. In a large bowl, place the ganache and let freeze for 1 hour 15 minutes while stirring frequently till very thick but spreadable.
- To make glaze: In a heavy small saucepan, melt marmalade over low heat. Take away from the heat then add in Grand Marnier and mix.
- Slice each cake into 2 layers of cake. On a plate, place the first cake later then brush with 1/4 of glaze. Spread over with 1 cup of ganache. Place the second layer on top then brush with 1/4 of glaze. Spread over with 3/4 cup of ganache. Place 1 1/2 baskets (about 2 1/2 cups) of berries on top. Spread over the third layer of cake with 1/2 cup of ganache. Invert over the berries with the chocolate side facing down. Brush with 1/4 of glaze then spread over with 1 cup of ganache. Place the fourth layer of cake on top and brush with the leftover glaze. Spread over the top of the cake with 3/4 cup of ganache. Add 1 cup of ganache into the pastry bag with medium star top fitted. Spread over the cake's sides with the leftover ganache, draw the icing spatula up for vertical lines. Around the bottom and top edges of the cake, pipe decorative ganache border. Let the cake freeze for 20 minutes. Top the cake with the leftover berries to cover completely. You can prepare this 1 day ahead. Use plastic wrap to loosely cover the cake and store in the fridge.
- Add mint sprigs for garnish. Serve the cake at room temperature.

Nutrition Information

- Calories: 996
- Sodium: 104 mg(4%)
- Fiber: 8 g(33%)
- Total Carbohydrate: 114 g(38%)
- Cholesterol: 171 mg(57%)
- Protein: 10 g(19%)
- Total Fat: 59 g(91%)
- Saturated Fat: 36 g(178%)

96. Chocolate Orange Fruitcake With Pecans

Serving: Serves 16 | Prep: | Cook: | Ready in:

Ingredients

- 2 1/2 cups large pecan pieces, toasted
- 1 cup (packed) chopped dried black Mission figs
- 1 cup (packed) chopped pitted prunes
- 1 cup (packed) chopped pitted dates
- 1/2 cup frozen orange juice concentrate, thawed
- 1/4 cup Grand Marnier or other orange liqueur
- 2 tablespoons grated orange peel
- 3 cups all purpose flour
- 3/4 cup (packed) unsweetened cocoa powder
- 2 1/2 teaspoons ground cinnamon
- 1 1/2 teaspoons baking powder
- 1 1/2 teaspoons baking soda
- 1 teaspoon salt

- 1 1-pound box dark brown sugar
- 6 ounces bittersweet (not unsweetened) or semisweet chocolate, coarsely chopped
- 1/2 cup (1 stick) unsalted butter, room temperature
- 4 ounces cream cheese, room temperature
- 4 large eggs, room temperature
- 3/4 cup purchased prune butter
- 1/2 cup plus 2 tablespoons (1 1/4 sticks) unsalted butter
- 1 pound bittersweet (not unsweetened) or semisweet chocolate, chopped
- 6 tablespoons orange juice concentrate, thawed
- Chopped candied fruit peel (optional)

Direction

- To make cake: Preheat the oven with the rack positioned in the bottom third to 325°F. Generously butter and spread flour on an angel food cake pan with 12 cups. In a large bowl, combine grated orange peel, Grand Marnier, orange juice concentrate, dates, prunes, chopped dried figs and toasted pecans. Allow to stand while stirring occasionally for 30 minutes.
- In a medium bowl, sift salt, baking soda, baking powder, cinnamon, cocoa and flour. In a processor, combine 6 ounces of chocolate and brown sugar then chop into small pieces.
- In a large bowl, beat cream cheese and butter by an electric mixer till blended. Beat in chocolate mix till fluffy. Beat in 1 egg at a time. Add in prune butter and beat. Add in 1/4 of dry ingredients and stir. Mix in 3 additions each of the leftover dry ingredients and fruit mixture.
- Place the batter into the prepped pan. Bake for 1 hour 55 minutes till a tester is attached with a few moist crumbs when being inserted near the middle. Let cool for 5 minutes. Turn then pan over and place onto rack; allow to stand for 5 minutes. Lift off the pan and let the cake cool completely. Use plastic to wrap and keep for 2 days at room temperature.
- To make glaze: In a heavy medium saucepan, melt butter over low heat. Stir in chocolate till smooth and melted. Add in orange juice concentrate and whisk.
- Put the cake on rack. Spread thickly over the sides and top of the cakes with some chocolate glaze. Store in the fridge for 15 minutes. Spread over the cake with the leftover glaze to completely cover. If preferred, sprinkle chopped candied fruit peel over. Store the cake for 30 minutes in the fridge till the glaze is set. You can prepare fruitcake for 3 weeks ahead. Use plastic to wrap the cake and store in the fridge.

Nutrition Information

- Calories: 860
- Cholesterol: 111 mg(37%)
- Protein: 10 g(19%)
- Total Fat: 52 g(80%)
- Saturated Fat: 24 g(120%)
- Sodium: 359 mg(15%)
- Fiber: 9 g(35%)
- Total Carbohydrate: 101 g(34%)

97. Chocolate Peanut Butter Terrine With Sugared Peanuts

Serving: Serves 8 | Prep: | Cook: |Ready in:

Ingredients

- 11 ounces bittersweet chocolate, finely chopped
- 1 ounce (2 tablespoons) unsalted butter
- 6 tablespoons creamy peanut butter
- 4 large egg yolks
- 1/4 cup granulated sugar
- 1 3/4 cups heavy whipping cream
- 4 ounces bittersweet chocolate, finely chopped
- 2 1/2 ounces (5 tablespoons) unsalted butter
- 2 teaspoons light corn syrup
- 1 large egg white

- 6 tablespoons granulated sugar
- 1 1/2 cups (7 1/2 ounces) unsalted peanuts

Direction

- Terrine: Spray nonstick spray on 8 1/2x4 1/2x2 3/4-in. loaf pan. Line plastic wrap on sprayed pan; leave 1 1/2-in. overhang on all the sides.
- Mix peanut butter, butter and chocolate in stainless-steel bowl. Put bowl above pan with simmering water; don't let bowl's bottom touch water. Heat till butter and chocolate melt, occasionally mixing. Take from above heat; whisk till smooth.
- Whip sugar and egg yolks for 1 minute on high speed till thick in a stand mixer's bowl with whip attachment. Take bowl from mixer stand. In 3 even additions, mix in chocolate mixture using wooden spoon; it'll be rather thick.
- Whisk cream till it begins to thicken in another bowl; fold cream in 4 even additions into chocolate mixture using a spatula. Spread batter in prepped pan. Use plastic wrap to cover, overhanging sides. Refrigerate for a minimum of 4 hours till firm.
- Unmold terrine: Fold back plastic wrap; invert pan onto wire rack. Pull a plastic wrap's corner to release terrine from pan. Lift off pan; remove plastic wrap carefully. Line parchment paper on a baking sheet; put rack into it. Put terrine in the fridge while making glaze.
- Chocolate glaze: Heat corn syrup, butter and chocolate in a stainless-steel bowl above a pan with simmering water, without bowl's bottom touching water, till butter and chocolate melt, occasionally mixing. Take off heat; whisk till smooth. Glaze should not be so thin it'll run off terrine yet pourable. Sit for 30 minutes in room temperature if glaze is too thin.
- Evenly and slowly put glaze on top of terrine; let it evenly stream down sides. Spread glaze to fully and smoothly cover terrine using an offset spatula; refrigerate for 30 minutes till glaze is set.

- Make sugared peanuts as glaze sets: Preheat an oven to 350°F. Whisk egg white till frothy in a bowl; whisk in sugar. Add peanuts; mix till coated with egg white mixture evenly.
- Spread peanuts on rimmed baking sheet in 1 layer; put in oven. Toast nuts for 15-20 minutes till golden brown and dry, mixing every 5 minutes.
- Serve: Put terrine on a serving platter; put sugared peanuts over. Cut terrine using a dry, hot knife.
- You can make terrine 2 days ahead; keep refrigerated. Sugared peanuts keep in room temperature in airtight container for 1 week.

Nutrition Information

- Calories: 1047
- Cholesterol: 276 mg(92%)
- Protein: 17 g(34%)
- Total Fat: 90 g(138%)
- Saturated Fat: 44 g(220%)
- Sodium: 61 mg(3%)
- Fiber: 6 g(24%)
- Total Carbohydrate: 62 g(21%)

98. Chocolate Whiskey Truffles Souffles With Caramel Sauce

Serving: Makes 8 servings | Prep: | Cook: |Ready in:

Ingredients

- 3/4 cup whipping cream
- 10 ounces bittersweet (not unsweetened) or semisweet chocolate, chopped
- 1/4 cup whiskey
- 1 1/2 cups whipping cream
- 1 vanilla bean, split lengthwise
- 3/4 cup sugar
- 1/4 cup water
- 4 large eggs, separated
- 1/4 cup plus 2 tablespoons sugar
- 1 1/2 tablespoons cornstarch

- 1 tablespoon unsweetened cocoa powder
- 2/3 cup milk (do not use low-fat or nonfat)
- 4 ounces bittersweet (not unsweetened) or semisweet chocolate, finely chopped
- 1 tablespoon unsalted butter
- 1/2 vanilla bean, split lengthwise
- 1/4 cup whiskey
- Additional sugar (for soufflé dishes)
- Powdered sugar

Direction

- Making truffles: In a heavy moderate-sized saucepan, add in cream and bring to a boil. Take away from heat. Put in chocolate and whisk until the whole mixture is smooth, also chocolate is melted. Mix whiskey in. Place in the fridge to chill for a minimum of 2 hours, until the mixture is stiff and chilled.
- Use a tablespoon to drop the truffle mixture on waxed paper. Use foil to line the baking sheet. Use your palms to roll each chocolate drop (dust your hands with free-sugar cocoa powder in case the truffle sticks to hands). Arrange on baking sheet. Put in the freezer to chill for an hour, until hard then cover it. (You can prepare for 1 week in advance, just keep it frozen)
- Making sauce: In a small bowl, put in cream. Scratch seeds from vanilla bean then combine bean and seeds into the cream.
- In a heavy medium saucepan, stir in water and sugar on low heat until sugar has dissolved. Raise the heat and boil the mixture until turns to deep amber color, no stirring. Use damp pastry brush to brush down sides of pan and twirl pan sometimes for 10 minutes. Take away from heat. Put in cream (the mixture will vigorously bubble up). Take the pan back to low heat and stir until caramel is smooth. Keep boiling about 2 minutes until the caramel is thickened and color deepens, while stirring sometimes. Transfer caramel into a small bowl thorough a strain. Put the sauce in the fridge to chill. (You may prepare sauce 1 week in advance. Cover and keep chilled)
- Making soufflés: In a medium bowl, blend yolks by whisking then set aside. In a medium stainless steel bowl, stir in cocoa, cornstarch and 1/4 cup sugar until there are not cornstarch lumps anymore. Stir in milk then put in butter and chocolate. Remove seeds from vanilla bean and put bean in.
- Put chocolate mixture bowl on saucepan of simmering water (do not let the bottom of the bowl touch the water). Whisk for about 2 minutes until the mixture is smooth. Take away from over water. Whisk some hot chocolate mixture gently into yolks. Pour the whisked yolk and chocolate mixture back to chocolate mixture bowl.
- Put in again over simmering water. Whip for 4 minutes until the mixture thickened and smooth as pudding consistency. Take off from water. Gently combine in whisky. Get rid of bean. Cool to quite warm.
- Set the oven to 450°F. Grease eight 2/3- to 3/4-cup custard cups or soufflé dishes with butter. Use sugar to dust all dishes. Place dishes on baking sheet. Put 1 truffle in per dish.
- In a medium bowl, beat whites by an electric mixer until creating soft peaks. Gently put in 2 tbsp. sugar then beat until firm but not dry.
- Mix whites into lukewarm soufflé base in 2 additions. Split soufflé mixture among prepared dishes, filling mostly to top. (You can prepare 1 week in advance. Use foil to cover the dish the place in the freezer to chill. Before baking, remove foil to open but do not thaw). Put soufflé on baking sheet in oven. Decrease temperature to 400°F. Bake for 17 minutes if it is unfrozen or 22 minutes if not, until dry-looking on top and puffed.
- Turn dishes to plates. Drizzle powdered sugar over. Serve while passing separately the chilled caramel sauce.

Nutrition Information

- Calories: 669
- Fiber: 3 g(13%)
- Total Carbohydrate: 70 g(23%)

- Cholesterol: 173 mg(58%)
- Protein: 7 g(15%)
- Total Fat: 40 g(62%)
- Saturated Fat: 24 g(120%)
- Sodium: 74 mg(3%)

99. Cinnamon Caramel Bread Puddings

Serving: Make 16 servings | Prep: | Cook: | Ready in:

Ingredients

- 20 3 1/2 x 3 1/2-inch slices cinnamon-raisin bread (not ends)
- 12 large eggs
- 2 1/2 cups whole milk
- 2 cups chilled whipping cream, divided
- 1 cup sugar
- 2 tablespoons vanilla extract
- 1 1/2 teaspoons finely grated orange peel
- Pinch of salt
- 2 tablespoons powdered sugar
- Purchased caramel sauce, warmed

Direction

- Cut bread to 3/4-in. cubes; put into very big bowl. Whisk 1 cup cream, milk, eggs and next 4 ingredients till sugar dissolves in big bowl. Pour egg mixture on bread; toss to coat. Use plastic to cover; to submerge bread in the egg mixture, put a plate on top. Chill for at least 4 hours – overnight.
- Mix bread mixture; let it stand for 30 minutes at room temperature.
- Preheat an oven to 375°F. Butter the 16 ramekins or 3/4-cup custard cups; divide to 2 roasting pans and divide bread mixture among cups. Pour hot water in pans until it reaches halfway up sides of cups.
- Bake puddings for 40 minutes till inserted tester in middle exits clean, edges are golden and puffed; allow puddings to stand for up to 2 hours at room temperature.
- Beat powdered sugar and leftover 1 cup cream using electric mixer till peaks form in medium bowl; serve puddings at room temperature/warm with warm caramel sauce and whipped cream.

Nutrition Information

- Calories: 310
- Saturated Fat: 8 g(40%)
- Sodium: 225 mg(9%)
- Fiber: 1 g(6%)
- Total Carbohydrate: 34 g(11%)
- Cholesterol: 176 mg(59%)
- Protein: 9 g(18%)
- Total Fat: 15 g(24%)

100. Citrus Pound Cake

Serving: Makes 8 servings | Prep: 20mins | Cook: 3.5hours | Ready in:

Ingredients

- 2 cups sifted cake flour (not self-rising; sift before measuring)
- 1 teaspoon baking powder
- 1/2 teaspoon salt
- 1 cup granulated sugar
- 1 tablespoon grated orange zest
- 1 teaspoon grated lemon zest
- 2 sticks (1/2 pound) unsalted butter, softened
- 4 large eggs, at room temperature 30 minutes
- 2 teaspoons fresh orange juice
- 1 teaspoon fresh lemon juice
- 1/2 teaspoon pure vanilla extract
- Garnish: confectioners sugar for dusting

Direction

- Preheat an oven with rack in center to 325°F; butter the 8 1/2x4 1/2-in. loaf pan.
- Sift salt, baking powder and flour together.

- Mix zests and sugar using electric mixer on low speed till sugar is colored evenly. Add butter; beat on high speed for 5 minutes till fluffy and pale.
- One by one, beat in eggs on medium speed, frequently scraping bowl's side down. Beat in vanilla and juices; mix in flour mixture on low speed just till incorporated.
- In loaf pan, spread batter; rap pan on counter a few times to remove air bubbles. Bake for 1-1 1/4 hours till inserted wooden pick in middle exits clean and golden; cool for 30 minutes in pan on rack. Around pan's edge, run a knife; invert cake onto rack. Fully cool, top side up.
- Cake improves in flavor if done at least 1 day ahead. You can make it 5 days ahead, kept at room temperature, tightly wrapped.

Nutrition Information

- Calories: 462
- Sodium: 230 mg(10%)
- Fiber: 1 g(3%)
- Total Carbohydrate: 52 g(17%)
- Cholesterol: 154 mg(51%)
- Protein: 6 g(12%)
- Total Fat: 26 g(39%)
- Saturated Fat: 15 g(77%)

101. Citrus Sponge Cake With Strawberries

Serving: | Prep: | Cook: | Ready in:

Ingredients

- Potato starch (for dusting cake pan)
- 2 teaspoons vegetable oil
- 1/2 cup matzoh cake meal
- 3/4 cup potato starch
- 8 extra-large eggs, separated, at room temperature
- 1 cup sugar
- 1/4 cup orange juice
- Juice of 1 large lemon
- 1 teaspoon freshly grated orange zest
- 1 teaspoon freshly grated lemon zest
- 1 1/2 teaspoons pure vanilla extract
- 1/2 teaspoon almond extract
- 1/4 teaspoon salt
- 3 pints strawberries, stemmed, washed, and thinly sliced
- 1/2 cup orange juice
- 1 tablespoon sugar

Direction

- Set an oven to 350°F and start preheating. Oil a 9-inch spring form pan lightly, then dust with potato starch.
- Sift together potato starch and cake meal on a piece of foil, then put aside.
- Whisk egg yolks in the bowl of an electric mixer at medium speed until thick and golden yellow, for 3 minutes. Slowly put in sugar. Carry on whisking 3 more minutes.
- Put in gradually lemon zest, orange zest, lemon juice and orange juice using the mixer at low speed. Put in almond extract and vanilla. Put the matzo meal mixture gradually into the batter. Gently combine until mixed thoroughly.
- Using the whisk attachment of the electric mixer, whisk egg whites in a clean bowl until foamy. Put in salt and whisk until the whites form glossy peaks. Use a spatula to fold the egg whites into the cake batter gently. Add the batter into the spring form pan and bake until a cake tester comes out clean, or for 50 minutes. In the pan, allow the cake to cool, then loosen the sides. Allow to cool entirely.
- Slice the cake into twelve wedges or halve the cake horizontally carefully using a serrated knife and slice into six wedges to have 12 wedges in total.
- Half an hour before serving the cake, toss orange juice and sugar together with strawberries. Scoop strawberries on top of each cake wedge, then serve.
- Tip: Serve the cake with ice cream or whipped cream to gild the lily.

Nutrition Information

- Calories: 249
- Saturated Fat: 1 g(7%)
- Sodium: 124 mg(5%)
- Fiber: 3 g(10%)
- Total Carbohydrate: 44 g(15%)
- Cholesterol: 167 mg(56%)
- Protein: 7 g(14%)
- Total Fat: 6 g(9%)

102. Classic Coconut Cake

Serving: Makes 10 servings | Prep: 30mins | Cook: 4hours | Ready in:

Ingredients

- Nonstick vegetable oil spray
- 2 cups all purpose flour
- 1 1/3 cups (loosely packed) sweetened flaked coconut
- 1 cup buttermilk
- 1 teaspoon baking soda
- 2 cups sugar
- 1 cup (2 sticks) unsalted butter, room temperature
- 5 large egg yolks
- 4 large egg whites, room temperature
- 3 1/3 cups powdered sugar
- 1 8-ounce package philadelphia-brand cream cheese, room temperature
- 1/2 cup (1 stick) unsalted butter, room temperature
- 2 teaspoons vanilla extract
- 1 cup (about) sweetened flaked coconut

Direction

- Cake: Preheat an oven to 350°F. Use nonstick spray to coat 2 9-in. diameter cake pans that have 1 1/2-in. high sides; line parchment paper rounds on bottom of pans.
- In medium bowl, mix coconut and flour. In small bowl, whisk baking soda and buttermilk. Beat butter and sugar using electric mixer for 2 minutes till fluffy and light in big bowl. Add egg yolks; beat to blend. In 3 additions, add flour mixture alternately with the buttermilk using 2 additions; beat to just blend after every addition. Beat 1/4 tsp. salt and egg whites using clean dry beaters till peaks form in another big bowl. Put 1/3 egg white mixture in batter; fold into batter to just blend. In 2 additions, fold in leftover egg white mixture; divide batter to pans.
- Bake cakes for 35 minutes till inserted tester in middle exits clean; cool cakes for 10 minutes in pans on racks. Around cake pan's sides, run small sharp knife; invert cake on racks. Peel off parchment carefully; fully cool cakes.
- Frosting: Beat vanilla, butter, cream cheese and sugar using electric mixer till blended in a big bowl. Put 1 cake layer on plate, flat side up; spread 1 cup frosting. Put 2nd layer on frosting, flat side up, spread frosting atop; spread leftover frosting on sides and top of cake. Sprinkle come coconut on cake's top; pat extra coconut on cake's sides. You can make it 1 day ahead. Use cake dome to cover; refrigerate. 1 hour before serving, stand in room temperature.

Nutrition Information

- Calories: 888
- Fiber: 3 g(11%)
- Total Carbohydrate: 112 g(37%)
- Cholesterol: 191 mg(64%)
- Protein: 8 g(17%)
- Total Fat: 47 g(72%)
- Saturated Fat: 28 g(141%)
- Sodium: 343 mg(14%)

103. Classic White Cake Layers

Serving: Makes two 9-inch round layers | Prep: | Cook: | Ready in:

Ingredients

- 2 cups all-purpose flour (spoon flour into dry-measure cup and level off)
- 2 teaspoons baking powder
- 1/4 teaspoon salt
- 12 tablespoons (1 1/2 sticks) unsalted butter, softened
- 1 1/2 cups sugar
- 2 teaspoons vanilla extract
- 6 large egg whites
- 3/4 cup milk
- Two 9-inch round cake pans, buttered and bottoms lined with buttered parchment or wax paper
- N/A parchment or wax paper

Direction

- Put rack in center of oven; preheat to 350°.
- Mix salt, baking powder and flour well in a bowl.
- Beat sugar and butter on medium speed for 5 minutes till light and very soft in a heavy-duty mixer's bowl with paddle attachment; beat in vanilla.
- By hand, whisk milk and egg whites till just combined in medium mixing bowl.
- Lower mixer speed to low; beat in 1/4 flour mixture then 1/3 milk mixture, pausing and scraping beater and bowl down after every addition. Beat in 1/4 flour then 1/3 milk mixture; scrape. Repeat with 1/4 more flour then leftover milk mixture; scrape. Beat in leftover flour mixture.
- Use a big rubber spatula to scrape bowl. Put batter into prepped pans; smooth tops.
- Bake layers till inserted toothpick in middle exits clean and are firm and well risen for 30-35 minutes; cool layers for 5 minutes in pans on racks. Unmold onto racks; right side up, finish cooling.
- Wrap layers in plastic then keep at room temperature if using the same day as being baked. For longer storage, double-wrap then freeze.

Nutrition Information

- Calories: 2388
- Saturated Fat: 58 g(288%)
- Sodium: 1351 mg(56%)
- Fiber: 7 g(30%)
- Total Carbohydrate: 340 g(113%)
- Cholesterol: 252 mg(84%)
- Protein: 35 g(71%)
- Total Fat: 101 g(156%)

104. Coconut Angel Food Cake

Serving: Makes 12 servings | Prep: | Cook: | Ready in:

Ingredients

- 1 1/4 cups egg whites (from about 9 large eggs), at room temperature
- 1/4 teaspoon salt
- 1 teaspoon cream of tartar
- 1 cup superfine sugar
- 2 teaspoons pure vanilla extract
- 2 teaspoons fresh lemon juice
- 1 cup sifted cake flour
- 1/3 cup dry unsweetened shredded coconut
- 1/3 cup fresh coconut shavings
- 1 bag (12 ounces) cranberries, fresh or frozen and thawed
- 2/3 cup granulated sugar
- 1 tablespoon grated orange zest
- 2/3 cup fresh orange juice
- 2 tablespoons orange-flavored liqueur
- 1/2 teaspoon cinnamon

Direction

- Cake: Heat an oven to 325°F. Beat salt and egg whites using electric mixer at medium for 2 minutes till frothy in a bowl. Add cream of tartar and beat for 5 minutes till soft peaks form. Put speed on high. 1 tbsp. at a time, add 1/2 cup sugar till whites make glossy, soft peaks. Beat in lemon juice and vanilla. Mix flour and leftover 1/2 cup sugar in another bowl. Sift 1/2 sugar-flour mixture on egg whites; thoroughly yet gently fold into batter using big spatula. Repeat twice using leftover sugar-flour mixture. In 2 batches, fold in dry coconut. Scrape batter into 10-in. ungreased angel food tube pan that has removable bottom; smooth top to even layer. Bake till cake springs back when pressed and top is lightly browned for 35 minutes. Flip pan upside down; rest on glass bottle's neck to cool. To loosen cake, run knife against pan's insides; remove pan. From bottom of pan, loosen cake; invert onto plate. Use plastic wrap to cover; keep in the fridge or in room temperature.
- Sauce: Boil all ingredients for 1 minute till lightly thick in a medium saucepan; cool. Cover; refrigerate for 1 hour. Sprinkle coconut shavings on cake's top before serving. Put 3 tbsp. sauce on the slices; serve.

105. Coconut Cream Pie

Serving: 8 | Prep: 25mins | Cook: 30mins | Ready in:

Ingredients

- 1 cup white sugar
- 1/2 cup all-purpose flour
- 1/4 teaspoon salt
- 3 cups milk
- 4 egg yolks
- 3 tablespoons butter
- 1 1/2 teaspoons vanilla extract
- 1 cup flaked coconut
- 1 (9 inch) pie shell, baked

Direction

- In a medium saucepan, mix together salt, flour and sugar over medium heat; slowly mix in milk. Cook and stir over medium heat till bubbly and thick. Decrease heat to low and cook for an additional 2 minutes. Remove pan from the heat.
- Put a strainer on top a clean mixing bowl; put aside.
- Slightly beat egg yolks. Pour slowly a cup of hot custard mixture into yolks, whisking constantly. Put the egg mixture back into the saucepan; then bring the entire mixture to a gentle boil. Cook and stir for 2 minutes before removing from heat. Pour the custard through the strainer immediately.
- Mix coconut, vanilla and butter into the hot mixture. Add hot filling into baked pie crust. Allow to cool and chill in the fridge for about 4 hours, until set.

Nutrition Information

- Calories: 399 calories;
- Total Fat: 18.8
- Sodium: 293
- Total Carbohydrate: 51.1
- Cholesterol: 121
- Protein: 6.9

106. Coconut Cupcakes With White Chocolate Frosting

Serving: Makes 12 cupcakes | Prep: | Cook: | Ready in:

Ingredients

- 1/2 cup coconut cream (not cream of coconut) or milk
- 3 large egg whites
- 1/2 teaspoon pure vanilla extract
- 1 1/2 cups cake flour
- 2 teaspoons baking powder

- 6 tablespoons (3 ounces) unsalted butter, softened
- 1/2 teaspoon salt
- 3/4 cup granulated sugar
- 1/2 cup desiccated or unsweetened coconut, finely ground in a food processor
- 1/2 cup sweetened dried coconut
- 6 ounces white chocolate, finely chopped
- 1 3/4 cups powdered sugar
- 1/4 cup milk
- 4 ounces (8 tablespoons) butter
- 1/2 teaspoon pure vanilla extract
- 1/4 teaspoon salt

Direction

- Cake: Preheat an oven to 350°F. Put oven rack into center position. Use nonstick spray to coat surface of 12-cup cupcake pan lightly; line paper liner/foil to line each cup.
- Whisk vanilla extract, egg whites and coconut cream together to combine in a small bowl. Sift baking powder and flour together over parchment paper or in another bowl.
- Whisk salt and butter till smooth and creamy in an electric mixer with a whisk; in a steady stream, add sugar while beating. Beat for 2-3 minutes at medium speed till fluffy and light, stopping to scrape bowl's sides down as needed.
- Add 1/3 coconut cream mixture and 1/3 dry ingredients; beat just till combined on low speed. Add leftover coconut cream mixture and dry ingredients in 2 alternation additions, beating between every addition to incorporate fully. Add sweetened dried coconut, final batch of dry ingredients and ground, dried coconut. Scrape bowl down; use a sturdy rubber spatula to mix one more time.
- Fill each cupcake cup to 2/3 full; knock pan 1-2 times on the countertop to even batter's surface and remove air bubbles. Put pan in oven; rotate pan 180° after 10-12 minutes. Bake till wooden skewer/cake tester exits with crumbs clinging on it and cake springs back when pressed lightly in the middle. Total baking time is around 20-22 minutes.
- Cool pan for 5 minutes on a cooling rack. Transfer cookies from pan onto rack; fully cool.
- Frosting: In a bowl, melt white chocolate above a saucepan of barely simmering water; be sure the bowl's bottom rests a few inches above water's surface. Mix chocolate till smooth; cool on countertop to room temperature.
- Sift powdered sugar into medium-sized bowl; mix in milk using a whisk till it is smooth and all sugar dissolves. Add salt, vanilla extract and butter; beat till shiny and smooth. Mix in cooled white chocolate with a rubber spatula.
- Put frosting into the fridge for 30 minutes till cool enough to frost cupcakes; you can keep it for 1 day in room temperature/in the fridge. Before spreading, softened refrigerated frosting in room temperature.

Nutrition Information

- Calories: 458
- Fiber: 1 g(5%)
- Total Carbohydrate: 56 g(19%)
- Cholesterol: 39 mg(13%)
- Protein: 4 g(8%)
- Total Fat: 25 g(39%)
- Saturated Fat: 18 g(88%)
- Sodium: 249 mg(10%)

107. Coconut Flans

Serving: Makes 8 | Prep: | Cook: | Ready in:

Ingredients

- 2 tablespoons vegetable oil
- 1 tablespoon plus 1/4 cup water
- 1 3/4 cups sugar
- 3/4 cup sweetened flaked coconut
- 1 13.5-ounce can unsweetened coconut milk
- 1 cup whole milk
- 1 vanilla bean, split lengthwise in half

- 8 large egg yolks
- 3 tablespoons triple sec

Direction

- Whisk 1 tbsp. water and oil to blend in small bowl; brush oil mixture inside 8 ramekins/3/4-cup custard cups. Mix leftover 1/4 cup water and 1 cup sugar in medium heavy saucepan on medium low heat till sugar is dissolved; boil without mixing for 9 minutes till syrup becomes deep amber color, brushing pan sides down with wet pastry brush, swirling sometimes. Divide caramel to prepped custard cups immediately; tilt each custard cup using oven mitts to coat bottom in caramel. Put cups in big roasting pan.
- Preheat an oven to 350°F. On baking sheet, spread coconut; toast in oven for 10 minutes till light golden, occasionally mixing. Maintain the oven temperature.
- Mix milk and coconut milk in another medium saucepan. From vanilla bean, scrape in seeds; add bean. Boil; take off heat. Cover; steep for 10 minutes. Discard vanilla bean. Beat 3/4 cup sugar and egg yolks using electric mixer for 4 minutes till pale and thick in big bowl; whisk hot milk mixture slowly into egg mixture then whisk in triple sec. Mix in 1/2 cup of toasted coconut.
- Divide custard to caramel-lined custard cups. To reach halfway up custard cup's sides, put hot water in roasting pan; bake for 50 minutes till custards only slightly move when cups are gently shaken and are nearly set; take custards from water. Slightly cool; chill overnight, uncovered.
- Around custards, run small sharp knife to loosen. Put plate on custard cup to unmold each custard. Grasp plate and custard cup filmy; invert, gently shaking, letting custard settle onto plate. Sprinkle leftover 1/4 cup toasted coconut on custards; serve.

Nutrition Information

- Calories: 426
- Cholesterol: 188 mg(63%)
- Protein: 5 g(10%)
- Total Fat: 21 g(33%)
- Saturated Fat: 14 g(68%)
- Sodium: 52 mg(2%)
- Fiber: 1 g(3%)
- Total Carbohydrate: 53 g(18%)

108. Coconut Pineapple Cake

Serving: Makes 8 servings | Prep: 1hours | Cook: 3hours | Ready in:

Ingredients

- 1 cup cake flour (not self-rising)
- 1/2 teaspoon salt
- 6 large eggs at room temperature
- 1 cup sugar
- 2 teaspoons vanilla
- 3/4 stick (6 tablespoons) unsalted butter, melted and cooled
- 1 (20-ounce) can crushed pineapple, including juice
- 2 tablespoons sugar
- 1 tablespoon cornstarch
- 1 teaspoon fresh lemon juice
- 2/3 cup water
- 1/4 cup sugar
- 3 tablespoons light rum
- Coconut buttercream
- 3 1/2 cups fresh coconut shavings (see how to crack and shave fresh coconut) or 2 2/3 cups sweetened flaked coconut (7-oz package)

Direction

- Cakes: Preheat an oven to 350°F. Butter 2 8-in., 2-in. deep square cake pans.
- Sift salt and flour into the bowl.
- Heat sugar and eggs, constantly whisking gently, in a big metal bowl above pot of simmering water till lukewarm.
- Take bowl off heat. Add vanilla; beat using an electric mixer on medium high speed, 10

minutes with handheld mixer, 5 minutes with standing mixer, till tripled in volume, pale and thick. In 2 batches, sift salt and flour on eggs, gently yet thoroughly folding after every batch. Fold in the melted butter till combined. Evenly divide batter to cake pans; smooth tops.

- Bake cakes in center of oven for 15 minutes till cakes are golden and tester exits clean; cool for 5 minutes in pans on racks. Invert onto racks; fully cool.
- Pineapple filling: Mix filling ingredients till cornstarch melts in a heavy saucepan; boil, constantly mixing. Simmer for 3 minutes, mixing. Fully cool filling, occasionally mixing.
- Rum syrup: Boil sugar and water in a heavy small saucepan, mixing till sugar melts; take off heat. Mix in rum. Put into a small bowl; chill till needed.
- Cake assembly: If needed, trim edges of cake; use a long-serrated knife to horizontally halve each to make 4 thin layers total. Put 1 cake layer onto cake plate, cut side up; brush some rum syrup on top. Spread 1/2 pineapple filling over. Put another cake layer over; brush syrup, then spread over with roughly 2/3 cup of butter cream. Place 3rd layer of cake on top, brush syrup and spread over with leftover pineapple. Put 4th layer over, cut side down; brush leftover syrup. Frost top and sides of cake using leftover butter cream; coat in coconut.
- You can make cake layers 2 days ahead, left unsplit; keep at room temperature, wrapped in plastic wrap well.
- You can prep pineapple filling 3 days ahead, covered, chilled.
- You can make rum syrup 1 week ahead, covered, chilled.
- You can assemble cake 1 day ahead, covered, chilled; before serving, bring to room temperature.

Nutrition Information

- Calories: 571
- Cholesterol: 162 mg(54%)
- Protein: 8 g(16%)
- Total Fat: 29 g(44%)
- Saturated Fat: 21 g(106%)
- Sodium: 212 mg(9%)
- Fiber: 5 g(21%)
- Total Carbohydrate: 71 g(24%)

109. Coconut And Macadamia Nut Banana Bread

Serving: Makes 5 loaves | Prep: | Cook: | Ready in:

Ingredients

- 2 1/2 cups all-purpose flour
- 3/4 teaspoon double-acting baking powder
- 1/2 teaspoon baking soda
- 1 teaspoon salt
- 1 1/2 sticks (3/4 cup) unsalted butter, softened
- 1 cup firmly packed light brown sugar
- 1/2 cup granulated sugar
- 1 1/2 teaspoons vanilla extract
- 3 large eggs
- 1 tablespoon freshly grated lemon zest
- 1 1/3 cups mashed ripe banana (about 3 large)
- 3 tablespoons sour cream
- 3/4 cup chopped macadamia nuts
- 1 cup sweetened flaked coconut, toasted lightly and cooled

Direction

- Sift the salt, baking soda, baking powder and flour into a bowl. Use an electric mixer to beat butter with sugars in a big bowl until the mixture turns light and fluffy, mix in vanilla and 1 egg at a time then the sour cream, banana and the zest. Add in the flour mixture, mix until just combined and mix in the coconut and macadamia nuts. Grease 5 5-3/4 x 3-1/4 inch loaf pans with butter and coat them with flour. Distribute the batter into the prepared pans. Set oven at 350°F, put the pans in the middle of the oven and bake until a tester exits clean, or for 35 to 40 minutes. Take the breads out from the pans and take them to a rack with right sides up and let cool.

Nutrition Information

- Calories: 292
- Protein: 4 g(8%)
- Total Fat: 15 g(23%)
- Saturated Fat: 7 g(37%)
- Sodium: 193 mg(8%)
- Fiber: 2 g(8%)
- Total Carbohydrate: 38 g(13%)
- Cholesterol: 52 mg(17%)

110. Coconut Chocolate Chip Cupcakes

Serving: Makes 20 | Prep: | Cook: | Ready in:

Ingredients

- 1 cup whole wheat pastry flour
- 1 cup unbleached all purpose flour
- 1/2 cup coconut milk powder (sifted, then measured)
- 1 teaspoon baking powder
- 1/2 teaspoon salt
- 1 1/4 cups (2 1/2 sticks) unsalted butter, room temperature
- 1 3-ounce package cream cheese, room temperature
- 1 1/2 cups sugar
- 1/2 teaspoon vanilla extract
- 4 drops coconut flavoring or 3/4 teaspoon coconut extract
- 5 large eggs
- 2 tablespoons whole milk
- 1 3/4 cups bittersweet chocolate chips (10 to 11 ounces)
- 1/2 cup (1 stick) unsalted butter, room temperature
- 1/2 cup coconut milk powder (sifted, then measured)
- 1/4 teaspoon salt
- 1/2 teaspoon vanilla extract
- 3 drops coconut flavoring or 1/2 teaspoon coconut extract
- 4 to 5 cups powdered sugar (16 to 20 ounces)
- 4 tablespoons (or more) whole milk
- Flaked sweetened coconut (optional)

Direction

- Cupcakes: Preheat an oven to 350°F. Line paper liners on 20 1/3-cup standard muffin cups. Into medium bowl, sift initial 5 ingredients. Beat cream cheese and butter using electric mixer till smooth in big bowl. Beat in sugar slowly; beat in coconut flavoring and vanilla extract. Beat in dry ingredients; it'll be stiff. One by one, add eggs; beat to blend after each. Beat in milk; mix in chocolate chips. In each paper liner, put scant 1/3 cup of batter. Bake cupcakes for 22 minutes till inserted tester in centers exits clean. Cool for 10 minutes. Turn out cupcakes from pan; cool on the rack.
- Frosting: Beat salt, coconut milk powder and butter using electric mixer till smooth in big bowl; beat in coconut flavoring and vanilla extract. 1 cup at 1 time, beat in enough of the powdered sugar to make very thick frosting. 1 tbsp. at 1 time, beat in milk till frosting thins enough to be spread.
- On cupcakes, spread frosting; if desired, sprinkle flaked coconut. You can make it 1 day ahead; keep at room temperature, airtight.

Nutrition Information

- Calories: 481
- Protein: 6 g(11%)
- Total Fat: 25 g(39%)
- Saturated Fat: 15 g(76%)
- Sodium: 169 mg(7%)
- Fiber: 2 g(7%)
- Total Carbohydrate: 62 g(21%)
- Cholesterol: 101 mg(34%)

111. Coconut Macadamia Crescents

Serving: Makes about 5 dozen | Prep: | Cook: |Ready in:

Ingredients

- 1 cup (2 sticks) unsalted butter, room temperature
- 3/4 cup powdered sugar, sifted
- 2 teaspoons vanilla extract
- 2 teaspoons coconut extract
- 2 1/4 cups sifted all purpose flour
- 1 teaspoon salt
- 1 cup chopped, roasted, salted macadamia nuts
- 1 egg white, beaten to blend
- 1 cup sweetened shredded coconut
- Additional powdered sugar

Direction

- Add butter into a medium bowl and beat it with an electric mixer until light. Add in 3/4 cup of powdered sugar little by little and beat together. Mix in extract. Mix in salt and flour then macadamia nuts. Let the dough chill in the fridge for half an hour.
- Set oven at 325°F and start preheating. Use parchment paper to line 3 big baking sheets. Pull off 1 tablespoon of dough, form 1/2-inch thick, 2-inch long crescent. Do the same with the rest of the dough. Brush egg white on top of the crescents and plunge the tops into coconut. Put the crescents with coconut side up on the prepared sheets, keep one inch apart from another. Bake them for about 20 minutes until they turn barely golden brown. Take the cookies on sheets on a rack and let cool. Sift more powdered sugar over. Cookies can be made 1 week prior. Keep them in an airtight container and store in the freezer. Heat up to room temperature before serving.

Nutrition Information

- Calories: 279
- Sodium: 125 mg(5%)
- Fiber: 1 g(6%)
- Total Carbohydrate: 23 g(8%)
- Cholesterol: 31 mg(10%)
- Protein: 3 g(6%)
- Total Fat: 20 g(31%)
- Saturated Fat: 10 g(51%)

112. Coconut Peach Layer Cake

Serving: Makes 12 servings | Prep: | Cook: |Ready in:

Ingredients

- 2 3/4 cups all purpose flour
- 1 teaspoon baking powder
- 1/2 teaspoon salt
- 3/4 cup buttermilk
- 1/4 cup sour cream
- 1 cup (2 sticks) unsalted butter, room temperature
- 1 2/3 cups sugar
- 1 cup canned sweetened cream of coconut (such as Coco López)*
- 4 large eggs, separated
- 2 teaspoons vanilla extract
- 3 cups sweetened flaked coconut
- 1/2 cup peach preserves
- 3 pounds peaches, peeled, cut into 1/4- to 1/2-inch-thick slices
- 1/2 cup sugar
- 2 tablespoons fresh lemon juice
- 3 cups chilled whipping cream
- 1/4 cup plus 2 tablespoons canned sweetened cream of coconut
- 1 1/2 teaspoons vanilla extract
- 1 peach, peeled, thinly sliced

Direction

- Cake: Preheat an oven to 350°F. Butter then flour 2 9-in. diameter cake pans that have 2-in.

high sides. Whisk salt, baking powder and flour to blend in medium bowl. Whisk sour cream and buttermilk in small bowl. Beat butter using electric mixer till fluffy in big bowl; beat in sugar slowly. Beat in vanilla, egg yolks and cream of coconut. In 3 additions, beat in dry ingredients, alternating with the buttermilk mixture in 2 batches. Beat egg whites till stiff yet not dry in another big bowl; fold into the batter.

- Divide batter to prepped pans; bake cakes for 45 minutes till inserted tester in middle exits clean. Cool cakes for 10 minutes in pans on racks. Turn onto rack; fully cool. Maintain the oven temperature.
- On big baking sheet, spread flaked coconut; bake for 14 minutes till lightly toasted, mixing once. Cool. You can make coconut and cakes 1 day ahead; separately cover in plastic wrap. Stand in room temperature.
- Filling: Mix preserves till melted in small saucepan on medium low heat; slightly cool. Toss lemon juice, sugar and peaches in big bowl. Add preserves; toss to mix.
- Frosting: Beat initial 3 ingredients till peaks form in big bowl.
- Drain the peach filling of extra juices; horizontally halve cakes. Put 1 cake layer on platter, cut side up; put 1/3 peach filling over. Spread filling with 1 cup frosting. Repeat layering twice; put final cake layer over, cut side down. Spread leftover frosting on sides and top of cake; fully cover cake in toasted coconut. Refrigerate for a minimum of 30 minutes – maximum of 1 day. Fan the peach slices on middle of cake; serve.

Nutrition Information

- Calories: 902
- Fiber: 5 g(20%)
- Total Carbohydrate: 111 g(37%)
- Cholesterol: 172 mg(57%)
- Protein: 9 g(19%)
- Total Fat: 49 g(75%)
- Saturated Fat: 33 g(167%)

- Sodium: 283 mg(12%)

113. Coeurs À La Crème With Blackberries

Serving: Makes 6 servings | Prep: | Cook: | Ready in:

Ingredients

- 3/4 pound cream cheese, softened
- 1 (8-ounce) container sour cream
- 3 tablespoons confectioners sugar, or to taste
- 1/2 teaspoon vanilla
- 1/2 teaspoon fresh lemon juice
- 2 (1/2-pint) containers blackberries (11 ounce)
- 1 tablespoon granulated sugar
- 1 tablespoon cassis (optional)
- 1/2 teaspoon fresh lemon juice
- 6 (1/3-cup) ceramic coeur à la crème molds and cheesecloth

Direction

- Coeurs: Beat pinch salt, juice, vanilla, confectioners' sugar, sour cream and cream cheese till smooth with an electric mixer. Through a fine sieve, force mixture into bowl to remove fine lumps.
- Line 1 dampened cheesecloth layer on molds; divide cheese mixture to molds. Smooth tops. On tops, fold overhanging cheesecloth; lightly press it. Refrigerate molds for minimum of 4 hours in shallow dish/pan to catch drips.
- Topping: Mash granulated sugar with 1/2 blackberries; mix in juice, cassis and leftover whole berries. Macerate for 20 minutes, occasionally mixing.
- Unmold coeurs; peel off cheesecloth carefully. Stand coeurs for 20 minutes before serving in room temperature. Put topping on coeurs.
- You can chill coeurs in molds for maximum of 2 days, covered.

114. Coffee Granita With Cardamom Whipped Cream

Serving: Makes 6 servings | Prep: 15mins | Cook: 3hours15mins | Ready in:

Ingredients

- 2 cups water, divided
- 1/2 cup plus 1 tablespoon sugar
- 1 1/2 tablespoons instant espresso powder
- 1/2 teaspoon vanilla extract
- 3/4 cup chilled heavy whipping cream
- 1/4 teaspoon ground cardamom

Direction

- Simmer 1/2 cup sugar and 1/2 cup water in small heavy saucepan on medium heat, constantly mixing till sugar is dissolved. Mix in vanilla extract and instant espresso powder; take off heat. Mix in leftover 1 1/2 cups water. Put into 9x9x2-in. metal baking pan and freeze for 1 hour; mix, mashing with back of fork the frozen parts. Cover; freeze for minimum of 1-2 hours – maximum of 1 day till firm. Scrape granite with fork, making icy flakes. Put granita in freezer.
- Beat leftover 1 tbsp. sugar, cardamom and cream till peaks form in big bowl. Divide granita to glasses/bowls; put whipped cream on granita.

115. Corn Bread

Serving: | Prep: 1hours | Cook: 1hours | Ready in:

Ingredients

- 1 can 1 can creamed corn
- 1 cup corn meal
- 1 cup flour
- 1/2 cup grated cheese
- 4 teaspoons baking powder
- 1 dash salt
- 2 cloves jalapenos

Direction

- Preparation
- Combine all the ingredients and put into a 9x13-inch greased pan.

116. Cornbread Muffins With Maple Butter

Serving: Makes 12 muffins | Prep: | Cook: | Ready in:

Ingredients

- 3/4 cup (1 1/2 sticks) unsalted butter, room temperature
- 3 1/2 tablespoons pure maple syrup (preferably grade B)
- 1 cup yellow cornmeal
- 1 cup unbleached all purpose flour
- 1/4 cup sugar
- 1 tablespoon baking powder
- 1/4 teaspoon salt
- 1 cup buttermilk
- 1 large egg
- 5 tablespoons unsalted butter, melted, cooled slightly

Direction

- To make maple butter: Use an electric mixer to beat the butter in a medium-sized bowl until it becomes creamy. Slowly beat in the maple syrup until smooth and blended well. You can make this a week ahead, keeping it covered and refrigerated.
- To make muffins: Heat up an oven to 375 degrees Fahrenheit. Butter 12 regular muffin cups (1/3 cup). In a medium bowl, sieve salt, baking powder, sugar, flour, and cornmeal. In another medium-sized bowl, whisk together egg and buttermilk, then whisk in the melted butter. Add buttermilk mixture into the dry ingredients, stirring until just combined. Be

sure not to over-mix. Equally divide the batter into the muffin cups. Bake until a tester is clean once inserted into the center, 15 minutes. The muffins will turn out pale. Cool the muffins on a rack for 10 minutes, then serve with the maple butter.

Nutrition Information

- Calories: 276
- Cholesterol: 60 mg(20%)
- Protein: 3 g(7%)
- Total Fat: 17 g(26%)
- Saturated Fat: 11 g(53%)
- Sodium: 184 mg(8%)
- Fiber: 1 g(3%)
- Total Carbohydrate: 28 g(9%)

117. Cornmeal Blini With Tomato Corn Salsa

Serving: Makes 64 | Prep: | Cook: | Ready in:

Ingredients

- 1 cup plus 2 tablespoons low-fat milk
- 2 tablespoons water
- 1/4 cup sugar
- 1 teaspoon dry yeast
- 3/4 cup unbleached all purpose flour
- 2/3 cup yellow cornmeal
- 1 teaspoon salt
- 1/2 cup buttermilk
- 2 large eggs, separated
- 5 teaspoons (about) vegetable oil
- 2 cups frozen corn, thawed, drained
- 1 1/2 pounds tomatoes, seeded, chopped
- 1/2 small red onion, finely chopped
- 6 tablespoons chopped fresh cilantro
- 2 jalapeño chilies, seeded, minced
- 1 tablespoon balsamic vinegar
- 1/2 cup nonfat plain yogurt

Direction

- Preparing the Blini: In a small saucepan, heat water and milk to room temperature (105 degrees F. to 115 degrees F.). Transfer into a large bowl. Stir in yeast and sugar. Leave to sit for ten minutes.
- In a medium bowl, mix salt, flour, and cornmeal to blend. Mix into the yeast mixture. Stir in egg yolks and buttermilk. Cover with plastic and allow to sit in a warm spot for about 2 hours until very spongy.
- In another medium bowl, beat the egg whites using an electric mixer until stiff but not dry. Carefully roll into the cornmeal mixture in two additions.
- Preheat an oven to 250 degrees F. Use one teaspoon of oil to rub a large nonstick skillet. Heat on medium-high heat. Work in batches while rubbing with more oil as needed. Transfer the batter by tablespoonfuls into the skillet and spread gently to form 2-inch rounds. Let to cook for about 2 minutes until bubbles start to break on surface and bottoms turn golden. Use a spatula to flip the blini over and let to cook for about 1 minute until golden. Spread onto large baking sheets in a single layer. Place in oven to keep warm.
- For the Salsa: In a medium bowl, stir all the ingredients apart from yogurt and blend. Add pepper and salt to taste. (You can prepare salsa and blini 8 hours ahead. Then cool the blini. Cover salsa and blini separately and refrigerate. Rewarm the blini while uncovered for about 10 minutes in oven at 350 degrees F prior to serving.)
- Pour a little amount of yogurt on top of blini. Distribute the salsa on top of blini. Spread onto platters then serve warm.

118. Cornmeal Cake With Sweet Rosemary Syrup And Blackberries

Serving: | Prep: | Cook: | Ready in:

Ingredients

- 1 stick (1/2 cup) unsalted butter, softened
- 1 cup sugar
- 1 cup yellow cornmeal
- 3/4 cup all-purpose flour
- 1 teaspoon baking powder
- 3/4 teaspoon salt
- 2 large eggs
- 1 large egg yolk
- 2/3 cup milk
- Sweet Rosemary Syrup
- lightly sweetened whipped cream
- 2 half-pints blackberries

Direction

- Cake: Preheat an oven to 350°F. Butter then flour 8x2-in. round cake pan.
- Beat sugar and butter using electric mixer till fluffy and light in a big bowl. Add leftover cake ingredients; beat till combined on low speed. Beat batter at high speed for 3 minutes till pale yellow.
- Put batter in prepped pan; bake in center of oven till tester exits with few crumbs adhering for 40 minutes.
- As cake bakes, make rosemary syrup.
- Cool cake for 10 minutes in pan on rack. Invert cake onto hand; put on rack, right side up. Brush 1/3 cup syrup slowly on cake while warm, letting syrup soak in then add more. Chill leftover syrup, covered, in a small pitcher. You can make syrup-soaked cake 1 day ahead; keep in room temperature, wrapped in plastic wrap.
- Cut cake to wedges; serve with leftover rosemary syrup, blackberries and whipped cream.

119. Cornmeal Cookies

Serving: Makes 8 servings | Prep: 20mins | Cook: 2.25hours | Ready in:

Ingredients

- 1 cup yellow cornmeal (not stone-ground)
- 3/4 cup all-purpose flour
- 1/2 teaspoon salt
- 7 tablespoons unsalted butter, softened
- 1/3 cup sugar
- 3/4 teaspoon pure vanilla extract
- 1 large egg plus 1 large egg yolk

Direction

- Preheat an oven with rack in center to 350°F.
- Whisk salt, flour and cornmeal. Beat vanilla, sugar and butter using electric mixer on medium speed for 5 minutes till fluffy and pale, occasionally scraping down bowl's side; beat in yolk and egg till combined well. Lower speed to low. In a slow stream, add cornmeal mixture, mixing just till combined. Shape dough to 5-in. square; chill for 30 minutes till firm while wrapped in a plastic wrap.
- Roll dough out to 7-in. (1/2-in. thick) square using the lightly floured rolling pin on lightly floured surface; use fork tines to score dough in 1 direction. Cut to 8 even strips, following scored marks; halve strips to make rectangles.
- Bake for 15-18 minutes on ungreased baking sheet till cookie's bottoms are pale golden. Put on rack; fully cool for 1 hour.
- You can make cookies 1 day ahead; keep at room temperature in airtight container.

Nutrition Information

- Calories: 254
- Fiber: 1 g(4%)
- Total Carbohydrate: 33 g(11%)
- Cholesterol: 73 mg(24%)
- Protein: 4 g(8%)
- Total Fat: 12 g(18%)
- Saturated Fat: 7 g(34%)
- Sodium: 142 mg(6%)

120. Cornmeal Pound Cake With Rosemary Syrup, Poached Pears, And Candied Rosemary

Serving: Makes 8 servings | Prep: | Cook: | Ready in:

Ingredients

- 3 cups water
- 2 cups sugar
- 1 cup dry or off-dry Riesling
- 3 fresh rosemary sprigs
- 1 vanilla bean, split lengthwise
- 1/4 teaspoon whole black peppercorns
- 8 Forelle pears or other small pears, peeled, stems left intact
- 1 cup all purpose flour
- 1 cup yellow cornmeal
- 1 cup (2 sticks) unsalted butter, room temperature
- 1 1/3 cups sugar
- 1/4 teaspoon salt
- 5 large eggs, beaten to blend in medium bowl
- 1 teaspoon vanilla extract
- 1 cup sugar
- 1/2 cup water
- 8 (4-inch-long) fresh rosemary sprigs
- Baker's sugar or other superfine sugar

Direction

- For Pears: Mix the first 6 ingredients in big saucepan on medium heat till sugar dissolves. Add pears; boil, occasionally turning pears. Lower heat to medium low and cover; simmer for 20 minutes till pears are tender. Chill pears in syrup for at least 3 hours till cold, uncovered. You can make it 2 days ahead; cover. Keep chilled.
- For Pound cake: Preheat an oven to 325°F. Butter then flour 9x5x3-in. metal loaf pan. Whisk cornmeal and flour to blend in medium bowl. Beat butter using electric mixer till fluffy and light in big bowl; beat in sugar slowly, then salt. By tablespoonfuls, drizzle in beaten eggs, constantly beating; beat in vanilla. Working in 3 additions, add dry ingredients; beat to just blend after each addition. Put batter in prepped pan.
- Bake cake for 1 hour 15 minutes till inserted tester in middle exits clean and brown on top; cool for 15 minutes in pan. Turn cake onto rack; fully cool. You can make it 1 day ahead. In foil, wrap; keep at room temperature.
- For Candied rosemary and syrup: Simmer 1/2 cup water and 1 cup sugar in medium saucepan on medium high heat, mixing till sugar dissolves. Add rosemary sprigs; simmer for 5 minutes till syrup slightly reduces, occasionally swirling pan. Transfer rosemary sprigs on rack using tongs; drain. Cover; put rosemary syrup aside.
- Into shallow bowl, put baker's sugar. One by one, add drained rosemary sprigs to sugar; turn to thickly coat. Place on paper towels; dry for at least 1 hour. You can make it 1 day ahead; allow syrup and sprigs to stand at room temperature.
- Cut dark cake ends off. Slice eight 1/2-3/4-in. thick cake slices. Diagonally halve each slice; on each plate, position 2 halves. Drain pears. On each plate, allow 1 pear to stand; drizzle reserved rosemary syrup on each dessert then garnish using candied rosemary sprig. Serve, separately with leftover syrup.

Nutrition Information

- Calories: 940
- Saturated Fat: 16 g(79%)
- Sodium: 131 mg(5%)
- Fiber: 7 g(27%)
- Total Carbohydrate: 167 g(56%)
- Cholesterol: 177 mg(59%)
- Protein: 8 g(16%)
- Total Fat: 27 g(42%)

121. Cranberry Oat Bars

Serving: 16 | Prep: 15mins | Cook: 15mins | Ready in:

Ingredients

- 2 cups fresh or frozen cranberries
- 3/4 cup sugar
- 2 tablespoons orange zest
- 1 1/2 cups all-purpose flour
- 1 1/2 cups rolled oats
- 1 cup packed light brown sugar
- 1 teaspoon baking powder
- 1/2 teaspoon salt
- 3/4 cup butter

Direction

- In a small saucepan, mix orange zest, white sugar and cranberries over medium high heat. Heat to a boil, then lower the heat and cook until the mixture has evaporated to only about 1 cup.
- Set the oven to 350°F (175°C), and start preheating. Coat a baking pan of 9x9 inches with oil, line with foil, then coat the foil with oil.
- In a medium bowl, mix salt, baking powder, brown sugar, oats and flour together. Use your hands or a pastry blender to cut in the butter until the mixture looks like coarse crumbs. Press firmly 1/2 the mixture into the prepared pan. Spread evenly the cranberry sauce over the base, crumble the rest of oat mixture on top.
- Bake in the oven for 10 - 15 minutes, until the top is golden brown. Allow to completely cool then cut into bars.

Nutrition Information

- Calories: 243 calories;
- Sodium: 161
- Total Carbohydrate: 38.6
- Cholesterol: 23
- Protein: 2.4
- Total Fat: 9.3

122. Cream Cheese Flan

Serving: Makes 8 to 10 servings | Prep: | Cook: | Ready in:

Ingredients

- 1 1/2 cups sugar
- 1 cup water, divided
- 1 8-ounce package cream cheese, room temperature
- 1 14-ounce can sweetened condensed milk
- 5 large eggs
- 1 large egg yolk
- 1 cup canned evaporated milk
- 1 teaspoon vanilla extract
- Pinch of salt

Direction

- Prepare the oven by preheating to 350 degrees F. In a heavy medium saucepan over medium-low heat, whisk 1/2 cup water and sugar until sugar dissolved. Raise the heat and boil without whisking, using a wet pastry brush to occasionally brush downsides of the pan and whirl the pan, until syrup becomes deep amber. Instantly transfer caramel to a glass baking dish (9x5x3-inch), slanting and turning the dish to coat the bottom and 2-inch up sides with caramel. Cool.
- In a large bowl, whisk cream cheese with an electric mixer until smooth. Slowly whisk in sweetened condensed milk, then the yolk and eggs. Add the rest 1/2 cup water, salt, vanilla, and evaporated milk; whisk to mix. Transfer custard to a caramel-lined dish. Put the dish in a metal baking pan (13x9x2-inch). Pour hot water to the pan enough to reach 1 1/2-inch up sides of the dish. Bake for about 1 hour until a knife poked into the center of the flan comes out clean. Take flan out of water bath and chill with no cover till cool; then keep in the refrigerator overnight, covered.
- Use a small sharp knife to run around the flan to loosen. Hold the platter and dish firmly and reverse, shaking carefully to unmold the flan

onto the platter. Pour the caramel syrup from the dish over the flan. Serve the flan, sliced.

Nutrition Information

- Calories: 497
- Total Fat: 20 g(31%)
- Saturated Fat: 11 g(54%)
- Sodium: 283 mg(12%)
- Total Carbohydrate: 69 g(23%)
- Cholesterol: 196 mg(65%)
- Protein: 12 g(24%)

Nutrition Information

- Calories: 238
- Cholesterol: 54 mg(18%)
- Protein: 3 g(6%)
- Total Fat: 18 g(28%)
- Saturated Fat: 11 g(55%)
- Sodium: 308 mg(13%)
- Fiber: 2 g(9%)
- Total Carbohydrate: 17 g(6%)

123. Cream Cheese – Yukon Gold Whipped Potatoes

Serving: Makes 10 servings | Prep: | Cook: |Ready in:

Ingredients

- 2 pounds Yukon gold potatoes, peeled and cut into 1-inch pieces
- 1/2 cup heavy cream
- 1/2 cup (1 stick) unsalted butter
- 2 tablespoons sour cream
- 4 ounces cream cheese, room temperature
- 3 tablespoons fresh lemon juice (from 1 medium lemon)
- 1 tablespoon freshly ground black pepper
- 1 tablespoon kosher salt

Direction

- Combine potatoes and cover with cold water in a medium, heavy pot; put on medium high heat. Cover; boil. Boil for 15 minutes till potatoes are pierced easily with a fork. Drain; pass through ricer/food mill into big mixing bowl. Put aside.
- Combine butter and heavy cream in small saucepan on medium heat. Put cream cheese, sour cream and cream mixture in potatoes; beat for 1 minute till fluffy and light. Mix in pepper, salt and lemon juice; serve hot.

124. Currant Scones

Serving: 12 | Prep: 20mins | Cook: 20mins |Ready in:

Ingredients

- 3/4 cup dried currants
- 4 3/4 cups all-purpose flour
- 1 tablespoon baking powder
- 3/4 teaspoon baking soda
- 1/2 cup white sugar
- 1 1/4 teaspoons salt
- 1 cup chilled unsalted butter, cut into 1/2-inch cubes
- 1 tablespoon chilled unsalted butter, cut into 1/2-inch cubes
- 1 1/2 cups buttermilk
- 1 teaspoon lemon zest
- 2 tablespoons melted butter
- 1/4 cup coarse sugar crystals

Direction

- Preheat an oven to 200 degrees C (400 degrees F). Line parchment paper onto a baking sheet.
- In a bowl, cover the currants with warm water and leave to moisten.
- In the bowl of a stand mixer, sift flour, baking soda, and baking powder. Combine salt and white sugar into the flour mixture with the paddle attachment at low speed. Pour in all the unsalted butter into the mixer bowl and

combine on low speed for about 30 seconds until the butter cubes reduce to the size of small peas.
- Drain the currants and discard the soaking water. Combine currants, lemon zest and buttermilk into flour mixture on low speed until dough begins to stick together.
- Spread out the dough onto a work surface that is lightly floured and then gently form into a rectangle of 18 inches long, 5 inches wide, and 1 1/2 inches thick. Brush the dough with the melted butter and drizzle sugar crystals on top.
- Use a sharp knife to chop dough in half crosswise. Chop each half into thirds and then chop each third diagonally to form 12 triangular-shaped scones. Transfer onto the baking sheet.
- Bake for about 18 minutes until the scones are golden brown lightly. Enjoy while still warm.

Nutrition Information

- Calories: 428 calories;
- Total Fat: 19
- Sodium: 493
- Total Carbohydrate: 58.7
- Cholesterol: 50
- Protein: 6.7

125. Currant And Spice Oatmeal Cookies

Serving: Makes about 45 cookies | Prep: | Cook: |Ready in:

Ingredients

- 2 large eggs
- 1 1/2 teaspoons vanilla extract
- 2/3 cup dried currants
- 1 2/3 cups all purpose flour
- 1 teaspoon baking soda
- 3/4 teaspoon salt
- 3/4 teaspoon ground cardamom
- 1/2 teaspoon ground cinnamon
- 1/4 teaspoon ground allspice
- 1 cup (2 sticks) unsalted butter, room temperature
- 1 1/2 cups (packed) dark brown sugar
- 2 cups old-fashioned oats

Direction

- Whisk vanilla and eggs to blend in small bowl. Stir in dried currants; cover. Let stand for 1 hour in room temperature.
- Preheat an oven to 350°F. Butter then flour 3 big baking sheets. Sift spices, salt, baking soda and flour into medium bowl. Beat butter using electric mixer till fluffy in big bowl. Add sugar; beat till smooth. Add currant mixture; beat to blend. Mix in flour mixture; stir in oats. By level tablespoonfuls, drop on prepped sheets, 1 1/2-in. apart. Slightly flatten cookies using moistened fingertips. 1 sheet at 1 time, bake for 12 minutes till cookies are golden brown; cool on sheets.

Nutrition Information

- Calories: 104
- Total Carbohydrate: 15 g(5%)
- Cholesterol: 19 mg(6%)
- Protein: 1 g(3%)
- Total Fat: 5 g(7%)
- Saturated Fat: 3 g(14%)
- Sodium: 59 mg(2%)
- Fiber: 1 g(3%)

126. Custard Gelato

Serving: Makes 1 1/2 quarts; serves 6 | Prep: | Cook: |Ready in:

Ingredients

- 2 1/4 cups whole milk

- Pinch of salt
- 2/3 cup sugar
- 6 egg yolks
- 2/3 cup heavy cream

Direction

- Heat salt and milk in medium saucepan on medium heat till bubbles form around pan's edges; put aside. Cover to keep it hot.
- Blend egg yolks and sugar till smooth and very thick in food processor/blender. Gradually add hot milk as machine runs; put mixture in saucepan. Cook on medium heat, constantly mixing with wooden spoon, till mixture slightly thickens and coats back of spoon for 6-8 minutes. Take pan off heat; set in bowl with ice water. Mix to cool mixture for 2 minutes. Cover; refrigerate till thoroughly chilled for 2 hours.
- Beat cream till soft peaks form in deep bowl. Fold whipped cream into custard mixture; put into ice cream maker. Follow manufacturer's instructions to freeze.

Nutrition Information

- Calories: 276
- Cholesterol: 191 mg(64%)
- Protein: 6 g(11%)
- Total Fat: 16 g(25%)
- Saturated Fat: 9 g(45%)
- Sodium: 105 mg(4%)
- Total Carbohydrate: 28 g(9%)

127. Damson Tartlets

Serving: Makes 6 servings | Prep: 45mins | Cook: 4hours | Ready in:

Ingredients

- 2 1/2 cups all-purpose flour
- 2 sticks (1/2 pound) cold unsalted butter, cut into 1/2-inch cubes
- 1 cup confectioners sugar
- 3 large egg yolks
- 1 pound damson plums or prune plums
- 1 3/4 cups sugar
- 2 tablespoons white wine
- 1 Turkish or 1/2 California bay leaf
- 1 cup heavy cream
- 1/2 vanilla bean, split lengthwise
- 1 tablespoon sugar
- 1/2 teaspoon grated lemon zest
- Equipment: 6 (4-inch) fluted tartlet pans

Direction

- Pastry dough: Pulse confectioners' sugar, butter and flour till it looks like coarse meal in food processor. Add egg yolks; pulse till dough forms.
- Put dough on lightly floured surface; halve. Shape each half to 4-in. 1-in. thick square; in plastic wrap, wrap. Freeze for minimum of 2 hours till solid.
- As pastry freezes, make compote: Simmer bay leaf, wine, sugar and whole plums in medium heavy saucepan on medium low heat till sugar dissolves, occasionally mixing, covered; don't boil over juices. Lower heat to low; simmer for 30 minutes till plums fall apart, occasionally mixing, covered. Put in a bowl; chill till cold, uncovered. Cover. Discard bay leaf and pits. If desired, add bit of confectioners' sugar to taste.
- Bake pastry: From 1 frozen square, grate coarsely pastry into tartlet pans, evenly dividing. Keep leftover dough for another time. Press dough flakes in tartlet pans to line sides and bottoms evenly. Use a fork to prick bottoms all over; freeze tartlets for minimum of 1 hour till firm.
- Preheat an oven with rack in center to 425°F.
- In shallow baking pan, put tartlets; put in oven. Lower oven temperature to 400°F; bake for 15-18 minutes till shells get golden all over.
- Put tartlet pans on rack; fully cool. Remove shells from pans.
- Cream filling: In a big bowl, put cream. From vanilla bean, scrape seeds into cream; beat in

zest and sugar using an electric mixer till cream holds stiff peaks then fold in 2 tbsp. plum compote; divide cream to tartlet shells. Put some leftover compote on top; serve. You'll have lots of compote remaining.
- Use black/slightly sweeter red plums for prune/damson plums and 2 tbsp. lemon juice for wine, greater acidity, if needed.
- You can freeze pastry for maximum of 1 month.
- Compote keeps for 2 weeks, chilled, covered.

Nutrition Information

- Calories: 1124
- Cholesterol: 228 mg(76%)
- Protein: 10 g(19%)
- Total Fat: 48 g(74%)
- Saturated Fat: 30 g(148%)
- Sodium: 27 mg(1%)
- Fiber: 7 g(27%)
- Total Carbohydrate: 170 g(57%)

128. Dark Chocolate Wedding Cake With Chocolate Orange Ganache And Orange Buttercream

Serving: Serves about 30 (including top tier) | Prep: | Cook: | Ready in:

Ingredients

- 1 3/4 cups unsweetened cocoa powder (not Dutch-process)
- 1 3/4 cups boiling water
- 4 ounces fine-quality bittersweet chocolate (not unsweetened), chopped
- one 8-ounce container sour cream
- 1 tablespoon plus 1 teaspoon vanilla extract
- 3 cups all-purpose flour
- 2 1/2 teaspoons baking soda
- 1 teaspoon salt
- 3 3/4 sticks (1 3/4 cups plus 2 tablespoons) unsalted butter, softened
- 1 3/4 cups granulated sugar
- 3/4 cup firmly packed light brown sugar
- 5 large eggs
- 1 cup heavy cream
- 8 ounces fine-quality bittersweet chocolate (not unsweetened), chopped
- 2 tablespoons unsalted butter, softened
- 2 teaspoons freshly grated orange zest
- 1 tablespoon Cointreau or other orange-flavored liqueur
- one 8-inch cardboard round*
- one 6-inch cardboard round*
- three 8-inch plastic straws
- 5 large egg yolks
- 1/4 cup sugar
- 1/2 cup fresh orange juice
- 1/2 stick (1/4 cup) unsalted butter, softened
- 1 1/2 teaspoons fresh lemon juice
- 1 1/4 cups sugar
- 1/2 cup water
- 5 large egg whites
- 1/2 teaspoon cream of tartar
- 6 1/2 sticks (3 1/4 cups) unsalted butter, cut into pieces and softened to cool room temperature
- 1/2 teaspoon salt
- 2 tablespoons freshly grated orange zest
- Note: A cake-decorating turntable* is extremely helpful for assembling and decorating a wedding cake.
- Decoration: fraises des bois (wild strawberries)** and small roses with some leaves attached (both fruit and flowers must be nontoxic and pesticide-free)
- *available at specialty cookware shops

Direction

- Prep cake: Cake Layers: Preheat an oven to 350°F. Line wax paper rounds on 2 9x2-in. buttered round cake pans and 2 7x2-in. buttered round cake pans. Butter paper. Use flour to dust pans; knock excess out.
- Whisk boiling water in a stream into cocoa powder till smooth in a bowl; mix in chopped

chocolate. Stand for 5 minutes. Mix it till chocolate melts and is smooth; cool. Whisk in vanilla and sour cream.

- Sift together salt, baking soda and flour into a bowl. Beat sugars and butter till fluffy and light in a standing electric mixer's big bowl. One by one, add eggs; beat well after each, scraping bowl's side down. Lower speed to low. Alternately in batches, add cocoa mixture and flour mixture, starting then ending with the flour mixture, beating till batter is well combined.
- Into each 7-in. pan, put 2 cups batter; smooth tops. Divide leftover batter, 3 3/4 cups each, to 9-in. pans; smooth tops. Put 1 7-in. layer and 9-in. layer on each rack, placing 7-in. layers in the oven's front part in lower third and middle of oven. Bake 9-in. layers for 35-40 minutes and 7-in. layers for 25-30 minutes till tester exits with crumbs adhering. Run thin knife around pans edges; invert cakes onto racks then peel paper off. Fully cool cakes. You can make cake layers 2 days ahead; keep, wrapped in plastic wrap well, at cool room temperature or 2 weeks ahead, frozen, wrapped in plastic wrap then foil well. Without unwrapping, defrost cake layers in room temperature.
- Ganache: Boil cream in a small saucepan; take off heat. Add liqueur, zest, butter and chocolate; stand for 3 minutes. Whisk till chocolate melts; chill ganache for 40 minutes till just cool.
- Beat ganache before using till just fluffy and light in an electric mixer's bowl; don't overbeat. It'll be grainy.
- Cake assembly: Put 1 9-in. layer on 8-in. cardboard round; evenly spread 2 cups ganache. Put leftover 9-in. layer over; to make even tier, press layers together gently. Put 1 7-in. layer on 6-in. cardboard round; in same manner, top with leftover ganache and leftover 7-in. layer.
- Use some buttercream to frost sides and top of 9-in. tier; while frosting 7-in. tier, chill. Chill both tiers till buttercream is firm.
- Halve straws; insert 1 straw piece into center of 9-in. tier all the way. Trim straw flush with tier's top; insert leftover 5 straw pieces in a circle in same manner, 1 1/2-in. from middle straw. Center a 7-in. tier still on cardboard over 9-in. tier. Use buttercream to fill gaps between tiers; put cake onto platter/cake stand. Chill cake for 6 hours minimum – 1 day maximum.
- Decoratively put roses and fraises des bois around sides and on top of cake; stand cake for 2-4 hours before serving in cool room temperature (the buttercream gets sensitive to warm temperatures). Including top tier, serves 30.
- Orange buttercream: Orange curd: Whisk sugar and yolks in a heavy small saucepan; whisk in pinch salt, butter and orange juice. Cook it on medium low heat, whisking, for 5-7 minutes till it just gets to boiling point; don't boil. Strain through fine sieve into bowl; whisk in the lemon juice. Cool curd, surface covered in plastic wrap; chill the orange curd, covered, for 4 hours minimum – 2 days maximum till cold.
- Buttercream: Boil water and sugar in a heavy saucepan, mixing till sugar dissolves; boil syrup, undisturbed, till candy thermometer reads 248°F. As syrup boils, beat pinch salt and whites till foamy in a standing electric mixer's big bowl; beat in the cream of tartar. Beat the whites till they hold stiff peaks; in a stream and avoiding side of bowl and beaters, beat in hot syrup. Beat it at medium speed for 15-20 minutes till fully cool. One piece at 1 time, beat in butter till smooth and thick; it'll look very thin and look like it is breaking initially, but as you beat more butter in, it'll thicken, be smooth and glossy. Beat in zest, salt and orange curd till smooth. You can make buttercream 4 days ahead; keep chilled in airtight container or freeze in an airtight container for 2 weeks ahead. Fully bring buttercream to room temperature; if frozen, it'll take a few hours. Before using, beat. It won't be smooth and glossy if buttercream is still too cold. Creates 8 cups.

129. Date & Blue Cheese Ball

Serving: Makes about 1 1/2 cups (360 ml) | Prep: | Cook: | Ready in:

Ingredients

- 8 oz/225 g of low-fat cream cheese (bar style), at room temperature
- 1 cup/115 g crumbled blue cheese, at room temperature
- 1 tbsp reduced-fat buttermilk
- 3 tbsp minced Medjool dates (5 to 6 pitted dates)
- 1 tbsp minced shallots
- 1 tsp grated lemon zest
- 1/4 tsp kosher or sea salt
- 1/4 tsp freshly ground pepper
- 2 tbsp minced fresh flat-leaf parsley
- 2 1/2 tbsp finely chopped toasted walnuts
- Crostini, Baked Pita Chips, Baked Bagel Chips, Marbled Rye Toasts, celery and carrot sticks

Direction

- Beat buttermilk, blue cheese and cream cheese at medium speed for 2 minutes till creamy and smooth in a stand mixer's bowl with paddle attachment. Add pepper, salt, lemon zest, shallots and dates; beat till combined well.
- Put cheese mixture on a big cling film/plastic wrap sheet; shape to a ball. Wrap ball in wrap; refrigerate for a minimum of 2 hours – overnight till well chilled.
- Mix walnuts and parsley in a shallow bowl/plate. Take cheese ball from fridge. Shape to well-formed ball with film/wrap still on. Unwrap cheese mixture; gently roll it in nut mixture till all sides are covered well. Immediately serve/cover then refrigerate till serving.
- You can prep cheese ball maximum of 2 days ahead; cover. Refrigerate.

130. Devil's Food Cake With Chocolate Spiderweb

Serving: Makes 8 to 10 servings | Prep: 1hours | Cook: 2.5hours | Ready in:

Ingredients

- 1 cup semisweet chocolate chips
- 2 cups all-purpose flour
- 1 1/4 teaspoons baking soda
- 1/2 teaspoon salt
- 1 cup boiling-hot water
- 3/4 cup unsweetened cocoa powder (not Dutch process)
- 1/2 cup milk
- 1 teaspoon pure vanilla extract
- 2 sticks unsalted butter, softened
- 1 1/4 cups packed dark brown sugar
- 3/4 cup granulated sugar
- 4 large eggs, warmed in very warm water 10 minutes
- 3 large egg whites
- 1 1/2 cups sugar
- 6 tablespoons water
- 1 1/2 tablespoons instant espresso powder (optional; see cooks' note, below)
- Equipment: 3 (9- by 2-inch) round cake pans; a pastry bag with writing tip (slightly less than 1/8 inch); a handheld electric mixer

Direction

- Cake: Preheat an oven with racks in lower and upper thirds to 350°F. Butter cake pans; line parchment paper rounds on bottoms. Dust pans using flour; knock excess out.
- Whisk salt, baking soda and flour in a small bowl.
- Whisk cocoa and boiling-hot water till smooth in another bowl; whisk in vanilla and milk.
- Beat sugars and butter using an electric mixer on medium high speed for 3 minutes till fluffy and light. One by one, add eggs; beat well after each. In 3 batches, mix in flour mixture alternating with cocoa mixture on low speed,

starting and ending with flour; mix just till combined.
- Divide batter to pans; smooth tops. Bake for 20-25 minutes till cake starts to pull away from pan sides and inserted wooden pick exits clean, switching pans positions halfway through.
- Cool cakes for 20 minutes in pans on racks. Turn onto racks; fully cool.
- As cake layers cool, make decorations: Trace 9-in. circle on parchment paper circle; draw spiderweb in the circle. Draw 2-3-in. spider next to web. Flip drawings onto baking sheet.
- Melt chocolate chips on heatproof bowl above saucepan of simmering water, stirring; slightly cool. Put in a pastry bag; pipe chocolate on web, starting with spokes, then on spider on parchment. Freeze for 1 hour till firm.
- Frosting: Put the frosting ingredients into big heatproof bowl set above pot with simmering water; beat using handheld mixer on low speed till sugar dissolves and is warm; beat for 7-10 minutes on high speed till fluffy and thick. Take bowl off heat; beat frosting for 5-10 minutes till slightly cool.
- Assemble cake: On serving plate, put a cake layer; spread some frosting on top. Put another cake layer over; spread some frosting. Put final cake layer over; frost sides and top of cake using leftover frosting.
- Cut off parchment portion with spider; put aside. Invert web on parchment on the cake; peel off paper carefully. Peel parchment off from spider; put spider onto web. Stand cake till chocolate decorations are soft in room temperature.
- You can make cake layers 2 days ahead, kept in room temperature, wrapped in plastic wrap well or frozen for 1 week.
- You can make chocolate decorations 1 day ahead, frozen.
- You can replace 2 tsp. pure vanilla extract for espresso powder in frosting. Egg whites in frosting might not get cooked fully.
- You can assemble and decorate cake 4 hours ahead, chilled; stand a minimum of 30 minutes before serving in room temperature.

Nutrition Information

- Calories: 840
- Total Fat: 34 g(52%)
- Saturated Fat: 20 g(101%)
- Sodium: 425 mg(18%)
- Fiber: 5 g(20%)
- Total Carbohydrate: 133 g(44%)
- Cholesterol: 155 mg(52%)
- Protein: 11 g(22%)

131. Devil's Food Cake With Peppermint Frosting

Serving: Makes 10 to 12 servings | Prep: | Cook: | Ready in:

Ingredients

- 2 2/3 cups all purpose flour
- 1 tablespoon baking powder
- 1 teaspoon baking soda
- 1 teaspoon salt
- 2 1/4 cups sugar
- 1 cup (2 sticks) unsalted butter, room temperature
- 3 large eggs
- 1 large egg yolk
- 1 1/4 cups unsweetened cocoa powder, sifted
- 2 cups ice water
- 1 1/3 cups heavy whipping cream
- 2 tablespoons light corn syrup
- 14 ounces bittersweet chocolate, chopped
- 12 ounces high-quality white chocolate (such as Lindt or Perugina), finely chopped
- 3 cups chilled heavy whipping cream, divided
- 1 1/2 teaspoons pure peppermint extract
- 2 1/4 cups sugar
- 1/2 cup water
- 3 large egg whites
- 1 tablespoon light corn syrup
- 1/2 teaspoon pure peppermint extract

- Bittersweet chocolate curls

Direction

- Cake: In middle of oven, put rack; preheat it to 350°F. Butter the 2 9-in. diameter cake pans that have 2-in. high sides. Dust pans using flour; tap extra out. Whisk initial 4 ingredients to blend in medium bowl. Beat butter and sugar using electric mixer till well blended in big bowl. One by one, beat in eggs; beat well after each. Beat in yolks. Add the cocoa; beat till blended well. In 3 batches, alternately with the ice water in 2 batches, add flour mixture, starting then ending with flour mixture, beating till smooth and just blended after every addition. Divide batter to prepped pans; smooth tops.
- Bake cakes for 40 minutes till inserted tester in middle exits clean; cool for 15 minutes in pans on racks. Invert cakes onto racks; fully cool. You can make it 1 day ahead. In foil, wrap; keep in room temperature.
- Dark chocolate ganache: Simmer corn syrup and cream in medium saucepan; take off heat. Add chocolate; whisk till smooth and melted. Put into small bowl; chill for 1 hour till firm enough to spread. You can make it 1 day ahead. Stand in room temperature for 30 minutes till soft enough to spread before using.
- White chocolate cream: In big heatproof bowl, put white chocolate. Simmer 1 cup cream in saucepan; put hot cream on white chocolate. Allow to stand for 1 minute; whisk till smooth. Whisk in extract and cover; chill for at least 4 hours till cold and thickens. You can make it 1 day ahead, chilled.
- Put 2 cups chilled cream in white chocolate cream; beat till peaks form and smooth. You can make it 3 hours ahead, chilled, covered. To thicken, rewhisk before using if needed.
- Horizontally halve each cake using long serrated knife. Put 1 cake layer, cut side up, on platter; spread cake with 1/3 dark chocolate ganache. In dollops, put 2 cups of white chocolate cream on cake; evenly spread to edges. Put 2nd cake layer on top, cut side down then spread 1/3 ganache then 2 cups of white chocolate cream. Repeat with leftover cream, ganache and 3rd cake layer, cut side up. Use 4th cake layer to cover, cut side down; chill as you make frosting.
- Peppermint frosting: Whisk corn syrup, egg whites, 1/2 cup water and sugar by hand to blend it well in a big heavy-duty stand mixer's bowl; put bowl with mixture above saucepan with gently simmering water. Constantly whisk with a hand whisk for 8-9 minutes till ribbons form when you lift whisk and it looks like marshmallow crème; whisk in peppermint extract. Take bowl from above water; attach bowl on heavy-duty stand mixer with whisk attachment. Beat at high speed for 7-8 minutes till it is very thick and barely warm to touch.
- Spread frosting on sides and top of cake using offset spatula, working quickly; sprinkle chocolate curls on sides and top. You can make it 1 day ahead. Use a cake dome to cover; chill.

Nutrition Information

- Calories: 1845
- Sodium: 623 mg(26%)
- Fiber: 7 g(29%)
- Total Carbohydrate: 180 g(60%)
- Cholesterol: 442 mg(147%)
- Protein: 20 g(39%)
- Total Fat: 128 g(197%)
- Saturated Fat: 75 g(377%)

132. Double Chocolate Layer Cake

Serving: Serves 12 to 14 | Prep: | Cook: | Ready in:

Ingredients

- 3 ounces fine-quality semisweet chocolate such as Callebaut

- 1 1/2 cups hot brewed coffee
- 3 cups sugar
- 2 1/2 cups all-purpose flour
- 1 1/2 cups unsweetened cocoa powder (not Dutch process)
- 2 teaspoons baking soda
- 3/4 teaspoon baking powder
- 1 1/4 teaspoons salt
- 3 large eggs
- 3/4 cup vegetable oil
- 1 1/2 cups well-shaken buttermilk
- 3/4 teaspoon vanilla
- 1 pound fine-quality semisweet chocolate such as Callebaut
- 1 cup heavy cream
- 2 tablespoons sugar
- 2 tablespoons light corn syrup
- 1/2 stick (1/4 cup) unsalted butter
- two 10- by 2-inch round cake pans

Direction

- For Cake layers: Preheat an oven to 300°F. Grease pans. Line wax paper rounds on bottoms; grease paper.
- Chop chocolate finely; mix with hot coffee in a bowl. Allow mixture to stand till smooth and chocolate melts, occasionally mixing.
- Sift salt, baking powder, baking soda, cocoa powder, flour and sugar into a big bowl. Beat eggs using electric mixer for 5 minutes with handheld mixer or 3 minutes with standing mixer, till lemon colored and slightly thick in another big bowl. Add melted chocolate mixture, vanilla, buttermilk and oil slowly; beat till well combined. Add sugar mixture; beat at medium speed till just combined well. Divide batter to pans; bake for 1 hour – 1 hour and 10 minutes in middle of oven till inserted tester in middle exits clean.
- Fully cool layers in pans on racks. Run the thin knife around pan's edges; invert layers onto racks. Remove wax paper carefully; fully cool layers. You can make cake layers 1 day ahead; keep at room temperature, wrapped in plastic wrap well.
- For Frosting: Chop chocolate finely. Boil corn syrup, sugar and cream in 1 1/2-2-qt. saucepan on moderately low heat, whisking till sugar dissolves; remove pan from heat. Add chocolate; whisk till chocolate melts. Cut butter to pieces; add to frosting, whisking till smooth.
- Transfer frosting into a bowl; cool, stirring occasionally till spreadable. You might have to chill frosting to get spreadable consistency depending on the chocolate used.
- Spread frosting on sides, top and between cake layers; cake keeps for 3 days, chilled while covered. Before serving, bring the cake to room temperature.

Nutrition Information

- Calories: 804
- Saturated Fat: 17 g(87%)
- Sodium: 570 mg(24%)
- Fiber: 7 g(29%)
- Total Carbohydrate: 112 g(37%)
- Cholesterol: 85 mg(28%)
- Protein: 10 g(19%)
- Total Fat: 42 g(64%)

133. Double Chocolate Brownies

Serving: Makes 16 | Prep: | Cook: | Ready in:

Ingredients

- 1/4 cup purchased chocolate syrup
- 2 ounces semisweet chocolate, chopped, or chocolate chips
- 1 8-ounce package cream cheese, room temperature
- 1 large egg
- 1/4 cup semisweet chocolate chips
- 1 tablespoon all purpose flour
- 1 cup (2 sticks) unsalted butter, room temperature

- 1 1/4 cups sugar
- 4 large eggs
- 1 teaspoon vanilla extract
- 1 1/3 cups all purpose flour
- 3/4 cup unsweetened cocoa powder
- 1/4 teaspoon baking powder
- 6 ounces semisweet chocolate, chopped, or chocolate chips
- 1 tablespoon vegetable oil

Direction

- Filling: Mix 2-oz. chopped chocolate and syrup in small heavy saucepan on low heat till chocolate melts; cool. Beat egg and cream cheese in medium bowl; mix in chocolate mixture. Blend in flour and 1/4 cup chocolate chips; put aside.
- Batter: Preheat an oven to 350°F. Grease square 9-in. baking pan that has 2-in. high sides; line waxed paper on bottom. Butter wax paper. Beat sugar and butter using electric mixer till fluffy in big bowl. One by one, add eggs; beat well after each. Beat in vanilla. Sift baking powder, cocoa and flour into medium bowl. Mix dry ingredients into the butter mixture.
- Put 1/2 chocolate batter in prepped pan; put filling over. Spread leftover batter over; bake the brownies for 40 minutes till inserted toothpick in middle exits clean. Put on rack; cool for 5 minutes. To loosen, run a sharp small knife around pan's edges; fully cool in pan.
- Glaze: Melt 6-oz. chocolate and oil in small heavy saucepan on low heat, constantly mixing.
- Slice cooled brownies to 16 2-in. squares; put on rack. Put warm glaze on brownies; stand till glaze sets. Put brownies onto platter.

Nutrition Information

- Calories: 385
- Saturated Fat: 14 g(70%)
- Sodium: 88 mg(4%)
- Fiber: 3 g(12%)
- Total Carbohydrate: 41 g(14%)
- Cholesterol: 104 mg(35%)
- Protein: 6 g(11%)
- Total Fat: 24 g(38%)

134. Dried Tart Cherry And Almond Muffins

Serving: Makes 10 | Prep: | Cook: |Ready in:

Ingredients

- 6 tablespoons orange juice
- 3/4 cup dried tart cherries (about 4 ounces)
- 1 cup plus 2 tablespoons all purpose flour
- 1/2 cup sugar
- 1 1/2 teaspoons baking powder
- 1/4 teaspoon salt
- 1 7-ounce package almond paste, crumbled
- 6 tablespoons (3/4 stick) unsalted butter, melted, hot
- 3 large eggs
- 1 1/2 teaspoons grated orange peel

Direction

- In middle of oven, put rack; preheat it to 375°F. Butter the 10 1/3-cup metal muffin cups. Simmer juice in small saucepan; take off heat. Add cherries; stand for 10 minutes till soft.
- Mix salt, baking powder, sugar and flour in medium bowl. Beat melted butter and almond paste using electric mixer till well blended with some small almond paste pieces in big bowl. One by one, add eggs; beat well after each. Mix in orange peel and cherry mixture. Add flour mixture; mix till just blended.
- Divide batter to prepped muffin cups; bake for 20 minutes till inserted tester in middle of muffins exits clean yet slightly moist to touch. You can make it 2 days ahead; cool. In foil, wrap muffins; keep in room temperature. Rewarm in the foil for 5 minutes in 350°F oven; serve warm.

Nutrition Information

- Calories: 306
- Sodium: 139 mg(6%)
- Fiber: 2 g(7%)
- Total Carbohydrate: 41 g(14%)
- Cholesterol: 74 mg(25%)
- Protein: 5 g(11%)
- Total Fat: 14 g(22%)
- Saturated Fat: 5 g(27%)

135. Dutch Sugar Cookies

Serving: Makes about 5 dozen | Prep: | Cook: | Ready in:

Ingredients

- 1 1/2 cups powdered sugar
- 1 cup (2 sticks) unsalted butter, room temperature
- 1 large egg
- 2 teaspoons vanilla extract
- 2 1/2 cups all purpose flour
- 1 teaspoon baking powder
- 1/2 teaspoon salt
- 4 ounces good-quality white chocolate (such as Lindt or Baker's), melted

Direction

- Beat butter and sugar using electric mixer till light in big bowl; beat in vanilla and egg. Add salt, baking powder and flour; mix to just combine. Halve dough. Gather each piece to ball; flatten to disks. In plastic, wrap; chill for 1 hour.
- Preheat an oven to 325°F. Roll 1 dough disk out to 1/8-in. thick on floured work surface. Cut out cookies using assorted cookie cutters; put cookies on ungreased baking sheets, 1-in. apart. Gather the dough scraps then reroll to 1/8-in. thick. Cut more cookies out.
- Bake cookies for 13 minutes till pale golden. Put cookies on rack; cool. Repeat using leftover dough disk.
- Put melted chocolate in pastry bag with 1/16-in. plain tip. Onto cookies, pipe chocolate; stand till chocolate sets. You can make ahead; keep for maximum of 1 week in room temperature in airtight container/freeze for maximum of 1 month.

Nutrition Information

- Calories: 298
- Cholesterol: 50 mg(17%)
- Protein: 3 g(7%)
- Total Fat: 16 g(25%)
- Saturated Fat: 10 g(50%)
- Sodium: 124 mg(5%)
- Fiber: 1 g(2%)
- Total Carbohydrate: 35 g(12%)

136. Easy Cranberry & Apple Cake

Serving: Serves 6 to 8 | Prep: | Cook: | Ready in:

Ingredients

- 12 ounces fresh cranberries, rinsed and picked over for stems
- 1 Granny Smith apple, peeled, cored, and medium-diced
- 1/2 cup light brown sugar, packed
- 1 tablespoon grated orange zest (2 oranges)
- 1/4 cup freshly squeezed orange juice
- 1 1/8 teaspoons ground cinnamon, divided
- 2 extra-large eggs, at room temperature
- 1 cup plus 1 tablespoon granulated sugar
- 1/4 pound (1 stick) unsalted butter, melted and slightly cooled
- 1 teaspoon pure vanilla extract
- 1/4 cup sour cream
- 1 cup all-purpose flour
- 1/4 teaspoon kosher salt

Direction

- Preheat an oven to 325°F.
- In a medium bowl, mix 1 tsp. cinnamon, orange juice, orange zest, brown sugar, apple and cranberries; put aside.
- Beat eggs for 2 minutes at medium high speed in an electric mixer's bowl with paddle attachment. Add sour cream, vanilla, butter and 1 cup granulated sugar with mixer on medium; beat till just combined. Add salt and flour slowly on low speed.
- Evenly put fruit mixture into 10-in. glass pie plate; put batter on fruit, fully covering it. Mix 1/8 tsp. cinnamon and leftover 1 tbsp. granulated sugar; sprinkle on batter. Bake till inserted toothpick in center of cake exits clean and fruit is bubbly around edges for 55-60 minutes. Serve at room temperature/warm.

Nutrition Information

- Calories: 515
- Total Fat: 19 g(30%)
- Saturated Fat: 11 g(57%)
- Sodium: 119 mg(5%)
- Fiber: 4 g(17%)
- Total Carbohydrate: 82 g(27%)
- Cholesterol: 115 mg(38%)
- Protein: 5 g(11%)

137. Egg Sponge

Serving: | Prep: | Cook: | Ready in:

Ingredients

- 3 tablespoons unsalted butter
- 6 tablespoons all-purpose flour
- 1 1/4 cups milk
- 4 large eggs, separated, the whites at room temperature

Direction

- Line wax paper on buttered 15 1/2x10 1/2x1-in. jellyroll pan; butter paper. Dust flour; knock excess out. Melt butter in a saucepan. Add flour; cook roux on medium low heat for 3 minutes, mixing. In a stream, add milk, whisking; simmer for 5 minutes, occasionally whisking. Put it into a big bowl. One by one, whisk in yolks; whisk well after each. Beat whites using an electric mixer till it holds stiff peaks in a bowl. Mix 1/3 whites into yolk mixture; gently yet thoroughly fold in leftover whites. Evenly spread batter in prepped pan; bake for 25 minutes till firm to touch and golden in center of preheated 350°F oven. Use buttered wax paper sheet, buttered side down, then a kitchen towel to cover egg sponge; invert baking sheet on towel. Invert sponge onto baking sheet, carefully removing wax paper from top. Trim 1/4-in. from egg sponge's short sides.

Nutrition Information

- Calories: 158
- Saturated Fat: 6 g(28%)
- Sodium: 70 mg(3%)
- Fiber: 0 g(1%)
- Total Carbohydrate: 9 g(3%)
- Cholesterol: 144 mg(48%)
- Protein: 7 g(13%)
- Total Fat: 11 g(16%)

138. Espresso Ganache Tartlets

Serving: Makes 6 servings | Prep: | Cook: | Ready in:

Ingredients

- 1/2 cup (1 stick) unsalted butter, room temperature
- 1/4 cup sugar
- 1 large egg
- 1 1/2 cups all purpose flour

- 1/4 teaspoon baking powder
- 1/8 teaspoon salt
- 1/4 cup hot water
- 1 tablespoon instant espresso powder
- 3/4 cup whipping cream
- 2 tablespoons sugar
- 10 ounces bittersweet (not unsweetened) or semisweet chocolate, chopped

Direction

- Crust: Beat sugar and butter using electric mixer till light in medium bowl; beat in egg. Add salt, baking powder and flour; beat till just blended. Divide dough to 6 3-in. diameter tartlet pans that have removable bottoms and 1-in. high sides. Press dough in pans with floured fingertips; refrigerate for 1 hour. Freeze for 10 minutes. Preheat an oven to 350°F. Bake the tartlets for 25 minutes till golden brown. Put on racks; fully cool.
- Filling: Mix espresso powder and 1/4 cup hot water till espresso is dissolved in small bowl. Simmer sugar and cream in medium heavy saucepan, mixing till sugar is dissolved; take off heat. Add chocolate; mix till smooth and melted. Stir in espresso mixture; put hot filling in tartlets. Chill till chocolate sets, for a minimum of 2 hours. You can make it 1 day ahead, kept refrigerated, covered. From tartlets, remove tart pan sides; put on plates. Serve.

Nutrition Information

- Calories: 624
- Protein: 7 g(14%)
- Total Fat: 40 g(61%)
- Saturated Fat: 24 g(121%)
- Sodium: 94 mg(4%)
- Fiber: 4 g(15%)
- Total Carbohydrate: 68 g(23%)
- Cholesterol: 105 mg(35%)

139. Fig And Fennel Bread

Serving: Makes two 12-inch-long loaves | Prep: | Cook: | Ready in:

Ingredients

- 1 1/4 cups warm water (105°F to 115°F)
- 1 tablespoon sugar
- 1 envelope dry yeast (2 1/4 teaspoons)
- 3 cups bread flour
- 1 8-ounce package dried Calimyrna figs, chopped (about 1 1/2 cups)
- 1 cup rye flour
- 2 tablespoons fennel seeds
- 1 tablespoon salt

Direction

- Mix yeast, sugar and 1 1/4 cups warm water in small bowl; stand for 10 minutes till it bubbles. Mix salt, fennel seeds, rye flour, 3/4 cup figs and bread flour in a heavy-duty mixer's bowl with paddle attachment. On lowest speed, mix; add yeast mixture slowly, mixing till all flour is incorporated. Or, vigorously mix by hand using a wooden spoon till dough comes together. Replace the paddle with dough hook; knead till elastic and smooth. Or, put dough on floured work surface to knead by hand then knead for 5 minutes till elastic and smooth. Put dough into oiled bowl; turn till coated. Use plastic wrap to cover then a kitchen towel; rise dough for 1 hour till doubled in volume in a draft-free warm area.
- Turn dough onto work surface; gently knead till deflated. Knead in leftover 3/4 cup figs. Halve dough; form each piece to 12-in. long loaf. Brush oil on rimmed baking sheet; put loaves on sheet, spacing apart. Use plastic to cover then kitchen towel; rise for 35 minutes till nearly doubled in volume in a draft-free, warm area.
- Preheat an oven to 375°F; bake the bread for 45 minutes till loaves sound hollow when you tap it and crust is golden; on rack, cool bread.

Nutrition Information

- Calories: 1060
- Fiber: 18 g(71%)
- Total Carbohydrate: 220 g(73%)
- Protein: 34 g(67%)
- Total Fat: 6 g(9%)
- Saturated Fat: 1 g(4%)
- Sodium: 1236 mg(51%)

140. Figgy Scones

Serving: Makes 20 scones | Prep: 25mins | Cook: 1hours | Ready in:

Ingredients

- 3/4 cup well-shaken buttermilk
- 1/4 cup pure maple syrup
- 1/2 cup plus 2 tablespoons heavy cream
- 3 1/2 cups all-purpose flour
- 3/4 cup sugar
- 1 teaspoon salt
- 1 teaspoon baking powder
- 1/2 teaspoon baking soda
- 2 sticks (1 cup) unsalted butter, cut into 1/2-inch cubes
- 1/2 lb dried Calmyrna figs, stems discarded and figs cut into 1/2-inch pieces (about 1 1/2 cups)
- 2 large egg yolks
- parchment paper

Direction

- In lower and upper oven thirds, put oven racks; preheat an oven to 400°F.
- Whisk 1/2 cup cream, syrup and buttermilk in small bowl. Mix baking soda, baking powder, salt, sugar and flour till combined in a stand mixer's bowl with paddle attachment on low speed/whisk in a big bowl. Add butter; blend with fingertips/pastry blender or mix till it looks like coarse meal with few roughly pea-sized small butter lumps. Stir in figs. Add buttermilk mixture; mix just till combined. Don't overmix.
- Line parchment paper on 2 big baking sheets; drop 10 1/4-cup batter mounds on each sheet, 1-in. apart.
- Whisk leftover 2 tbsp. cream and yolks; brush on scone's tops. Use all egg wash.
- Bake for 20-25 minutes till scones are golden and puffed, switching baking sheets positions halfway through baking.
- Put on rack; cool to warm.
- Best eaten same day as made.

Nutrition Information

- Calories: 244
- Cholesterol: 53 mg(18%)
- Protein: 3 g(6%)
- Total Fat: 13 g(20%)
- Saturated Fat: 8 g(39%)
- Sodium: 174 mg(7%)
- Fiber: 1 g(4%)
- Total Carbohydrate: 30 g(10%)

141. Flaxseed, Fig, And Walnut Crackers

Serving: Makes about 40 crackers | Prep: | Cook: | Ready in:

Ingredients

- 1/3 cup whole flaxseed
- 1/4 cup ground flaxseed or flaxseed meal (available in the vitamin section of most supermarkets)
- 1 1/2 cups whole-wheat flour
- 1/2 teaspoon baking powder
- 1/4 teaspoon kosher salt
- 1 tablespoon plus 1 teaspoon brown sugar
- 4 tablespoons unsalted butter, at room temperature
- 1/4 cup walnuts, chopped
- About 7 dried figs, chopped (1 cup)

- 1/2 cup soy milk

Direction

- Preheat an oven to 325°F.
- Mix the sugar, salt, baking powder, flour and whole and ground flaxseed in a mixing bowl.
- Put butter and blend on medium speed with paddle attachment till mixture resembles coarse crumbs.
- Fold the soy milk, figs and walnuts, and combine till dough is velvety.
- In plastic wrap, wrap dough and refrigerate for 10 minutes.
- Unroll 1/2 of dough on a floured area to 1/8-inch thick or slimmer. Cut it as though on grid to create 2-inch squares, then using a spatula, turn them on to unoiled baking sheet. Redo with another dough half.
- Let the crackers bake for 20 minutes till golden brown. Allow to cool, then serve.
- Tip: serve crackers along with almond butter, fruit spread or omega-3-rich pumpkin butter. Other strategies for boosting kids' omega-3 intake: Drizzle ground flaxseed or wheat germ on their favorite cereal; fold pumpkin seeds, sunflower seeds, or walnuts into a peanut-and-M&M trail mix; cook with hemp oil, canola oil, or pumpkin oil; or use omega-3-enriched eggs, which contain more EFAs than regular ones.

Nutrition Information

- Calories: 46
- Saturated Fat: 1 g(4%)
- Sodium: 19 mg(1%)
- Fiber: 1 g(5%)
- Total Carbohydrate: 5 g(2%)
- Cholesterol: 3 mg(1%)
- Protein: 1 g(3%)
- Total Fat: 3 g(4%)

142. Flourless Chocolate Cake With Coffee Liqueur

Serving: Makes 12 servings | Prep: | Cook: |Ready in:

Ingredients

- 1 pound semisweet chocolate, chopped
- 1 cup (2 sticks) unsalted butter
- 1/4 cup coffee liqueur
- 1 teaspoon vanilla extract
- 7 large eggs, room temperature
- 1 cup sugar
- Powdered sugar

Direction

- Preheat an oven to 350°F. Butter the 9-in. diameter springform pan that has 2 3/4-in. high sides; line parchment paper on bottom of pan. Mix vanilla, coffee liqueur, butter and chocolate in big heavy saucepan on low heat till smooth and melted; cool to lukewarm. Beat 1 cup sugar and eggs using electric mixer till pale for 6 minutes, thick and slowly dissolving ribbon forms when you lift beaters. Fold 1/3 egg mixture in lukewarm chocolate mixture; fold leftover egg mixture into the chocolate mixture.
- On baking sheet, put prepped pan; put batter in prepped pan. Bake for 55 minutes till inserted tester in cake exits with moist crumbs attached; cool for 5 minutes. Press down cake edges gently; fully cool in pan. You can prep cake 1 day ahead; use plastic wrap to cover. Refrigerate. 1 hour before continuing, stand in room temperature.
- To loosen cake, run knife around the pan sides; remove pan sides. Put cake on platter; remove the parchment paper. Sprinkle powdered sugar on cake. Serve.

Nutrition Information

- Calories: 449
- Total Fat: 29 g(45%)
- Saturated Fat: 17 g(87%)

- Sodium: 48 mg(2%)
- Fiber: 2 g(9%)
- Total Carbohydrate: 45 g(15%)
- Cholesterol: 149 mg(50%)
- Protein: 5 g(11%)

143. Fougasse

Serving: 20 | Prep: | Cook: |Ready in:

Ingredients

- 1 1/2 cups warm water (110 degrees F/45 degrees C)
- 1 teaspoon active dry yeast
- 4 cups all-purpose flour
- 1/2 tablespoon dried basil
- 1/2 tablespoon ground savory
- 1/2 tablespoon dried thyme
- 1/2 tablespoon dried rosemary
- 2 tablespoons sea salt
- 4 tablespoons olive oil
- 2 tablespoons cornmeal

Direction

- Into a big bowl, pour water. Scatter yeast in the water and rest without moving till melted. Mix in 2 tablespoons oil, sea salt, a tablespoon herbs and a cup flour till well incorporated. Stir in flour, a cup at one time, till a thick and somewhat sticky dough forms.
- Transfer dough to a lightly floured area and knead till pliable and smooth. Shape into a round and put into a greased bowl. Turn dough to coat the top. Put a clean dishtowel to cover the bowl and allow to rise till doubled for an hour.
- Deflate dough and halve. Form into uneven ovals, approximately 1 1/2-inch thick. On top of 2 baking sheets, scatter cornmeal; turn the dough onto pans. Brush olive oil on every loaf and scatter the rest of the herbs over. Make a few slits in the bread, slicing through dough using a knife. Put clean dishtowels to cover the loaves. Allow to rise once more for 20 minutes till dough starts to rise once more.
- Into the prepped 220°C or 450°F oven, put the baking sheets. Immediately splash a bit of water onto oven floor to make steam, then latch the door of the oven. Bake for 20 minutes till golden.

Nutrition Information

- Calories: 120 calories;
- Sodium: 529
- Total Carbohydrate: 20.1
- Cholesterol: 0
- Protein: 2.8
- Total Fat: 3

144. Four Layer Pumpkin Cake With Orange Cream Cheese Frosting

Serving: Makes 12 servings | Prep: | Cook: |Ready in:

Ingredients

- Nonstick vegetable oil spray
- 3 cups all purpose flour
- 2 teaspoons baking powder
- 1 teaspoon baking soda
- 1 teaspoon Chinese five-spice powder*
- 1/2 teaspoon fine sea salt
- 1 cup (2 sticks) unsalted butter, room temperature
- 2 cups (packed) golden brown sugar
- 3 large eggs, room temperature
- 1 15-ounce can pure pumpkin
- 1/3 cup whole milk
- 1 cup (2 sticks) unsalted butter, room temperature
- 2 8-ounce packages cream cheese, room temperature
- 1 tablespoon finely grated orange peel
- 2 cups powdered sugar, sifted

- Chopped walnuts or walnut halves, toasted

Direction

- Cake: Put rack in oven's bottom third; preheat it to 350°F. Spray nonstick spray on 2 9-in. cake pans that have 1 1/2-in. sides. Line parchment on bottoms; spray parchment.
- Whisk the flour and following 4 ingredients in big bowl. Beat butter till smooth using electric mixer in another big bowl; beat in brown sugar. One by one, add eggs; beat to blend between the additions. Beat in pumpkin. Alternately with milk in 2 batches, put dry ingredients in butter mixture in 3 batches, beating to blend between the additions. Divide batter to pans.
- Bake cakes for 40 minutes till inserted tester in middle exits clean; cool for 15 minutes in pans on rack. To loosen, run knife around cakes; invert cakes on racks. Remove parchment. Flip cakes onto racks, using tart pan bottom for aid, top sides up; fully cool. You can make it 1 day ahead. In plastic, wrap cakes; keep in room temperature.
- Frosting: Beat butter using electric mixer till smooth in big bowl. Add orange peel and cream cheese; beat till smooth. Add powdered sugar; beat at low speed till smooth.
- From cakes, trim rounded tops. Horizontally halve each cake using long serrated knife. Put 1 cake layer on big platter, cut side up. In dollops, put 2/3 cup frosting on cake; spread to edges. Repeat twice with frosting and cake; put leftover, cut side down, cake layer over. Spread leftover frosting on sides and top of cake; the layer will be thin. You can make it 2 days ahead. Use cake dome to cover; chill. 1 hour before serving, stand in room temperature.
- Use walnuts to decorate cake; serve.

145. Frozen Almond Cappuccino Dacquoise

Serving: | Prep: | Cook: |Ready in:

Ingredients

- 1 cup shelled natural almonds (about 5 ounces), toasted lightly and cooled
- 1 1/4 cups sugar
- 2 1/2 teaspoons cornstarch
- 5 large egg whites
- 1/4 teaspoon cream of tartar
- 1/4 teaspoon salt
- 4 1/2 cups well-chilled heavy cream
- 1/3 cup instant espresso powder
- 6 tablespoons sugar
- 2 tablespoons Kahlúa or other coffee-flavored liqueur
- 1/2 pint raspberries

Direction

- Preheat an oven to 250°F. Line parchment paper/foil on 2 buttered baking sheets; trace 3 13x4-in. rectangles on paper/foil, 1 on 1 sheet then 2 on other.
- Meringue layers: Grind 1/2 cup sugar, cornstarch and almonds fine in a food processor. Use an electric mixer to beat salt, cream of tartar and egg whites till it holds soft peaks in a big bowl; in a slow stream, beat in leftover 3/4 cup sugar till meringue holds glossy, stiff peaks. Thoroughly yet gently fold in almond mixture; put in pastry bag with 1/2-in. plain tip. Pipe meringue on prepped foil, filling in rectangles, beginning on inside edge of rectangle.
- Bake meringue layers in lower and upper thirds of oven for 1-1 1/4 hours till meringues are dry when touched and firm, switching sheets positions in oven halfway through the baking. Cool meringues on the sheets on the racks. Slide foil off the sheets; peel meringues off foil carefully. You can make meringue layers 1 day ahead, kept in room temperature, tightly wrapped.

- Cut cardboard piece 2-in. larger than meringue layers; wrap in foil.
- Filling: Use an electric mixer to beat filling ingredients till it holds stiff peaks in a big bowl.
- Assembling cake: Place 1 meringue layer on cardboard, smooth side down; spread 1/2-in. thick filling layer over with long, metal spatula. Repeat layers with some filling and another meringue the same way; put leftover meringue layer with smooth side up, on filling. Spread thin filling layer on sides and top of dacquoise; put leftover filling in a pastry bag with star tip. Decoratively pipe leftover filling around dacquoise; put raspberries onto dacquoise. Freeze the dacquoise for 6 hours till hard, uncovered. You can make dacquoise 2 days ahead, frozen then wrapped in plastic wrap then foil after about 6 hours.
- Stand dacquoise before serving for 30 minutes in the fridge. Slice dacquoise using an electric knife/serrated knife.

Nutrition Information

- Calories: 305
- Cholesterol: 73 mg(24%)
- Protein: 4 g(7%)
- Total Fat: 23 g(36%)
- Saturated Fat: 13 g(63%)
- Sodium: 64 mg(3%)
- Fiber: 1 g(6%)
- Total Carbohydrate: 21 g(7%)

146. Frozen Lemon Cream Meringue Cake

Serving: | Prep: | Cook: | Ready in:

Ingredients

- 4 large egg whites at room temperature
- 1 cup sugar
- 1 stick (1/2 cup) unsalted butter
- 3/4 cup sugar
- 1/2 teaspoon cornstarch
- 1/2 cup fresh lemon juice (about 2 lemons)
- 1 tablespoon freshly grated lemon zest
- 1 whole large egg plus 6 large egg yolks
- 1 cup plain yogurt
- 1 1/2 teaspoons unflavored gelatin
- 3 tablespoons orange-flavored liqueur
- 1 1/2 cups heavy cream
- lemon slices and unsprayed lemon leaves for garnish

Direction

- For the meringue layers: Line foil or parchment paper on a buttered baking sheet then use the bottom and the top of a 9-in.-square pan as a guide to trace 2 squares on it; there will be one slightly larger square. Beat a pinch of salt and the whites by an electric mixer in a large bowl till soft peaks form. Beat in 1 tbsp. of sugar at a time till the whites hold stiff, glossy peaks. Place the meringue into a pastry bag with a 1/2-in. tip fitted. Pipe to fill the squares and smooth the tops. Bake the meringues for 1 hour in the center of an oven that has been preheated to 275°F till very pale golden in color and firm when slightly touched. Take the meringues with parchment out of the baking sheets. Cool then carefully peel off the parchment. Trim the meringue layers using a serrated knife to fit the smaller square inside the pan's bottom and fit the larger one inside the pan's top. Save the trimmings.
- Use vegetable oil to oil the pan and line plastic wrap on it, let about 5-in. overhang all around. On the lined pan, place the smaller layer of meringue with the smooth side facing down. Crumble the reserved meringue trimmings then stir in the lemon cream. Transfer the filling into the pan and smooth it then place the leftover layer of meringue on top with the smooth side facing up, gently press. Enclose the cake by folding the plastic-wrap overhang

over the top. Wrap the cake well and store in the freezer overnight till frozen solid.
- For the icing: Sprinkle over the orange-flavored liqueur with gelatin in a small saucepan and allow to soften for 1 minute. Heat and stir the mixture to dissolve the gelatin over low heat. Beat cream in a bowl till stiff peaks form then beat in the gelatin mixture in a stream till the icing holds stiff peaks.
- Unwrap and unmold the cake onto a serving plate, remove the plastic wrap. Spread over the sides and top of the cake with a thin icing layer. Place the leftover icing into a pastry bag with a decorative tip fitted (like basketwork one) then pipe over the cake. Let the cake chill for no longer than 1 1/2 hours. Place leaves and slices of lemon to decorate and use a serrated knife to slice into squares.
- For the lemon cream: Melt the butter with lemon juice, cornstarch and sugar in a heavy saucepan over moderately low heat; stir to dissolve the sugar. Lightly whisk the yolks and the whole egg together in a bowl then add the butter mixture in a stream whisking. Place the mixture onto the pan and cook while constantly whisking for 3-5 minutes over moderately low heat till the surface appears the first bubble and the curd is thickened enough to form the mark from the whisk. Immediately place the curd into a bowl and use plastic wrap to cover its surface and allow to cool. Cover the curd with plastic wrap and let chill till cold, for 1 hour. Add the yogurt into the curd and whisk, let the lemon cream chill and serve it as a filling for the frozen lemon cream meringue cake or serve with berries. Make about 3 cups.

Nutrition Information

- Calories: 265
- Total Carbohydrate: 26 g(9%)
- Cholesterol: 129 mg(43%)
- Protein: 4 g(7%)
- Total Fat: 17 g(25%)
- Saturated Fat: 10 g(49%)
- Sodium: 39 mg(2%)
- Fiber: 0 g(0%)

147. Frozen Meyer Lemon Cream With Blackberry Sauce

Serving: Makes 6 servings | Prep: | Cook: | Ready in:

Ingredients

- 1/2 cup plus 2 tablespoons sugar
- 5 tablespoons plus 1 1/2 teaspoons strained fresh Meyer lemon juice
- 3 large egg yolks
- 1 tablespoon light corn syrup
- 1 cup chilled heavy whipping cream
- 1 3/4 teaspoons finely grated Meyer lemon peel, divided
- 1 cup frozen unsweetened blackberries, thawed

Direction

- Whisk corn syrup, egg yolks, 5 tbsp. lemon juice and 1/2 cup sugar to blend in small metal bowl; put bowl above saucepan with boiling water. Whisk for 3 minutes till fluffy, thick and inserted thermometer in mixture reads 180°F. Put bowl with yolk mixture above bigger bowl filled with water and ice; cool mixture for 8 minutes, occasionally mixing.
- Meanwhile, beat 1 tbsp. sugar, 1 1/2 tsp. lemon peel and cream using electric mixer till stiff peaks form in medium bowl; fold cooled yolk mixture in 3 additions into cream. Cover; freeze for 4 hours till firm.
- Mix 1/4 tsp. lemon peel, 1 1/2 tsp. lemon juice, leftover 1 tbsp. sugar, berries and accumulated juices in small bowl; allow to stand for 10 minutes. Mash 1/2 berries coarsely to thicken juices in bowl. Into small bowls, scoop lemon cream; put 1 rounded tbsp. berry sauce on each top. Serve.

Nutrition Information

- Calories: 269
- Cholesterol: 147 mg(49%)
- Protein: 3 g(5%)
- Total Fat: 17 g(26%)
- Saturated Fat: 10 g(50%)
- Sodium: 22 mg(1%)
- Fiber: 1 g(5%)
- Total Carbohydrate: 28 g(9%)

148. Frozen White Chocolate And Raspberry Mousse Torte

Serving: Makes 12 servings | Prep: | Cook: | Ready in:

Ingredients

- 1 (9-ounce) box chocolate wafer cookies, broken into pieces
- 1/2 cup (1 stick) unsalted butter, melted
- 1/3 cup Chambord (black raspberry-flavored liqueur) or crème de cassis (black currant-flavored liqueur)
- 1 1/2 teaspoons unflavored gelatin
- 2 (12-ounce) packages frozen unsweetened raspberries, thawed, drained, juices reserved
- 1/2 cup sugar
- 12 ounces good-quality white chocolate (such as Lindt or Baker's finely chopped
- 2 cups chilled whipping cream
- 3/4 cup powdered sugar
- 1 teaspoon vanilla extract
- 1 1/2-pint basket raspberries
- Chocolate Leaves

Direction

- Crust: use processor to grind pieces of cookie finely. Put in the butter; process to moisten crumbs. Force the mixture on base and midway up the sides of springform pan, 9-inch across with 2 3/4-inches high sides. Put in freezer while prepping the mousse.
- Mousse: put liqueur in a medium, heavy saucepan. Scatter top of liqueur with gelatin; rest for 20 minutes to soften gelatin.
- Firmly force raspberries through sieve right in a big measuring cup. Put sufficient reserved juices in cup with puree to reach 1 2/3 cups mixture of berry. To gelatin mixture, put half cup of sugar and berry mixture. Mix on moderately-low heat for 3 minutes to barely dissolve gelatin and sugar. Take off from heat. Put in the white chocolate; mix to melt. Turn the mixture of raspberry into a big bowl. Refrigerate for 2 hours till thick yet not set, mixing frequently.
- In a bowl, whip powdered sugar, vanilla and cream to form firm peaks. Fold to raspberry mixture the cream in 3 increments. Turn the mousse into crust; even the top. Freeze for not less than 6 hours to firm. May be done 4 days in advance. Freeze with cover.
- Slice on pan sides; remove pan sides. Put the torte onto a platter. Place raspberries around torte top edge. Jazz up using Chocolate Leaves.

Nutrition Information

- Calories: 568
- Total Carbohydrate: 64 g(21%)
- Cholesterol: 71 mg(24%)
- Protein: 5 g(11%)
- Total Fat: 33 g(50%)
- Saturated Fat: 19 g(95%)
- Sodium: 166 mg(7%)
- Fiber: 7 g(28%)

149. Fudgy Chocolate Chunk Brownies With Walnuts

Serving: Makes about 15 | Prep: | Cook: | Ready in:

Ingredients

- 1 cup (2 sticks) unsalted butter

- 8 ounces bittersweet (not unsweetened) or semisweet chocolate, chopped
- 3 ounces unsweetened chocolate, chopped
- 1/2 cup all purpose flour
- 1 1/2 teaspoons baking powder
- 1/2 teaspoon salt
- 1 cup plus 2 tablespoons sugar
- 3 large eggs
- 3 1/4 teaspoons instant espresso powder or instant coffee powder
- 1 tablespoon vanilla extract
- 1 1/4 cups chopped toasted walnuts
- 6 ounces bittersweet (not unsweetened) or semisweet chocolate, coarsely chopped

Direction

- Preheat an oven to 350°F. Butter the 13x9x2-in. glass baking dish. In heavy medium saucepan, melt the first 3 ingredients on low heat, mixing till smooth; take away from the heat. Cool for 10 minutes.
- Sift salt, baking powder and flour into medium bowl. Beat vanilla, espresso powder, eggs and sugar using electric mixer till blended in big bowl. Add melted chocolate mixture; beat till smooth. Add dry ingredients; mix till just blended. Fold in 6-oz. coarsely chopped chocolate and walnuts.
- Put batter in prepped pan; smooth top. Bake for 30 minutes till inserted tester in middle exits with moist crumbs attached and the top looks dry. Put pan on rack; completely cool. (You can make it 1 day ahead; use foil to cover. Keep at room temperature.) Slice brownies to squares; serve.

Nutrition Information

- Calories: 427
- Saturated Fat: 15 g(76%)
- Sodium: 135 mg(6%)
- Fiber: 3 g(13%)
- Total Carbohydrate: 39 g(13%)
- Cholesterol: 70 mg(23%)
- Protein: 5 g(11%)
- Total Fat: 31 g(47%)

150. Fudgy Meringue Cookies

Serving: Makes about 16 | Prep: 30mins | Cook: 2hours | Ready in:

Ingredients

- Nonstick vegetable oil spray
- 1 cup bittersweet chocolate chips (do not exceed 61% cacao; about 6 ounces), divided
- 1 1/2 cups powdered sugar, divided
- 1/3 cup unsweetened cocoa powder
- 2 teaspoons cornstarch
- 2 large egg whites, room temperature
- 1/2 teaspoon vanilla extract
- 1/8 teaspoon cream of tartar

Direction

- Put 1 rack into bottom third and top third of oven; preheat it to 350°F. Use nonstick spray to coat 2 big rimmed baking sheets. Cook 1/2 cup chocolate chips in 15-sec intervals till chocolate softens in small microwave-safe bowl; mix till smooth and melted. Cool chocolate for 10 minutes to lukewarm. Whisk cornstarch, cocoa and 1/2 cup sugar to blend in small bowl.
- Beat cream of tartar, 1/8 tsp. salt, vanilla and room-temperature egg whites using electric mixture till soft peaks form in medium bowl. In 4 additions, add leftover 1 cup sugar, beating after each addition to just blend; beat for 2 minutes till meringue is glossy like marshmallow crème and thick. Beat in cocoa mixture then fold in melted chocolate; fold in 1/2 cup of chips.
- By rounded tablespoonfuls, drop batter on prepped sheets, 3-in. apart; bake cookies for 7 minutes. Reverse sheets; bake for 6 minutes till cracked and looks dry. Cook cookies for 5 minutes on sheets. Put cookies on racks; fully cool.

Nutrition Information

- Calories: 107
- Protein: 1 g(3%)
- Total Fat: 4 g(6%)
- Saturated Fat: 2 g(10%)
- Sodium: 9 mg(0%)
- Fiber: 1 g(5%)
- Total Carbohydrate: 20 g(7%)

151. German Lebkuchen Cake With White Chocolate Frosting

Serving: Makes 12 servings | Prep: | Cook: |Ready in:

Ingredients

- 2 to 3 large oranges
- 1/2 cup honey
- 2/3 cup orange juice
- 3/4 cup (1 1/2 sticks) unsalted butter, room temperature
- 3/4 cup firmly packed golden brown sugar
- 1 tablespoon vanilla extract
- 1 1/4 teaspoons ground cinnamon
- 3/4 teaspoon ground cloves
- 3/4 teaspoon ground nutmeg
- 3/4 teaspoon ground allspice
- 1/2 teaspoon salt
- 2 large eggs, room temperature
- 1 3/4 cups all purpose flour
- 1 1/2 teaspoons baking soda
- 3/4 teaspoon baking powder
- 2/3 cup half and half
- 1 tablespoon lemon juice
- 2/3 cup dried currants
- 12 ounces imported white chocolate (such as Lindt), chopped
- 1 cup (2 sticks) unsalted butter, room temperature
- 12 ounces cream cheese, room temperature
- 3 cups toasted sliced almonds
- Orange slices or orange peel ribbon

Direction

- Syrup: Remove peel from oranges, orange part only, in strips using vegetable peeler. Mince peel to get 3 tbsp. Mix 2 tbsp. orange peel, (keep leftover 2 tbsp. peel for cake) orange juice and honey in medium heavy saucepan; boil for 10 minutes till reduced to 3/4 cup. Put aside honey syrup.
- Cake: Preheat an oven to 350°F. Butter the 9-in. square baking pan that has 2-in. high sides; line waxed paper on bottom. Butter pan; use flour to dust pan. Beat initial 8 ingredients using electric mixer till fluffy in big bowl; stir in reserved 2 tbsp. minced orange peel. One by one, add eggs; beat well after each. Sift baking powder, baking soda and flour into medium bowl. Stir lemon juice and half and half in small bowl. Alternately with the half and half mixture, beat dry ingredients into butter mixture, starting then ending with the dry ingredients; stir in currants. Put batter in prepped pan; bake for 50 minutes till inserted toothpick in middle exits clean. Cake won't rise to pan's top. Cool cake for 20 minutes. Around pan sides, run small sharp knife to loosen/ turn out cake onto rack; cool. Peel paper off. You can make it 1 day ahead; separately cover cake and syrup. Stand in room temperature.
- Frosting: Melt chocolate on top of double boiler above simmering water, occasionally mixing till smooth; cool it to barely lukewarm. Beat cream cheese and butter till light using electric mixer. Add 1/4 cup honey syrup and chocolate; beat till light and smooth. Chill for 20 minutes till thick enough to spread, occasionally mixing.
- Horizontally halve cake; put bottom layer on platter, cut side up. Brush 1/4 cup honey then spread 1 1/4 cups of frosting. Brush leftover 1/4 cup syrup on top cake layer's cut side; put cake on filled layer, cut side down. Put 2/3 cup frosting aside for garnish. Spread leftover frosting on sides and top of cake; around sides,

press almonds. Put leftover 2/3 cup frosting in pastry bag with small star tip; decoratively pipe frosting around cake's top edge. Chill cake for 1 hour till frosting sets. Use orange slices to garnish. You can make it 1 day ahead; cover. Chill. Stand before serving for 2 hours in room temperature.

Nutrition Information

- Calories: 937
- Sodium: 433 mg(18%)
- Fiber: 7 g(27%)
- Total Carbohydrate: 78 g(26%)
- Cholesterol: 144 mg(48%)
- Protein: 15 g(31%)
- Total Fat: 66 g(102%)
- Saturated Fat: 31 g(153%)

152. Gilded Sesame Cookies

Serving: Makes about 2 1/2 dozen cookies | Prep: 30mins | Cook: 1.75hours | Ready in:

Ingredients

- 1 1/4 cups all-purpose flour
- 1/2 teaspoon baking powder
- 1/4 teaspoon salt
- 1 stick (1/2 cup) unsalted butter, softened
- 1/2 cup sugar
- 1/2 cup well-stirred tahini
- 1 teaspoon pure vanilla extract
- 1/3 cup sesame seeds (preferably hulled)
- 1/4 teaspoon gold or silver luster dust (optional)
- parchment paper

Direction

- Whisk salt, baking powder and flour in a small bowl.
- Beat sugar and butter using an electric mixer on medium high speed for 3 minutes till fluffy and pale in a big bowl; beat in vanilla and tahini. Lower speed to low; in 2 batches, add flour mixture, mixing till crumbly dough forms. Put dough on plastic wrap sheet; press to disk. Chill dough for a minimum of 1 hour till firm, wrapped in plastic wrap.
- Put the oven racks into lower and upper thirds of oven; preheat an oven to 350°F. Line parchment paper on 2 big baking sheets.
- Mix luster dust (optional) and sesame seeds in small bowl.
- Roll dough to 1-in. balls; one by one, roll balls in seeds to coat. Put on lined baking sheets, 2-in. apart. Bake for 12-15 minutes till cookies start to crack and are puffed, switching sheets positions halfway through baking. Cool for 10 minutes on sheets; cookies are fragile when hot. Transfer from parchment onto rack; fully cool.
- It's best to get hulled sesame seeds for this recipe. They're delicate and pale ivory in color.
- You can chill dough for maximum of 1 day.
- Cookies keep for 5 days in room temperature in airtight container. Luster dust in nontoxic, but it's best to use it only for decorative purposes. Use coloring that is extremely safe.

153. Ginger Cake

Serving: Makes 1 large loaf cake or 3 mini-loaves | Prep: 20mins | Cook: 3hours | Ready in:

Ingredients

- 10 oz stem ginger in syrup*, drained, reserving 1/4 cup syrup, and coarsely chopped (1 cup); or see cooks' note, below
- 1 1/2 cups all-purpose flour
- 2 sticks (1 cup) unsalted butter, softened
- 1/4 teaspoon salt
- 2/3 cup packed dark brown sugar
- 4 large eggs, separated
- 1 (8 1/2- by 4 1/2- by 2 1/2-inch) loaf pan, or see cooks' note, below

Direction

- In center place, set the oven rack and preheat the oven to 325°F.
- Butter and flour the loaf pan, tapping out extra flour.
- In a food processor, pulse the 1/2 cup flour and ginger till ginger is nicely chopped.
- In a big bowl with electric mixer, beat the salt and butter till creamy. Put the brown sugar, a bit at a time, and whisk till fluffy and light. Put the yolks, 1 by 1, whisking thoroughly after every addition. Whisk in saved ginger syrup, then mix in the chopped ginger mixture.
- In a separate bowl with cleaned beaters, mix a pinch of salt and whites till they barely hold stiff peaks.
- Into batter, fold a quarter of whites carefully yet thoroughly, then into batter, sift a quarter of leftover cup flour and fold softly yet well. Put the leftover egg whites alternating with flour in 3 batches, folding in exactly the same manner.
- Into the loaf pan, scoop the batter, scattering evenly. Let bake for 1 1/4 to 1 1/2 hours till a wooden skewer or pick pricked in middle of cake comes out clean. Allow to cool on a rack for 10 minutes, then trace a thin knife around the edge of the pan and invert the cake onto rack to cool fully for an hour.

Nutrition Information

- Calories: 1152
- Total Fat: 69 g(107%)
- Saturated Fat: 41 g(207%)
- Sodium: 372 mg(16%)
- Fiber: 4 g(16%)
- Total Carbohydrate: 118 g(39%)
- Cholesterol: 411 mg(137%)
- Protein: 18 g(37%)

154. Ginger Cream

Serving: 32 | Prep: | Cook: 10mins | Ready in:

Ingredients

- 1½ cups low-fat vanilla yogurt
- ½ cup whipping cream
- ¼ cup candied ginger, finely chopped

Direction

- Line cheesecloth on sieve; put above a bowl, with minimum of 1/2-in. clearance from bottom. Add yogurt; cover. Drain for 1 1/2 hours in the fridge.
- Discard whey. Whip cream using chilled beaters to soft peaks in chilled bowl. To one side, push cream; add drained yogurt. Use a rubber spatula to fold in; fold in candied ginger.

Nutrition Information

- Calories: 24 calories;
- Fiber: 0
- Total Carbohydrate: 3
- Protein: 1
- Total Fat: 1
- Saturated Fat: 1
- Cholesterol: 5
- Sugar: 2
- Sodium: 9

155. Ginger Honey Cookies

Serving: Makes 14 cookies | Prep: 15mins | Cook: 45mins | Ready in:

Ingredients

- 1 1/4 cups all-purpose flour
- 1 teaspoon baking soda
- 1/4 cup finely chopped crystallized ginger
- 1/4 teaspoon salt

- 1 stick unsalted butter, softened
- 1/2 cup packed light brown sugar
- 1 large egg
- 1/4 cup mild honey

Direction

- Preheat an oven with racks in lower and upper thirds to 350°F.
- Whisk salt, ginger, baking soda and flour in a bowl.
- Beat brown sugar and butter using an electric mixer on medium high speed till fluffy and pale in big bowl; beat in honey and egg till combined. Lower speed to low; stir in flour mixture.
- Drop 14 heaping dough tablespoons on 2 ungreased baking sheets, 2-in. apart.
- Bake for 10-14 minutes total till golden, switching sheets position halfway through baking; cookies will spread out flat. Fully cool on sheets on rack.
- Cookies keep for 3 days in room temperature in an airtight container.

Nutrition Information

- Calories: 165
- Fiber: 0 g(2%)
- Total Carbohydrate: 25 g(8%)
- Cholesterol: 31 mg(10%)
- Protein: 2 g(3%)
- Total Fat: 7 g(11%)
- Saturated Fat: 4 g(21%)
- Sodium: 102 mg(4%)

156. Ginger Whipped Cream

Serving: Makes about 2 cups | Prep: 5mins | Cook: 5mins | Ready in:

Ingredients

- 1 cup chilled whipping cream
- 1 1/2 tablespoons sugar
- 1 teaspoon vanilla extract
- 2 tablespoons chopped crystallized ginger

Direction

- Beat vanilla extract, sugar and chilled whipping cream to soft peaks in bowl; mix in chopped crystallized ginger then cover. Chill for 6 hours.

Nutrition Information

- Calories: 220
- Saturated Fat: 12 g(58%)
- Sodium: 28 mg(1%)
- Fiber: 0 g(0%)
- Total Carbohydrate: 13 g(4%)
- Cholesterol: 66 mg(22%)
- Protein: 1 g(3%)
- Total Fat: 18 g(28%)

157. Gingerbread Bars

Serving: Makes 24 | Prep: | Cook: | Ready in:

Ingredients

- 2 cups all purpose flour
- 2 teaspoons ground ginger
- 1 teaspoon ground cinnamon
- 1/4 teaspoon ground nutmeg
- 1/4 teaspoon ground cloves
- 1/2 teaspoon baking soda
- 1/2 teaspoon salt
- 10 tablespoons (1 1/4 sticks) unsalted butter, room temperature
- 3/4 cup (packed) dark brown sugar
- 7 1/2 tablespoons sugar, divided
- 2 large eggs
- 1/4 cup light (unsulfured) molasses

Direction

- Preheat an oven to 350°F. Butter and flour a baking sheet, 15x10x1-inch in size. In a medium bowl, put 2 cups of flour; to a small bowl, put the 2 tablespoons flour and set aside. To flour in medium bowl, put salt, baking soda and spices; beat to combine. In a big bowl, mix 6 tablespoons sugar, brown sugar and butter with electric mixer till fluffy. Mix in the eggs, one by one, then the molasses. To butter mixture, put the dry ingredients and mix to incorporate. In prepped pan, scatter the batter evenly. On top of the batter, sift the reserved 2 tablespoons flour equally, then scatter leftover 1 1/2 tablespoons sugar equally.
- Let the gingerbread bake for 22 minutes till golden brown and tester pricked into middle comes out clean; cool fully in pan on the rack. Slice gingerbread crosswise making 4 strips, then slice every strip into 6 portions, creating 2 dozen bars, each approximately 31/2x13/4 inches. Can be prepared 2 days in advance. Keep airtight at room temperature.

Nutrition Information

- Calories: 139
- Protein: 2 g(3%)
- Total Fat: 5 g(8%)
- Saturated Fat: 3 g(16%)
- Sodium: 82 mg(3%)
- Fiber: 0 g(1%)
- Total Carbohydrate: 22 g(7%)
- Cholesterol: 28 mg(9%)

158. Gingerbread Christmas Pudding With Orange Hard Sauce

Serving: Makes 8 to 10 servings | Prep: | Cook: | Ready in:

Ingredients

- 1 1/2 cups powdered sugar
- 1/2 cup (1 stick) unsalted butter, room temperature
- 2 tablespoons brandy
- 1 teaspoon grated orange peel
- Nonstick vegetable oil spray
- 11/4 cups all purpose flour
- 1 tablespoon ground ginger
- 2 teaspoons ground cinnamon
- 1 teaspoon baking powder
- 1/2 teaspoon salt
- 1/2 teaspoon baking soda
- 1/4 teaspoon ground cloves
- 3/4 cup sugar
- 6 tablespoons (3/4 stick) unsalted butter, room temperature
- 3 large eggs
- 1/2 cup orange marmalade
- 1/4 cup mild-flavored (light) molasses
- 1 teaspoon grated orange peel

Direction

- Sauce: Mix all ingredients to blend well in small bowl; you can make it 4 days ahead, refrigerated, covered. Before serving, bring to room temperature.
- Pudding: Use nonstick spray to coat center tube and inside of 6-8-cup pudding mold/Bundt cake pan; butter generously. Sift flour and following 6 ingredients in medium bowl. Use electric mixer to beat butter and sugar till well blended in big bowl; one by one, beat eggs in then orange peel, molasses and marmalade. Add flour mixture; beat till just blended. Put batter in prepped mold; tightly cover mold with foil.
- Put steamer rack in big pot; put pudding mold onto rack. Put enough water in pot to reach halfway up mold's sides. Boil water; lower heat to medium. Cover the pot; steam pudding for 1 hour 15 minutes till inserted tester near middle exits clean; to maintain level, add extra boiling water if needed. Remove mold from pot with oven mitts; uncover. Stand for 10 minutes. To loosen, cut around sides and top center of pudding. Turn pudding onto rack;

cool for 20 minutes. You can make it 1 day ahead, fully cooled. Return to mold and cover; chill. Steam to heat through for 45 minutes; turn out of mold. Put pudding on platter. Slice pudding to wedges and serve with sauce.

Nutrition Information

- Calories: 633
- Protein: 7 g(14%)
- Total Fat: 25 g(38%)
- Saturated Fat: 14 g(68%)
- Sodium: 316 mg(13%)
- Fiber: 2 g(7%)
- Total Carbohydrate: 97 g(32%)
- Cholesterol: 123 mg(41%)

159. Gingerbread Puddings With Candied Apples

Serving: Makes 8 servings | Prep: | Cook: | Ready in:

Ingredients

- 8 cups unsweetened apple cider or apple juice
- 1 1/2 pounds Granny Smith apples, peeled, cored, cut into 1/3-inch cubes (about 4 1/2 cups)
- 3/4 cup (packed) golden brown sugar
- 1 3/4 cups all purpose flour
- 1 tablespoon ground ginger
- 1 teaspoon baking soda
- 1 teaspoon ground cinnamon
- 1/4 teaspoon salt
- 1/4 teaspoon ground cloves
- 1/4 teaspoon finely ground black pepper
- 1/2 cup (1 stick) unsalted butter, room temperature
- 3/4 cup (packed) golden brown sugar
- 1 large egg
- 3/4 cup mild-flavored (light) molasses
- 1/2 cup boiling water
- 3 cups whole milk
- 2 4-inch-long pieces fresh ginger (about 4 ounces), peeled, thickly sliced
- 1 tablespoon whole black peppercorns
- 4 large eggs
- 3/4 cup sugar
- 1 teaspoon vanilla extract
- 1 teaspoon ground ginger
- Pinch of salt
- Ice cream or crème fraîche*
- *Available at some supermarkets and at specialty foods stores.

Direction

- Candied apple garnish: Boil all ingredients in big pot on high heat, mixing till sugar is dissolved. Lower heat to medium; simmer for 2 hours till cider thickly coats apples and apples are translucent and soft, mixing occasionally. Put into bowl; cool. You can make it 1 week ahead; cover. Chill. Before serving, bring to room temperature.
- Gingerbread: Preheat an oven to 350°F. Butter the 9x9x2-in. metal baking pan. Whisk initial 7 ingredients to blend in medium bowl. Beat butter using electric mixer till fluffy in big bowl. Add egg and brown sugar; beat till blended. Beat in the molasses; beat in flour mixture. Mix in 1/2 cup of boiling water using rubber spatula; put batter in prepped pan.
- Bake gingerbread for 40 minutes till inserted tester in middle exits clean; put pan on rack. Fully cool gingerbread in pan. You can make it 1 day ahead. Use foil to cover pan; stand in room temperature.
- Puddings: Preheat an oven to 325°F. Simmer peppercorns, fresh ginger and milk in medium heavy saucepan; take off heat. Whisk salt, ground ginger, vanilla, sugar and eggs to blend in medium bowl; whisk hot milk mixture slowly into egg mixture. Into medium bowl, strain custard; discard strainer solids.
- Slice enough gingerbread to 1/2-in. cubes to get 5 1/3 cups; keep leftover gingerbread for another time. Divide the gingerbread cubes to 8 ramekins/3/4-cup custard cups. In each cup, put custard on gingerbread, evenly dividing.

Stand so gingerbread absorbs some custard for 15 minutes.
- In roasting pan, put cups; to reach halfway up cup's sides, put hot water in pan. Use foil to cover pan; bake puddings for 1 hour till set. Take out of water bath.
- Serve puddings in room temperature/warm, topped with ice cream and candied apple garnish.

Nutrition Information

- Calories: 805
- Total Fat: 18 g(28%)
- Saturated Fat: 10 g(51%)
- Sodium: 389 mg(16%)
- Fiber: 4 g(18%)
- Total Carbohydrate: 152 g(51%)
- Cholesterol: 156 mg(52%)
- Protein: 11 g(22%)

160. Gingered Peach Pavlovas

Serving: Makes 6 | Prep: | Cook: | Ready in:

Ingredients

- 1/2 cup sugar, divided
- 2 teaspoons cornstarch
- 2 large egg whites, room temperature
- 1/8 teaspoon cream of tartar
- 1/4 teaspoon vanilla extract
- 2 cups water
- 1 1/4 cups sugar
- 3 tablespoons fresh lemon juice
- 1 2-inch piece fresh ginger, peeled, thinly sliced
- 3 firm but ripe large peaches, peeled, halved, pitted
- 1/2 cup (generous) fresh raspberries (about half of 6-ounce basket)
- 1/2 cup (generous) fresh blackberries (about half of 6-ounce basket)
- 1/2 cup chilled heavy whipping cream
- 1 1/2 tablespoons sugar

Direction

- Meringues: Put rack in middle of oven; preheat it to 250°F. Line parchment paper on baking sheet. Whisk cornstarch and 1 1/2 tbsp. sugar to blend in small bowl; put aside.
- Beat cream of tartar and egg whites using electric mixer till soft peaks form in big bowl; beat in vanilla. 1 tbsp. at a time, beat in leftover 6 1/2 tbsp. sugar slowly; beat till stiff peaks form. Above meringue, sift cornstarch mixture; fold in gently till just incorporated with a rubber spatula.
- In 6 mounds, 1/4 cup each, put meringue on prepped baking sheet, spacing apart. Create indentation in middle of every mound using back of spoon, making each meringue to 3-in. diameter nest. Bake the meringues for 55 minutes till barely golden and crisp outside yet soft inside. Put meringues on rack using metal spatula; fully cool. You can make it 1 day ahead; keep in airtight container in 1 layer in room temperature.
- Peaches: Boil sliced ginger, fresh lemon juice, 1 1/4 cups sugar and 2 cups water in a big saucepan, mixing till sugar is dissolved. Lower heat to medium; simmer for 5 minutes. Put peeled peach halves in syrup in saucepan; take off heat. Cool peaches in syrup to room temperature, occasionally turning. Put peaches with syrup in medium bowl; cover. Chill till cold. You can make peaches 1 day ahead, kept refrigerated.
- Take peaches from syrup; cut each half to 6 wedges. Put syrup aside.
- Berries and topping: In small bowl, put all berries; add 4 tbsp. peach syrup. Toss till coated.
- Beat 1 1/2 tbsp. sugar and cream using electric mixer till soft peaks form in medium bowl.
- On each of the 6 plates, put 1 meringue; put whipped cream in middle of each meringue. Put berry mixture and 6 peach wedges on top of each.

Nutrition Information

- Calories: 446
- Saturated Fat: 9 g(47%)
- Sodium: 36 mg(2%)
- Fiber: 3 g(11%)
- Total Carbohydrate: 76 g(25%)
- Cholesterol: 60 mg(20%)
- Protein: 4 g(8%)
- Total Fat: 16 g(25%)

161. Glazed Chocolate Cake With Sprinkles

Serving: Makes1 (9-inch) cake | Prep: 25mins | Cook: 2.25hours | Ready in:

Ingredients

- 1 cup all-purpose flour
- 1/3 cup unsweetened Dutch-process cocoa powder
- 1 teaspoon baking soda
- 1/2 teaspoon baking powder
- 1/4 teaspoon salt
- 1 stick unsalted butter, softened
- 1 cup packed light brown sugar
- 2 large eggs at room temperature 30 minutes
- 1 teaspoon pure vanilla extract
- 1 cup whole milk
- 1/4 cup heavy cream
- 3 1/2 oz bittersweet chocolate (not more than 60% cacao if marked), finely chopped
- 2 teaspoons light corn syrup
- Colorful confectionary sprinkles and/or nonpareils
- a 9- by 2-inch round cake pan

Direction

- How to make cake: turn the oven to 350 degrees F and place the rack in the middle section. Grease the bottom and sides of the pan and line with a piece or round parchment paper.
- Sift together baking powder, cocoa powder, baking soda, salt and flour in a mixing bowl.
- Use a hand mixer to whisk brown sugar and butter in a big mixing bowl on medium-high power until fluffy and light, about 3-5 minutes. Put in the eggs one at a time, beat well after every addition. Add in vanilla. Lower speed to medium-low and put the milk and flour mixture alternately by batch in, start and end with flour mixture (batter will look curdled).
- Put the batter in cake pan and smoothen the top. Bake until the sides start to pull away from the pan and a toothpick test comes out clean, about 35-40 minutes. Let it cool for 5 minutes in the pan, and then put the cake upside down on a rack and let it cool thoroughly, for about an hour.
- How to make glaze: simmer cream in a small saucepan on medium heat. Pour chocolate in a mixing bowl and put cream on top, let it sit for a minute. Gradually beat until smooth, and add in corn syrup. Cool thoroughly while gently stirring from time to time, half an hour (glaze will become thick).
- Slowly remove the parchment paper from the cake. Put the glaze in the middle of the cake and use a spatula to spread the glaze to the edges. Top with nonpareils and/or sprinkles.
- Note from the chef: Cake can be made 2 days beforehand and stored at room temperature (glaze will not remain shiny).

Nutrition Information

- Calories: 3563
- Total Fat: 178 g(274%)
- Saturated Fat: 102 g(510%)
- Sodium: 2802 mg(117%)
- Fiber: 55 g(219%)
- Total Carbohydrate: 499 g(166%)
- Cholesterol: 781 mg(260%)
- Protein: 69 g(137%)

162. Glowing Jack O' Lantern Cookies

Serving: | Prep: | Cook: |Ready in:

Ingredients

- 1/3 cup hard candies
- 1/2 cup (1 stick) butter, at room temperature
- 1 cup sugar
- 1 egg
- 1 teaspoon lemon zest, optional
- 1 teaspoon lemon juice
- red and yellow liquid coloring or orange paste coloring
- 2 cups all-purpose flour
- 1 teaspoon baking powder
- 1/2 teaspoon salt

Direction

- Preheat an oven to 350°F. Line Silpat mat/foil/parchment (not wax paper since it will stick) on 2 baking sheets.
- If wrapped, unwrap candies; put into heavy ziplock bag. Crush with bottom of saucepan/flat side of meat tenderizer to crush them into powder.
- Beat sugar and butter till creamy in a big mixing bowl; blend in food coloring, lemon juice, lemon zest (if using) and egg. Start with 6 drops of red and 5 drops yellow liquid coloring/dab of orange paste; to get desired shade, add more. Mix well till combined fully.
- Add salt, baking powder and flour to bowl; stir well.
- Roll 1/2 of dough out on lightly floured surface; use a cookie cutter/freehand with a paring knife's tip to cut out 8 large jack-o'-lantern shapes; create short, fat pumpkins with 4-in. wide by 3-in. high or tall, thin pumpkins with 2-3-in. wide and 4-in. tall. Variety is good. Use a knife to cut out a mouth, nose and big eyes in each; don't create lots of teeth, they break off. Be aware that the mouth, nose and eyes should be wide enough to hold melted candy. Lift pumpkins with a spatula carefully; put onto prepped baking sheets. Push back mouth, nose and eye openings using a paring knife's tip so they're as wide as possible but not losing dough bridges between features. Repeat using leftover dough half.
- Generously sprinkle candy powder into mouth, nose and eyes openings directly to parchment using the small spoon's tip; try to keep candy off cookie's surface.
- Bake, carefully watching, for 8-10 minutes. Once candy melts, remove; don't let cookie's surface brown. They should be very pale and set.
- Cool cookies on baking sheets. Or, lift parchment off sheets carefully then put whole sheet on cooling racks, only if racks are large enough to hold sheet. Peel off parchment carefully when cookies are fully cool.

163. Golden Eggs

Serving: 12 eggs or about 12 muffin-sized cakes | Prep: | Cook: |Ready in:

Ingredients

- Nonstick baking spray
- 3 cups all-purpose flour
- 1 tablespoon baking powder
- 1 teaspoon salt
- 1 teaspoon nutmeg
- 1/2 pound (2 sticks) unsalted butter, at room temperature
- 2 cups sugar
- 5 large eggs, at room temperature
- 1 teaspoon vanilla extract
- 1 1/4 cups nonfat buttermilk
- 8 tablespoons (1 stick) unsalted butter, melted
- 1 cup sugar and 1 teaspoon cinnamon mixed together in a small shallow bowl

Direction

- Preheat an oven to 325°F. Spray nonstick spray on molds; you can use a muffin pan or any

other small baking molds. This recipe uses egg-shaped molds.
- Sift together nutmeg, salt, baking powder and flour; put aside.
- Whip together sugar and butter till fluffy and light in an electric mixer fitted with the whisk or paddle attachment.
- This may takes up to 10 minutes, varies on butter temperature.
- Stop then scrape down bowl sides to ensure incorporating all butter into sugar while whipping away.
- Keep scraping and whipping, it can take a while.
- One by one, add eggs, whipping after each egg till egg is incorporated into batter fully.
- Also scrape down bowl every now and again.
- Add vanilla.
- Alternate adding buttermilk and flour mixture, mixing slowly once all eggs are incorporated.
- When they are well incorporated but not overbeaten, fold batter several times with a rubber spatula to ensure that batter is smooth and everything is distributed evenly.
- Distribute batter into molds; fill every cavity a little less than half full.
- Bake for approximately 15 minutes; ensure to check if cake springs back when touched and look for a very light golden-brown color, baking times varies on mold's size.
- While warm, unmold these little cakes; dunk into melted butter quickly. Dredge in sugar and cinnamon.

164. Golden Onion Pie

Serving: Makes 8 (first course) servings | Prep: 30mins | Cook: 4.5hours | Ready in:

Ingredients

- 1 1/2 teaspoons active dry yeast
- 1/3 cup warm whole milk (105-115°F)
- 1/4 teaspoon sugar
- 2 cups all-purpose flour
- 1/2 teaspoon salt
- 1 large egg
- 1/2 stick unsalted butter, melted and cooled
- 3 1/2 pounds onions, thinly sliced
- 1/4 pounds bacon, finely chopped
- 1/2 stick unsalted butter
- 1 cup sour cream
- 2 large egg yolks
- Equipment: a 9-inch springform pan
- Accompaniment: green salad with mustard vinaigrette

Direction

- Dough: Mix sugar, milk and yeast by hand in a bowl/stand mixer's bowl with paddle attachment; stand for 5 minutes till foamy. Start again with new yeast if it doesn't foam.
- Add butter, egg, salt and flour; stir/mix on low speed till dough forms. Upper speed on medium high; knead by hand for 5 minutes/beat for 3 minutes.
- Lightly sprinkle flour on dough; use kitchen towel, that isn't terry cloth, to cover bowl. Rise for 1 1/2-2 hours till doubled in warm room temperature in draft-free place.
- As dough rises, make filling: Cook bacon, 1/2 tsp. pepper, 1 tsp. salt and onions in butter in 12-in. heavy skillet on medium high heat for 20 minutes till onions are soft, occasionally mixing, covered.
- Uncover; cook for 20-30 minutes till onions are golden, occasionally mixing; cool onions.
- Whisk yolks and sour cream; mix into onions.
- Bake pie: Preheat an oven with rack in center to 375°F.
- Roll dough to 12-in. round with lightly floured rolling pin on lightly floured surface; fit dough, slightly stretching if needed to hang on edge, into springform pan. Evenly spread filling in it. On filling, fold dough edges; leave some filling visible in middle. Stand pie for 20 minutes in room temperature.
- Bake for 1 1/4 hours till filling is bubbly and crust is golden brown; before serving, slightly cool.

- You can slowly rise dough for 8-12 hours in the fridge, in bowl covered in plastic wrap; before using, bring to room temperature.
- You can cook onion mixture 3 days ahead, chilled. Before adding yolks and sour cream, bring to room temperature.
- You can make pie 1 day ahead, chilled. Reheat for 30 minutes in 350°F oven, covered.

Nutrition Information

- Calories: 441
- Saturated Fat: 13 g(67%)
- Sodium: 278 mg(12%)
- Fiber: 4 g(18%)
- Total Carbohydrate: 45 g(15%)
- Cholesterol: 125 mg(42%)
- Protein: 10 g(20%)
- Total Fat: 25 g(39%)

165. Grapefruit Pie

Serving: Makes 6 to 8 servings | Prep: | Cook: | Ready in:

Ingredients

- 9 (2 1/4-inch by 4 3/4-inch) graham crackers
- 2 tablespoons sugar
- 5 tablespoons unsalted butter, melted
- 1/4 teaspoon salt
- 1 cup sugar
- 3 tablespoons cornstarch
- 1 (3-ounce) box strawberry-flavored Jell-O
- 2 large or 3 medium red grapefruits
- 3/4 cup chilled heavy cream
- 2 tablespoons sugar

Direction

- Prep crust: heat the oven to 350°F. Use butter to grease a pie plate, 9-inch in size.
- Grind graham crackers for a minute using food processor to crumbs. Put in butter, salt and sugar, and pulse machine for 2 to 3 minutes till mixture turns into fine crumbs. Force mixture smoothly to base and up the pie plate sides. Bake for 10 minutes in the center of the oven till golden brown in color. Let crust cool in the pan on a rack.
- Prep filling: mix cornstarch, 1 1/2 cups of water and sugar in a two-quart saucepan. Place on medium heat and simmer for 6 to 7 minutes, mixing continuously till mixture is clear and thick. Put in Jell-O and mix for a minute to dissolve. Take off from heat and let come to room temperature.
- Slice peel and all white pith off grapefruit with sharp knife and slice segments off membranes. Put the segments to the filling, then put to crust and refrigerate till firm, for not less than 3 hours to a day.
- Whip sugar and cream with electric mixer in medium size bowl, to hold soft peaks. Evenly smear on top of filling to serve.

Nutrition Information

- Calories: 543
- Sodium: 273 mg(11%)
- Fiber: 2 g(8%)
- Total Carbohydrate: 84 g(28%)
- Cholesterol: 66 mg(22%)
- Protein: 4 g(8%)
- Total Fat: 23 g(35%)
- Saturated Fat: 13 g(66%)

166. Grapes With Kir Sabayon

Serving: Serves 6 | Prep: | Cook: | Ready in:

Ingredients

- 3 large egg yolks
- 1/4 cup sugar
- Pinch of salt
- 1/2 cup dry white wine
- 1/2 cup chilled whipping cream
- 5 tablespoons crème de

- 2 cups red seedless grapes
- 2 cups white seedless grapes

Direction

- Beat salt, sugar and yolks using electric mixer/whisk in nonaluminum medium metal bowl; put bowl above saucepan of simmering water without touching water. Beat in wine slowly; beat for 9 minutes till candy thermometer reads 160°F and mixture mounds in spoon. Put bowl into bigger bowl with water and ice; whisk till cool. Take from above water.
- Beat cream till stiff peaks form in another medium bowl. Add crème de cassis; beat till peaks form. Fold into egg mixture and cover; refrigerate. You can prep it 1 day ahead.
- In bowl, mix grapes; divide 6 bowls. Put sabayon over.

167. Greek Honey And Anise Twists (Koulourakia)

Serving: Makes about 5 dozen | Prep: | Cook: | Ready in:

Ingredients

- 1/3 cup honey
- 4 tablespoons anise-flavored liqueur, such as Marie Brizard
- 2 tablespoons fresh lemon juice
- 4 1/4 cups all purpose flour
- 1 1/2 teaspoons salt
- 1 teaspoon baking powder
- 1 cup (2 sticks) unsalted butter, room temperature
- 1 cup sugar
- 3 large eggs
- 1 1/2 tablespoons aniseed
- 2 teaspoons finely grated lemon peel
- Sesame seeds

Direction

- Mix juice, 2 tbsp. liqueur and honey in small bowl; put aside glaze.
- Preheat an oven to 350°F. Butter baking sheets lightly. Mix baking powder, salt and flour in medium bowl. Beat sugar and butter using electric mixer till fluffy in big bowl. One by one, add eggs; beat well after each. Beat in lemon peel, aniseed and leftover 2 tbsp. liqueur; mix in dry ingredients slowly.
- Roll dough between work surface and palms to 7-in. ropes, 1 tbsp. dough at 1 time. Shape to twists/bow ties; put on prepped baking sheets, evenly spacing. Brush glaze on cookies; sprinkle sesame seeds. Bake the cookies for 15 minutes till pale golden. Put cookies on racks; brush cookies with glaze lightly. Cool. You can make it ahead; keep for a maximum of 1 week in room temperature in airtight container/frozen for 1 month maximum.

Nutrition Information

- Calories: 323
- Protein: 5 g(10%)
- Total Fat: 13 g(20%)
- Saturated Fat: 8 g(38%)
- Sodium: 194 mg(8%)
- Fiber: 1 g(4%)
- Total Carbohydrate: 46 g(15%)
- Cholesterol: 65 mg(22%)

168. Green Curry Chicken

Serving: Serves 6 | Prep: | Cook: | Ready in:

Ingredients

- 4 tablespoons fish sauce (nam pla)
- 1 tablespoon minced garlic
- 1 tablespoon sugar
- 1 teaspoon ground black pepper
- 1 1/2 pounds skinless boneless chicken tenders

- 1 tablespoon vegetable oil plus additional oil (for frying)
- 3 tablespoons Thai green or red curry paste
- 2 cups canned unsweetened coconut milk
- 1 cup chicken stock or canned low-salt chicken broth
- 1/4 cup (packed) golden brown sugar
- 1 10-ounce package ready-to-use fresh spinach
- 1 cup fresh basil leaves
- 3 large egg whites
- 1/2 cup cornstarch
- 2 tablespoons all purpose flour
- 1/4 cup water
- Steamed rice

Direction

- In a medium bowl, mix 2 tbsp. of fish sauce, pepper, sugar, and garlic. Add the chicken and refrigerate it for 1 hour.
- Put 1 tbsp. of oil in a medium saucepan and heat it over medium heat. Add the curry paste and cook for 2 minutes until fragrant. Mix in the sugar, 2 tbsp. of fish sauce, stock, and coconut milk. Simmer for 10 minutes until the sauce is slightly thickened and the flavors are well-blended; keep warm.
- In a pot filled with boiling water, cook the spinach for 3 minutes until soft. Drain the spinach well and allow it to cool, squeezing until dry. Place the spinach into a blender. Add the basil and 1/4 cup of sauce. Puree the mixture.
- Beat the cornstarch, 1/4 cup of water, flour, and egg whites in a large bowl using the electric mixer until smooth. Drain the chicken and add it into the batter, stirring until coated. Pour oil into the heavy large pot until it reaches a depth of 3-inches. Heat the oil to 350°F. Working in batches, deep-fry the chicken for 2 minutes, flipping often until golden and cooked through. Transfer the chicken into the paper towels using the tongs.
- Add the spinach puree to the sauce, and then bring it to a boil. Remove it from the heat. Top the steamed rice with the chicken, and then pour over the sauce. Serve.

Nutrition Information

- Calories: 612
- Saturated Fat: 18 g(92%)
- Sodium: 1630 mg(68%)
- Fiber: 3 g(12%)
- Total Carbohydrate: 48 g(16%)
- Cholesterol: 48 mg(16%)
- Protein: 24 g(48%)
- Total Fat: 37 g(58%)

169. Green Tea Cheesecake With Raspberries And Raspberry Mint Tisane

Serving: Makes 8 servings | Prep: | Cook: |Ready in:

Ingredients

- 1 cup (generous) ground shortbread cookies (about 6 ounces)
- 2 8-ounce packages cream cheese, room temperature (do not use whipped or "light" products)
- 1/2 cup (packed) fromage blanc*
- 3/4 cup plus 2 tablespoons sugar
- 4 large eggs
- 2 teaspoons Japanese green tea powder** or 2 teaspoons finely ground green tea from about 4 tea bags
- 2 1/2-pint containers fresh red raspberries
- 2 1/2-pint containers fresh golden raspberries
- 1 bunch fresh mint
- Boiling water

Direction

- To make cake: Preheat the oven to 325°F. Get a springform pan with 8-in. diameter and firmly press cookie crumbs onto its bottom only, not the sides. Use 3 layers of heavy-duty foil to tightly wrap outside the pan. In a large bowl, beat sugar, fromage blanc and cream cheese with an electric mixer till smooth. One at a time, add eggs; beat till incorporated before the next addition. Add green tea powder and beat till smooth. Pour over the prepped crust in pan with batter. In a roasting pan, place cake and pour in enough hot water to fill 1/2 of the springform pan.

- Bake for 1 hour till set but the middle still slightly moves when you shake the pan gently. Take the cake out of the roasting pan and let cool at room temperature for 1 hour. Store in the fridge overnight, uncovered. You can prepare this 2 days ahead. Keep in the fridge, covered.
- To make tisane: Place into each of 8 heatproof glasses with 3 mint leaves and 5 raspberries (mix of golden and red). Add boiling water to fill glasses and allow to steep for 5 minutes.
- Loosen cake by cutting around sides of the pan and remove the sides. Transfer cake onto a platter. Add some raspberries to garnish the cake. Slice into wedges. Serve each cake piece with a glass of tisane and a few raspberries.
- You can find fromage blanc at specialty foods stores, cheese stores and some supermarkets.
- Green tea powder can be found at Japanese markets.
- The tisane can be served with rock candy swizzle sticks for a touch of whimsy even though tisane does not really need sweetening.

Nutrition Information

- Calories: 542
- Protein: 11 g(23%)
- Total Fat: 30 g(46%)
- Saturated Fat: 14 g(70%)
- Sodium: 329 mg(14%)
- Fiber: 13 g(52%)
- Total Carbohydrate: 62 g(21%)
- Cholesterol: 158 mg(53%)

170. Grilled Flatbreads

Serving: Makes 8 servings | Prep: 1hours | Cook: 2hours30mins | Ready in:

Ingredients

- 1 1/4 ounce envelope active dry yeast
- 1 tablespoon olive oil plus more for brushing
- 5 cups (or more) all-purpose flour
- 1 tablespoon kosher salt plus more for seasoning
- 1 tablespoon (about) Tabil Spice Blend
- Freshly ground black pepper

Direction

- Sprinkle yeast on 2 cups of warm (105-115°) water in stand mixer's bowl with paddle fitted in it; allow to sit for 10 minutes till yeast dissolves. Stir in 1 tbsp. oil. Add 1 tbsp. salt and 5 cups flour; beat for 1 minute till dough forms.
- Put dough on floured work surface; knead for 5 minutes till smooth. As needed, add extra flour by spoonfuls for soft yet slightly sticky dough. Put dough into lightly oiled, big bowl; turn till coated. Use a kitchen towel to cover bowl; allow the dough to rise for 1 hour till doubled in volume in a warm place.
- Onto floured work surface, turn out dough; divide to 8 even pieces. Roll to balls; arrange 2-in. apart. Use a kitchen towel to cover; let rest for 15 minutes.
- Prep grill for medium-high heat; brush oil on 4 baking sheets lightly. Roll dough to 9-in. round, working with 1 dough ball at a time. Put 2 dough rounds onto each prepped sheet. Lightly brush with oil; season with pepper, salt and spice blend.
- Brush oil on grill rack; working in batches, put flatbreads on rack, spice side down. Brush with oil; season with pepper and salt. Grill for 1-1 1/2 minutes per side till cooked through and lightly charred in spots. Put on a work surface; cut to wedges.

171. Ham Mousse With Hollandaise

Serving: Makes 8 (first course) servings | Prep: | Cook: | Ready in:

Ingredients

- 2 large eggs, separated
- 9 ounces cooked ham, trimmed and finely ground in a food processor (2 cups)
- Pinch of freshly grated nutmeg
- Pinch of white pepper
- Pinch of cayenne
- 1/2 teaspoon salt
- 1 cup chilled heavy cream
- 2 tablespoons medium-dry Sherry
- Garnish: watercress sprigs
- Accompaniment: Hollandaise
- an 8- by 4- by 2 1/2-inch (1-quart) metal loaf pan

Direction

- Set the oven to 300°F for preheating.
- In a bowl, whisk the yolks first before whisking in white pepper, salt, cayenne, ham, and nutmeg.
- In a separate bowl, whisk the Sherry and cream using an electric mixer until the mixture holds soft peaks. Fold the mixture into the ham gently and thoroughly.
- Whisk egg whites and a pinch of salt using the cleaned beaters in a separate bowl until frothy. Fold the mixture into the ham gently and thoroughly.
- Spread the mousse into the well-buttered loaf pan. Place it into the hot water bath in the middle of the oven and let it bake, uncovered for 1 1/2 hours until the toothpick inserted in its center comes out unstained and when the mousse is firm to the touch.
- Allow the loaf pan with mousse to cool on a rack for 40 minutes. Use a thin knife to run the dull side or run a small spatula around edges to invert mousse onto the plate.
- Take note that this mousse can be prepared a day ahead. Just keep it chilled and covered loosely in a plastic wrap.

172. Hazelnut Crunch Cake With Honeyed Kumquats

Serving: Makes 10 servings | Prep: | Cook: |Ready in:

Ingredients

- 1 cup sugar
- 1/4 cup water
- 2 cups unhusked hazelnuts, toasted
- 55 kumquats (about 21 ounces)
- 1 1/2 cups Chardonnay
- 3/4 cup sugar
- 3/4 cup honey
- 10 whole star anise* or whole cloves
- 1 vanilla bean, split lengthwise
- 1 cup unhusked hazelnuts, toasted
- 2 cups all purpose flour
- 1 tablespoon baking powder
- 1 1/2 teaspoons Chinese five-spice powder**
- 3/4 teaspoon salt
- 3/4 cup (1 1/2 sticks) unsalted butter, room temperature
- 1 1/2 cups sugar
- 3 large egg yolks
- 1 tablespoon vanilla extract
- 1 teaspoon almond extract
- 1 1/4 cups whole milk
- 5 large egg whites
- 1 1/2 8-ounce containers mascarpone
- 1 1/2 cups chilled whipping cream
- 3 tablespoons sugar
- 4 teaspoons Cognac or brandy
- 1 tablespoon vanilla extract
- *Brown, star-shaped seedpods; available in the spice section of some supermarkets, specialty foods stores, and at Asian markets.
- **A spice blend that usually contains ground aniseed, cinnamon, star anise, cloves, or

ginger; available in the spice section of most supermarkets.

Direction

- Making the nut crunch: Line foil on the baking tray. In a heavy medium saucepan, mix the 1/4 cup water and sugar on medium-low heat, until the sugar has been dissolved. Turn up the heat and boil without mixing, until the syrup turns deep amber in color. Use wet pastry brush to brush down the sides, then swirl the pan from time to time. Stir in nuts. Pour on the foil and let it fully cool. Chop the nut crunch coarsely, then put it aside.
- For the kumquats: Cut cross on each kumquat, beginning at the rounded end to within 1/4-inch of the stem end. In a heavy big saucepan, boil the star anise, honey, sugar and wine, then mix until the sugar has been dissolved. Scrape in the seeds from the vanilla bean, then put in the bean. Put in kumquats and let it simmer for about 8 minutes, until nearly tender. Move the kumquats to a plate using a slotted spoon and let it cool. Take off the seeds and chop enough kumquats finely to get 2/3 cup (set aside the leftover kumquats). Boil the kumquat syrup gently until it reduces to 1 1/4 cups for approximately 12 minutes, then let it cool.
- For the cake: Set an oven to preheat to 350 degrees F. Use foil to line the 17x11x3/4-inch or 15 1/2 x 10 1/2 x 1-inch baking tray, then butter and flour the foil. In a processor, grind the nuts and flour finely, then move to a medium bowl. Whisk in the salt, spice and baking powder. In a big bowl, beat the sugar and butter using an electric mixer until well combined. Beat in extracts and yolks. Beat in the dry ingredients alternately with milk in few additions, just until blended. In a separate big bowl, beat the whites using clean dry bitters until it becomes stiff yet not dry. Fold 1/3 of the whites into the batter to make it light, then fold in the rest of the whites. Evenly spread the batter in the prepped pan.
- Let the cake bake for 28 minutes for 15 1/2 x 10 1/2-inch cake and about 20 minutes for 17x11-inch cake, until an inserted tester in the middle exits clean. Let the cake cool for 20 minutes in the pan on a rack. To loosen, run a knife around the cake. Flip the cake on the rack lined with foil and let it fully cool. Slice the hazelnut cake crosswise into three even pieces.
- For the frosting: In a big bowl, mix together all the ingredients and beat it until it forms soft peaks (avoid overbeating because the mixture will curdle).
- Put one piece of cake on the platter. Spread 3/4 cup of the frosting on top and sprinkle it with 1/3 cup nut crunch and 1/3 cup chopped kumquats, then drizzle 2 tbsp. kumquat syrup on top. Put the 2nd piece of cake over and spread it with 3/4 cup of the frosting, then sprinkle 1/3 cup nut crunch and 1/3 cup chopped kumquats, then drizzle 2 tbsp. kumquat syrup on top. Put the 3rd piece of cake on top. Spread the leftover frosting over the top and sides of the cake. Drain the leftover kumquats, take off the seeds and any pulp that was attached. Put kumquats on top of the cake and arrange it like flowers. Do ahead: This can be prepared one day in advance, covered, and chilled. Store the kumquat syrup and leftover nut crunch at room temperature. Press the rest of the nut crunch around the sides of the cake and drizzle 2 tbsp. syrup on top of the cake, then serve.

Nutrition Information

- Calories: 1161
- Sodium: 475 mg(20%)
- Fiber: 8 g(33%)
- Total Carbohydrate: 130 g(43%)
- Cholesterol: 172 mg(57%)
- Protein: 16 g(33%)
- Total Fat: 64 g(99%)
- Saturated Fat: 25 g(126%)

173. Hazelnut And Chocolate Pithiviers

Serving: Serves 8 | Prep: | Cook: |Ready in:

Ingredients

- 1 17 1/4-ounce package frozen puff pastry sheets (2 sheets), thawed
- 6 tablespoons (3/4 stick) unsalted butter, room temperature
- 1/2 cup sugar
- 3/4 cup hazelnuts (about 3 ounces), toasted, husked, finely ground
- 2 tablespoons all purpose flour
- 1 teaspoon vanilla extract
- 2 large eggs
- 1 3/4 ounces bittersweet (not unsweetened) or semisweet chocolate, cut into small pieces

Direction

- Preheat an oven to 400°F and cut 1 pastry sheet to 9 1/2-in. diameter round. Put on big heavy cookie sheet; chill.
- Cream sugar and butter using electric mixer till fluffy in medium bowl; mix in vanilla, flour and nuts. Mix in 1 egg. Evenly spread filling on chilled pastry round; leave 1/2-in. border on edge. Put chocolate pieces on filling, evenly spacing; chill for 15 minutes.
- Beat leftover egg in small bowl to blend. Cut 2nd pastry sheet to 9 1/2-in. diameter round; brush beaten egg on border of filled pastry. Put 2nd pastry round over; to seal, firmly press edges together. Decoratively crimp edges; brush beaten egg on pastry. In middle, cut small vent hole. Score half circles in top of pastry using small sharp knife's tip, 1/2-in. apart, starting in vent then ending on crimped edge. You can make it 1 day ahead; cover. Refrigerate.
- Bake pastry for 25 minutes till golden brown and puffed; cool on cookie sheet for 10 minutes. Put pastry on platter. Cut to wedges; serve in room temperature/warm.

Nutrition Information

- Calories: 585
- Cholesterol: 69 mg(23%)
- Protein: 8 g(16%)
- Total Fat: 42 g(64%)
- Saturated Fat: 13 g(67%)
- Sodium: 172 mg(7%)
- Fiber: 2 g(9%)
- Total Carbohydrate: 48 g(16%)

174. Homemade Butter And Buttermilk

Serving: Makes about 2 cups butter and 4 cups (32 ounces) buttermilk | Prep: | Cook: |Ready in:

Ingredients

- 6 cups heavy cream, preferably organic
- 1/4 teaspoon fine sea salt
- Special equipment: 5-quart stand mixer (or larger)

Direction

- Put cream in a 5-qt. electric stand mixer's bowl with whisk attachment. Use plastic wrap to tightly cover mixer and top of bowl. Beat cream for 10-12 minutes till it holds soft peaks on medium high speed; increase speed to high. Beat for 5 minutes longer till it separates to thin, liquid buttermilk and pale-yellow, thick butter.
- Through colander, strain mixture into big bowl. Knead butter vigorously in colander using hands for 5 minutes till creamy and dense, squeezing out leftover buttermilk.
- Put butter in big bowl; keep buttermilk. Knead salt into butter using hands. Roll to logs; wrap in plastic wrap or put into airtight container then refrigerate. Butter keeps for up to 1 month frozen/1 week refrigerated.

- Through fine-mesh sieve, strain buttermilk; cover. Refrigerate for 1 week.

Nutrition Information

- Calories: 308
- Saturated Fat: 21 g(103%)
- Sodium: 70 mg(3%)
- Total Carbohydrate: 2 g(1%)
- Cholesterol: 122 mg(41%)
- Protein: 2 g(4%)
- Total Fat: 33 g(51%)

175. Honey, Date, And Pecan Tart

Serving: Makes 8 servings | Prep: | Cook: | Ready in:

Ingredients

- 1 1/4 cups unbleached all purpose flour
- 1/2 cup (1 stick) chilled unsalted butter, cut into 1/2-inch cubes
- 1/4 teaspoon salt
- 3 to 4 tablespoons ice water
- 2 large eggs, separated
- 6 tablespoons sugar, divided
- 2 tablespoons honey
- 1 tablespoon bourbon
- 1/2 teaspoon vanilla extract
- 1/8 teaspoon salt
- 2 tablespoons all purpose flour
- Pinch of baking soda
- 1 cup chopped pitted Medjool dates
- 2/3 cup coarsely chopped pecans
- Whipped cream

Direction

- Preparing the crust: In a processor, blend the salt, butter and flour using on/off turns, until the mixture looks like coarse meal. Pour in 3 tbsp ice water and blend using the on/off turns, until it forms moist clumps. If dry, pour in more water by teaspoonfuls. Gather the dough into a ball and flatten it into a disk. Use plastic to wrap it and let it chill for a minimum of an hour to a maximum of one day. Set an oven to preheat to 425 degrees F. On a surface that's lightly floured, roll out the dough to 13-inch round. Move to a 9-inch tart pan with a removable bottom. Slice off all of the overhang except for the 1/4-inch and leave the dough sides higher than the sides of the pan. Let the crust freeze for 15 minutes. Use dried beans and foil to line the crust. Let it bake for about 20 minutes, until the sides become set. Take off the beans and foil. Let the crust bake for about 15 minutes until it turns golden in color, then prick using a fork if the crust is bubbling. Let the crust cool on a rack. Lower the oven temperature to 325 degrees F.
- Making the filling: In a big bowl, whisk the salt, vanilla, bourbon, honey, 4 tbsp sugar and yolks, until it becomes thick. Beat in baking soda and flour, followed by pecans and dates. In a medium bowl, whisk the egg whites until it forms soft peaks. Put in 2 tbsp sugar and beat it until it becomes stiff yet not dry. Fold the whites to the date mixture in 3 additions. Spread the crust with the filling, then bake the tart for about 40 minutes, until the filling is just set in the middle and turns deep brown and puffed. Let the tart cool for a minimum of 30 minutes on a rack. You may serve it at room temperature or warm with whipped cream. Do ahead: This tart can be prepared a day in advance with cover and allow to stand at room temperature.

Nutrition Information

- Calories: 396
- Total Fat: 19 g(30%)
- Saturated Fat: 8 g(41%)
- Sodium: 139 mg(6%)
- Fiber: 3 g(13%)
- Total Carbohydrate: 53 g(18%)
- Cholesterol: 77 mg(26%)
- Protein: 5 g(11%)

176. Honey Glazed Bunny Rolls

Serving: Makes 12 Rolls | Prep: | Cook: |Ready in:

Ingredients

- 1 cup milk
- 1/4 cup honey
- a 1/4-ounce package active dry yeast (2 1/2 teaspoons)
- 1/2 stick (1/4 cup) unsalted butter, melted
- 2 large egg yolks
- 4 cups bread flour
- 2 teaspoons salt
- 2 tablespoons honey
- 1/2 stick (1/4 cup) unsalted butter
- 2/3 cup confectioners' sugar
- 12 dried currants, halved

Direction

- Heat honey and milk in small saucepan on low heat till lukewarm, mixing; take off heat. Mix in yeast; stand for 5 minutes till foamy. Add yolks and butter; whisk till well combined.
- Put milk mixture in standing electric mixer's bowl/big bowl, if kneading by hand. Slowly add salt and flour to milk mixture; mix till incorporated. Knead dough with dough hook for 2 minutes till smooth. Or, knead dough by hand for 10-15 minutes till smooth on lightly floured surface.
- Put dough in lightly oiled big bowl; turn to coat in oil. Rise dough in the fridge overnight till doubled in bulk, covered in plastic wrap. Or, rise dough for 2 hours till doubled in bulk in a warm place.
- Grease the 2 baking sheets. Punch dough down; divide to 12 pieces. Shape each piece to egg shape; put pieces on prepped baking sheets. On each piece, hold scissors perpendicular to baking sheet, points down, and creating 1/2-in. long snip at wide end's base to make a bunny tail. Make narrow 2-in. long snip on every side, beginning near wide end then cutting towards narrow end to make 2 bunny ears on every piece. Make 2 holes in the narrow end using a wooden pick then firmly pressing a currant half in each hole with pick to make eyes on every piece.
- Brush 1/2 warm glaze on rolls; rise for 45 minutes or less till doubled in bulk in a warm place, loosely covered with plastic wrap; if dough is cold, rising takes longer.
- Preheat oven to 400°F.
- Heat leftover glaze till warm on low heat; brush rolls. Bake rolls on lower and upper thirds of oven for 20 minutes, switching sheet positions in oven halfway through the baking, till golden. Put on racks; cool.
- Serve rolls in room temperature/warm.
- Heat glaze ingredients on low heat till butter melts, occasionally mixing, in a small saucepan; take off heat. Keep glaze warm, covered.

Nutrition Information

- Calories: 315
- Saturated Fat: 6 g(28%)
- Sodium: 224 mg(9%)
- Fiber: 1 g(5%)
- Total Carbohydrate: 50 g(17%)
- Cholesterol: 53 mg(18%)
- Protein: 7 g(14%)
- Total Fat: 10 g(15%)

177. Honey Orange Madeleines

Serving: Makes about 18 | Prep: | Cook: |Ready in:

Ingredients

- Melted butter
- 2 large eggs
- 1/3 cup honey

- 1/4 cup sugar
- 1 1/2 teaspoons grated orange peel
- 1/2 teaspoon orange flower water
- 1/2 teaspoon vanilla extract
- 1 cup all purpose flour
- 3/4 cup (1 1/2 sticks) unsalted butter, melted, room temperature
- Sugar

Direction

- Preheat an oven to 400°F. Brush melted butter on madeleine mold; dust flour. Mix grated orange peel, 1/4 cup sugar, honey, and eggs in an electric mixer's bowl; put above saucepan with simmering water. Don't let bowl touch water. Mix for 2 minutes till just lukewarm; take from above water. Beat using electric mixer for 12 minutes till tripled in volume and pale yellow. Add vanilla extract and orange flower water. Mix in flour slowly on low speed, occasionally scraping bowl. Put 1/3 batter in medium bowl. Fold 3/4 cup of melted butter slowly into batter in the medium bowl; don't fold in water on bottom of butter. Fold mixture gently into leftover batter; it'll slightly thicken.
- Put batter in madeleine mold, filling nearly to top; bake for 10 minutes, turning the pan halfway through cooking, till cookies are springy to the touch. Onto rack, invert pan, then use the tip of knife to pry out cookies lightly. Sprinkle sugar on cookies. Wipe molds out; brush melted butter. Dust flour; repeat using leftover batter. Fully cool on rack. You can make it 1 day ahead; keep in room temperature in airtight containers.

Nutrition Information

- Calories: 133
- Total Fat: 8 g(13%)
- Saturated Fat: 5 g(25%)
- Sodium: 9 mg(0%)
- Fiber: 0 g(1%)
- Total Carbohydrate: 14 g(5%)
- Cholesterol: 41 mg(14%)
- Protein: 2 g(3%)

178. Hot Milk Cakes With Strawberries And Cream

Serving: Makes 6 servings | Prep: | Cook: | Ready in:

Ingredients

- Nonstick vegetable oil spray
- 2 extra-large eggs
- 2/3 cup plus 1/2 cup sugar
- 3/4 teaspoon vanilla extract, divided
- 1 cup plus 2 tablespoons self-rising flour
- 2/3 cup whole milk
- 5 tablespoons unsalted butter
- 1 pound large strawberries, hulled, thinly sliced lengthwise
- 1/2 cup chilled heavy whipping cream
- 1 tablespoon powdered sugar

Direction

- Set oven to 425°F; preheat. Prepare six 3/4 cup custard cups by spraying nonstick spray on each cup. In a medium bowl of an electric mixer, whisk eggs on high speed for about 3 minutes until thickened. Slowly beat in 2/3 cup of sugar and whisk until pale yellow and thickened, for about 1 minute more. Whisk in 1/2 teaspoon of vanilla then beat in flour for 30 seconds. In a small saucepan, allow butter and milk to boil while stirring until the butter is melted. Pour hot milk mixture into the batter, beating until smooth and blended for about 30 seconds. Distribute batter into the prepared cups. Transfer cups on the rimmed baking sheet.
- Bake until the top of the cakes risen (a rounded tall peak will form on each center), becomes pale golden and firm when touched, for about 16 minutes. For at least 20 minutes, cool in the cups. Note: You can do this 8 hours in advance. Completely cool the cups and set aside at room temperature with cover.

- In a medium bowl, add strawberries and the rest of the 1/2 cup of sugar; toss to coat and set aside for 20 minutes allowing to form the juices. In a separate medium bowl, whisk powdered sugar, cream, and the rest of the 1/4 teaspoon of vanilla with an electric mixer until it forms a peak.
- Take out room temperature or warm cakes from cups and place into the bowls. Slice the rounded top of every cake and scoop few berries and the juices on top. Cover the berries with cake tops. Add whipped cream on top and add the remaining juices and berries for garnishing. Serve.

Nutrition Information

- Calories: 568
- Fiber: 2 g(9%)
- Total Carbohydrate: 66 g(22%)
- Cholesterol: 158 mg(53%)
- Protein: 7 g(15%)
- Total Fat: 32 g(49%)
- Saturated Fat: 17 g(84%)
- Sodium: 334 mg(14%)

179. Hurry Up Black Bean Dip

Serving: Makes 6 to 8 servings | Prep: | Cook: | Ready in:

Ingredients

- 1 medium red onion, chopped
- 2 (16-ounce) cans black beans, drained and rinsed
- 2 tablespoons balsamic vinegar
- 1 tablespoon fresh orange or lime juice
- 1 tablespoon chopped fresh cilantro
- 1 tablespoon olive oil
- 1 garlic clove, peeled
- 1 teaspoon ground cumin
- Salt and freshly ground pepper, to taste
- Tortilla chips and, if you're with that sort of crowd, assorted cut-up raw vegetables

Direction

- Set aside a tablespoon of red onion in a cup for garnish.
- Puree cumin, garlic, oil, cilantro, orange juice, vinegar, remaining red onion and beans in a food processor or blender.
- Move the dip in a bowl; sprinkle pepper and salt. Add the reserved red onion on top then serve with vegetables and tortilla chips.

Nutrition Information

- Calories: 174
- Saturated Fat: 0 g(2%)
- Sodium: 422 mg(18%)
- Fiber: 11 g(44%)
- Total Carbohydrate: 29 g(10%)
- Protein: 10 g(19%)
- Total Fat: 3 g(4%)

180. Ice Cream Cone Cake

Serving: Makes about 20 servings | Prep: 3hours | Cook: 4.5hours | Ready in:

Ingredients

- 3 cups all-purpose flour
- 1 tablespoon baking powder
- 1 1/2 teaspoons salt
- 3 sticks (3/4 pound) unsalted butter, softened
- 1 3/4 cups sugar
- 4 large eggs at room temperature 30 minutes
- 1 1/2 teaspoons pure vanilla extract
- 1 1/2 cups whole milk
- 7 flat-bottomed wafer cones
- 1 1/2 cups whole milk
- 9 large egg yolks
- 3/4 cup sugar
- 1/4 teaspoon salt

- 3 1/2 ounces fine-quality bittersweet chocolate (no more than 60% cacao if marked), chopped
- 6 sticks (1 1/2 pound) unsalted butter, softened
- 1 tablespoon pure vanilla extract
- 2 cups coarsely crushed 2-inch chocolate wafers (28 small cookies)
- Equipment: 2 (8- by 2-inch) round cake pans; a small offset spatula; 2 large pastry bags each fitted with 1/3-inch star tip
- 1 small offset spatula
- 2 large pastry bags each fitted with 1/3-inch star tip

Direction

- Cake and cones: Preheat an oven with racks in lower and upper thirds to 350°F. Butter pans. Line parchment on bottoms; butter then lightly flour pans.
- Sift salt, baking powder and flour into a bowl.
- Beat sugar and butter using, paddle attachment for stand mixer, electric mixer on medium high speed for 5 minutes in stand mixer, 10 for a handheld, till fluffy and pale. One by one, beat in eggs then vanilla; beat for 5 minutes till incorporated thoroughly. Lower speed to low. Alternately with milk, add flour mixture in 4 additions, starting and finishing with flour mixture; mix just till batter is smooth.
- Stand cones in 12-cup muffin pan, open ends up; fill cones with batter to 2/3 full. Divide leftover batter to cake pans.
- Bake for 25-35 minutes for cakes, 15-22 minutes for cones, cakes in lower oven third and cones in upper oven third, till inserted wooden pick in middle of cake exits clean; cool cakes in pans for 5 minutes on big rack. Put cones on another rack; fully cool. Invert cakes onto rack; fully cool.
- Buttercream: Boil milk in a medium saucepan. Whisk salt, sugar and yolks till well combined in a bowl; in a slow stream, add milk, continuously whisking. Put into saucepan; cook on medium low heat for 5-10 minutes till an instant-read thermometer reads 175°F and custard thickens, constantly mixing with a wooden spoon. Don't boil. Through fine-mesh sieve, strain into metal bowl. Refrigerate for a minimum of 1 hour till cold, covered.
- Melt chocolate; cool to warm.
- Using cleaned beaters/whisk attachment for stand mixer, beat butter on high speed for 4 minutes for handheld, 2 minutes in stand mixer, till fluffy and light. Lower speed to medium; add cold custard slowly. Add vanilla; increase speed to high. Beat for 4 minutes with handheld, 2 minutes in stand mixer, till buttercream is smooth.
- Put 1 1/4 cups buttercream into bowl; mix in warm melted chocolate to create chocolate buttercream. Put 2 cups vanilla buttercream into another bowl; to create cookies-and-cream filling, fold in crushed wafers.
- Assemble cake: Using a big serrated knife, horizontally halve cakes; put 1 cake layer on a plate/cake stand, cut side up. Spread 1 cup of cookies-and-cream buttercream on top with offset spatula; put another, cut side down, cake layer over. Spread 1 cup of cookies-and-cream buttercream. Put another, cut side up, cake layer over; spread leftover cookies-and-cream buttercream. Put leftover, cut side down, cake layer over; spread top and sides of cake with 2 1/2 cups of vanilla buttercream in total.
- Put leftover vanilla buttercream and chocolate buttercream in different pastry bags.
- Lengthwise halve each cone with a serrated knife. Attach the flat sides of cones on cake's side with cone's tops touching. In case one breaks, you'll have another cone.
- Pipe 2 tbsp. buttercream over every other cone, touching cake's top, holding the pastry bag full of vanilla buttercream on cake vertically to look like soft-serve ice cream. In same manner, pipe chocolate buttercream over leftover cones.
- You can bake cones and cake 1 day ahead; keep in room temperature, wrapped in plastic wrap tightly.

- Set into ice bath and mix for 5 minutes till cold to quick-chill the custard for the vanilla buttercream.
- You can make vanilla buttercream, without cookies and chocolate, 2 days ahead, covered, chilled. Before using, bring to room temperature.
- Pipe vanilla buttercream first then the chocolate if you only have 1 pastry bag.

Nutrition Information

- Calories: 680
- Saturated Fat: 29 g(146%)
- Sodium: 361 mg(15%)
- Fiber: 3 g(11%)
- Total Carbohydrate: 55 g(18%)
- Cholesterol: 234 mg(78%)
- Protein: 8 g(16%)
- Total Fat: 50 g(76%)

181. Iced Lemon Cookies

Serving: Makes About 3 Dozen | Prep: | Cook: | Ready in:

Ingredients

- 1/2 cup sugar
- 6 tablespoons (3/4 stick) unsalted butter, room temperature
- 2 teaspoons vanilla extract
- 1 teaspoon grated lemon peel
- 3 large eggs
- 2 cups all purpose flour
- 2 teaspoons baking powder
- 1 tablespoon butter
- 3 cups powdered sugar, sifted
- 2 tablespoons (or more) water
- 2 tablespoons lemon juice
- 1 teaspoon vanilla extract

Direction

- For the cookies: Turn the oven to 350°F to preheat. Use foil to line 2 baking sheets. In a big bowl, beat together grated lemon peel, vanilla extract, unsalted butter, and sugar with an electric mixer until combined. Add 1 egg each time, beating thoroughly between additions (the mixture may seem curdled). Keep beating for 1 minute. In a small bowl, mix together baking powder and flour. Add to the butter mixture and mix until a soft sticky dough forms.
- In a pastry bag that has a 3/8-in. wide round tip, add the dough. On the prepared sheets, pipe rings with 2-in. diameter, keeping distance between each. Dip your fingertips into water, and press each ring on the ends into a smooth ring. Bake for about 20 minutes until turning golden brown. In the meantime, make the icing.
- For the icing: In a heavy medium-sized saucepan, heat butter over low heat until melted. Add vanilla extract, lemon juice, 2 tablespoons water, and sugar and stir until the mixture has fully heated and the sugar has melted. If the icing is too thick to brush, add additional water to thin.
- Take the cookies out of the oven. Immediately brush over the hot cookies with warm icing. Let the iced cookies stay on the sheets to cool for 2 minutes. Remove onto a rack to fully cool (You can prepare this 1 day in advance. Put in an airtight container to store).

Nutrition Information

- Calories: 287
- Total Carbohydrate: 50 g(17%)
- Cholesterol: 64 mg(21%)
- Protein: 4 g(8%)
- Total Fat: 8 g(12%)
- Saturated Fat: 5 g(23%)
- Sodium: 80 mg(3%)
- Fiber: 1 g(2%)

182. Inside Out Carrot Cake Cookies

Serving: Makes about 13 cookies | Prep: | Cook: | Ready in:

Ingredients

- 1 1/8 cups all-purpose flour
- 1 teaspoon cinnamon
- 1/2 teaspoon baking soda
- 1/2 teaspoon salt
- 1 stick (1/2 cup) unsalted butter, softened
- 1/3 cup plus 2 tablespoons packed light brown sugar
- 1/3 cup plus 2 tablespoons granulated sugar
- 1 large egg
- 1/2 teaspoon vanilla
- 1 cup coarsely grated carrots (2 medium)
- 1 scant cup walnuts (3 ounces), chopped
- 1/2 cup raisins (2 1/2 ounces)
- 8 ounces cream cheese
- 1/4 cup honey

Direction

- Preparation: Set oven racks in the lower thirds and upper of the oven and prepare the oven by preheating to 375 degrees F. Prepare 2 buttered baking sheets.
- In a bowl, combine salt, baking soda, cinnamon, and flour.
- In a bowl, use an electric mixer to whisk vanilla, egg, sugars, and butter on medium speed for about 2 minutes until pale and fluffy. Whisk in raisins, nuts, and carrots at low speed then put in flour mixture and whisk until just blended.
- Place 1 1/2 tablespoon batter each cookie on baking sheets with 2-inch apart then bake for a total of 12-16 minutes, switching the position of sheets halfway through baking, until cookies springy when touched and lightly browned. Cool cookies for 1 minute on sheets on racks then place cookies onto racks and cool fully.
- While baking cookies, place honey and cream cheese in a food processor and process until smooth.
- Put a generous tablespoon of cream cheese filling on each flat side of cookies in between to sandwich together.

Nutrition Information

- Calories: 307
- Saturated Fat: 8 g(42%)
- Sodium: 193 mg(8%)
- Fiber: 1 g(5%)
- Total Carbohydrate: 35 g(12%)
- Cholesterol: 52 mg(17%)
- Protein: 4 g(8%)
- Total Fat: 18 g(27%)

183. Jack Stein's Mashed Potatoes

Serving: Serves 6 to 8 | Prep: | Cook: | Ready in:

Ingredients

- 2 1/4 pounds russet potatoes, peeled, cut into 1 1/2-inch pieces
- 8 tablespoons (1 stick) butter
- 2 large onions, chopped
- 2 large garlic cloves, chopped
- 6 tablespoons (or more) milk

Direction

- Cook potatoes for 15 minutes till tender in pot with boiling salted water.
- Meanwhile, melt 2 tbsp. butter on high heat in big heavy skillet. Add onions; sauté for 8 minutes till golden. Add garlic; sauté for 30 seconds.
- Drain potatoes; put in same pot. Mix till potatoes look dry on low heat. Put in bowl; add 6 tbsp. butter and 6 tbsp. milk. Beat potatoes using electric mixer till smooth; if

desired, add more milk. Add onion mixture; beat till just blended. Season with pepper and salt to taste.

Nutrition Information

- Calories: 302
- Saturated Fat: 10 g(50%)
- Sodium: 19 mg(1%)
- Fiber: 3 g(12%)
- Total Carbohydrate: 37 g(12%)
- Cholesterol: 42 mg(14%)
- Protein: 5 g(10%)
- Total Fat: 16 g(25%)

184. Key Lime Cheesecake With Tropical Dried Fruit Chutney

Serving: Makes 12 servings | Prep: | Cook: | Ready in:

Ingredients

- 2/3 cup all purpose flour
- 2/3 cup sweetened flaked coconut
- 1/3 cup sugar
- 1/4 cup (1/2 stick) unsalted butter, melted
- 3 8-ounce packages cream cheese, room temperature
- 1/2 cup sour cream
- 1 cup sugar
- 5 large eggs
- 3 tablespoons fresh Key lime juice
- 2 teaspoons finely grated Key lime peel
- 3/4 teaspoon vanilla extract
- Tropical Dried-Fruit Chutney

Direction

- Crust: Preheat an oven to 350°F. Mix sugar, coconut and flour to blend in medium bowl. Drizzle with butter; mix till crumbs stick together. Firmly press on bottom of 9-in. diameter springform pan and bake crust for 25 minutes till golden brown; cool crust. On work surface, stack 3 big 18-in. wide and heavy-duty foil sheets; in middle, put cake pan. Snugly wrap foil around pan sides; maintain the oven temperature.
- Filling: Beat cream cheese using electric mixer till smooth in big bowl; beat in sour cream. Beat in sugar. One by one, beat in eggs, scraping bowl's sides down occasionally. Beat in vanilla, lime peel and lime juice; put batter on crust. Put wrapped cheesecake in big roasting pan. To reach halfway up cheesecake pan's sides, put hot water in roasting pan; cover cheesecake pan, not the roasting pan, with foil loosely.
- Put cheesecake into oven, still in water bath; bake for 1 hour. Uncover; bake for 20 minutes till just set in middle when cake pan is shaken gently. Remove cake from water. Put directly into fridge; chill overnight, uncovered.
- To loosen, cut around cake; remove pan sides. Cut cake; serve it with chutney.

Nutrition Information

- Calories: 411
- Cholesterol: 155 mg(52%)
- Protein: 7 g(14%)
- Total Fat: 29 g(44%)
- Saturated Fat: 16 g(82%)
- Sodium: 255 mg(11%)
- Fiber: 1 g(3%)
- Total Carbohydrate: 33 g(11%)

185. Key Lime Coconut Cake

Serving: Makes 8 servings | Prep: 20mins | Cook: 2hours | Ready in:

Ingredients

- 1 cup sweetened flaked coconut
- 1 stick unsalted butter, softened
- 1 1/4 cups granulated sugar

- 1 tablespoon grated Key lime zest
- 2 large eggs
- 1 3/4 cups self-rising flour
- 3/4 cup whole milk
- 1/4 cup fresh Key lime juice, divided
- 1 cup confectioners sugar
- 1 tablespoon rum (optional)

Direction

- Heat the oven with rack the center to 350°F. Liberally grease a round cake pan, 9- by 2-inch in size, with butter and line one parchment paper round on bottom.
- In small baking pan, let coconut toast in oven for 8 to 12 minutes, mixing one or two times, till golden. Cool down. Keep oven on.
- Use electric mixer to whip granulated sugar, zest and butter till fluffy. Whip eggs in, 1 by 1. Mix flour and half cup of coconut, put aside the rest for topping. Mix 2 tablespoons of lime juice and milk. Whisk milk and flour mixtures to mixture of egg on low speed alternating in batches, starting and finishing with flour.
- Scoop the batter to pan and even the top. Bake for 40 to 45 minutes, till golden and an inserted wooden pick in the middle gets out clean. Cool down till warm, then remove from pan and throw the parchment.
- Mix leftover 2 tablespoons of lime juice, rum in case using and confectioners' sugar, and put on top of cake. Scatter leftover coconut on top.

Nutrition Information

- Calories: 460
- Fiber: 2 g(8%)
- Total Carbohydrate: 74 g(25%)
- Cholesterol: 79 mg(26%)
- Protein: 5 g(11%)
- Total Fat: 17 g(26%)
- Saturated Fat: 11 g(55%)
- Sodium: 386 mg(16%)

186. Key Lime Mousse

Serving: Makes 4 servings | Prep: 20mins | Cook: 2.25hours | Ready in:

Ingredients

- 1/2 tablespoon grated Key lime zest
- 1/2 cup fresh Key lime juice
- 1/2 cup sugar
- Pinch of salt
- 3 large eggs
- 3/4 stick unsalted butter, cut into bits
- 2/3 cup chilled heavy cream

Direction

- In a small heavy saucepan, stir eggs, salt, sugar, juice and zest together. Put in butter and cook on medium low heat for 5 minutes, while whisking often until thick enough to hold marks of whisk. Use a fine mesh sieve to force the mixture through into a bowl then put in an ice bath for chilling quickly for 5 minutes, while stirring sometimes.
- Beat cream until form stiff peaks, then gently fold into custard but thoroughly. Scoop into glasses and place in the fridge to refrigerate for minimum of 2 hours and maximum of 12 hours.

Nutrition Information

- Calories: 447
- Sodium: 144 mg(6%)
- Fiber: 0 g(1%)
- Total Carbohydrate: 29 g(10%)
- Cholesterol: 239 mg(80%)
- Protein: 6 g(12%)
- Total Fat: 35 g(55%)
- Saturated Fat: 21 g(106%)

187. Kouign Amann

Serving: Makes 12 | Prep: | Cook: | Ready in:

Ingredients

- 2 tablespoons (30 g) European-style butter (at least 82% fat), melted, slightly cooled, plus more for bowl
- 1 tablespoon (10 g) active dry yeast
- 3 cups (400 g) all-purpose flour, plus more for surface
- 3 tablespoons (40 g) sugar
- 1 teaspoon (5 g) kosher salt
- 12 ounces (340 g) chilled unsalted European-style butter (at least 82% fat), cut into pieces
- 1/2 cup (100 g) sugar
- 1 teaspoon (5 g) kosher salt
- All-purpose flour
- 3/4 cup (150 g) sugar, divided
- Nonstick vegetable oil spray

Direction

- Preparation
- Dough
- Brush butter on big bowl. Whisk 1/4 cup very warm water, 110-115°F, and yeast to melt in another big bowl; stand for 5 minutes till yeast begins to foam. Add 3/4 cup cold water, 2 tbsp. butter, 1 tsp. salt, 3 tbsp. sugar and 3 cups flour; mix till you get a shaggy dough. Turn onto lightly floured surface; knead for 5 minutes till dough is slightly tacky, soft and supple; as needed, add flour.
- Proof dough twice
- Put dough in prepped bowl; turn to coat in butter. Use plastic wrap to cover bowl; put in draft-free, warm spot. Rise dough for 1-1 1/2 hours till doubled in size. Resting and rising is called proofing. Punch dough down; lightly knead inside bowl a few times. Cover with plastic wrap; chill for 45-60 minutes in fridge till dough doubles in size.
- Form and chill dough.
- Turn dough onto lightly floured surface; pat to 6x6-in. square then wrap in plastic. Chill in freeze for 30-35 minutes till dough is very firm yet not frozen; you want it as firm as chilled butter block in 5th step.
- Mix and make butter block
- Use an electric mixer at low speed to beat 1 tsp. salt, 1/2 cup sugar and 12-oz. butter for 3 minutes till waxy looking and homogenous; scrape butter mixture onto big parchment sheet. Form to 1/4-in. thick 12x6-in. rectangle.
- Wrap butter block and chill
- Wrap up butter neatly; press out air. Gently roll packet to push butter into the corners with rolling pin and make evenly thick rectangle; chill for 25-30 minutes in fridge till firm yet pliable.
- Roll dough out and enclose the butter block
- Roll dough to 19x7-in. 50% longer than butter block and bit wider rectangle on lightly floured surface. Put butter block onto upper 2/3 of dough; leave thin border along sides and top. Like a letter, fold dough: Bring lower 1/3 dough up then over lower butter half. Fold exposed upper 1/2 of dough and butter on lower half; butter shouldn't break, just bend. Press dough edges to seal, enclosing the butter.
- Do 1st turn
- Counterclockwise, rotate dough package 90°F so flap opening is towards your right. Roll dough out to 3/8-in. thick 24x8-in. rectangle, dusting flour if needed. Like a letter, fold rectangle to thirds like in step 6, bring up lower third then the upper third down to complete the first turn. Lightly dust dough with flour then wrap in plastic; chill in freeze for 30 minutes till firm yet not frozen. Put in fridge; chill for 1 hour till very firm. Freezing dough first lessens chilling time.
- 2nd and 3rd turns.
- With flap opening on your right, put dough on surface; roll dough to 3/8-in. thick 24x8-in. rectangle, dusting flour if needed. Same as before, fold to thirds; counterclockwise rotate 90°F so flap opening in on the right; roll to 24x8-in. rectangle again. Sprinkle 2 tbsp. sugar on dough's surface; fold to thirds. Lightly dust flour then wrap in plastic; chill in freezer for

30 minutes till firm yet not frozen. Put in fridge; chill for 1 hour till very firm.
- Roll out then cut dough.
- With flap opening on your right, put dough on surface; roll dough to rectangle slightly bigger than 16x12-in., dusting flour if needed; trim it to 16x12-in. Slice to 12 squares to get 4x3 grid. From surface and dough, brush extra flour.
- Form then proof Kouign Amann
- Use nonstick spray to coat muffin cups lightly. Evenly dividing, sprinkle total of 1/4 cup of sugar on squares; gently press to adhere. Flip; repeat with 1/4 cup more sugar, gently pressing to adhere. Shake excess off. Lift corners of every square; press into middle. Put each into muffin cup. Use plastic to wrap pans; chill for 8-12 hours in fridge; dough with puff with layers that are slightly separated.
- Baking
- Preheat an oven to 375°F. Unwrap the pans; sprinkle leftover 2 tbsp. sugar, evenly dividing, on kouign-amann. Bake for 25-30 minutes till sugar is deeply caramelized and pastry gets golden brown all over; be sure dough is cold when baking pastries. Remove from pan immediately. Put on wire rack; cool.
- Best eaten same day baked; keep leftovers in room temperature in airtight container and reheat for 5 minutes in 300°F oven.

Nutrition Information

- Calories: 453
- Protein: 4 g(8%)
- Total Fat: 27 g(41%)
- Saturated Fat: 16 g(80%)
- Sodium: 212 mg(9%)
- Fiber: 1 g(5%)
- Total Carbohydrate: 51 g(17%)
- Cholesterol: 66 mg(22%)

188. Lavender Honey And Yogurt Pie

Serving: Makes 8 servings | Prep: | Cook: | Ready in:

Ingredients

- 11 whole graham crackers (to yield about 1 1/3 cups crumbs)
- 5 tablespoons unsalted butter, melted
- 1/2 cup old-fashioned rolled oats (not quick-cooking)
- 3 tablespoons firmly packed light brown sugar
- 1/8 teaspoon salt
- 1 envelope unflavored gelatin
- 3 tablespoons cold water
- 1 cup whole-milk yogurt
- 1/2 cup lavender honey
- 1 1/2 cups heavy cream, chilled
- 2 medium-size ripe peaches, peeled, pitted, and cut into 1/4-inch-thick slices
- 2 tablespoons lavender honey
- 1/4 teaspoon ground cinnamon

Direction

- Crust: Preheat an oven to 350°F. Process graham crackers till finely ground in a food processor. Mix salt, brown sugar, oats, melted butter and crumbs till moist in a medium-sized bowl; press on bottom of 9-in. pie plate and all way up sides, tightly packing with fingertips so it's compacted and even. Bake for 6-8 minutes till crisp; fully cool on wire rack. You can wrap crust in plastic and freeze for 1 month.
- Filling: Sprinkle gelatin on cold water in stainless-steel small bowl; soften for 2 minutes. Whisk honey and yogurt in medium-sized bowl.
- Put 2-in. water to bare simmer in small saucepan; put bowl with gelatin above pan without touching water. Heat for 30-60 seconds till it melts, constantly whisking. Whisk into yogurt mixture till smooth.
- Use electric mixer to whip heavy cream till it holds stiff peaks in a big bowl; fold yogurt

mixture gently into whipped cream without deflating cream. Scrape in prepped pie shell and cover in plastic wrap; refrigerate for 6 hours – 1 day till fully set.
- Topping: Mix cinnamon, honey and peach slices in medium-sized bowl when ready to serve; slice pie to wedges. Serve every slice with several peaches alongside.

Nutrition Information

- Calories: 455
- Saturated Fat: 16 g(79%)
- Sodium: 161 mg(7%)
- Fiber: 2 g(7%)
- Total Carbohydrate: 52 g(17%)
- Cholesterol: 84 mg(28%)
- Protein: 5 g(10%)
- Total Fat: 27 g(42%)

189. Lemon Aioli

Serving: 8 | Prep: 15mins | Cook: | Ready in:

Ingredients

- 1/2 cup sour cream
- 1/2 cup mayonnaise
- 1 lemon, zested and juiced, or to taste
- 1 tablespoon olive oil
- 1 tablespoon finely chopped parsley
- 1 tablespoon finely chopped chives
- 1 clove garlic, minced
- 1/4 teaspoon dry mustard
- salt and ground black pepper to taste

Direction

- In a bowl, mix pepper, sour cream, mayonnaise, salt, lemon zest, dry mustard, lemon juice, garlic, olive oil, chives, and parsley together until smooth.

Nutrition Information

- Calories: 148 calories;
- Total Fat: 15.7
- Sodium: 106
- Total Carbohydrate: 2.7
- Cholesterol: 12
- Protein: 0.8

190. Lemon Butter Cookies

Serving: 12 | Prep: | Cook: | Ready in:

Ingredients

- 1/2 cup butter, softened
- 1/2 cup white sugar
- 1 egg
- 1 1/2 cups all-purpose flour
- 2 tablespoons fresh lemon juice
- 1 teaspoon lemon zest
- 1/2 teaspoon baking powder
- 1/8 teaspoon salt
- 1/3 cup granulated sugar for decoration

Direction

- In a big bowl, use an electric mixer to beat sugar and butter together until the mixture is creamy. Beat in egg until fluffy and light. Mix in salt, baking powder, lemon peel and juice, and flour. Cover and chill until firm, for 2 hours.
- Set the oven to 175°C or 350°F to preheat.
- On a work surface coated well with flour, roll out a small amount of dough at a time using a floured rolling pin into 1/4-inch thick while keeping the leftover dough in the fridge. Use a 3-in. round cookie cutter to cut, then remove to ungreased cookie sheet. Use sugar to sprinkle over.
- Bake until edges are browned slightly, about 8-10 minutes, then allow to cool on cookie sheets for a minute. Transfer to wire racks and

let cool thoroughly. Keep in an airtight container.

Nutrition Information

- Calories: 185 calories;
- Total Fat: 8.2
- Sodium: 105
- Total Carbohydrate: 26.1
- Cholesterol: 36
- Protein: 2.2

191. Lemon Buttermilk Chess Tartlets

Serving: Makes 8 tartlets | Prep: | Cook: | Ready in:

Ingredients

- 1 recipe pâte brisée
- 1/2 stick (1/4 cup) unsalted butter, softened
- 1 cup granulated sugar
- 3 large eggs
- 1/4 cup buttermilk
- 2 tablespoons cornmeal
- 1 teaspoon freshly grated lemon zest plus thin strips of lemon zest tied into knots for garnish
- 3 tablespoons fresh lemon juice
- 1/4 teaspoon salt
- confectioners' sugar for dusting the tartlets

Direction

- Roll dough out on a floured surface to 1/8-in. thick; fit into the 8 tartlet tins, each 3/4-in. deep, 3 3/4-in. across top. Roll a rolling pin on tin's edges to trim extra dough; chill shells for about 30 minutes.
- Cream sugar and butter using an electric mixer till fluffy and light in a bowl. One by one, beat in eggs; beat well after each. Beat in salt, lemon juice, grated zest, cornmeal and buttermilk; divide mixture to tartlet shells. Bake tartlets on the baking sheet for 15 minutes on lower third of preheated 425°F oven. Lower oven temperature to 350°F; bake tartlets till set and golden for 10-15 minutes. Cool tartlets in tins on racks till they can get handled. Remove from tins; fully cool on racks. You can make them 1 day ahead and kept loosely covered in a cool place. Lightly dust confectioners' sugar on tartlets; garnish with lemon zest knots.

192. Lemon Cheesecake Squares With Fresh Berries

Serving: Makes 16 squares | Prep: | Cook: | Ready in:

Ingredients

- 9 whole graham crackers
- 5 tablespoons butter
- 1 8-ounce package cream cheese, room temperature
- 1/3 cup sugar
- 1 large egg
- 3 tablespoons sour cream
- 2 tablespoons fresh lemon juice
- 2 teaspoons finely grated lemon peel
- 1 teaspoon vanilla extract
- Fresh berries

Direction

- For Crust: Preheat an oven to 350°F. Fold 16-in. long foil piece to 8x16-in. strip. Put in 8x8x2-in. metal baking pan; on 2 sides, leave overhang. Repeat with another foil sheet in opposing direction, fully lining pan. Butter the foil.
- In heavy-duty plastic bag, put graham crackers; finely crush crackers with mallet/rolling pin. Melt butter on low heat in medium skillet. Remove from heat. Add crumbs; toss to coat. Evenly press crumbs on bottom of prepped pan; bake crust for 12 minutes till deep golden. While prepping filling, cool crust.

- For Filling: Beat sugar and cream cheese using electric mixer till smooth in big bowl. Beat in sour cream and egg, then vanilla, lemon peel and lemon juice; spread batter on crust.
- Bake cheesecake for 30 minutes till set in middle and slightly puffed; fully cool in pan on rack. Chill the cheesecake for at least 2 hours till cold. You can make it 1 day ahead, kept chilled, covered.
- Lift cheesecake from pan, using foil overhang as aid. Cut to 16 squares; put on platter. Put berries on top of each square. Chill for up to 3 hours till serving; serve chilled.

Nutrition Information

- Calories: 140
- Sodium: 94 mg(4%)
- Fiber: 0 g(1%)
- Total Carbohydrate: 11 g(4%)
- Cholesterol: 38 mg(13%)
- Protein: 2 g(4%)
- Total Fat: 10 g(15%)
- Saturated Fat: 6 g(28%)

193. Lemon Crisps

Serving: 48 | Prep: | Cook: | Ready in:

Ingredients

- 1 (18.25 ounce) package lemon cake mix with pudding
- 1 cup crisp rice cereal
- 1/2 cup butter
- 1 egg

Direction

- Set the oven to 180°C or 350°F to preheat.
- Melt margarine or butter on low heat.
- Stir all of ingredients together including margarine or butter, mixing well.
- Form dough into balls, 1-inch size, and arrange on a grease-free cookie sheets, spaced 2 inches apart. Use your thumb to press balls flat.
- Bake until edges turn golden, about 9 minutes. Allow to cool on cookie sheets for a minute. Transfer to wire racks to cool.

Nutrition Information

- Calories: 66 calories;
- Cholesterol: 12
- Protein: 0.8
- Total Fat: 3.3
- Sodium: 97
- Total Carbohydrate: 8.4

194. Lemon Crostata

Serving: Makes 8 servings | Prep: 1.5hours | Cook: 5.5hours | Ready in:

Ingredients

- 3/4 cup whole almonds with skins (1/4 pound), toasted and cooled
- 2 cups all-purpose flour, divided
- 10 tablespoons unsalted butter, softened
- 1/2 cup sugar
- 1 large egg, lightly beaten
- 1/2 teaspoon pure vanilla extract
- 3/4 teaspoon pure almond extract
- 2 teaspoons grated lemon zest
- 1/2 teaspoon salt
- 5 large egg yolks
- 3/4 cup plus 1 tablespoon sugar, divided
- 1 tablespoon grated lemon zest
- 1/2 cup fresh lemon juice
- 6 tablespoons unsalted butter, cut into bits
- 3/4 teaspoon salt
- Equipment: an 8-inch springform pan; a pastry/pizza wheel

Direction

- Dough: Pulse 1/4 cup flour and almonds till finely ground, not to a paste, in a food processor.
- Beat sugar and butter using an electric mixer till fluffy and pale; chill 1 tbsp. beaten egg for egg wash. Beat leftover egg into the butter mixture; beat in almond and vanilla extracts. Mix in leftover 1 3/4 cups flour, salt, zest and almond mixture on low speed till dough just forms. Halve the dough; shape each half to 5-6-in. disk. Separately wrap disks in plastic wrap; chill for a minimum of 30 minutes till firm.
- Filling: Beat 3/4 cup sugar and yolks using cleaned beaters for 5 minutes till tripled in volume and very thick; put in medium heavy saucepan. Mix in salt, butter, juice and zest; cook on medium low heat for 6 minutes till it starts to bubble and curd thickens enough to hold whisk's marks, frequently whisking. Put lemon curd in a bowl; chill for a minimum of 1 hour till cold, surface covered using parchment paper.
- Bake crostata: Preheat an oven with rack in center to 375°F; butter springform pan generously.
- Keeping other piece chilled, roll 1 dough piece to 12-in. round between 2 parchment sheets; dough will get very tender. Remove top parchment sheet; invert dough in springform pan. Patch dough with your fingers; it tears easily. Press dough 1-in. up the side and on bottom of pan; trim excess.
- Chill shell. Roll leftover dough to 12-in. round between parchment sheets; remove top parchment sheet. Cut dough to 10 1/3-in. wide strips using a pastry wheel; slide onto baking sheet, still on parchment. Chill for 30-45 minutes till firm.
- Bake shell for 15-20 minutes till edge is golden and bottom is pale golden; cool shell for 30 minutes in pan on rack.
- Spread filling in shell; put 5 strips on filling, 1-in. apart. Put leftover 5 strips diagonally across initial strips, 1-in. apart, to make a lattice that has diamond-shaped spaces. Flush with shell's edge, trim all strip edges. Brush egg wash on lattice top; sprinkle leftover tbsp. sugar on crostata.
- Bake crostata for 25-30 minutes till filling is bubbly and pastry is golden; fully cool for 2 hours in pan on rack. Juices will thicken.
- You can chill dough for a maximum of 2 days.
- Best eaten same day as made; can get baked 1 day ahead, covered when cool, chilled. Serve in room temperature.

Nutrition Information

- Calories: 571
- Protein: 9 g(18%)
- Total Fat: 33 g(52%)
- Saturated Fat: 16 g(82%)
- Sodium: 325 mg(14%)
- Fiber: 3 g(11%)
- Total Carbohydrate: 61 g(20%)
- Cholesterol: 200 mg(67%)

195. Lemon Layer Cake

Serving: 12 | Prep: 30mins | Cook: 30mins | Ready in:

Ingredients

- 1 (18.25 ounce) package white cake mix
- 1 1/4 cups white sugar
- 5 tablespoons cornstarch
- 3 egg yolks
- 2 tablespoons grated lemon zest
- 3 lemons, juiced
- 2 cups boiling water
- 3 tablespoons butter

Direction

- Follow package directions to prep then bake cake mix for 3 8-in. round pans; fully cool cakes. Split every cake in half to create 6 layers.
- Lemon custard: Mix cornstarch and sugar in a big saucepan/double boiler; then stir well.

Mix in lemon juice, lemon zest and egg yolks. Whisk in boiling water slowly; cook on medium heat till thick, constantly mixing. Take off heat; mix in butter. Put aside; cool.
- Put bottom cake layer onto serving plate; spread about 1/5 lemon custard over. Repeat the layers. Frost sides and top with Seven Minute Frosting.

Nutrition Information

- Calories: 319 calories;
- Sodium: 306
- Total Carbohydrate: 60.3
- Cholesterol: 59
- Protein: 3
- Total Fat: 8.7

196. Lemon Snow Pudding With Basil Custard Sauce

Serving: Makes 6 servings | Prep: 30mins | Cook: 3.5hours | Ready in:

Ingredients

- 1 (1/4-ounce) envelope unflavored gelatin
- 1/4 cup cold water
- 1 cup boiling-hot water
- 3/4 cup sugar
- 1 tablespoon grated lemon zest
- 1/3 cup fresh lemon juice
- 3 large egg whites at room temperature 30 minutes
- 2 cups whole milk
- 1/3 cup sugar
- 1 cup packed basil leaves
- 3 large egg yolks
- Garnish: basil leaves

Direction

- Snow pudding: Mix gelatin in cold water in big bowl; stand for 5 minutes. Mix in juice, lemon zest, sugar and hot water till sugar melts. Put bowl into an ice bath; mix often for 45 minutes till it has a raw egg white-like consistency, thick and cold.
- Beat gelatin mixture using electric mixer on medium high speed for 1-2 minutes till very frothy. Beat whites till they hold soft peaks in another bowl.
- Put whites in gelatin mixture; beat on high speed for 5 minutes, longer for hand-held mixer, till thick enough to make a flat, wide ribbon that holds shape over mixture when you lift beater and tripled in volume. Put it into a big serving bowl; chill for 3 hours till set.
- As snow pudding sets, make custard: Boil pinch salt, sugar and milk in a small saucepan, mixing till sugar melts. Take off heat; mix in basil. Steep for 30 minutes, covered.
- Put yolks into small bowl. Through sieve, strain milk mixture into another bowl; press on hard then discard basil. Put into saucepan. Whisk 1/2 cup of warm milk mixture into the yolks; whisk into leftover milk in saucepan. On medium-low heat, cook till instant-read thermometer reads 170°F and custard coats spoon's back, constantly mixing with a wooden spoon.
- Put custard sauce into a bowl; chill for 2 hours till cold, occasionally mixing.
- Assembly: Put snow pudding into bowls/glasses; put custard sauce over.
- Egg whites won't be fully cookies.
- You can chill, separately, custard sauce and snow pudding for maximum of 1 day, tightly covered.

Nutrition Information

- Calories: 234
- Saturated Fat: 2 g(12%)
- Sodium: 71 mg(3%)
- Fiber: 0 g(1%)
- Total Carbohydrate: 42 g(14%)
- Cholesterol: 100 mg(33%)
- Protein: 7 g(14%)

- Total Fat: 5 g(8%)

197. Lemon Souffles With Boysenberries

Serving: Makes 6 | Prep: | Cook: 40mins | Ready in:

Ingredients

- 6 teaspoons seedless boysenberry jam
- 24 frozen boysenberries or blackberries
- 2 tablespoons finely grated lemon peel
- 3/4 cup sugar, divided
- 1 tablespoon cornstarch
- 3/4 cup whole milk
- 3 large eggs, separated
- 2 tablespoons (1/4 stick) butter
- 5 tablespoons fresh lemon juice
- Powdered sugar

Direction

- Preheat an oven to 400°F. Butter the 6 3/4-cup ramekins then coat in sugar. On bottom of every ramekin, put 4 frozen berries and 1 tsp. jam. Put on baking sheet. Mash 1/2 cup sugar and lemon peel in medium heavy saucepan; whisk in cornstarch and then yolks and milk. Add 2 tbsp. butter; boil on medium heat, constantly whisking. Boil for 1 minuet till thick pudding forms, constantly whisking. Put into big bowl; stir in lemon juice. Season with salt to taste.
- Beat egg whites using electric mixer to soft peaks in medium bowl; beat in 1/4 cup of sugar slowly till stiff yet not dry. Fold whites into the warm lemon pudding. Put mixture on berries; fill it to the top. Bake for 14 minutes till golden around edges, set and puffed; sift powdered sugar over.

198. Lemon Thyme Madeleines With Lemon Vodka Syrup

Serving: Makes about 42 madeleines | Prep: | Cook: | Ready in:

Ingredients

- 2 cups cake flour (not self-rising)
- 1 teaspoon baking powder
- 1/2 teaspoon salt
- 3 tablespoons plus 1 teaspoon freshly grated lemon zest (from about 7 large lemons)
- 1 1/2 tablespoons finely chopped fresh thyme leaves
- 2 sticks (1 cup) unsalted butter, softened
- 2 teaspoons fresh lemon juice
- 2 cups sugar
- 6 large eggs
- 1/4 cup water
- 1/4 cup sugar
- 1/4 cup lemon vodka
- 1/4 cup fresh lemon juice
- 2 teaspoons finely chopped fresh thyme leaves

Direction

- For making madeleines: Heat oven to 325 degrees F beforehand. Butter and flour a madeleine pan generously (preferably non-stick), remove excess flour.
- Whisk thyme, zest, salt, baking powder, and flour together in a bowl.
- In the second bowl, use an electric mixer to beat sugar, lemon juice, and butter together till mixture gets fluffy and light. Add eggs in, one egg at a time, beating well after every addition; add flour mixture, beating till just combined.
- In the prepared madeleine molds, pour some of batter. Smooth the surfaces and scrape back and forth over molds and return excess batter to bowl using a spatula. (This will get rid of any air pockets and guarantee that molds are not overfilled.) Wipe edges of pan to remove excess batter.

- Allow madeleines to bake for 20-25 minutes in the middle of the oven, or till tops turn golden and edges get browned. Loosen edges and remove madeleines to a rack set over a baking dish. Continue to make more madeleines in pan, cleaned, buttered, and floured, with remaining batter following the same steps above.
- For making lemon syrup: While the first batch of madeleines is baking, bring syrup ingredients to a boil in a small saucepan, stirring, then remove from heat.
- Use some of hot syrup to brush over warm madeleines and continue with remaining madeleines when they are done, keep syrup warm.

Nutrition Information

- Calories: 118
- Fiber: 0 g(1%)
- Total Carbohydrate: 16 g(5%)
- Cholesterol: 38 mg(13%)
- Protein: 2 g(3%)
- Total Fat: 5 g(8%)
- Saturated Fat: 3 g(15%)
- Sodium: 47 mg(2%)

199. Lemon Glazed Butter Cake

Serving: Makes 6 servings | Prep: 10mins | Cook: 3hours | Ready in:

Ingredients

- 1 1/2 cups all-purpose flour
- 1 1/2 teaspoons baking powder
- Rounded 1/4 teaspoon salt
- 1/2 cup plus 1 tablespoon whole milk
- 1 tablespoon grated lemon zest
- 1/2 teaspoon pure vanilla extract
- 1 stick unsalted butter, softened
- 3/4 cup granulated sugar
- 3 large eggs at room temperature 30 minutes
- 1 cup confectioners sugar
- 1/4 cup fresh lemon juice
- Garnish: confectioners sugar for dusting

Direction

- Heat the oven with rack in the center to 350°F. Use butter to grease a round cake pan, 8-by 2-inch in size and dust with flour.
- Mix baking powder, salt and flour. Mix zest, vanilla and milk.
- Use electric mixer to whip granulated sugar and butter on moderate speed for 2 minutes till fluffy and pale. Put in the eggs, 1 by 1, whipping thoroughly after every increment.
- Stir in mixture of flour on low speed in 3 additions, alternately with mixture of milk, starting and finishing with mixture of flour and combining till each increment is just blended.
- Put the batter to cake pan and even the top, then gently tap against the counter to get rid of any air bubbles. Bake for 35-40 minutes till golden in color and an inserted wooden pick in the cake middle gets out clean. Cool for 10 minutes in pan.
- Mix lemon juice and confectioners' sugar till smooth.
- Transfer cake to rack place on baking sheet, then invert once more. Brush all of glaze on surface and side of cake. Cool fully.
- Note: Cake may be glazed a day in advance and store at room temperature.

Nutrition Information

- Calories: 477
- Cholesterol: 136 mg(45%)
- Protein: 7 g(15%)
- Total Fat: 19 g(29%)
- Saturated Fat: 11 g(55%)
- Sodium: 237 mg(10%)
- Fiber: 1 g(4%)
- Total Carbohydrate: 71 g(24%)

200. Lemon Lattice White Chocolate Cake

Serving: Serves 12 | Prep: | Cook: | Ready in:

Ingredients

- 3/4 cup fresh lemon juice
- 2 tablespoons cornstarch
- 1 cup plus 2 tablespoons sugar
- 3 large eggs
- 6 large egg yolks
- 1/2 cup plus 1 tablespoon unsalted butter, cut into small pieces
- 2 tablespoons grated lemon peel
- 2 1/4 cups whipping cream
- 4 1/2 ounces imported white chocolate (such as Lindt), chopped
- 3/4 teaspoon vanilla extract
- 2 3/4 cups sifted all purpose flour
- 1 teaspoon baking powder
- 3/4 teaspoon salt
- 4 ounces imported white chocolate (such as Lindt), chopped
- 1 cup whipping cream
- 1/2 cup plus 2 tablespoons milk
- 1 teaspoon vanilla extract
- 1/2 cup (1 stick) unsalted butter, room temperature
- 2 cups sugar
- 4 large eggs, separated

Direction

- Lemon curd: Mix cornstarch and lemon juice in medium heavy saucepan, mixing till cornstarch is dissolved. Whisk in leftover ingredients; cook on medium heat for 7 minutes till it starts to boil, smooth and thick, constantly mixing. Put in medium bowl; to avoid forming a skin, directly put plastic wrap on curd's surface. Refrigerate for 6 hours till chilled. You can prep it days ahead.
- Frosting: Mix chocolate and 1/2 cup cream in small heavy saucepan on low heat till it is smooth and chocolate melts; put into big bowl. Whisk in vanilla and leftover 1 3/4 cups cream; refrigerate for 6 hours till well chilled. You can prep it 1 day ahead.
- Cake: Put rack in middle of oven; preheat it to 350°F. Butter the 3 9-in. diameter cake pans that have 1 1/2-in. high sides; line waxed paper on bottoms. Butter paper. Use flour to dust pans; tap excess out. Sift salt, baking powder and flour into medium bowl then repeat sifting.
- Mix 1/2 cup cream and chocolate till it is smooth and chocolate melts in a medium heavy saucepan on low heat; mix in vanilla, milk and leftover 1/2 cup cream.
- Beat 1 cup sugar and butter using electric mixer till fluffy in big bowl; beat in yolks. Mix dry ingredients, alternately with the white chocolate mixture, into butter mixture, starting then ending with dry ingredients. Beat egg whites with electric mixer with clean dry beaters to soft peaks in medium bowl. Beat in leftover 1 cup sugar slowly; beat till stiff yet not dry. In 2 additions, fold whites into the cake batter. Divide batter to prepped cake pans; bake for 24 minutes till cakes start to pull away from pan's sides and inserted tester in middle exits clean. Cool cakes for 10 minutes in pans on racks. Turn out cakes on racks; peel waxed paper off. Fully cool. You can prep it 4 hours ahead; cover. Stand in room temperature.
- Beat frosting using electric mixer till stiff peaks form in another big bowl. On platter, put 1 cake layer; evenly spread 2/3 cup of lemon curd on cake layer. Spread 3/4 cup of frosting on curd; put 2nd cake layer over. Spread 2/3 cup curd on cake then 3/4 cup frosting; put 3rd cake layer over. Evenly frost sides and tops of cake using 3 cups frosting.
- Put leftover lemon curd into pastry bag with no. 2 star tip; around cake's top, pipe circle of curd, 1/2-in. from edge. Pipe diagonal lines inside circle, making lattice pattern, evenly spaced; keep leftover curd for another time. Put leftover frosting in a clean pastry bag with no. 2 star tip then pipe ruffled border around

bottom and top cake edges. You can prep it maximum of 6 hours ahead, refrigerated. 30 minutes before serving, stand in room temperature.

Nutrition Information

- Calories: 835
- Fiber: 1 g(4%)
- Total Carbohydrate: 91 g(30%)
- Cholesterol: 321 mg(107%)
- Protein: 11 g(22%)
- Total Fat: 49 g(75%)
- Saturated Fat: 29 g(144%)
- Sodium: 270 mg(11%)

201. Lemon Raspberry Cupcakes

Serving: Makes 12 | Prep: | Cook: | Ready in:

Ingredients

- 3/4 cup (12 tablespoons) unsalted butter, room temperature
- 3 cups powdered sugar, divided
- 4 1/2 teaspoons finely grated lemon peel, divided
- 2 large eggs
- 1 1/4 cups self-rising flour
- 1/4 cup buttermilk
- 4 tablespoons fresh lemon juice, divided
- 12 teaspoons plus 1 tablespoon seedless raspberry jam
- Fresh raspberries (for garnish)

Direction

- Preheat an oven to 350°F. Line paper liners on 12 muffin cups. Beat 3 tsp. lemon peel, 1 1/2 cups powdered sugar and butter using electric mixer till blended in big bowl; beat till pale yellow and fluffy. One by one, add eggs; beat to blend after each addition. Beat in 1/2 flour. Add 2 tbsp. lemon juice and buttermilk; beat to blend, then beat in leftover flour.
- Into each muffin liner, drop 1 rounded tbsp. batter; put 1 tsp. raspberry jam on top. Cover with leftover batter, dividing evenly.
- Bake cupcakes for 23 minutes till inserted tester halfway into centers exits clean; in pan on rack, cool cupcakes. Meanwhile, whisk 1 1/2 tsp. lemon peel, 2 tbsp. lemon juice and leftover 1 1/2 cups powdered sugar in small bowl. Spoon 1/2 icing on 6 cupcakes. Whisk 1 tbsp. raspberry jam into leftover icing; spoon on leftover cupcakes. Let it stand for 30 minutes till icing sets; use raspberries to garnish.

Nutrition Information

- Calories: 303
- Saturated Fat: 8 g(38%)
- Sodium: 182 mg(8%)
- Fiber: 1 g(2%)
- Total Carbohydrate: 46 g(15%)
- Cholesterol: 62 mg(21%)
- Protein: 3 g(5%)
- Total Fat: 12 g(19%)

202. Lillet Marshmallows

Serving: Makes about 64 marshmallows | Prep: 25mins | Cook: 3.75hours | Ready in:

Ingredients

- 3 (1/4-ounce) envelopes unflavored gelatin
- 3/4 cup Lillet Blanc, divided
- 1 1/2 cups sugar
- 1 cup light corn syrup
- 1/4 cup water
- About 1/2 cup confectioners sugar for dusting and dredging
- Equipment: a stand mixer fitted with whisk attachment; a candy thermometer

Direction

- Apply a bit of oil to an 8-inch baking pan.
- In the bowl of a mixer, drizzle gelatin on top of half a cup of Lillet let it soften while syrup is prepared.
- In a heavy pot, mix left 1/4 cup of Lillet, a pinch of salt, water, corn syrup and sugar. Let it boil on medium heat but do not stir, until thermometer reads 238-240 degrees. Take away from heat.
- Put hot syrup in the gelatin mixture slowly down the side of bowl in a slow stream while the mixer is on low speed. Turn up the speed to high and beat for 11-13 minutes until mixture becomes very thick and when the beater is lifted, a thick ribbon is formed.
- Scrape the marshmallow in the baking pan, it will be quite gooey, then smoothen the top with a spatula lightly covered in oil. Let it stand without a cover at room temperature for 2-3 hours until the surface is not sticky anymore and using your fingertips you can carefully move the marshmallow away from the pan sides.
- Strain confectioner's sugar using a sieve on a cutting board. Pull the sides of marshmallow from the edge of the pan with the help of a spatula and invert on the cutting board. Sprinkle confectioner's sugar on top. Slice marshmallow in 1-inch squares.
- Coat marshmallow in confectioner's sugar completely.
- It's ideal to make the marshmallows on a dry day. Sugared marshmallows can last up to a week when placed inside an airtight container, layered in sheets of parchment paper, and kept in a dry place at room temperature.

Nutrition Information

- Calories: 40
- Protein: 0 g(1%)
- Total Fat: 0 g(0%)
- Saturated Fat: 0 g(0%)
- Sodium: 4 mg(0%)
- Total Carbohydrate: 10 g(3%)

203. Lime And Lemon Friands

Serving: Makes 12 friands | Prep: | Cook: | Ready in:

Ingredients

- 14 tablespoons butter, melted, divided
- 3/4 cup slivered almonds (about 4 ounces)
- 1/2 cup all purpose flour
- 6 large egg whites
- 2 cups powdered sugar plus additional for sprinkling
- 1 tablespoon finely grated lemon peel
- 1 tablespoon finely grated lime peel

Direction

- Preheat an oven to 400°F. Brush 1 tbsp. melted butter on 12 1/3-cup muffin cups. Pulse flour and almonds till almonds are finely ground in processor. Beat egg whites till frothy in big bowl. Sift 2 cups sugar on egg whites. Add leftover 13 tbsp. melted butter and ground almond mixture; fold to just blend. Divide batter to muffin cups; sprinkle lime peel and lemon peel on tops.
- Bake cakes for 20 minutes till centers spring back when you touch it and golden; cool for 5 minutes. Around molds, run thin knife; invert cakes onto rack. You can make it 8 hours ahead. Cool then cover; keep in room temperature.
- Sprinkle powdered sugar on tops of cakes; serve in room temperature/warm.

Nutrition Information

- Calories: 279
- Total Carbohydrate: 26 g(9%)
- Cholesterol: 36 mg(12%)
- Protein: 4 g(9%)
- Total Fat: 18 g(28%)

- Saturated Fat: 9 g(44%)
- Sodium: 30 mg(1%)
- Fiber: 1 g(6%)

204. Limoncello Tiramisu (Tiramisu Al Limoncello)

Serving: Makes 12 servings or more | Prep: | Cook: | Ready in:

Ingredients

- 5 large eggs
- 5 or 6 lemons
- 1 cup sugar
- 1 1/2 cups limoncello liqueur
- 1 cup water
- 1 pound (2 cups) Mascarpone, at room temperature
- 40 ladyfingers (preferably imported Italian savoiardi), or more as needed
- A double boiler, with a large stainless-steel bowl and a wide saucepan to hold it; a large flexible wire whisk; a shallow-rimmed pan for moistening the savoiardi with syrup
- For assembling the tiramisù: a shallow casserole or baking dish with 3-quart capacity, such as a 9-by-13-inch Pyrex pan

Direction

- So water level is right under mixing bowl's bottom when sitting in pan, put water into double-boiler pan. Separate eggs; put yolks into big bowl of double boiler then whites into separate stainless-steel bowl to whip with electric mixer/by hand.
- From 2 or more lemons, use a fine grater to remove zest to get 2 tbsp. zest. Squeeze out then strain juice of these and other lemons to measure 3/4 cup fresh lemon juice.
- Tiramisu base: Heat water to steady simmer in double boiler. Beat 1/2 cup limoncello, 1/4 cup sugar and egg yolks till well blended, off heat; put bowl above simmering water. Constantly whisk, scraping whisk around bottom and sides of bowl frequently as egg mixture heats into frothy sponge and expands for around 5 minutes or more. Take bowl off double boiler pan when sponge thickens to make ribbon when dropped onto surface; cool.
- Meanwhile, boil 1/2 cup sugar, 1 cup water, all lemon juice and leftover 1 cup limoncello in a saucepan; boil, mixing to dissolve sugar. Cook for 5 minutes, let the alcohol evaporate; fully cool syrup.
- Mix mascarpone to soften with a wooden spoon in another big bowl. Drop in grated lemon zest; beat till creamy and light. By hand/machine, beat leftover 1/4 cup sugar and egg whites till it has medium firm peaks.
- Scrape 1/3 cooked limoncello sponge/zabaglione on mascarpone when it's cool; fold using big rubber spatula. In 2-3 additions, fold in leftover zabaglione; in several additions, fold in whipped egg whites till limoncello-mascarpone cream is evenly blended and light.
- No deeper than 1/4-in. put some cooled syrup in shallow-rimmed pan to moisten savoiardi/ladyfingers. Roll ladyfinger in syrup, one by one; put into baking dish/casserole. Briefly wet each cookie; it'll fall apart if it soaks up a lot of syrup. Put moistened ladyfingers in tight, neat rows, fully filling pan's bottom. You should fit 20 ladyfingers in 1 layer.
- Put 1/2 mascarpone cream-limoncello on lady fingers; smooth it to cover them and fill pan. Dip then put 2nd ladyfingers layer in pan; fully cover with leftover cream.
- Use spatula to smooth cream; seal tiramisu airtight using plastic wrap. Refrigerate for 6 hours – 2 days before serving/put in freeze for about 2 hours. Serve: Cut tiramisu to desired portions. Transfer each from the pan onto dessert plates.

205. Little Lemony Ricotta Cheesecake

Serving: Makes 6 servings | Prep: | Cook: | Ready in:

Ingredients

- Nonstick vegetable oil spray
- 2/3 cup sugar
- 1/2 cup fresh lemon juice
- 4 teaspoons finely grated lemon peel
- 2 8-ounce packages cream cheese, room temperature
- 1 cup whole-milk ricotta cheese
- 2 extra-large eggs
- 2/3 cup purchased lemon curd

Direction

- Preheat the oven to 425 degrees F. With nonstick baking spray, coat eight 3/4-cup ramekins or custard cups. Use an electric mixer to whisk lemon juice, lemon peel and sugar in a big bowl until sugar crystal vanishes/dissolves, for about a minute. Beat ricotta cheese and cream cheese until smooth, for about a minute (some little curds from ricotta may remain). Beat in eggs until mixed well.
- Pour and divide the batter onto prepared ramekins. Put ramekins on rimmed baking sheet. Bake until it inflates, done in the middle, and pale golden on top, for about 18 minutes. Refrigerate until cold, for about 2 hours. DO AHEAD: this can be made a day before. Cover with wrap and keep refrigerated.
- Pour lemon curd and spread over cold cheesecakes. Serve.

Nutrition Information

- Calories: 540
- Total Carbohydrate: 35 g(12%)
- Cholesterol: 201 mg(67%)
- Protein: 12 g(25%)
- Total Fat: 40 g(62%)
- Saturated Fat: 21 g(107%)
- Sodium: 345 mg(14%)
- Fiber: 0 g(2%)

206. Low Fat Banana Bread

Serving: 12 | Prep: 10mins | Cook: 45mins | Ready in:

Ingredients

- 1 1/2 cups all-purpose flour
- 1 cup white sugar
- 1 teaspoon baking soda
- 1 teaspoon salt
- 1 egg
- 1/2 cup light mayonnaise
- 3 ripe bananas, mashed
- 1 teaspoon vanilla extract

Direction

- Preheat the oven to 175 °C or 350 °F. Oil and flour a loaf pan of 9x5-inch in size. In a bowl, mix salt, baking soda, sugar and flour together.
- In a mixing bowl, whisk the egg. Mix in vanilla extract, bananas and mayonnaise till equally combined. Mix in flour mixture till all dry lumps are gone. Put batter into prepped loaf pan.
- In the prepped oven, let bake for 45 minutes till a toothpick pricked into the middle comes out clean. Allow to cool down in the pan for 10 minutes prior to transferring to cool fully on wire rack.

Nutrition Information

- Calories: 171 calories;
- Sodium: 398
- Total Carbohydrate: 38.1
- Cholesterol: 16
- Protein: 2.5
- Total Fat: 1.3

207. Mace Cake

Serving: Makes 10 to 12 (dessert) servings | Prep: 20mins | Cook: 1.5hours | Ready in:

Ingredients

- 4 large eggs
- 2 1/2 cups sugar
- 2 cups all-purpose flour
- 2 teaspoons baking powder
- 1/2 teaspoon salt
- 1 tablespoon plus 1/2 teaspoon ground mace
- 1 cup whole milk
- 1 stick (1/2 cup) unsalted butter
- Accompaniment: lightly sweetened whipped cream

Direction

- In the center position of the oven, put oven rack; preheat the oven to 350°F. Butter then flour 13x9-in. baking pan; knock extra flour out.
- Beat 2 cups sugar and eggs using an electric mixer on high speed for 14-16 minutes if using handheld or 8 minutes if using a stand mixer, till thick enough to make a ribbon that takes 2 seconds to dissolve when you lift beater and tripled in volume in a big bowl.
- Whisk 1 tbsp. mace, salt, baking powder and flour.
- Boil butter and milk in a heavy small saucepan; remove from heat.
- Add flour mixture into egg mixture; mix just till combined. Mix in hot milk mixture till combined and thin.
- Mix leftover 1/2 tsp. mace and leftover 1/2 cup sugar in a small bowl.
- Spread batter in baking pan; evenly sprinkle with mace sugar. As cake bakes, sugar will form a crust. Bake for 25-30 minutes till inserted skewer/wooden pick in center exits clean and is pale golden.
- Cool cake till warm for at least 30 minutes in pan on a rack; cut to squares. Serve in room temperature/warm.
- Cake keeps for 3 days at room temperature in an airtight container.

Nutrition Information

- Calories: 413
- Cholesterol: 101 mg(34%)
- Protein: 6 g(12%)
- Total Fat: 12 g(19%)
- Saturated Fat: 7 g(35%)
- Sodium: 231 mg(10%)
- Fiber: 1 g(3%)
- Total Carbohydrate: 71 g(24%)

208. Madeleines With Lavender Honey

Serving: Makes about 24 | Prep: | Cook: | Ready in:

Ingredients

- 9 tablespoons (1 stick plus 1 tablespoon) unsalted butter
- 4 large egg whites, room temperature
- 1 1/3 cups powdered sugar
- 6 tablespoons all purpose flour
- 1/4 cup almond flour or almond meal
- 1 tablespoon lavender honey
- Madeleine pan

Direction

- Preheat an oven to 350°F. Butter every madeleine mold in pan. Dust in flour; tap out extra. Melt 9 tbsp. unsalted butter on medium heat in medium skillet; cook for 3-4 minutes till butter is golden brown, mixing often. Put aside browned butter.
- Beat almond flour, all-purpose flour, sugar and egg whites using electric mixer till smooth and blended in medium bowl. In microwave-

safe small bowl, put honey; heat for 5-10 seconds just to warm. Beat honey into batter then add browned butter; beat it to blend. Put 1 tbsp. batter in each prepped madeleine mold.

- Bake madeleines for 12 minutes till inserted tester in middle exits clean and tops are just dry; cool for 5 minutes. Tap madeleines gently out of molds. Put on rack; slightly cool.
- Prep extra madeleines: Wash pan; fully cool. Butter then flour molds; fill as mentioned above. Serve the madeleines warm.

209. Maida Heatter's Chocolate Cookies With Gin Soaked Raisins

Serving: Makes about 12 large cookies | Prep: | Cook: 10hours | Ready in:

Ingredients

- 1/2 cup golden raisins
- 1/3 cup gin
- 3 cups sifted confectioners sugar (sift before measuring)
- 2/3 cup sifted unsweetened cocoa powder, preferably Dutch-process (sift before measuring)
- 1 teaspoon instant espresso powder
- 2 tablespoons all-purpose flour (unsifted)
- 3/4 teaspoon salt
- 3 large egg whites
- 1/2 teaspoon vanilla
- 8 oz pecans (2 1/4 cups), toasted, cooled, and coarsely chopped

Direction

- Mix gin and raisins in a cup; stand to macerate for a minimum of 8 hours.
- Preheat an oven to 350°F. Butter then flour 2 big baking sheets; shake extra flour off.
- Using an electric mixer on low speed, mix salt, flour, espresso powder, cocoa and confectioners' sugar. Add vanilla and egg whites; mix till smooth.
- In sieve, drain raisins without pressing; put raisins in dough with pecans. Mix till combined thoroughly; dough will be sticky and thick.
- For each cookie, drop 1/4 cup dough onto baking sheet, minimum of 3-in. apart, working quickly; pat down every mound gently to 1/2-in. thick.
- 1 sheet at 1 time, bake cookies in center of oven till centers are set and cookies look cracked for 15-17 minutes, rotating the sheet halfway through baking; cool cookies for 1 minute on sheet. Carefully transfer to rack; fully cool.
- You may soak raisins in gin for a maximum of 1 week.
- Cookies keep for 5 days in room temperature in airtight container.

Nutrition Information

- Calories: 280
- Total Fat: 14 g(22%)
- Saturated Fat: 2 g(8%)
- Sodium: 161 mg(7%)
- Fiber: 4 g(15%)
- Total Carbohydrate: 36 g(12%)
- Protein: 4 g(8%)

210. Maida's Skinny Whipped Cream

Serving: Makes about 3 cups cream, 16 servings, 3 tablespoons each | Prep: | Cook: | Ready in:

Ingredients

- 1/4 cup reduced-fat sour cream
- 1/2 cup heavy whipping cream
- 2 large egg whites
- 1/4 cup sugar

Direction

- Whisk sour cream till smooth in a small bowl; put aside.
- Whip heavy cream by machine/by hand till it holds soft peaks.
- Meringue: Boil a saucepan half full of water on medium heat. Lower heat so water gently boils.
- Gently whisk sugar and egg whites in an electric mixer's heatproof bowl above a pan of simmering water till sugar dissolves and egg whites are hot; whip by machine with whisk attachment at medium speed till it is cool and rises in volume. Don't overwhip; meringue can get grainy.
- Use a fingertip to test if meringue is still warm. Remove bowl from mixer when meringue rises well in volume before cooled to room temperature; put above a bowl with cold tap water. Mix meringue above cold water using a big rubber spatula till cool when tester using a fingertip.
- If it separates, whisk cream quickly; whisk in sour cream. Fold in meringue using a big rubber spatula.
- Best for any dessert that needs a spoonful of whipped cream.
- Scrape into a shallow bowl if prepping cream ahead; cover in plastic wrap. Keep refrigerate for a few hours only; any longer and it'll separate.

211. Majestic And Moist New Year's Honey Cake

Serving: Serves 8–10 | Prep: | Cook: | Ready in:

Ingredients

- 3 1/2 cups all-purpose flour
- 1 tablespoon baking powder
- 1 teaspoon baking soda
- 1/2 teaspoon salt
- 4 teaspoons ground cinnamon
- 1/2 teaspoon ground cloves
- 1/2 teaspoon ground allspice
- 1 cup vegetable oil
- 1 cup honey
- 1 1/2 cups granulated sugar
- 1/2 cup brown sugar
- 3 eggs
- 1 teaspoon vanilla extract
- 1 cup warm coffee or strong tea
- 1/2 cup fresh orange juice
- 1/4 cup rye or whisky (see Note)
- 1/2 cup slivered or sliced almonds (optional)
- I like this cake best baked in a 9-inch angel food cake pan, but you can also make it in a 10-inch tube or bundt cake pan, a 9-by-13-inch sheet pan, or three 8-by-4 1/2-inch loaf pans.

Direction

- Set an oven to preheat to 350 degrees F. Grease the pans lightly. For gift honey cakes, use cake collars that were designed to fit a particular loaf pan. For angel food and tube pans, line the bottom using parchment paper that's lightly greased. This will make the cake appear professional and irresistible.
- Whisk together the spices, salt, baking soda, baking powder and flour in a big bowl. Create a well in the middle, then add whiskey or rye, orange juice, coffee, vanilla, eggs, sugars, honey and oil.
- Mix together the ingredients well using an electric mixer or a strong wire whisk on low speed to create a thick batter and be sure that no ingredients will be stuck on the bottom of the bowl.
- Scoop the batter in the prepped pan and sprinkle almonds on top of the cake evenly. Put the cake pan on two baking trays that were piled together and let it bake until the cake bounces back once touched lightly in the middle. For the sheet-style cakes, bake it for 40-45 minutes; for loaf cakes, 45-55 minutes; for tube and angel cake pans, let it bake for 60-70 minutes. This batter is liquidy and it will depend on your oven; it might need an

additional time. The cake must bounce back once lightly pressed.
- Allow the cake to stand for 15 minutes prior to taking it out of the pan. Turn it upside down on a wire rack to let it fully cool.
- Note: You may use coffee or orange juice as a replacement for whiskey.

Nutrition Information

- Calories: 919
- Cholesterol: 60 mg(20%)
- Protein: 11 g(22%)
- Total Fat: 31 g(47%)
- Saturated Fat: 2 g(12%)
- Sodium: 663 mg(28%)
- Fiber: 4 g(15%)
- Total Carbohydrate: 155 g(52%)

212. Maple Crunch Layer Cake

Serving: Makes 14 servings | Prep: | Cook: | Ready in:

Ingredients

- Vegetable oil
- 1 cup pure maple syrup
- 1/2 cup sugar
- 2 teaspoons apple cider vinegar
- 2 teaspoons baking soda
- 1 cup coarsely chopped walnuts (about 4 ounces)
- Nonstick vegetable oil spray
- 2 1/2 cups all purpose flour
- 2 teaspoons baking powder
- 1 teaspoon baking soda
- 1/2 teaspoon salt
- 1/4 teaspoon ground cinnamon
- 1/2 cup (1 stick) unsalted butter, room temperature
- 1/2 cup (packed) golden brown sugar
- 1 cup pure maple syrup
- 2 large eggs
- 2 teaspoons vanilla extract
- 1/2 cup buttermilk
- 1/2 cup pure maple syrup
- 4 large egg whites
- 2 cups (4 sticks) unsalted butter, cut into 1/2-inch-thick slices, room temperature

Direction

- For the candy: Line aluminum foil on baking sheet; grease foil with vegetable oil. In heavy medium saucepan, mix apple cider vinegar, sugar, and maple syrup till sugar is dampened. Fasten a candy thermometer. Avoid mixing, boil the mixture over moderately-high heat and boil till temperature reads 300°F, brushing down sides of pan with dampen pastry brush from time to time and twirling the pan, for 7 minutes. Take pan away from heat; stir in the baking soda, then the nuts, mixture will froth up.
- On prepped baking sheet, quickly put the maple candy and scatter to even half-inch thickness, the candy will start to firm briskly. Allow to sit for a minimum of 30 minutes till candy toughens. This can be done a day in advance. Using plastic wrap, tightly cover the baking sheet and keep the candy at room temperature.
- For the cake: Preheat an oven to 350°F. With nonstick spray, coat 2 8-inch diameter with 2-inch high sides cake pans. Line parchment paper on pan bases; grease the parchment. In medium bowl, beat cinnamon, salt, baking soda, baking powder and flour to incorporate.
- In big bowl, whisk butter using electric mixer till fluffy. Put in golden brown sugar and whisk till fluffy and incorporated. Slowly whisk in maple syrup, batter may seem lumpy. Whisk in eggs, one by one, then the vanilla extract. Whisk in the dry ingredients in 3 additions alternately with buttermilk in 2 additions. Distribute batter among prepped pans.
- Let the cakes bake for 30 minutes till tester pricked into middle comes out clean. Allow

the cakes to cool for 5 minutes. Transfer cakes to racks, remove parchment paper, and cool cakes fully. Can be done a day in advance. Tightly wrap; keep at room temperature.

- For the buttercream: In small saucepan, boil maple syrup. Meantime, whisk egg whites with electric mixer in big bowl till stiff peaks create. Do not allow hot maple syrup to touch the beaters, put quarter cup syrup into egg whites, whisking to incorporate. Slowly whisk in leftover hot maple syrup. Keep whisking for 15 minutes till whites are cool and stiff. Put in the butter, a slice at a time, whisking to incorporate after each addition, buttercream may separate and flatten; continue beating till smooth once more.
- Slice sufficient maple candy into quarter-inch portions to get a cup; tightly wrap the rest of maple candy in plastic. On a platter, put a layer of cake. Scatter a cup buttercream on top of cake. Scatter a cup maple candy pieces over; lightly push the candy to stick. Put the other cake layer on top. Smoothly scatter the rest of buttercream over the top and sides of the cake. Can be done a day in advance. Cover using a cake dome; refrigerate. Bring to room temperature prior to proceeding.
- Slice enough of the rest of the maple candy into quarter-inch portions to get 2 cups. Mince sufficient maple candy to get 2 tablespoons. Push the quarter-inch portions onto the sides of cake. On top edge, scatter minced maple candy. Serve the cake in 2 hours.

Nutrition Information

- Calories: 691
- Total Carbohydrate: 72 g(24%)
- Cholesterol: 114 mg(38%)
- Protein: 6 g(12%)
- Total Fat: 44 g(67%)
- Saturated Fat: 22 g(110%)
- Sodium: 407 mg(17%)
- Fiber: 1 g(5%)

213. Maple Walnut Coffeecake

Serving: | Prep: | Cook: | Ready in:

Ingredients

- 1 1/2 cups all-purpose flour
- 1 cup walnuts
- 2/3 cup firmly packed light brown sugar
- 3/4 stick (6 tablespoons) unsalted butter, softened
- 1 1/2 teaspoons cinnamon
- 1/4 teaspoon salt
- 1/4 cup pure maple syrup
- 2 cups all-purpose flour
- 1 1/4 teaspoons double-acting baking powder
- 3/4 teaspoon baking soda
- 1 teaspoon salt
- 1 stick (1/2 cup) unsalted butter, softened
- 2/3 cup firmly packed light brown sugar
- 1/4 cup pure maple syrup
- 1 1/2 teaspoons maple extract
- 1/2 teaspoon vanilla extract
- 2 large eggs
- 3/4 cup sour cream
- confectioners' sugar for sprinkling the coffeecake

Direction

- Crumb mixture: Blend salt, cinnamon, butter, brown sugar, walnuts and flour till it is crumbly and nuts are ground in a food processor. Add syrup; pulse motor till it is well combined.
- Preheat an oven to 350°F. Butter then lightly flour 9-in. pan.
- Batter: Sift salt, baking soda, baking powder and flour into a bowl. Cream brown sugar and butter till it is fluffy and light using an electric mixer in another bowl; beat in vanilla, maple extract and maple syrup. One by one, beat in eggs; beat well after each. Alternately with sour cream, add flour mixture to butter mixture, starting and ending with flour

mixture. Beat after every addition till it just combines.
- Put 1/2 batter in pan, evenly spreading; sprinkle 1/2 crumb mixture. Evenly spread leftover batter on crumb mixture; sprinkle leftover crumb mixture over. Bake cake for 50-60 minutes in center of oven till tester exits clean. Cool cake for 5 minutes in pan on rack; remove pan sides. Put cake on rack, removing bottom of pan; fully cool cake. Sprinkle confectioners' sugar over. You can make coffee cake 1 day ahead, kept wrapped up in plastic wrap.

Nutrition Information

- Calories: 294
- Cholesterol: 49 mg(16%)
- Protein: 4 g(8%)
- Total Fat: 13 g(19%)
- Saturated Fat: 7 g(35%)
- Sodium: 183 mg(8%)
- Fiber: 1 g(4%)
- Total Carbohydrate: 42 g(14%)

214. Maple And Chocolate Chip Shortbread

Serving: Makes 16 | Prep: 25mins | Cook: 2hours | Ready in:

Ingredients

- 3/4 cup (1 1/2 sticks) unsalted butter, room temperature, plus additional for pan
- 7 tablespoons finely ground maple sugar, divided
- 1/4 teaspoon coarse kosher salt
- 1 1/2 cups all purpose flour
- 1/4 cup (about) bittersweet chocolate chips
- 2 teaspoons pure maple syrup (preferably Grade B)

- Test kitchen tip: If maple sugar is coarse, grind it in a food processor until it resembles granulated sugar.

Direction

- Preheat an oven to 300°F. Butter the 9-in. diameter tart pan that has removable bottom. Beat coarse salt, 6 tbsp. maple sugar and room-temperature butter using electric mixer till fluffy, light and sugar melts in big bowl. Add flour; beat till just blended. Evenly pat dough on bottom of prepped pan. In random pattern, press chocolate chips in the dough, spacing the chips 1/2-in., apart, while being visible. Brush maple syrup on dough; evenly sprinkle leftover 1 tbsp. maple sugar.
- Bake shortbread for 55 minutes till firm to touch and golden brown. Put pan on rack; cool it for 10 minutes. Push the tart pan bottom up gently, releasing shortbread. Slice warm shortbread to 16 wedges; fully cool shortbread wedges. Serve.

Nutrition Information

- Calories: 148
- Saturated Fat: 6 g(30%)
- Sodium: 32 mg(1%)
- Fiber: 0 g(2%)
- Total Carbohydrate: 15 g(5%)
- Cholesterol: 23 mg(8%)
- Protein: 1 g(3%)
- Total Fat: 10 g(15%)

215. Maple Glazed Sour Cream Doughnuts With Sugared Walnut Streusel

Serving: Makes about 24 doughnuts and 24 doughnut holes | Prep: | Cook: | Ready in:

Ingredients

- 1 large egg white
- 1/4 cup sugar
- 1 teaspoon ground cinnamon
- 1 1/2 cups chopped walnuts (about 6 ounces)
- 3 1/2 cups all purpose flour
- 1 tablespoon baking powder
- 1 teaspoon ground cinnamon
- 1 teaspoon salt
- 1/2 teaspoon baking soda
- 1 cup sugar
- 2 large eggs
- 2 teaspoons (packed) finely grated orange peel
- 1/2 teaspoon vanilla extract
- 1/3 cup melted unsalted butter, cooled briefly
- 1 cup sour cream
- 2 cups powdered sugar
- 1/4 teaspoon maple extract
- 5 tablespoons (about) heavy whipping cream
- Canola oil (for deep-frying)

Direction

- To make streusel: Set oven to 300°F to preheat. Use parchment paper to line rimmed baking sheet. In a bowl, whisk egg white for about 1 minute until frothy. Whisk in cinnamon and sugar. Fold in the nuts. Spread the mixture on the prepared sheet. Bake for about 12 minutes until starting to dry. Stir with metal spatula to break up the nuts. Keep baking for about 10 minutes until coating and nuts are golden brown and dry; let cool on sheet. Move the streusel to work surface. Chop nuts to get small (rice-size) bits. Move into shallow bowl.
- To make doughnuts: in medium bowl, whisk the first 5 ingredients to blend. Beat eggs and sugar using electric mixer in large bowl for about 3 minutes until very thick. Beat in vanilla and orange peel. Beat in butter gradually; beat in the sour cream in 2 increments. Fold in dry ingredients gently in 4 increments (dough will become lightly sticky). Put aside for 1 hour with a cover.
- To make glaze: In medium bowl, combine maple extract and powdered sugar. Put in 4 tablespoons cream; and whisk until it gets smooth. Whisk in extra cream, 1 teaspoon each time, to form a medium-thick glaze. Allow to stand with a cover for up to 3 hours.
- Slightly sprinkle flour over 2 rimmed baking sheets. On slightly floured surface, press out 1/3 of dough to get the thickness of 1/2- to 2/3-inch. Cut out dough rounds using round cutter 2 1/2-inch in diameter. Place on the floured sheets. Repeat the process with the rest of dough in 2 more batches. Collect all the dough scraps. Press out the dough; cut more dough rounds until no scraps left.
- Cut out middle of each dough round using round cutter measuring 1-inch-diameter to make doughnut holes and doughnuts.
- Line several layers of paper towels to 2 baking sheets. In large deep skillet, add oil to depth of 1 1/2 inches. Insert deep-fry thermometer and heat oil to reach 365°F to 370°F. Fry doughnut holes for about 2 minutes in 2 batches, turning once, until golden brown. Transfer to paper towels using slotted spoon. Fry doughnuts, 3 or 4 pieces each time, for about 1 minute per side, until golden brown. Move doughnuts to paper towels using slotted spoon. Let doughnut holes and doughnuts cool completely.
- Spread 1 side of doughnut with glaze, one by one, then dip the glazed side into streusel. Place doughnuts on rack with streusel side up. Allow glaze to set for minimum of 30 minutes. Use the same glaze to coat doughnut holes and dip them into streusel.

Nutrition Information

- Calories: 261
- Protein: 4 g(8%)
- Total Fat: 12 g(18%)
- Saturated Fat: 4 g(21%)
- Sodium: 161 mg(7%)
- Fiber: 1 g(4%)
- Total Carbohydrate: 36 g(12%)
- Cholesterol: 32 mg(11%)

216. Mascerated Berries With Vanilla Cream

Serving: Makes 6 servings | Prep: | Cook: | Ready in:

Ingredients

- 6 cups fresh mixed berries (scant 2 pounds), divided
- 3/4 cup sugar
- 1/4 cup fresh orange juice
- 1 vanilla bean, halved lengthwise, or 1 1/2 teaspoons vanilla extract
- 1 cup chilled heavy cream
- 1/3 cup sour cream
- 1/4 cup sugar

Direction

- Preparing the berries: Mash 1 cup of berries with orange juice and sugar in a big bowl using the back of a wooden spoon or a potato masher, until the sugar starts to dissolve. Stir in leftover 5 cups of berries gently and allow it to sit at room temperature for 1 to 2 hours, tossing from time to time, until the berries become juicy.
- Making the vanilla cream: Scrape the seeds from the vanilla bean into a medium bowl. Add sugar, sour cream and chilled cream and beat it using an electric mixer or a whisk until it forms soft peaks. Do ahead: This cream can be prepared 30 minutes in advance. Put cover and let it chill.

Nutrition Information

- Calories: 382
- Total Fat: 18 g(27%)
- Saturated Fat: 11 g(53%)
- Sodium: 23 mg(1%)
- Fiber: 4 g(14%)
- Total Carbohydrate: 57 g(19%)
- Cholesterol: 61 mg(20%)
- Protein: 2 g(4%)

217. Mashed Potatoes With Black Olives

Serving: Serves 6 | Prep: | Cook: | Ready in:

Ingredients

- 3 1/2 pounds red-skinned potatoes, peeled, cut into 1-inch pieces
- 2/3 cup milk
- 4 1/2 tablespoons butter
- 2/3 cup chopped pitted brine-cured black olives (such as Kalamata)
- 2 tablespoons chopped Italian parsley
- 3 tablespoons olive oil

Direction

- In big pot with salted boiling water, let potatoes cook for 15 minutes, till extremely tender. Allow to drain. Turn potatoes onto big mixing bowl. Put in butter and milk. Whip with electric mixer, till consistency of potatoes are smooth. Mix olives in. Add pepper and salt to season. Turn onto serving bowl. Scatter parsley over; sprinkle with oil.

Nutrition Information

- Calories: 362
- Saturated Fat: 7 g(35%)
- Sodium: 112 mg(5%)
- Fiber: 4 g(17%)
- Total Carbohydrate: 48 g(16%)
- Cholesterol: 26 mg(9%)
- Protein: 6 g(13%)
- Total Fat: 18 g(27%)

218. Maytag Blue Cheese Souffles With Black Corinth Grapes And Muscat Grape Reduction

Serving: Serves 6 as a cheese course or first course | Prep: | Cook: | Ready in:

Ingredients

- 3 cups Muscat grapes or other grapes (about 1 1/4 pounds)
- 1/2 cup water
- 3 tablespoons finely chopped walnuts (preferably black walnuts*)
- 1/2 cup milk
- 2 tablespoons unsalted butter
- 1/4 cup all-purpose flour
- 1 large egg yolk
- 1/4 pound Maytag Blue cheese**
- 2 large egg whites
- 2 individual brioches (each about 3 inches in diameter)
- 1 tablespoon unsalted butter
- 1 cup black Corinth grapes (Champagne grapes)
- *available at some specialty foods shops and by mail order from American Spoon Foods, tel. (800) 222-5886
- **available at specialty foods and cheese shops and by mail order from Maytag Dairy Farms, tel. (800) 247-2458

Direction

- Grape reduction: Simmer grapes in water in 1 1/2-qt. saucepan for 30 minutes, uncovered. Through fine sieve, put mixture into bowl; to get as much liquid as you can, press on solids hard. Put liquid in cleaned pan; gently boil till reduces to 1/2 cup. Keep sauce, covered, warm. You can make sauce 1 day ahead, covered, chilled. Before serving, reheat sauce to warm.
- Souffles: Preheat an oven to 400°F.
- Butter 6 2 1/2 x 1 1/4-in. or 1/4-cup ramekins. Coat in walnuts; knock out extra walnuts.
- Heat butter and milk in a different 1 1/2-qt. saucepan on medium heat till butter melts; boil. All at once, add flour; vigorously whisk till it boils. Put mixture into bowl; whisk till it doesn't release steam. Whisk in yolk; it'll be stiff. Break 1/2 maytag blue to small pieces; mix into flour mixture using rubber spatula.
- Beat whites using an electric mixer till they hold stiff peaks in a bowl; whisk 1/2 whites to lighten into cheese mixture. Add leftover whites; gently whisk till incorporated. It'll be dense.
- Divide batter to ramekins; put into roasting pan. To reach halfway up ramekin's sides, put hot water in roasting pan; bake soufflés in center of oven for 30 minutes till golden brown and puffed.
- As soufflés bake, make brioche toasts: From brioches, cut 6 1/2-in. thick slices; cut round from each slice using 2 1/2-in. round cutter. Heat butter till foam subsides in 10-12-in. nonstick skillet on medium high heat; sauté brioche rounds for 30 seconds per side till golden. Break leftover 1/2 Maytag Blue to chunks.
- In middle of each of the 6 plates, put brioche toast. One by one, invert soufflés onto big plate; turn right side up. Put a soufflé over each brioche round; put sauce around soufflés. Put leftover cheese and grapes on plates.

Nutrition Information

- Calories: 728
- Saturated Fat: 11 g(53%)
- Sodium: 857 mg(36%)
- Fiber: 5 g(21%)
- Total Carbohydrate: 104 g(35%)
- Cholesterol: 144 mg(48%)
- Protein: 24 g(47%)
- Total Fat: 25 g(38%)

219. Mexican Chocolate Icebox Cake

Serving: Serves 12 | Prep: | Cook: | Ready in:

Ingredients

- 60 sponge-cake-type ladyfingers (from three 3-ounce packages)
- 2 3/4 cups chilled whipping cream
- 4 ounces unsweetened chocolate, chopped
- 1/4 cup sugar
- 1 cup plus 2 tablespoons powdered sugar
- 1/2 cup unsalted butter, room temperature
- 2 teaspoons vanilla extract
- 1 teaspoon ground cinnamon
- 1 ounce semisweet chocolate, grated

Direction

- Line ladyfingers on bottom of 9-in. diameter springform pan; line ladyfingers on pan's sides, standing ladyfingers rounded side out, side by side. Mix 1/4 cup sugar, unsweetened chocolate and 3/4 cup whipping cream till smooth and chocolate melts in small heavy saucepan on low heat; take off heat. Cool it to room temperature.
- Beat 1 tsp. vanilla, butter and 1 cup powdered sugar using electric mixer till blended in big bowl; beat in the cooled chocolate mixture. Use clean dry beaters to beat cinnamon, 1 tsp. vanilla, 2 tbsp. powdered sugar and leftover 2 cups cream till firm peaks form. Into chocolate mixture, fold 1/2 whipped cream mixture.
- In ladyfinger-lined pan, spread 1/2 chocolate fillings; put ladyfingers layer over then leftover chocolate filling. Spread/pipe leftover whipped cream mixture on filling; sprinkle grated semisweet chocolate. Refrigerate for 3 hours till firm. You can make it 1 day ahead; cover, kept refrigerated. Remove the pan sides from cake; serve.

Nutrition Information

- Calories: 562
- Sodium: 103 mg(4%)
- Fiber: 2 g(9%)
- Total Carbohydrate: 54 g(18%)
- Cholesterol: 203 mg(68%)
- Protein: 9 g(17%)
- Total Fat: 35 g(54%)
- Saturated Fat: 21 g(103%)

220. Mexican Chocolate Cherry Rounds

Serving: Makes about 5 dozen | Prep: | Cook: | Ready in:

Ingredients

- 6 ounces unsweetened chocolate, chopped
- 2 cups plus 2 tablespoons all purpose flour
- 1 tablespoon ground cinnamon
- 2 teaspoons baking powder
- 1 teaspoon salt
- 1/4 teaspoon cayenne pepper
- 1/4 teaspoon ground cloves
- 1 3/4 cups sugar
- 1/2 cup (1 stick) unsalted butter, room temperature
- 3 large eggs
- 1 teaspoon vanilla extract
- 2/3 cup powdered sugar
- 60 (about) candied cherry halves

Direction

- Mix chocolate till smooth on top of double boiler above simmering water; cool.
- Mix flour with following 5 ingredients in a medium bowl. Beat butter and 1 3/4 cups sugar using electric mixer till light in big bowl. One by one, beat in eggs then chocolate and vanilla; add dry ingredients slowly, beating till just combined. Chill dough for 2 hours till firm.
- Preheat an oven to 350°F. Butter 2 big baking sheets lightly. In shallow pan, put powdered sugar. Shape dough to 1-in. balls. Roll every ball to coat in sugar; shake excess sugar off.

Put cookies onto prepped baking sheets, 1 1/2-in. apart. Into middle of each cookie, press 1 cherry half; bake for 10 minutes till cookies crack and puff yet soft. Put cookies on rack; fully cool. You can prep ahead; keep for up to 1 week in room temperature in airtight container/frozen for up to 1 month.

Nutrition Information

- Calories: 319
- Saturated Fat: 7 g(37%)
- Sodium: 208 mg(9%)
- Fiber: 3 g(13%)
- Total Carbohydrate: 48 g(16%)
- Cholesterol: 50 mg(17%)
- Protein: 5 g(10%)
- Total Fat: 12 g(19%)

221. Meyer Lemon Budino

Serving: Makes 6 servings | Prep: | Cook: | Ready in:

Ingredients

- 1/2 cup plus 2 tablespoons sugar
- 3 large eggs, separated
- 1/4 cup all purpose flour
- 1/4 cup fresh Meyer lemon juice
- 2 tablespoons fresh regular lemon juice
- 2 tablespoons finely grated Meyer lemon peel
- 3/4 cup plus 2 tablespoons whole milk
- 1/4 teaspoon salt
- Whipped cream (optional)

Direction

- Preheat an oven to 350°F. Butter 6 ramekins or 3/4-cup custard cups. Whisk lemon peel, lemon juice, flour, egg yolks and 1/2 cup sugar till well blended in big bowl; whisk in milk.
- Beat salt and egg whites using electric mixer till frothy in medium bowl. Add leftover 2 tbsp. sugar slowly and beat till soft peaks form. Working in 2 additions, fold beaten egg whites into the lemon mixture; divide it to prepped custard cups. In roasting pan, place custard cups; pour hot water in roasting pan until it reach halfway up custard cup's sides. Bake puddings for 30 minutes till springs back when touched lightly and tops are golden. Remove cups from water. Serve cold/warm with whipped cream (optional).

Nutrition Information

- Calories: 161
- Saturated Fat: 1 g(7%)
- Sodium: 148 mg(6%)
- Fiber: 0 g(2%)
- Total Carbohydrate: 28 g(9%)
- Cholesterol: 97 mg(32%)
- Protein: 5 g(10%)
- Total Fat: 4 g(6%)

222. Meyer Lemon Shortcakes With Meyer Curd And Mixed Citrus

Serving: 8 servings | Prep: | Cook: | Ready in:

Ingredients

- 2 large eggs
- 2 large egg yolks
- 1/3 cup sugar
- 1/3 cup fresh Meyer lemon juice or regular fresh lemon juice
- 1 tablespoon (packed) finely grated Meyer lemon peel or regular lemon peel
- 1/4 teaspoon (generous) coarse kosher salt
- 6 tablespoons (3/4 stick) unsalted butter, cut into 1/4-inch cubes
- 1 3/4 cups unbleached all purpose flour
- 1/4 cup sugar
- 3 1/2 teaspoons baking powder

- 1/2 teaspoon coarse kosher salt
- 2 teaspoons (packed) finely grated Meyer lemon peel or regular lemon peel
- 3 tablespoons chilled unsalted butter, cut into 1/2-inch cubes
- 1 cup plus 2 tablespoons chilled heavy whipping cream
- 1 tablespoon raw sugar*
- 1 cup chilled heavy whipping cream
- 2 tablespoons sugar
- Mixed Citrus "Marmalade"
- Powdered sugar

Direction

- To make Meyer lemon curd: In a moderate-sized metal bowl, whisk together coarse salt, lemon peel, lemon juice, sugar, egg yolks and eggs to blend well. Place this bowl over simmering water in a saucepan and do not let the bottom of bowl touch water. Whisk the mixture continuously about 5-6 minutes without boiling, until thickened and an instant-read thermometer stuck into the mixture reaches 170 degrees F to 172 degrees F. Take the bowl away from simmering water. Whisk into the curd with butter with 2-3 cubes at one time, letting butter melt before adding more while whisking until curd is smooth. Press directly onto the surface of curd with plastic wrap and chill overnight.
- To make biscuits: Set the oven to 375°F. Use parchment paper to line rimmed baking sheet. In a medium bowl, whisk together coarse salt, baking powder, sugar and flour to mix well, then stir in lemon peel. Put in butter cubes and use your fingertips to rub until the mixture looks like coarse meal. Put in 1 cup of cream and stir just until dough starts to clump together, then gather dough together. On a surface covered lightly with flour, turn dough out and press it out to 7-in. round with the thickness about 1 inch. Cut out round with a 2 1/4-in.-diameter cookie cutter dipped into flour. Reshape dough scraps and cut out more dough rounds until enough 8 rounds totally.
- Turn the biscuits to prepared baking sheet with 1-in. space between each other. Use leftover 2 tbsp. of heavy whipping cream to brush the top of biscuits, then sprinkle raw sugar over top. Bake biscuits for 20 minutes, until turn golden and tester tucked into the center comes out clean. Turn the biscuits to rack and allow them to cool thoroughly.
- To make topping: In a medium bowl, use an electric mixer to beat together 2 tbsp. of sugar and 1 cup of cream until forming peaks.
- Halve the biscuits horizontally and put on a plate with the bottom half of each biscuit. Put 1 heaping tbsp. of lemon curd on top of each and then liberal spoonful of Mixed Citrus Marmalade. Top with whipped cream topping, then use top half of biscuit to cover each. Dust powdered sugar over top of shortcakes.

223. Meyer Lemon Soufflé

Serving: Makes 8 servings | Prep: 30mins | Cook: 2hours | Ready in:

Ingredients

- 1 cup whole milk
- 4 large eggs, separated, plus 2 additional large egg whites
- 1/2 cup plus 2 tablespoons sugar plus additional for sprinkling
- 1/2 teaspoon pure vanilla extract
- 2 tablespoons cornstarch
- 1 1/2 teaspoons finely grated Meyer lemon or other lemon zest
- 1/3 cup fresh Meyer lemon or other lemon juice
- 1/2 teaspoon salt
- 1/2 teaspoon cream of tartar
- a 7-inch soufflé dish (6-cup capacity; 3 inches deep); a 7-inch round plus a 32- by 8-inch strip of parchment paper or wax paper

Direction

- Simmer milk in 1 1/2-2-qt. heavy saucepan; take off heat.
- Beat vanilla, sugar and yolks using an electric mixer on high speed for 3-6 minutes till pale and thick in medium bowl. Lower speed to low; add cornstarch, mixing till incorporated. In a slow stream, add hot milk, mixing till smooth.
- Put custard in same saucepan; boil, constantly whisking. Lower heat; simmer for 2 minutes, constantly mixing. It'll be thick. Take off heat. Put into a big bowl; whisk in juice and zest. Use parchment/wax paper round to cover surface; cool for 1 hour to room temperature.
- In lower oven third, put oven rack; preheat the oven to 375°F.
- Butter soufflé dish; sprinkle sugar, turning it to coat all sides. Knock out excess.
- Beat salt and egg whites using cleaned beaters on medium high speed till foamy in another big bowl. Add cream of tartar; put speed on high. Beat till egg whites hold stiff peaks.
- Mix 1/4 whites to lighten into lemon custard; thoroughly yet gently fold in leftover whites. Put mixture in prepped soufflé dish; tightly wrap paper strip around soufflé dish's outside, making collar that extends a minimum of 4-in. above rim then tape overlapping ends together.
- Bake the soufflé for 35-45 minutes till golden in spots and puffed; remove collar. Immediately serve.
- You can make lemon custard, with no egg whites, 1 day ahead, directly covered with wax paper/parchment, chilled.

Nutrition Information

- Calories: 129
- Sodium: 196 mg(8%)
- Fiber: 0 g(0%)
- Total Carbohydrate: 20 g(7%)
- Cholesterol: 96 mg(32%)
- Protein: 5 g(10%)
- Total Fat: 3 g(5%)
- Saturated Fat: 1 g(7%)

224. Mi Tierra Biscochitos

Serving: Makes 36 to 48 cookies | Prep: | Cook: | Ready in:

Ingredients

- 6 cups well-sifted flour
- 3 teaspoons baking powder
- 1 teaspoon salt
- 1 1/2 cups sugar, plus 1/4 cup mixed with 1 tablespoon cinnamon, on a plate
- 2 teaspoons anise seed
- 1 pound lard
- 2 eggs, beaten
- 1/2 cup brandy or sweet wine

Direction

- Blend anise seed, 1 1/2 cups sugar, salt, baking powder and flour on low speed in an electric mixer's bowl. In small batches, add lard, increasing mixer speed to medium till lard is incorporated well. Lower speed to low; add brandy and beaten eggs.
- Use plastic wrap to cover mixing bowl; refrigerate it for 24 hours.
- Preheat an oven to 350°F when ready to bake cookies. Shape dough to ping-pong-ball-size pieces; on each of the 4 cookie sheets, put 12 balls. Dip fork in dry flour; press balls twice to make crisscross pattern. You should get a 1/4-in. high cookie. Bake till bottoms and edges are golden brown, for 12 minutes.
- Remove from oven. One by one, drop baked cookies into cinnamon and sugar mixture using a spoon and spatula; gently roll to coat. Put aside; cool.

225. Mile High Chocolate Cake With Vanilla Buttercream

Serving: Makes 16 servings | Prep: | Cook: | Ready in:

Ingredients

- 1 1/4 cups hot water
- 3/4 cup natural unsweetened cocoa powder (such as Scharffen Berger)
- 2/3 cup sour cream
- 2 2/3 cups all purpose flour
- 2 teaspoons baking powder
- 1 teaspoon baking soda
- 1/2 teaspoon salt
- 3/4 cup (1 1/2 sticks) unsalted butter, room temperature
- 1/2 cup solid vegetable shortening (preferably nonhydrogenated), room temperature
- 1 1/2 cups sugar
- 1 cup (packed) dark brown sugar
- 3 large eggs
- 1 tablespoon vanilla extract
- 5 large egg whites
- 1 2/3 cups sugar, divided
- 1 vanilla bean, split lengthwise
- 1/3 cup water
- 1 pound (4 sticks) unsalted butter, diced, room temperature
- 5 ounces high-quality milk chocolate (such as Lindt), chopped
- 5 ounces bittersweet chocolate (54% to 60% cacao), chopped
- 1 1/4 cups heavy whipping cream
- 2 tablespoons light corn syrup
- 2 tablespoons (1/4 stick) unsalted butter, cut into 1/2-inch cubes, room temperature
- Candy thermometer
- Instant-read thermometer
- Offset spatula

Direction

- For Cake: Butter the 3 8-in. diameter cake pans that have 1 1/2-in. high sides. Line parchment paper round on bottom of each pan; butter parchment. Use flour to dust pans; tap excess out. Whisk sour cream, cocoa powder and 1 1/4 cups hot water till smooth in medium bowl; put aside for 20-30 minutes till cool.
- Put rack in middle of oven; preheat it to 325°F. Into another medium bowl, sift next 4 ingredients. Beat shortening and butter using electric mixer till smooth and well blended in big bowl. Add both sugars; beat for 5 minutes till fluffy and light. Add eggs, one at a time; beat till blended well after each addition. Stir in vanilla. Add flour mixture in 3 batches alternately with the cocoa mixture in 2 batches, starting and finishing with flour mixture, beating just till incorporated. Divide the batter, 2 3/4 cups batter to each, to prepped pans; smooth tops.
- Bake cakes for 50-55 minutes till inserted tester in middle exits clean; cool cakes for 20 minutes in pans on racks. To loosen, run knife around cake's sides. Invert cakes onto racks; fully cool. (You can make it 1 day ahead. Wrap in plastic; keep at room temperature.
- For Vanilla buttercream: Mix 1/3 cup sugar and egg whites in a stand mixer's big bowl with whisk attachment fitted in it. Scrape in seeds from the vanilla bean.
- Mix 1/3 cup water and leftover 1 1/3 cups sugar in medium saucepan. Stir on medium heat till sugar dissolves. Put candy thermometer on pan's side, being sure the thermometer's bulb is immersed in syrup. Raise heat; boil for 5 minutes till temperature reaches soft-ball stage, 238-240°F. Remove syrup from heat immediately; use it within 2 minutes.
- Meanwhile, beat the egg white mixture at medium speed till slightly opaque and very soft peaks form.
- Adjust mixer speed on high. In a steady slow stream, pour hot syrup down bowl's side into egg white mixture; beat till meringue makes stiff peaks. Cool meringue in bowl for 30 minutes till lukewarm and instant-read thermometer reads 100°F. Don't beat.
- Beat meringue again in stand mixer at medium speed. Add butter slowly, 2-3 tbsp. at a time, constantly beating until absorbed

before adding the next. Beat till buttercream is smooth. If the buttercream looks curdled or broken, put mixer bowl with buttercream on medium heat over a stove burner then whisk for 5-10 seconds with a big whisk to slightly warm the mixture, then remove from heat and vigorously whisk/attach bowl onto stand mixer then beat the mixture again on medium speed. Repeat warming and beating buttercream mixture as many times as needed till it isn't curdled and is smooth.

- Horizontally halve each cake to make 6 cake layers using serrated knife; trim domed cake's tops to make even layers if needed. Position one cake layer on a platter. By tablespoonfuls, drop 3/4 cup buttercream on top of cake layer; evenly spread with offset spatula up to edges. Put 2nd cake layer on top; spread with 3/4 cup buttercream. Repeat with 3 more cake layers, spreading each with 3/4 cup buttercream, slightly pressing to adhere. Put 6th cake layer on top; don't spread buttercream on top cake layer. Chill the cake for at least 1 hour.
- For Chocolate glaze: In medium bowl, mix both chocolates. Simmer corn syrup and cream in heavy saucepan then pour hot cream mixture on chocolate; allow to stand for 2 minutes. Whisk the chocolate mixture till smooth and melted. Add butter; whisk till melted. Chill glaze for 30-45 minutes till glaze thickly drips when slowly poured from spoon and slightly thick.
- By teaspoonfuls, spoon glaze around cake's top edge, arranging drips 2-in. apart, letting glaze slowly drip down cake's sides. Spoon leftover glaze on top middle of cake; smooth using offset spatula, fully covering top. Chill cake for at least 1 hour till glaze sets. You can make it 1 day ahead. Use foil to tent; keep chilled. Allow the cake to stand 1 hour before serving at room temperature.

226. Milk Chocolate Mousse

Serving: Makes 2 cups | Prep: | Cook: |Ready in:

Ingredients

- 2 tablespoons brewed coffee
- 5 ounces milk chocolate, coarsely chopped
- 1 tablespoon dark rum (optional)
- 3/4 cup heavy cream

Direction

- Gently simmer water in a small pot on medium heat. Mix rum (optional), coffee and chocolate in a metal medium bowl that may sit over pot with water without touching water. Put bowl over; heat till chocolate melts, mixing often. Take off heat when smooth. Put aside; cool till not warm to touch.
- Whip cream for 1 minute to soft peaks on high speed.
- Fold 1/2 cream into chocolate till some streaks remain and chocolate is combined yet not incorporated fully. Working in 2 batches, add leftover cream; mixing to incorporate fully when you add the final batch.
- Put it into dessert dishes to set to serve alone or leave it in bowl to scoop for serving. Refrigerate for minimum of 1 hour to maximum of 48 hours till set.

Nutrition Information

- Calories: 229
- Cholesterol: 46 mg(15%)
- Protein: 2 g(5%)
- Total Fat: 18 g(28%)
- Saturated Fat: 11 g(56%)
- Sodium: 30 mg(1%)
- Fiber: 1 g(3%)
- Total Carbohydrate: 15 g(5%)

227. Milk Chocolate Mousse With Port Ganache And Whipped Crème Fraîche

Serving: Makes 8 servings | Prep: | Cook: | Ready in:

Ingredients

- 1 1/4 cups plus 1/2 cup (or more) ruby Port
- 1/2 cup heavy whipping cream
- 2 tablespoons (1/4 stick) unsalted butter
- 4 ounces high-quality milk chocolate (such as Lindt, Perugina, or Valrhona), chopped
- 1 tablespoon sugar
- 2 large eggs, separated
- 2 tablespoons water
- 10 tablespoons chilled heavy whipping cream, divided
- 1 tablespoon sugar
- 6 ounces high-quality milk chocolate (such as Lindt, Perugina, or Valrhona), chopped
- 1/3 cup chilled heavy whipping cream
- 1/3 cup chilled crème fraîche*

Direction

- To prepare the ganache: Using a heavy medium saucepan, boil 1 1/4 cups of Port for about 9 minutes or until it reduces to 1/4 cup.
- In a small saucepan, simmer butter and cream. Turn off heat. Add chocolate to the mixture and whisk together until smooth. Add 2 tablespoons for Port reduction to the chocolate mixture, then stir. Add 1 tablespoon of sugar and 1/2 cup of Port to the Port reduction. Boil for 6 to 7 minutes or until syrup thickly coats spoon.
- To prepare mousse: In a heavy medium saucepan, whisk yolks, 2 tablespoons of cream, 2 tablespoons of water, and sugar. Cook and stir over medium-low for 5 minutes or until custard becomes thick enough to coat the spoon; do not boil. Turn off heat. Add chocolate and stir the mixture until smooth. Transfer to a medium bowl. In a separate medium bowl and using an electric mixer, beat egg whites until soft peaks appear. In 2 additions, fold egg whites into the chocolate mixture. In another medium bowl, mix 8 tablespoons of cream until peaks appear. Fold whipped cream into the chocolate mixture. Cover and refrigerate for 6 hours. DO AHEAD: The mousse can be made 1 day in advance, but make sure to keep it chilled.
- To prepare whipped crème fraîche: In a medium bowl and using an electric mixer, beat cream until soft peaks appear. Fold in crème fraîche.
- In 10-second intervals, rewarm ganache in the microwave oven until it becomes warm. Rewarm Port syrup too; if syrup is too thick, thin with Port by 1/2 teaspoonfuls.
- In a small saucepan, pour water and bring almost to boiling. Prepare 8 plates, and on the center of each plate, place 2 tablespoons of warm ganache. Dip tablespoon into hot water in the saucepan; remove excess water. On one edge of the mouse, pull tablespoon in horizontal position, creating a scoop with oval shape. Place 1 scoop of mousse in center of the ganache. Repeat procedure for each plate, dipping spoon into hot water and removing excess water every time you take a scoop from the mousse. Using a smaller spoon, repeat the same procedure to scoop whipped crème fraîche, and place the scoop of crème fraîche alongside mousse on each plate. Drizzle each plate with warm Port syrup around ganache.

228. Milk Chocolate Soufflés With Nougat Whip

Serving: Makes 8 individual soufflés | Prep: | Cook: | Ready in:

Ingredients

- 12 ounces high-quality milk chocolate (such as Lindt, Perugina, or Valrhona), chopped
- 1/2 cup heavy whipping cream
- 2 large egg yolks
- Pinch of salt

- 6 large egg whites, room temperature
- 2 tablespoons sugar
- 1 large egg white, room temperature
- 1 1/2 tablespoons honey
- 1/3 cup chilled heavy whipping cream
- 1 tablespoon amaretto or other almond liqueur
- 1/4 cup whole almonds, toasted, chopped
- 8 3/4-cup soufflé dishes

Direction

- Souffles: Butter the 8 3/4-cup soufflé dishes. Sprinkle sugar; tilt cups to fully coat. Tap extra out. Put prepped soufflé dishes on big baking sheet.
- Mix cream and chocolate in big metal bowl above saucepan with barely simmering water till it is smooth and chocolate melts. Take bowl from above water. Mix salt and egg yolks into chocolate mixture. Beat egg whites using electric mixer till soft peaks form in another big bowl. Add 2 tbsp. sugar slowly, beating till semi-firm peaks form. Fold 1/4 beaten egg whites using rubber spatula into the chocolate mixture to lighten it. Fold leftover egg whites, in 2 additions, into chocolate mixture. Divide chocolate mixture to prepped soufflé dishes, fully filling dishes. You can make it 2 days ahead; refrigerate till cold, uncovered. Cover; keep chilled.
- Nougat whip: Beat egg white using electric mixer till soft peaks form in medium bowl. Add honey slowly, beating for 3 minutes till soft peaks form.
- Mix amaretto and cream in another medium bowl; beat till soft peaks form and thick. Fold almonds and whipped cream mixture into meringue. You can make it 2 hours ahead. Cover; chill.
- Put rack in middle of oven; preheat to 400°F. Bake the soufflés on baking sheet, 18 minutes if chilled, 16 minutes at room temperature, till tops feel firm and puffed.
- Immediately serve soufflés, passing the nougat whip alongside.

229. Mincemeat Soufflé

Serving: Serves 6 | Prep: | Cook: | Ready in:

Ingredients

- 4 large eggs, separated
- 1/3 cup plus 1/4 cup sugar
- 3 1/2 tablespoons all purpose flour
- 1 1/4 cups whole milk
- 1/2 cup purchased mincemeat from jar
- 2 1/2 teaspoons grated orange peel
- 1 teaspoon vanilla extract

Direction

- Beat 1/3 cup sugar and yolks using electric mixer for 3 minutes till thick in medium bowl; beat in flour. Simmer milk in medium heavy saucepan. Whisk hot milk slowly into yolk mixture; put into saucepan. Constantly whisk on medium heat for 2 minutes till custard boils and thickens; take off heat. Whisk in vanilla, peel and mincemeat; cool it to lukewarm.
- Preheat an oven to 400°F then butter 6- to 7-cup soufflé dish. Beat egg whites using clean dry beaters till soft peaks form in big bowl. Add leftover 1/4 cup sugar slowly; beat till you make glossy medium-firm peaks. Fold 1/3 egg whites into the mincemeat mixture; in 2 additions, fold in leftover whites. Put soufflé mixture gently in prepped dish; bake for 35 minutes till soufflé is deep golden and puffed. Immediately serve.

230. Mini Chocolate Sandwich Cookies

Serving: Makes about 200 sandwiches | Prep: 1.5hours | Cook: 3hours | Ready in:

Ingredients

- 2 cups all-purpose flour

- 1/2 teaspoon salt
- 1 1/2 sticks (3/4 cup) unsalted butter, softened
- 2/3 cup sugar
- 2 whole large eggs plus 2 large egg yolks
- 3 oz fine-quality semisweet chocolate, finely chopped, melted, and cooled
- 2 oz fine-quality bittersweet chocolate (not unsweetened), finely chopped, melted, and cooled
- 2 large eggs
- 1 cup confectioners sugar
- 1 1/2 sticks (3/4 cup) unsalted butter, cut into bits
- 4 oz fine-quality bittersweet chocolate (not unsweetened), finely chopped
- an instant-read thermometer

Direction

- In a bowl, whisk salt and flour until combined.
- In another big bowl, whisk together sugar and butter until fluffy and pale using an electric mixer set at medium high speed for 2 minutes if using a stand mixer with the paddle attachment or for 4 minutes if using a hand mixer. Mix in chocolate, yolks and whole eggs until combined. Lower the speed to low and add in the flour mixture. Mix well until combined.
- Set oven to 350 degrees F and place the oven racks in the upper and lower thirds of the oven.
- Put batter by the half a teaspoonfuls on two ungreased cookie sheets 1 inch apart. Let it bake for 7-8 minutes until puffed up. Halfway through baking, turn the pans. Take cookies off pans using a metal spatula and place them on the racks to completely cool. Bake the left dough in the same manner once the cookie sheets have cooled.
- In the top pot of double boiler or a big metal bowl set on a pot with simmering water whisk chocolate, butter, confectioner's sugar and eggs. Whisk until thermometer reads 170 degrees F. Remove bowl, or top pot of double boiler, and set in a bigger bowl with cold water and ice. Stir occasionally until it becomes cold. Take away from ice water and beat for 3 minutes using clean beaters at medium high speed until it becomes fluffy and pale.
- On the flat side of the cookie, spread half a teaspoon of filling. Form a sandwich by placing a second cookie's flat side over the filling. Repeat the process for the rest of the cookies.
- Cookies can last up to 4 days inside an airtight container layered in sheets of wax paper and kept at room temperature.

Nutrition Information

- Calories: 30
- Saturated Fat: 1 g(6%)
- Sodium: 8 mg(0%)
- Fiber: 0 g(0%)
- Total Carbohydrate: 3 g(1%)
- Cholesterol: 9 mg(3%)
- Protein: 0 g(1%)
- Total Fat: 2 g(3%)

231. Mini Crab Cakes

Serving: 18 | Prep: 20mins | Cook: 20mins | Ready in:

Ingredients

- 1 (16 ounce) can fancy lump crabmeat, well drained and picked through for cartilage
- 1 egg, lightly beaten
- 1 cup Dannon Oikos Plain Greek Nonfat Yogurt
- 1/4 cup finely chopped red bell pepper
- 1/4 cup thinly sliced green onion
- 1 teaspoon finely grated zest of one lemon
- Fresh cracked pepper to taste
- 1 cup plain or panko breadcrumbs, divided
- Cooking spray
- 2 tablespoons chopped parsley
- 2 tablespoons chopped basil
- 2 tablespoons lemon juice

Direction

- Combine 1/2 cup breadcrumbs, lemon zest fresh cracked pepper, green onion, red pepper, 1/3 cup yogurt, egg and crabmeat.
- Use a small ice cream scoop or tablespoon to shape mini crab cakes then coat crab cakes in the reserved breadcrumbs, put them on a parchment lined baking sheet. Grease lightly with cooking spray.
- Bake in a preheated oven at 400°F until lightly golden, about 12 to 15 minutes.
- Blend together basil, chopped parsley, lemon juice and remaining yogurt. Add cracked black pepper for seasoning. Enjoy the crab cakes with sauce.

Nutrition Information

- Calories: 56 calories;
- Cholesterol: 30
- Protein: 7.9
- Total Fat: 0.8
- Sodium: 134
- Total Carbohydrate: 5.4

232. Mint Brownies

Serving: Makes 20 small brownies | Prep: | Cook: |Ready in:

Ingredients

- 1/2 cup (1 stick) unsalted butter
- 2 ounces unsweetened chocolate, chopped
- 2 large eggs
- 1 cup sugar
- 1/2 cup all purpose flour
- 1/2 teaspoon peppermint extract
- 1/2 teaspoon vanilla extract
- Pinch of salt
- 1/2 cup chopped pecans
- 1 cup sifted powdered sugar
- 4 tablespoons (1/2 stick) unsalted butter, room temperature
- 1 tablespoon whole milk
- 1/4 teaspoon peppermint extract
- 4 ounces semisweet chocolate, chopped

Direction

- To make brownies, set oven to 350 degrees F and start preheating. Coat an 8x8x2" metal baking pan with a thin layer of butter. In a small saucepan, mix chocolate and butter on low heat until smooth. Put aside. In a large bowl, whisk sugar and eggs for about 5 minutes with an electric mixer until it is lightened in color and forms a fluffy texture. Combine salt, vanilla extract, peppermint, flour and chocolate mixture and stir until nicely blended. Stir in nuts.
- Pour into the greased pan. Bake for about 25 minutes until a tester comes out with wet crumbs after being inserted into the middle. Let chill slightly.
- In a bowl, whip extract, milk, 2 tablespoons of butter and powdered sugar together until it turns creamy to make toppings. Lather on top while brownies are still warm. Let cool for 60 minutes until set.
- In a small saucepan, mix 2 tablespoons of butter and chocolate on low heat until smoothened. Let cool slightly. Spread evenly over the peppermint topping. Chill, covered, for 60 minutes till set. Slice into 20 squares. (Or you can make this 8 hours ahead. Foil-covered and let sit at room temperature).

Nutrition Information

- Calories: 203
- Fiber: 1 g(5%)
- Total Carbohydrate: 22 g(7%)
- Cholesterol: 37 mg(12%)
- Protein: 2 g(4%)
- Total Fat: 13 g(19%)
- Saturated Fat: 7 g(33%)
- Sodium: 24 mg(1%)

233. Minted Blueberries With Lemon Cream

Serving: Serves 2 | Prep: | Cook: | Ready in:

Ingredients

- 2 tablespoons water
- 2 tablespoons sugar
- 1/2 pint picked-over blueberries
- 1 1/2 teaspoons chopped fresh mint leaves
- 1/2 cup well-chilled heavy cream
- 1 teaspoon finely grated fresh lemon zest

Direction

- Simmer 1 tbsp. sugar and water for 1 minute till sugar dissolves in a very small saucepan. Toss mint and blueberries in a small bowl. Chill blueberry mixture till cold for 15 minutes, covered. Divide blueberries to 2 martini glasses.
- Beat leftover 1 tbsp. sugar and cream using electric mixer till it holds stiff peaks in a chilled bowl; fold in zest. Put lemon cream over blueberries.

Nutrition Information

- Calories: 297
- Saturated Fat: 14 g(69%)
- Sodium: 25 mg(1%)
- Fiber: 2 g(8%)
- Total Carbohydrate: 25 g(8%)
- Cholesterol: 82 mg(27%)
- Protein: 2 g(4%)
- Total Fat: 22 g(34%)

234. Mixed Fruit Pavlovas

Serving: Makes 10 servings | Prep: | Cook: | Ready in:

Ingredients

- 3 egg whites
- 3/4 cup plus 2 tablespoons sugar
- 1/2 teaspoon cornstarch
- 1 1/2 cups pastry cream
- 1/2 cup heavy cream
- 1 cup apricot glaze
- 3 to 4 cups assorted seasonal fruit such as sliced peaches, apricots, or plums; berries; or grapes
- 2 cups raspberry sauce
- 1/2 cup powdered sugar

Direction

- Meringues: Preheat an oven to 150°F. Line parchment paper on 2 big baking sheets. On each sheet, trace 5 circles using 3-in. diameter ring mold/bowl as guide. Flip paper so making are under. Whisk egg whites till frothy in a big metal bowl. Whisk in sugar slowly then cornstarch. To bowl, attach candy thermometer; put it above saucepan of simmering water. Keep whisking till thermometer reads 130°F. Take bowl off heat; beat mixture using electric mixer on medium high speed for 5-7 minutes till it holds stiff peaks and cools. Put mixture into a pastry bag with big star tip.
- Pipe meringue on 1 traced circle, starting at middle, working in a spiral outward. Pipe 2nd layer to make outer wall in ring around edge; in same manner, fill leftover circles.
- Bake meringues for 3 hours till dry outside yet soft inside. Put pan on rack; cool for 5 minutes. From parchment, peel meringues. Allow to cool completely on rack. You can make meringues ahead; keep for 2 weeks in airtight container in cool, dry place/frozen for maximum of 3 months in airtight container.
- Filling: Beat cream till stiff peaks form using electric mixer.
- Whisk pastry cream till smooth in big bowl. To lighten, whisk in 1/3 whipped cream; fold in leftover whipped cream.

- Assembly and serving: Boil apricot glaze in small saucepan on medium heat, occasionally mixing. Keep warm.
- Put each meringue onto serving plate; use 3 tbsp. pastry cream mixture to fill. Mound fruit over cream; brush glaze on fruit. Scoop raspberry sauce alongside on the plate. Dust powdered sugar on pavlovas; immediately serve.

235. Mocha Rum Cake

Serving: | Prep: | Cook: | Ready in:

Ingredients

- cocoa powder for dusting
- 3 cups all-purpose flour
- 1 1/2 teaspoons baking soda
- 3/4 teaspoon salt
- 3/4 pound fine-quality bittersweet chocolate (not unsweetened), chopped
- 3 sticks (1 1/2 cups) unsalted butter, cut into pieces
- 1/3 cup dark rum
- 2 cups strong brewed coffee
- 2 1/4 cups granulated sugar
- 3 large eggs, beaten lightly
- 1 1/2 teaspoons vanilla extract
- confectioners' sugar for dusting
- lightly sweetened whipped cream

Direction

- Preparation:
- Preheat the oven to 300 degrees F. Butter the 4.5-in.-deep (twelve cups) Kugelhupf or Bundt pan and dust using the cocoa powder, remove the redundant by knocking.
- Mix salt, baking soda and flour together in the bowl. In the big metal bowl positioned above the saucepan of barely simmering water, melt the butter and chocolate, mixing till becoming smooth. Take the chocolate out of the heat and mix granulated sugar, coffee and rum in. Using the electric mixer to whip in the flour, half cup at a time, scraping down side, and whip in the vanilla and eggs till the batter becomes well-combined. Add the batter to the prepped pan.
- Bake the cake in the oven center roughly 1 hour plus 50 minutes or till the tester comes out clean. Allow the cake to cool down totally in the pan on the rack and turn it onto the rack. Cake may be made 3 days ahead and kept it well-wrapped and chilled.
- Dust the cake using the confectioners' sugar and serve along with the whipped cream.

236. Mocha And Raspberry Trifle

Serving: Serves 12 | Prep: | Cook: | Ready in:

Ingredients

- 3 tablespoons water
- 2 tablespoons sugar
- 3 tablespoons Cognac or other brandy
- 2 cups whole milk
- 1 tablespoon instant espresso powder
- 1 vanilla bean, split lengthwise
- 6 large egg yolks
- 3/4 cup sugar
- 1/4 cup cornstarch
- 3 ounces bittersweet (not unsweetened) or semisweet chocolate, chopped
- 1 3/4 cups chilled whipping cream
- 2 purchased 8-inch-diameter, 1- to 1 1/4-inch-thick round sponge cakes, each cut horizontally in half
- 3/4 cup raspberry preserves (about 10 ounces)
- 2 cups fresh or frozen raspberries (unthawed)
- 2 cups fresh raspberries
- 2 tablespoons red currant jelly, melted with 1 tablespoon water
- 1 1/2 teaspoons sugar
- Red currant bunches or red grape clusters (optional)

Direction

- Syrup: Boil sugar and 3 tbsp. water in small saucepan on medium high heat, mixing till sugar dissolves. Take off heat; stir in cognac then cool.
- Mocha pastry cream: In medium heavy saucepan, mix espresso powder and milk. From vanilla bean, scrape in seeds; add bean. Simmer; take off heat. Discard bean. Beat sugar and yolks using electric mixer for 3 minutes till very thick in big bowl. Mix in cornstarch and beat to blend well. Beat hot milk mixture slowly into egg mixture. Put it into saucepan; whisk on medium heat for 3 minutes till it boils. Take off heat. Add chocolate; whisk till it is smooth and chocolate melts. Put into medium bowl. Press plastic wrap directly on pastry cream's surface; refrigerate for 3 hours till cold. You can make it 2 days ahead. Cover the syrup; keep in room temperature. Keep the pastry cream refrigerated
- Whisk the cold pastry cream till smooth. Beat whipping cream using electric mixer till medium-stiff peaks form in big bowl. In another medium bowl, put 1 1/2 cups of whipped cream; to use as topping, put aside. Mix 1/3 leftover whipped cream from big bowl to lighten into pastry cream. Fold leftover whipped cream from big bowl in 2 additions into pastry cream.
- Assembly: On bottom of 8-in. diameter, 3-qt. trifle bowl, put 1 cake layer; brush 1/4 syrup on cake. Spread 3 tbsp. raspberry preserves on cake. Spread with 1 cup pastry cream. Put 1/2 cup frozen/fresh raspberries on pastry cream. Repeat layering with 1 1/2 cups frozen/fresh raspberries, pastry cream, preserves, syrup and leftover cake layers thrice.
- Spread the reserved 1 1/2 cups of whipped cream on trifle; put 2 cups fresh raspberries on whipped cream. Brush the red currant jelly mixture on raspberries lightly; sprinkle 1 1/2 tsp. sugar. Garnish, if desired, with grape clusters/red currant bunches. Cover; refrigerate for 3 hours. You can make it 8 hours ahead, kept refrigerated.

Nutrition Information

- Calories: 394
- Fiber: 4 g(14%)
- Total Carbohydrate: 55 g(18%)
- Cholesterol: 153 mg(51%)
- Protein: 5 g(10%)
- Total Fat: 17 g(27%)
- Saturated Fat: 10 g(49%)
- Sodium: 68 mg(3%)

237. Mocha Chip Cookies

Serving: Makes about 4 1/2 dozen | Prep: | Cook: | Ready in:

Ingredients

- 1 1/4 cups all purpose flour
- 1 cup whole wheat flour
- 1 tablespoon baking soda
- 1 cup unsalted butter, room temperature
- 3/4 cup sugar
- 3/4 cup (packed) golden brown sugar
- 2 large eggs
- 2 teaspoons instant coffee powder
- 2 teaspoons vanilla extract
- 1 12-ounce package semisweet chocolate chips
- 1 cup chopped toasted walnuts

Direction

- Preheat the oven to 375°F. Combine in medium bowl with baking soda and both flours. Whip both sugars and butter using electric mixer in big bowl till light. Whip in coffee powder, vanilla and eggs. Whip flour mixture in. Mix in nuts and chocolate chips.
- Drop tablespoonfuls of dough to unoiled baking sheets, 2-inch space away. Bake for 9 minutes, till golden brown yet remain soft. Let

cool for 2 minutes on sheets. Turn onto racks and cool down.

Nutrition Information

- Calories: 319
- Sodium: 202 mg(8%)
- Fiber: 2 g(9%)
- Total Carbohydrate: 38 g(13%)
- Cholesterol: 43 mg(14%)
- Protein: 4 g(8%)
- Total Fat: 19 g(29%)
- Saturated Fat: 9 g(47%)

238. Molasses Crinkles

Serving: 48 | Prep: | Cook: | Ready in:

Ingredients

- 3/4 cup shortening
- 1 cup packed brown sugar
- 1 egg
- 1/4 cup molasses
- 2 1/4 cups all-purpose flour
- 2 teaspoons baking soda
- 1/4 teaspoon salt
- 1/2 teaspoon ground cloves
- 1 teaspoon ground cinnamon
- 1 teaspoon ground ginger
- 1/3 cup granulated sugar for decoration

Direction

- Cream brown sugar and shortening. Mix in molasses and egg and combine thoroughly.
- Mix ginger, cinnamon, cloves, salt, baking soda and flour. To the shortening mixture, put flour mixture and combine thoroughly. Place a cover and refrigerate dough for a minimum of 2 to 3 hours.
- Preheat the oven to 175°C or 350°F. Oil the cookie sheets.
- Roll dough forming rounds to the size of big walnuts. Roll rounds in sugar and on the prepped baking sheets, set 3-inch away. Allow to bake for 10 to 12 minutes in the preheated oven. Allow to cool for a minute prior to putting to a wire rack to keep cooling.

Nutrition Information

- Calories: 79 calories;
- Protein: 0.7
- Total Fat: 3.4
- Sodium: 68
- Total Carbohydrate: 11.7
- Cholesterol: 4

239. Moscato Zabaglione With Cornmeal Cookies

Serving: Makes 6 servings | Prep: | Cook: | Ready in:

Ingredients

- 1/2 cup (1 stick) unsalted butter, room temperature
- 1/2 cup sugar
- 1 teaspoon grated lemon peel
- 1/2 teaspoon salt
- 2 large egg yolks
- 1/2 cup yellow cornmeal
- 1 1/4 cups all purpose flour
- 2/3 cup golden raisins (about 4 ounces)
- Powdered sugar
- Zabaglione
- 6 large egg yolks
- 1/3 cup sugar
- 3/4 cup Italian Moscato or Essencia

Direction

- Preparation: To make cookies: In a large bowl, use an electric mixer and whisk 1/2 cup sugar and butter until fluffy. Whisk in salt and lemon peel then the egg yolks. Whisk in

cornmeal then flour. Mix in raisins. Knead the dough just to mix; place onto a sheet of plastic wrap. Roll the dough into a log (2x9-inch) using plastic. Let it chill for 3 hours or up to 1 day until firm.
- Prepare the oven by preheating to 325 degrees F. Use parchment paper to line a large baking sheet. Cut the dough log into rounds with a thickness of 1/4-inch. Transfer rounds to prepared baking sheet and arrange them with 1-inch space apart and reforming into rounds if uneven. Bake cookies for about 15 minutes until edges turn golden. Place onto a rack. Sprinkle with powdered sugar and fully cool. (You can prepare this 3 days in advance. Keep airtight at room temperature.)
- To make zabaglione: In a large metal bowl, beat sugar and egg yolks to mix; slowly mix in Moscato. Place the bowl over the saucepan with simmering water (prevent the bowl from touching the water). Stir for about 4 minutes until the mixture turns foamy and thick and thermometer poked into the mixture reads 160 degrees F. Split up zabaglione among 6 wine glasses. Serve right away passing cookies alongside.

240. Nectarine Cake Squares

Serving: Makes 6 to 8 servings | Prep: | Cook: | Ready in:

Ingredients

- 1 1/2 cups all-purpose flour
- 1 1/2 teaspoons baking powder
- 1/2 teaspoon baking soda
- 1/4 teaspoon salt
- 1 stick (1/2 cup) unsalted butter, softened
- 1 cup plus 3 tablespoons granulated sugar
- 1 teaspoon vanilla
- 1/4 teaspoon almond extract
- 2 large eggs
- 1/2 cup sour cream
- 2 medium firm-ripe nectarines (14 to 16 ounces), quartered lengthwise and pitted
- 1 tablespoon fresh lemon juice
- 2 teaspoons confectioners sugar for dusting

Direction

- Preheat and oven to 350 degrees Fahrenheit. Butter then flour a 13x9x2 inch metal baking pan and knock the excess flour.
- In a small bowl, sift together salt, baking soda, baking powder, and flour. In a large bowl, use an electric mixer to beat together 1 cup granulated sugar and butter at a medium-high speed for about 2 minutes or until light and fluffy. Beat in almond and vanilla extract. Add the eggs one at a time, mixing until just combined at a low speed after every addition. Alternately add sour cream and flour mixture in 3 batches until just combined, mixing after every addition. Spread the batter onto the pan and smooth out the top.
- Cut nectarines into 1/8 inch slices lengthwise and toss with remaining 3 Tbsp. granulated sugar and lemon juice in a bowl. Slightly overlapping, arrange slices in 4 crosswise rows over the batter. Cover cake surface with buttered wax paper to help fruit glaze and bake in the middle of the oven for 15 minutes. Remove the paper and bake for 20 - 25 minutes more, until tester comes out clean when inserted.
- Generously dust with confectioner's sugar while the cake is still warm, and cool completely on a rack.

Nutrition Information

- Calories: 499
- Protein: 7 g(13%)
- Total Fat: 21 g(33%)
- Saturated Fat: 13 g(63%)
- Sodium: 328 mg(14%)
- Fiber: 2 g(8%)
- Total Carbohydrate: 72 g(24%)
- Cholesterol: 113 mg(38%)

241. Nectarine Golden Cake

Serving: Makes 8 servings | Prep: 15mins | Cook: 1.5hours | Ready in:

Ingredients

- 1 cup all-purpose flour
- 2 teaspoons baking powder
- Rounded 1/4 teaspoon salt
- 1 stick unsalted butter, softened
- 3/4 cup plus 1/2 tablespoon sugar, divided
- 2 large eggs
- 1 teaspoon pure vanilla extract
- 1/8 teaspoon pure almond extract
- 2 nectarines, pitted and cut into 1/2-inch-thick wedges
- 1/2 teaspoon grated nutmeg
- Equipment: a 9-inch springform pan

Direction

- Preheat an oven with a rack in the middle to 350 degrees F. Butter a springform pan lightly.
- Whisk salt, baking powder, and flour together.
- Beat 3/4 cup of sugar and butter using an electric mixer until it turns pale and fluffy. Add the eggs one at a time and beat the mixture well after each addition. Beat in the extracts. Mix in the flour mixture until just combined in a low speed.
- Spread the batter in the pan evenly and scatter the nectarines on top. Stir together the remaining 1/2 tablespoon of sugar and nutmeg then, sprinkle over the top. Bake for 45 - 50 minutes until the cake is golden brown and firm yet tender on top when touched lightly (the cake will rise over the fruit). Cool for 10 minutes in the pan and remove the sides from the pan and cool to warm.

Nutrition Information

- Calories: 271
- Total Carbohydrate: 36 g(12%)
- Cholesterol: 77 mg(26%)
- Protein: 4 g(7%)
- Total Fat: 13 g(20%)
- Saturated Fat: 8 g(39%)
- Sodium: 183 mg(8%)
- Fiber: 1 g(4%)

242. New York Style Crumb Cake

Serving: 12 servings | Prep: | Cook: |Ready in:

Ingredients

- 1 cup (packed) dark brown sugar
- 1/2 cup sugar
- 1 1/2 tablespoons ground cinnamon
- 1/2 teaspoon salt
- 1 cup (2 sticks) unsalted butter, melted, warm
- 2 1/2 cups all purpose flour
- 2 1/2 cups all purpose flour
- 1 teaspoon baking soda
- 3/4 teaspoon baking powder
- 1/2 teaspoon salt
- 3/4 cup (1 1/2 sticks) unsalted butter, room temperature
- 1 1/2 cups sugar
- 2 large eggs
- 1 1/3 cups sour cream
- 1 teaspoon vanilla extract

Direction

- Topping: Whisk salt, cinnamon and both sugars to blend in medium bowl. Add warm melted butter; mix to blend. Add flour; toss till moist clumps form and looks slightly wet with a fork. Put aside.
- Cake: Put rack in middle of oven; preheat it to 350°F. Butter the 13x9x2-in. glass baking dish and sift salt, baking powder, baking soda and flour into medium bowl. Beat room-temperature butter using electric mixer till smooth in big bowl. Add sugar; beat till fluffy and light. One by one, add eggs; beat till blended well after each. Add vanilla extract and sour cream; beat till just blended. In 3

additions, add flour mixture; beat till just incorporated after every addition. Put cake batter in prepped baking dish; evenly spread with offset/rubber spatula. Squeeze small topping handfuls together to make small clumps; evenly drop topping clumps on cake batter, fully covering. It'll be thick.
- Bake cake for 1 hour till topping is slightly crisp and deep golden brown and inserted tester in middle exits clean; cool cake for minimum of 30 minutes in dish on rack. You can make it 1 day ahead; fully cool. Cover; stand in room temperature.
- Cut cake to squares; serve at room temperature/slightly warm.

243. Old Fashioned Chocolate Chip Cookies

Serving: Makes about 42 | Prep: | Cook: | Ready in:

Ingredients

- 1 cup (packed) golden brown sugar
- 1/2 cup sugar
- 1/2 cup solid vegetable shortening, room temperature
- 1/2 cup (1 stick) unsalted butter, room temperature
- 2 large eggs
- 1 teaspoon vanilla extract
- 3 cups all purpose flour
- 1 teaspoon baking soda
- 1 teaspoon salt
- 1 12-ounce package semisweet chocolate chips

Direction

- Set oven to preheat at 350°F. Use an electric mixer to beat together both sugars, shortening and butter in large bowl till fluffy and light. Beat eggs and vanilla into the mixture. Mix together the salt, baking soda and flour in large bowl. Add all these dry ingredients into the mixture of butter and mix till incorporated. Stir chocolate chips into the mixture.
- On heavy large baking sheets, drop heaping tablespoonfuls of the dough 2 inches apart. Bake to a golden brown, for about 12 minutes. Transfer the baking sheets to racks; let them cool down for 5 minutes. Transfer the cookies to racks; cool thoroughly.

Nutrition Information

- Calories: 145
- Total Fat: 7 g(11%)
- Saturated Fat: 4 g(18%)
- Sodium: 75 mg(3%)
- Fiber: 1 g(3%)
- Total Carbohydrate: 20 g(7%)
- Cholesterol: 15 mg(5%)
- Protein: 2 g(3%)

244. Onion Fennel Flatbread

Serving: MAKES 4 | Prep: | Cook: | Ready in:

Ingredients

- 1/4 cup (1/2 stick) plus 2 teaspoons unsalted butter, room temperature
- 1 1/2 cups finely chopped onion
- 1 cup warm water (105 °F. to 115 °F.)
- 1 envelope quick-rising yeast
- 1 teaspoon sugar
- 1 1/4 teaspoons salt
- 4 teaspoons fennel seeds
- 3 cup (about) all purpose flour

Direction

- Melt 1/4 cup butter on medium low heat in medium heavy skillet. Add onion; sauté for 15 minutes till very tender. Put into a big electric mixer's bowl with dough hook.
- Put 1 cup warm water in onion; mix in salt, sugar and yeast. Crush 2 tsp. fennel seeds

using mortar and pestle. Put in onion mixture; 1/2 cup at a time, mix in enough flour to create medium-soft dough. Knead the dough for 4 minutes till elastic and smooth on floured surface; leave dough on floured work surface. Use towel to cover; stand for 20 minutes till starting to rise.

- Butter a big heavy baking sheet. Briefly knead dough; divide dough to 4 even pieces. Shape each piece to ball; flatten to 3/4-in. thick 5-in. diameter round. Put rounds on prepped baking sheet; rub leftover 2 tsp. butter on tops. Evenly sprinkle leftover 2 tsp. whole fennel seeds on rounds; gently press to adhere. Use towel to cover; rise for 30 minutes till puffy in a draft-free warm area.
- Meanwhile, preheat an oven to 450°F. Bake the breads for 25 minutes till golden; serve warm.

Nutrition Information

- Calories: 501
- Fiber: 5 g(19%)
- Total Carbohydrate: 80 g(27%)
- Cholesterol: 36 mg(12%)
- Protein: 12 g(23%)
- Total Fat: 15 g(23%)
- Saturated Fat: 9 g(44%)
- Sodium: 545 mg(23%)

245. Orange Angel Food Cake With Caramel Sauce And Tropical Fruit Compote

Serving: Makes 10 servings | Prep: | Cook: | Ready in:

Ingredients

- 1 cup sugar
- 1/3 cup water
- 1 cup heavy whipping cream
- 2 tablespoons (1/4 stick) unsalted butter
- 3/4 teaspoon ground cardamom
- Pinch of salt
- 1 1/4 cups powdered sugar
- 1 cup cake flour
- 1/4 teaspoon salt
- 1 1/3 cups egg whites (about 9 large)
- 1 1/2 teaspoons cream of tartar
- 1 cup superfine sugar
- 1 tablespoon finely grated orange peel
- 1 1/2 teaspoons vanilla extract
- 2 blood oranges
- 3 ripe passion fruits
- 1 kiwi, peeled, quartered lengthwise, then cut crosswise into 1/2-inch slices
- 1 cup 1/2-inch cubes mango
- 1/2 cup 1/2-inch cubes pineapple
- 1 to 2 tablespoons sugar
- 1 tablespoon chopped fresh mint
- Pinch of salt

Direction

- Sauce: Mix 1/3 cup water and sugar in medium heavy saucepan on moderately low heat till sugar is dissolved. Put heat on medium high; boil without mixing for 5 minutes till syrup is deep amber, occasionally brushing pan's sides down using wet pastry brush, swirling pan. Take off heat. Add cream carefully; it'll vigorously bubble. Put pan on low heat; mix till sauce is smooth and caramel bits are dissolved. Take off heat; add pinch of salt, cardamom and butter. Mix till butter melts; cool. You can make it 1 week ahead; cover and chill. Rewarm on low heat/bring to room temperature before using.
- Cake: Preheat an oven to 350°F. Sift salt, flour and powdered sugar thrice; put into medium bowl.
- Beat egg whites using electric mixer till foamy in big bowl. Add cream of tartar and beat till soft peaks form and whites are opaque. Add superfine sugar slowly, beating till fluffy peaks form and whites are shiny and thick. Peaks should gently droop over; don't overbeat. Add vanilla and orange peel; beat till just blended. Sift 1/4 flour mixture on whites; fold flour mixture gently into whites using big rubber spatula. In 3 extra additions, repeat

using leftover flour mixture. Put batter in 10-in. diameter ungreased angel food cake pan that has 4-in. high sides and removable bottom; smooth top. Don't use nonstick pan.

- Bake cake for 50 minutes till springy to touch and golden. Invert pan on work surface immediately if pan has feet. Alternatively, invert center pan's tube onto bottle/funnel's neck. Fully cool cake.
- Tap pan's bottom edge on work surface gently while rotating pan till cake loosens; put on platter. You can make it 8 hours ahead. Use cake dome to cover; stand in room temperature.
- Compote: Cut all white pith and peel from oranges. Cut between the membranes to release the orange segments into bowl using sharp small knife, working above bowl to catch juices. From membranes, squeeze leftover juice into bowl. Cut each in half/thirds if orange segments are big. Halve passion fruits; scoop pulp out. Put into orange segments. Add pinch of salt, mint, sugar and leftover fruits; gently toss to mix. You can make it 2 hours ahead, chilled, covered.
- Cut cake; put on plates. Put compote next to it; put caramel over.

Nutrition Information

- Calories: 520
- Sodium: 190 mg(8%)
- Fiber: 2 g(9%)
- Total Carbohydrate: 78 g(26%)
- Cholesterol: 78 mg(26%)
- Protein: 7 g(14%)
- Total Fat: 22 g(34%)
- Saturated Fat: 13 g(64%)

246. Orange Chocolate Chip Cupcakes With Chocolate Frosting

Serving: Makes 12 cupcakes | Prep: 15mins | Cook: 1.25hours | Ready in:

Ingredients

- 5 tablespoons unsalted butter, softened
- 1/2 cup sugar
- 1 large egg
- Finely grated zest of 1 navel orange
- 1/2 teaspoon vanilla
- 1 cup all-purpose flour
- 1 1/2 teaspoons baking powder
- 1/8 teaspoon salt
- 1/2 cup whole milk
- 1 1/4 cups semisweet mini chocolate chips (7 1/2 oz)
- 1/4 cup heavy cream
- a muffin tin with 12 (1/2-cup) muffin cups, plus paper liners

Direction

- Preheat an oven to 350°F.
- Beat sugar and butter using an electric mixer till fluffy and light in big bowl; beat in vanilla, zest and egg.
- Sift salt, baking powder and flour together; mix on low speed into butter mixture, alternating with milk, starting then ending in flour mixture.
- Fold in 1/2 cup of chips; divide batter to lined muffin cups.
- Bake in center of oven for 20-25 minutes till tester exits clean and pale golden. Turn cupcakes onto rack; fully cool.
- Simmer cream in small heavy saucepan. Add leftover 3/4 cup chips; whisk till smooth. On cupcakes, spread frosting.

Nutrition Information

- Calories: 246
- Saturated Fat: 7 g(36%)

- Sodium: 117 mg(5%)
- Fiber: 1 g(4%)
- Total Carbohydrate: 31 g(10%)
- Cholesterol: 41 mg(14%)
- Protein: 3 g(6%)
- Total Fat: 12 g(19%)

247. Orange Soufflé

Serving: Makes 6 servings | Prep: | Cook: |Ready in:

Ingredients

- 1 cup whole milk
- 1/4 cup plus 3 tablespoons granulated sugar
- 2 tablespoons cornstarch
- 1 1/2 teaspoons finely grated fresh orange zest
- 1 tablespoon unsalted butter
- 1 tablespoon fresh orange juice
- 1 tablespoon Grand Marnier or other orange liqueur
- 4 large eggs, separated
- 1/4 teaspoon salt
- Confectioners sugar for dusting

Direction

- In center position, put oven rack; preheat the oven to 400°F. Butter 9 1/2-in. glass deep-dish pie plate.
- Boil zest, cornstarch, 1/4 cup granulated sugar and milk, constantly whisking, in 2-qt. heavy saucepan on medium heat; boil for 1 minute, whisking. Take off heat; whisk in liqueur, juice and butter till butter melts. Whisk in yolks till blended.
- Beat salt and whites using electric mixer on medium speed till they hold soft peaks in a big bowl. Little by little, add leftover 3 tbsp. granulated sugar; beat till whites hold stiff peaks.
- Fold 1/4 whites to lighten into yolk mixture; thoroughly yet gently fold in leftover whites. Use a rubber spatula to spread in pie plate;

bake for 16-18 minutes till golden and puffed. Dust confectioners' sugar; immediately serve.

Nutrition Information

- Calories: 171
- Sodium: 163 mg(7%)
- Fiber: 0 g(0%)
- Total Carbohydrate: 22 g(7%)
- Cholesterol: 133 mg(44%)
- Protein: 6 g(11%)
- Total Fat: 6 g(10%)
- Saturated Fat: 3 g(15%)

248. Orange Tapioca Pudding

Serving: Makes 6 servings | Prep: 1hours | Cook: 2hours | Ready in:

Ingredients

- 2 navel oranges
- 2 tablespoons orange liqueur such as Grand Marnier or Cointreau
- 1/3 cup plus 3 tablespoons sugar, divided
- 1/3 cup tapioca pearls (preferably 1/8 inch; not quick-cooking)
- 3 cups whole milk
- 2 large eggs, separated
- 1/2 cup chilled heavy cream

Direction

- Finely grate to measure 1 tsp of orange zest. Use a sharp knife to cut then discard the leftover white pith and peel from oranges. Cut into membrane-free segments then drop them into a bowl, squeeze membrane juices to measure enough 3 tbsp. then add into the segments. Place in 2 tbsp. of sugar and liqueur then toss with the segments. Allow to macerate for 20 minutes.
- Meanwhile, in a heavy medium saucepan, cook and stir 1/8 tsp of salt, 1/3 cup of sugar, grated zest, milk and tapioca over medium

heat to dissolve the sugar. Let boil while stirring occasionally then lower to medium-low heat and simmer gently for 10 minutes, constantly stir till thick. Through a sieve set over saucepan, drain the segments of oranges then transfer the liquid into tapioca, save the segments. Simmer gently for 20-30 minutes, constantly stir till tapioca pearls turn translucent completely.

- In a metal bowl, whisk egg yolks together then whisk in hot pudding slowly. Set the bowl in an ice bath and stir occasionally till cool to quick-chill. The pudding will be thickened.
- Use an electric mixer to beat a pinch of salt with egg whites till soft peaks form. Place in the leftover tbsp. of sugar then beat white till stiff peaks form.
- In a separate bowl, beat cream using clean beaters till stiff peaks form. Gently but thoroughly fold whites then cream into the pudding.
- Place the orange segments into 6 small bowls, ramekins or glasses and place pudding on top. Cover and let chill for at least 1 hour.
- Note: The egg whites in this recipe are not cooked. This may be of concern if salmonella is a problem in your area.
- You can chill the pudding for up to 3 days.

Nutrition Information

- Calories: 296
- Protein: 7 g(14%)
- Total Fat: 13 g(20%)
- Saturated Fat: 7 g(37%)
- Sodium: 84 mg(4%)
- Fiber: 1 g(4%)
- Total Carbohydrate: 37 g(12%)
- Cholesterol: 101 mg(34%)

249. Orange Almond Cake With Chocolate Icing

Serving: Serves 10 | Prep: | Cook: | Ready in:

Ingredients

- 3 large oranges
- 2 cups plus 2 tablespoons all purpose flour
- 1 cup whole almonds
- 2 teaspoons baking powder
- 1/2 teaspoon salt
- 2 cups plus generous 1 tablespoon sugar
- 1 cup unsalted butter, room temperature
- 4 large eggs
- 1 cup whole milk
- 1/2 teaspoon vanilla extract
- 1/4 teaspoon almond extract
- 1 1/2 cups fresh orange juice
- Chocolate Icing
- Additional whole almonds
- Small orange-slice triangles
- Fresh mint leaves

Direction

- Preheat an oven to 350°F. Butter the three 9-in. diameter cake pans that have 1 1/2-in. high sides. Dust with flour; tap excess out. Remove peel in strips, orange part only, from oranges using vegetable peeler. Chop peel coarsely to get 1/2 cup. Blend salt, baking powder, 1 cup almonds and flour till finely ground in processor. Transfer into medium bowl. Blend orange peel and 2 cups sugar till peel is minced finely in processor.
- Beat butter using electric mixer till blended in big bowl. Add sugar mixture; beat till fluffy. Beat in eggs, one at a time. Mix both extracts and milk in small bowl. Working in 3 additions each, beat flour mixture alternately with the milk mixture into egg mixture on low speed; divide batter to prepped pans.
- Bake cakes for 25 minutes till inserted tester in middle exits clean; cool cakes for 5 minutes in pans on racks. Turn cakes out onto racks; fully cool. Boil leftover generous 1 tbsp. sugar and 1

1/2 cups of fresh orange juice in small saucepan for 8 minutes till reduced to 1/2 cup. Brush warm juice mixture over cooled cake tops.
- Put 1 cake layer on cake platter, orange syrup side up; spread with 1 cup chocolate icing. Top with the second cake layer; spread with 1 cup icing. Put 3rd cake layer over, syrup side up; spread leftover icing on sides and tops of cake. (You can make it 1 day ahead; use cake dome to cover. Keep at room temperature.) Put mint leaves, orange triangles and extra almonds around cake's top edge; slice cake. Serve.

250. Orange Almond Cream Cake

Serving: Makes 8 to 10 servings | Prep: | Cook: |Ready in:

Ingredients

- 2 cups whole milk
- 1 tablespoon grated orange peel
- 6 large egg yolks
- 2/3 cup sugar
- 1/2 cup all purpose flour
- 1/4 cup (1/2 stick) unsalted butter, cut into 1/2-inch cubes, room temperature
- 4 teaspoons vanilla extract
- 1 cup sugar
- 1 cup water
- 3 tablespoons Grand Marnier or other orange-flavored liqueur
- 1 cup whole milk
- 2 tablespoons (1/4 stick) unsalted butter
- 2 cups sifted cake flour (sifted, then measured)
- 2 teaspoons baking powder
- 1/2 teaspoon salt
- 4 large eggs
- 1 3/4 cups sugar, divided
- 2 teaspoons vanilla extract
- 4 teaspoons grated orange peel, divided
- 8 large navel oranges
- 2 cups chilled heavy whipping cream
- 1/2 cup coarsely crushed amaretti cookies (Italian macaroons)*
- 1/4 cup apricot jam, melted

Direction

- Cream filling: Simmer orange peel and milk in medium heavy saucepan; take off heat. Beat yolks using electric mixer to blend in big bowl. Add sugar as machine runs; beat for 4 minutes till it is thick and light yellow. Add flour; beat till combined well. Beat in the hot milk mixture slowly; put custard back to same saucepan. Cook on medium heat for 3 minutes till it thickens and boils, constantly mixing. Take off heat. Whisk in vanilla and butter. Put cream filling in medium bowl; press surface with plastic wrap. Refrigerate the cream filling overnight. You can make it 2 days ahead, kept refrigerated.
- Syrup: Boil 1 cup water and sugar in small saucepan, mixing to melt sugar; boil, occasionally swirling pan, for 5 minutes. Slightly cool. Mix in Grand Marnier and cover; chill till cold. You can make it 2 days ahead, kept chilled.
- Cake: In middle of oven, put rack; preheat it to 350°F. Butter the 2 9-in. diameter cake pans that have 1 1/2-in. high sides; line parchment paper round on each pan. Bring butter and milk almost to boil in the small saucepan; take off heat. Sift salt, baking powder and flour into medium bowl.
- Beat egg using electric mixer for 2 minutes on high speed in big bowl. 1 tbsp. at a time, beat in 1 1/2 cups of sugar slowly; beat for 5 minutes till thick and light yellow, occasionally scraping down sides. Lower speed to medium high then add vanilla; in steady stream, beat in the hot milk mixture slowly. Add dry ingredients immediately; beat just till blended and thin, scraping bowl's sides down occasionally. Stir in 3 tsp. orange peel; divide batter to prepped pans quickly.
- Bake for 30 minutes till spring back when center is pressed, pulls away from pan's sides

and are golden. Cool for 10 minutes in pan on rack. Invert cakes; peel parchment paper off. Flip cakes on rack, right side up; fully cool. You can make it 1 day ahead. In plastic, wrap; stand in room temperature.

- Cut off white pith and peel from oranges using small sharp knife; cut between the membranes to release the segments above a strainer set above a big bowl. Put orange segments on paper towels; drain.
- Beat 1/4 cup sugar and cream till cream holds peaks in big bowl. Into cream filling, fold 1/2 cup of whipped crema; fold in leftover 1 tsp. grated orange peel and crushed amaretti. Horizontally halve each cake layer to make 4 layers using serrated knife. Put 1 cake, cut side up, on plate; generously brush 6 tbsp. syrup. Spread with 3/4 cup filling. Put 20 orange segments in 1 layer on filling; repeat layering twice with orange segments, filling, syrup and cake. Put leftover cake layer over, cut side down; brush syrup on cake. Use 1 cup whipped cream to fill pastry bag with big star tip. Spread leftover whipped cream on sides and top of cake; in rosettes, pipe cream around cake's top edge. Use orange segments to cover center; brush melted apricot jam on oranges. Refrigerate it for 3 hours. You can make it 1 day ahead, kept refrigerated.

Nutrition Information

- Calories: 1056
- Total Carbohydrate: 160 g(53%)
- Cholesterol: 345 mg(115%)
- Protein: 15 g(30%)
- Total Fat: 41 g(62%)
- Saturated Fat: 23 g(115%)
- Sodium: 365 mg(15%)
- Fiber: 5 g(20%)

251. Panettone With Candied Fruit

Serving: Makes 2 (8-inch) or 8 (3 1/2-inch) loaves | Prep: | Cook: |Ready in:

Ingredients

- 1/4 teaspoon sugar
- 1 teaspoon active dry yeast
- 2/3 cup all-purpose flour
- 1 teaspoon active dry yeast
- 2 large egg yolks
- 1 tablespoon sugar
- 1 1/3 cups flour
- 3 1/2 cups flour
- 9 large egg yolks
- 1/3 cup plus 1 tablespoon milk
- 2 tablespoons honey
- 3/4 cup sugar
- 20 tablespoons (2 1/2 sticks) unsalted butter
- 2 teaspoons salt
- 1 teaspoon vanilla extract
- 1 cup mixed candied fruit (such as glacéed cherries and citron, orange, or lemon peel), diced
- 1 cup golden raisins
- *Available at baking supply stores and www.sugarcraft.com.
- 2 (8-inch) or 8 (3 1/2-inch) paper panettone molds*

Direction

- Biga: Mix sugar and 1/3 cup warm (105-115°F) water in a standing mixer's bowl with dough hook; mix in yeast. Allow to stand for 5 minutes till yeast melts. Add flour; mix on low speed for 2 minutes till smooth. Use plastic wrap to cover bowl; rise for 3 hours till tripled in volume in draft-free, warm area. You can make it 5 days ahead. Mix down start; cover. Chill. Before using, bring to room temperature.
- Start dough: Mix yeast and 1/4 cup warm, 105-115°F, water in a small bowl; stand for 5 minutes till yeast melts. Attach bowl with biga on standing mixer with dough hook. Add

yeast mixture; mix on low speed for 2 minutes till combined. Add flour, sugar and egg yolks; mix on medium speed for 5 minutes till smooth and shiny. Use plastic wrap to cover bowl; rise for 3 hours till tripled in volume in draft-free, warm place.

- Finish dough then bake bread: Attach bowl with dough in standing mixer with dough hook. Add 10 tbsp. butter, 1/4 cup sugar, honey, milk, egg yolks and flour; mix on medium speed for 3 minutes till blended. Add leftover sugar, vanilla and salt; mix on medium speed for 5 minutes till well blended.
- 1 tbsp. at once, add leftover 10 tbsp. butter as mixer runs; dough will pull away from bowl's sides, shiny and smooth. Add raisins and candied fruit; mix for 1 minute till blended. Shape dough to ball; put into big bowl. Use clean kitchen towel to cover; rise for 3 hours till doubled in volume in a draft-free, warm area.
- Preheat an oven to 350°F. Butter the 8 3 1/2-in. or 2 8-in. paper panettone molds. Punch dough down; turn onto work surface. Halve dough to 2 pieces; shape each to ball. Divide dough to 8 small balls if using small molds. In each mold, put 1 ball; use clean kitchen towel to cover. Rise for 1 hour till dough springs back when poked and risen part the rim in a draft-free, warm place.
- Bake for 45-50 minutes till golden brown. Stick 2 skewers through each mold's base to cool; suspend the bread upside down by resting the skewers on 2 containers that are taller than bread. This avoids deflating bread while it cools.
- Wrap in plastic wrap well then in tissue/parchment paper when loaves are cool; keep in room temperature.

Nutrition Information

- Calories: 5243
- Fiber: 26 g(102%)
- Total Carbohydrate: 775 g(258%)
- Cholesterol: 1460 mg(487%)
- Protein: 100 g(201%)
- Total Fat: 198 g(305%)
- Saturated Fat: 93 g(467%)
- Sodium: 3196 mg(133%)

252. Paskha Cheese

Serving: Makes10 generous servings | Prep: | Cook: | Ready in:

Ingredients

- 1/3 cup brandy
- 1 cup loosely packed golden raisins (5 ounces)
- 2 pounds farmer cheese*
- 2 hard-boiled large egg yolks (reserve whites for another use if desired)
- 1 stick (1/2 cup) unsalted butter, softened
- 3/4 cup sugar
- 1 cup sour cream
- 2 teaspoons vanilla
- 1/4 teaspoon salt
- 1 cup chilled heavy cream
- a wooden paskha cheese mold** or a clean 2-quart terra-cotta flowerpot with a drainage hole and a plate slightly smaller than top of pot; cheesecloth; 2 lb of weights such as large soup or vegetable cans

Direction

- Over low heat, heat the brandy along with raisins in a small saucepan until warm. Take out from the heat source and allow to steep for about 15 minutes until the raisins are softened.
- Force yolks and cheese through a medium-mesh sieve or a potato ricer into a bowl.
- Use an electric mixer at medium speed to beat sugar and butter together in a large bowl for about 2 minutes until fluffy and pale. Add salt, vanilla, sour cream and cheese mixture and beat until blended. Then use cleaned beaters to beat cream in a bowl until it holds soft peaks. Gently fold raisins and whipped cream along

with the remaining brandy into the cheese mixture but thoroughly.
- Line a single layer of cheesecloth onto the mold (or flowerpot) and leave about 2- to 3-inch overhang on all sides. Then ladle the cheese mixture into the mold, and fold the ends of the cheesecloth over the top. Place a lid on the cheesecloth and add weights on top of lid (or on top of foil and small plate in case you are using flowerpot). Refrigerate the mold on a huge plate (to hold the drips) for at least 24 hours.
- Take out the lid from mold and open the cheesecloth. Then invert a serving plate atop mold and invert the mold on top of the plate. Then unlock the hinges, open the mold and remove the cheesecloth. Cover the cheese loosely with plastic wrap and leave to sit for 30 minutes at room temperature.

Nutrition Information

- Calories: 1225
- Saturated Fat: 54 g(269%)
- Sodium: 1619 mg(67%)
- Fiber: 1 g(2%)
- Total Carbohydrate: 34 g(11%)
- Cholesterol: 322 mg(107%)
- Protein: 59 g(119%)
- Total Fat: 94 g(144%)

253. Pavlova With A Passionfruit Curd

Serving: makes 4 servings | Prep: | Cook: | Ready in:

Ingredients

- 4 egg whites
- 2/3 cup superfine sugar
- 1 teaspoon white wine vinegar
- 1 tablespoon hot water
- 1 1/4 cups heavy cream
- 2 eggs, plus 2 extra yolks
- 5 tablespoons fresh passionfruit pulp
- 1 oz. unsalted butter cut into small dice
- 1/4 cup superfine sugar

Direction

- Preheat an oven to 300°. Oil a big baking parchment piece on a baking sheet. Whisk hot water, vinegar, sugar and egg whites for 5 minutes till soft, white peaks form on highest speed in a food mixer's bowl. Put mixture into 8-in. round on oiled paper/put 4 high rounds to make individual pavlovas on the paper. Cook in middle of oven till crisp for 1 hour 10 minutes; individual pavlovas take 1 hour. On wire rack, cool.
- Passionfruit curd: Constantly mix all ingredients in a bowl above a pan with simmering water till it looks like thin custard and begins to thicken; cook for 10 minute till it thickens more, still mixing. Immediately take off heat to not overcook. Put curd into a clean container/jar; cool. Cover; refrigerate.
- Serve: Whip cream to soft peaks; put onto pavlova base, spreading it out with a palette knife to edges. Put spoonful of cream over each pavlova for individual pavlovas; put passionfruit curd on top.

Nutrition Information

- Calories: 535
- Cholesterol: 197 mg(66%)
- Protein: 7 g(15%)
- Total Fat: 35 g(54%)
- Saturated Fat: 21 g(107%)
- Sodium: 104 mg(4%)
- Fiber: 0 g(0%)
- Total Carbohydrate: 49 g(16%)

254. Pb&j Crumble Bars

Serving: Makes 24 bars | Prep: | Cook: | Ready in:

Ingredients

- 3/4 stick (6 tablespoons) unsalted butter, softened
- 6 tablespoons peanut butter
- 1/2 cup packed light brown sugar
- 1 large egg
- 1 1/2 cups all-purpose flour
- 1/2 teaspoon salt
- 1/2 cup grape jelly

Direction

- In center position, put oven rack; preheat an oven to 350°F. Line foil on 9-in. square baking pan.
- Use an electric mixer on medium speed to beat brown sugar, peanut butter and butter for 2 minutes till fluffy in a big bowl. Add egg; beat till combined. Mix in salt and flour on low speed till dough forms.
- Keep 1 cup dough for the topping; evenly press leftover dough on bottom of baking pan. In an even layer, spread jelly over dough; crumble reserved dough coarsely on jelly layer. Bake for 30-35 minutes till top is golden; fully cool for 45 minutes in pan on rack. Cut to bars.

Nutrition Information

- Calories: 117
- Saturated Fat: 2 g(12%)
- Sodium: 56 mg(2%)
- Fiber: 0 g(2%)
- Total Carbohydrate: 16 g(5%)
- Cholesterol: 15 mg(5%)
- Protein: 2 g(4%)
- Total Fat: 5 g(8%)

---

255. Peach Ice Cream Pie With Amaretti Cookie Crust

Serving: Makes 8 to 10 servings | Prep: 1hours30mins | Cook: 11hours |Ready in:

Ingredients

- Nonstick vegetable oil spray
- 1 1/3 cups finely ground amaretti cookies (Italian macaroons) plus 1/2 cup coarsely crushed cookies
- 1 tablespoon sugar
- 2 pinches of salt
- 1/4 cup (1/2 stick) unsalted butter, melted
- 3 pounds firm but ripe peaches, halved, pitted, cut into 3/4-inch-wide wedges
- 1 cup (packed) plus 1 tablespoon golden brown sugar, divided
- 1 1/2 tablespoons fresh lemon juice
- 2 1/4 quarts vanilla ice cream (9 cups)
- 2/3 cup chilled heavy whipping cream
- Even easier: Use purchased peach ice cream instead of mixing up your own.
- Ingredient info: Amaretti cookies are available at supermarkets and Italian markets.

Direction

- Preheat an oven to 350°F. Use nonstick spray to coat 9-in. glass pie dish. In medium bowl, mix pinch salt, 1 tbsp. sugar and finely ground cookie crumbs. Add lukewarm melted butter; stir to blend. Press the crumbs up sides and on bottom of dish; bake for 10 minutes till golden around edges. Fully cool in dish on the rack.
- Preheat a broiler. Line foil on rimmed baking sheet; use nonstick spray to coat. In even layer, put peaches on sheet; broil for 3-5 minutes till starting to brown, closely watching to prevent burning. Sprinkle 1/4 cup of brown sugar on peaches; broil for 2-3 minutes till sugar caramelizes and melts, rotating sheet to evenly cook. Put juices and peaches in bowl; leave burned parts behind. Add pinch salt, lemon juice and 3/4 cup brown sugar to peaches; mix

till sugar is dissolved. Cover; chill for 2 hours till cold.
- Soften ice cream slightly in microwave in 20-sec intervals on low power; put in big bowl. Add broiled-peach mixture. To incorporate peaches, fold; peaches will break apart. Put 2/3 ice cream in cooled crust; smooth the top. Freeze leftover peach ice cream and pie separately with a cover for 4 hours till firm. Scoop leftover ice cream into bowl in level scoops using medium-sized ice cream scoop; put on top of pie, in concentric circles. Freeze pie. You can make it days ahead, kept frozen, covered.
- Beat leftover 1 tbsp. brown sugar and cream using electric mixer till peaks form in medium bowl. Sprinkle the coarsely crushed amaretti cookies on pie; cut to wedges. Put dollop of the brown sugar whipped cream over; serve.

Nutrition Information

- Calories: 841
- Cholesterol: 149 mg(50%)
- Protein: 10 g(19%)
- Total Fat: 49 g(76%)
- Saturated Fat: 26 g(128%)
- Sodium: 295 mg(12%)
- Fiber: 4 g(15%)
- Total Carbohydrate: 97 g(32%)

256. Peach Sabayon With Balsamic Peaches

Serving: Makes 4 dessert servings | Prep: | Cook: | Ready in:

Ingredients

- 3 medium peaches (1 lb total), halved, pitted, and each half cut into 6 wedges
- 2 teaspoons balsamic vinegar
- 1/4 cup sugar
- 4 large egg yolks
- 1/3 cup dry white wine
- 3 tablespoons peach brandy
- an instant-read thermometer

Direction

- Gently toss 1 tbsp. sugar, vinegar and peaches; macerate for 30 minutes.
- Use a handheld electric mixer on medium high speed to beat leftover 3 tbsp. sugar, brandy, wine and yolks in a big metal bowl above saucepan with barely simmering water for 7 minutes till sabayon reads 140°F on thermometer when peaches macerate for 15 minutes; beat above simmering water for 4 minutes till it makes thick ribbon when you lift beaters and triples in volume. Take bowl from saucepan.
- Divide juice and peaches to 4 bowls; put sabayon over.

257. Peach And Mascarpone Cheesecake With Balsamic Syrup

Serving: Makes 10 Servings | Prep: | Cook: | Ready in:

Ingredients

- 7 whole graham crackers, broken into pieces
- 1/3 cup sugar
- 5 tablespoons unsalted butter, diced
- 3 (8-ounce) packages mascarpone cheese
- 1 cup sugar
- 3 tablespoons all purpose flour
- 3 large eggs
- 1/2 teaspoon vanilla extract
- 2 large peaches (about 1 pound), peeled, pitted, diced
- 1/2 cup balsamic vinegar
- 1/2 cup sliced peaches

Direction

- Crust: Preheat an oven to 350°F. Blend butter, sugar and graham cracker pieces till moist clumps form in processor; press on bottom, not the sides, of 9-in. diameter springform pan then bake for 12 minutes till golden brown. Put crust on rack; cool. Maintain the oven temperature.
- Filling: Beat flour, sugar and mascarpone using electric mixer till blended in big bowl. One by one, beat in eggs; add vanilla extract. In mini processor/blender, puree diced peaches till smooth. Into batter, beat peach puree; put filling in crust. Bake for 1 hour 5 minutes till middle is softly set and edges are dry and raised. Directly put hot cheesecake in fridge; chill overnight, uncovered.
- In small saucepan, boil balsamic vinegar for 4 minutes till reduced to 1/4 cup; cool syrup. Around cheesecake, cut; remove pan sides. Put peach slices over; drizzle balsamic vinegar syrup. Serve.

Nutrition Information

- Calories: 491
- Saturated Fat: 17 g(87%)
- Sodium: 319 mg(13%)
- Fiber: 1 g(5%)
- Total Carbohydrate: 46 g(15%)
- Cholesterol: 146 mg(49%)
- Protein: 7 g(15%)
- Total Fat: 32 g(49%)

258. Peaches Under Meringue

Serving: Makes 4 servings | Prep: 10mins | Cook: 10mins | Ready in:

Ingredients

- 2 ripe peaches, halved and pitted
- 3 tablespoons plus 1 teaspoon sugar, divided
- 1 large egg white
- 2 tablespoons finely chopped sesame candy or crushed amaretti

Direction

- Set the broiler to preheating.
- Arrange the peaches on a baking sheet, cut-side up. Sprinkle 1 tsp. of sugar all over the peaches. Position it inside the broiler 4-5-inches away from the heat and broil for 2-4 minutes until the tops start to brown.
- In a deep bowl, whisk the egg white and a pinch of salt using the electric mixer with a speed of medium-high until foamy. Add the remaining 3 tbsp. of sugar gradually, whisking well until the white holds stiff and glossy peaks. Mix in sesame candy.
- Spoon a dollop of meringue onto each of the peach halves. Broil the peaches for 30 seconds. Switch the broiler off, leaving the peaches inside the oven for 30-60 seconds until the tips of the meringue turn browned.
- Take note that the egg white in this procedure is not fully cooked.

Nutrition Information

- Calories: 100
- Saturated Fat: 1 g(5%)
- Sodium: 14 mg(1%)
- Fiber: 1 g(6%)
- Total Carbohydrate: 21 g(7%)
- Protein: 2 g(4%)
- Total Fat: 2 g(3%)

259. Peanut Butter Cupcakes

Serving: 24 | Prep: 10mins | Cook: 12mins | Ready in:

Ingredients

- 2 cups brown sugar
- 1/2 cup shortening
- 1 cup peanut butter

- 2 eggs
- 1 1/2 cups milk
- 1 teaspoon vanilla extract
- 2 1/2 cups all-purpose flour
- 1 teaspoon baking soda
- 2 teaspoons cream of tartar
- 1 pinch salt

Direction

- Preheat an oven to 175°C/350°F. Grease then flour/line paper liners on a cupcake pan.
- Mix peanut butter, shortening and brown sugar till fluffy and light in a big bowl. One by one, beat in eggs; mix in vanilla. Mix salt, baking soda, cream of tartar and flour; alternately with milk, mix into batter. Put into prepped muffin cups.
- In the preheated oven, bake till cupcake's tops spring back when pressed lightly for 15-20 minutes; cool for a minimum of 10 minutes in pan. Transfer to a wire rack; fully cool.

Nutrition Information

- Calories: 209 calories;
- Total Fat: 10.5
- Sodium: 118
- Total Carbohydrate: 24.8
- Cholesterol: 17
- Protein: 5.1

260. Peanut Butter Pie

Serving: 8 | Prep: | Cook: | Ready in:

Ingredients

- 1 (9 inch) prepared graham cracker crust
- 1 (8 ounce) package cream cheese, softened
- 1/2 cup creamy peanut butter
- 1/2 cup confectioners' sugar
- 1 (16 ounce) container frozen whipped topping, thawed
- 15 miniature chocolate covered peanut butter cups, unwrapped

Direction

- Stir the peanut butter, confectioners' sugar and cream cheese together until silky. Fold in half of the whipped topping. Scoop the mixture into the graham cracker shell.
- Put the remaining whipped topping on top of the peanut butter mixture and decorate with peanut butter cups. Refrigerate for at least 2 hours or overnight before serving.

Nutrition Information

- Calories: 605 calories;
- Cholesterol: 32
- Protein: 9.5
- Total Fat: 43.1
- Sodium: 367
- Total Carbohydrate: 49.5

261. Peanut Butter Swirl Brownies

Serving: | Prep: | Cook: | Ready in:

Ingredients

- 1 1/4 cups unsalted butter, softened
- 1 cup chunky peanut butter
- 1/2 cup firmly packed light brown sugar
- 3 large eggs
- 8 ounces cream cheese, softened
- 4 ounces unsweetened chocolate, chopped
- 2 cups granulated sugar
- 1 teaspoon vanilla
- 7/8 cup all-purpose flour

Direction

- Cream brown sugar, peanut butter, and 1/2 stick of the butter in a bowl, and whisk in the cream cheese, a small amount at a time and 1 of the eggs, whisking until the mixture is smooth. Melt chocolate with 1 stick of the remaining butter in a small saucepan over low heat, whisking until the mixture is smooth, and allow the chocolate mixture to cool. Cream granulated sugar and the remaining 1 stick of butter in a separate bowl, whisking until the mixture is fluffy and light, and whisk in the remaining 2 eggs, 1 egg at a time, whisking thoroughly between each addition. Mix in the sifted flour, vanilla, and the chocolate mixture, and add the batter into a 13x9-in. baking pan coated with butter. Drop the peanut butter mixture in dollops into the batter, marble the batter by swirling the peanut butter mixture, bake the brownies in the center of the preheated 350° oven until a tester will come out with crumbs sticking to it and the brownies slightly shrink from the sides of the pan, about 45-50 minutes, let them cool, and then slice into squares.

Nutrition Information

- Calories: 320
- Protein: 5 g(10%)
- Total Fat: 21 g(33%)
- Saturated Fat: 11 g(54%)
- Sodium: 49 mg(2%)
- Fiber: 1 g(6%)
- Total Carbohydrate: 29 g(10%)
- Cholesterol: 59 mg(20%)

262. Peanut Butter Tart With Caramel Peanut Glaze

Serving: Makes 12 servings | Prep: | Cook: |Ready in:

Ingredients

- 1 1/4 cups all purpose flour
- 3 tablespoons sugar
- 1/2 teaspoon ground cinnamon
- 7 tablespoons chilled unsalted butter, cut into pieces
- 1 large egg yolk
- 2 teaspoons whipping cream
- 3/4 teaspoon vanilla extract
- 1/3 cup plus 2 tablespoons (packed) golden brown sugar
- 3 tablespoons plus 1/4 cup chilled whipping cream
- 2 tablespoons (1/4 stick) unsalted butter
- 3 ounces cream cheese, room temperature
- 1/4 cup creamy peanut butter, room temperature
- 1 teaspoon vanilla extract
- 1/2 cup (packed) golden brown sugar
- 6 tablespoons (3/4 stick) unsalted butter
- 1/4 cup water
- 4 tablespoons whipping cream
- 2 tablespoons light corn syrup
- 3/4 cup chopped lightly salted roasted peanuts

Direction

- Crust: Blend initial 3 ingredients to mix in processor. Add butter; cut in till coarse meal form with on/off turns. Add vanilla extract, cream and egg yolk; process till moist clumps form. Bring dough to ball; flatten to disk. In plastic, wrap; chill for minimum of 1 hour – maximum of 1 day.
- Preheat an oven to 350°F. Roll dough out to 11-in. round on lightly floured surface. Put dough in 9-in. fluted tart pan that has removable bottom. To make double-thick sides, fold in overhang. Use fork to pierce dough all over; freeze for 15 minutes.
- Bake crust for 25 minutes till golden brown. Put on rack; fully cool. You can make it 1 day ahead; kept in room temperature, airtight.
- Filling: Mix butter, 3 tbsp. cream and 1/3 cup brown sugar till sugar is dissolved in medium saucepan on medium heat; fully cool.
- Beat vanilla, peanut butter and cream cheese using electric mixer till smooth in medium bowl; mix in the brown sugar mixture.

- Beat 1/4 cup cream and leftover 2 tbsp. brown sugar using electric mixer till peaks form in another medium bowl; fold into the peanut butter mixture. Put in curst; use spatula to smooth top. Chill for 3 hours till set.
- Caramel-peanut glaze: Mix corn syrup, 2 tbsp. cream, 1/4 cup water, butter and brown sugar till sugar is dissolved in medium heavy saucepan on medium heat. Put heat on high; boil without mixing for 7 minutes till candy thermometer reads 238°F. Take off heat. Mix in peanuts and leftover 2 tbsp. cream; cool for 15 minutes to lukewarm.
- Put glaze on filling; smooth using spatula. Chill tart for 30 minutes till set. You can make it 1 day ahead, kept chilled. Cut to wedges; serve.

Nutrition Information

- Calories: 413
- Saturated Fat: 15 g(73%)
- Sodium: 43 mg(2%)
- Fiber: 1 g(6%)
- Total Carbohydrate: 35 g(12%)
- Cholesterol: 77 mg(26%)
- Protein: 6 g(12%)
- Total Fat: 29 g(45%)

263. Peanut Butter And Chocolate Chunk Brownies

Serving: Makes about 25 | Prep: | Cook: | Ready in:

Ingredients

- 6 tablespoons (3/4 stick) unsalted butter, room temperature
- 1/2 cup nutty old-fashioned-style or freshly ground peanut butter
- 1 1/4 cups (packed) golden brown sugar
- 2 large eggs
- 2 teaspoons vanilla extract
- 3/4 cup all purpose flour
- 1 teaspoon baking powder
- 1/4 teaspoon salt
- 4 ounces bittersweet (not unsweetened) or semisweet chocolate, coarsely chopped

Direction

- Preheat an oven to 350°F. Butter 8-in. square baking pan generously, then dust with flour. Beat butter using electric mixer till smooth in big bowl. Mix to blend if oil separates from peanut butter. Add peanut butter in butter; beat till blended well, occasionally scraping down bowl's sides. Beat in brown sugar. Add eggs, one at a time; beat well after each addition. Beat in vanilla. Sift salt, baking powder and flour into medium bowl. Add into peanut butter mixture and beat till blended; mix in chocolate.
- Transfer batter into pan; smooth top using spatula. Bake for 33 minutes till the inserted toothpick 2-in. from pan's edge exits with moist crumbs attached. Put pan on rack; fully cool. (You can make it 3 days ahead; cover. Keep at room temperature.)
- Slice brownies to squares.

Nutrition Information

- Calories: 139
- Total Carbohydrate: 18 g(6%)
- Cholesterol: 22 mg(7%)
- Protein: 2 g(5%)
- Total Fat: 7 g(11%)
- Saturated Fat: 3 g(16%)
- Sodium: 48 mg(2%)
- Fiber: 1 g(3%)

264. Peanut Dacquoise With Peanut Butter Mousse

Serving: Makes 8 to 10 servings | Prep: 1hours30mins | Cook: 7hours |Ready in:

Ingredients

- 1 1/4 cups roasted spanish salted peanuts with skin (6 to 6 1/2 ounces), divided
- 3/4 cup sugar, divided
- 6 large egg whites
- 1/8 teaspoon cream of tartar pinch of coarse kosher salt
- 1/2 cup chunky natural-style peanut butter
- 1/4 cup (packed) golden brown sugar
- Pinch of coarse kosher salt
- 1 cup chilled heavy whipping cream, divided
- 1 tablespoon sugar
- 1 teaspoon vanilla extract
- 1/4 cup natural unsweetened cocoa powder
- 1/4 cup sugar
- 1 cup heavy whipping cream
- 1 1/3 cups bittersweet chocolate chips

Direction

- For meringue layers: Set oven to 275 degrees F and start preheating. Line parchment paper on a big baking tray. On the parchment, draw three 10-inch x 4 1/2-inch rectangles; turn parchment over. In a processor, finely grind 1/4 cup sugar and 1 cup nuts. Coarsely chop the remaining 1/4 cup nuts then put aside.
- In a big bowl, with an electric mixer, whisk coarse salt, cream of tartar, and egg whites until foamy. As the mixer is running, slowly pour in the remaining 1/2 cup of sugar, whisking till meringue is glossy and stiff. Put in coarsely chopped nuts and ground nut mixture; stir kindly just to blend.
- Use a spoon to transfer 2 cups meringue onto every rectangle on the parchment; evenly spread to fill the rectangles. (Remaining meringue can be used to bake as cookies.)
- Bake meringues till they are entirely golden brown; dry to touch yet still lightly soft, about 1 1/2 hours. Remove to rack and let cool completely.
- For mousse: In a medium bowl, use an electric mixer to whisk coarse salt, brown sugar and peanut butter to combine. With mixer running, slowly whisk in 1/4 cup cream. Put in another 1/4 cup cream, whisk just to combine. In another medium bowl, beat vanilla, sugar and the remaining 1/2 cup cream till peaks form; in 3 additions, stir into peanut butter mixture. Let chill until it is ready to use.
- For glaze: In a medium saucepan, beat sugar and cocoa powder to blend nicely. Slowly pour in 1/4 cup water, beating until smooth. Slowly beat in heavy cream. Heat to a boil on medium heat, beating often. Decrease to low heat. Put in chocolate and beat until smooth and melted. Let rest at room temperature for 2 hours, mixing from time to time, till the mixture is lightly thickened and cool.
- Let meringues stay on parchment, trim the edge of every meringue with a big serrated knife to get the initial 10-inch x 4 1/2-inch size. With the thin knife, slide between paper and meringues to loosen. Using a spoon, evenly distribute 1/4 cup glaze into the top of two meringue rectangles, spread to cover top. Let chill 30 minutes till chocolate sets. Arrange one glazed meringue on a plate; spoon 1/2 mousse (scant 1 1/4 cups) over top and spread out in even layer. Arrange another glazed meringue rectangle over top of the previous one; spread with the rest of mousse. Place the unglazed meringue rectangle over top of all. Stream 1/2 cup glaze down the center of top meringue. Spread glaze over the top meringue with icing spatula, letting glaze drip down sides. Smooth all sides and the top to evenly cover with a thin layer. Keep in the fridge about 30 minutes till glaze is set. Spread the rest of glaze over top of dacquoise; rapidly smooth all sides and the top in even layer. If wanted, slightly sprinkle fleur de sel over top. Allow to chill for no less than 3 hours. (Note: You can make the cake 3 days in advance; use cake dome to cover and keep chilled.)

Nutrition Information

- Calories: 720
- Protein: 15 g(29%)
- Total Fat: 50 g(77%)

- Saturated Fat: 22 g(112%)
- Sodium: 207 mg(9%)
- Fiber: 5 g(21%)
- Total Carbohydrate: 64 g(21%)
- Cholesterol: 82 mg(27%)

265. Pecan Caramel Cheesecake

Serving: | Prep: | Cook: | Ready in:

Ingredients

- seven 5- by 2 1/2-inch graham crackers
- 1/2 cup coarsely chopped pecans, toasted and cooled
- 3/4 stick (6 tablespoons) unsalted butter, melted and cooled
- 2 pounds cream cheese, softened
- 1 1/2 cups firmly packed light brown sugar
- 1/4 cup all-purpose flour
- 4 large eggs
- 1/2 cup sour cream
- 2 teaspoons vanilla extract
- 1/2 teaspoon salt
- 1 cup granulated sugar
- 1 cup heavy cream
- 1 tablespoon unsalted butter
- 1 teaspoon vanilla extract
- 1 cup pecan halves, toasted lightly and cooled

Direction

- Crust: Grind pecans and graham crackers fine in a food processor; mix with butter in a bowl. Press on bottom of 9x2 1/2-in. springform pan; chill the crust for 30 minutes.
- Preheat an oven to 325°F.
- Filling: Beat cream cheese using electric mixer till fluffy and light in a bowl. Slowly add brown sugar, beating till well combined. Beat in flour. One by one, add eggs; beat well after each. Add salt, vanilla and sour cream; beat till well combined.
- Put filling in curst; bake in center of oven till edges are set yet center slightly trembles for 1 hour. Cheesecake sets while cooling. Turn off oven; cool cheesecake for 2 hours in oven with the oven door propped 6-in. open till fully cool.
- Topping: Cook 1/2 cup sugar in a heavy dry saucepan till melted on medium low heat; cook sugar till deep caramel, swirling pan. Add cream and leftover 1/2 cup sugar; simmer till caramel is dissolved, sometimes mixing. Simmer without mixing till candy thermometer reads 225°F; take off heat. Mix in vanilla and butter; cool it to room temperature.
- Put topping on cheesecake, gently spreading; decoratively put pecans over. Chill cheesecake overnight, covered. Remove pan side.

Nutrition Information

- Calories: 314
- Cholesterol: 84 mg(28%)
- Protein: 4 g(8%)
- Total Fat: 23 g(35%)
- Saturated Fat: 11 g(56%)
- Sodium: 195 mg(8%)
- Fiber: 1 g(3%)
- Total Carbohydrate: 25 g(8%)

266. Pecan Praline Trellis

Serving: Makes 1 loaf | Prep: | Cook: | Ready in:

Ingredients

- 3 tablespoons plus 2 1/4 cups (or more) unbleached all purpose flour
- 1 1/2 teaspoons instant or rapid-rise yeast (measured from 1 envelope)
- 3 tablespoons warm water (105°F to 115°F)
- 1/2 cup plus 1 tablespoon sour cream
- 4 1/2 tablespoons sugar
- 3 large egg yolks
- 1 tablespoon vanilla extract

- 3/4 teaspoon salt
- 4 1/2 tablespoons unsalted butter, cut into 4 pieces, room temperature
- 1 1/2 cups pecans (about 6 ounces)
- 1 1/2 teaspoons vegetable oil
- 1/8 teaspoon fine sea salt
- 6 tablespoons (3/4 stick) unsalted butter, room temperature
- 1 1/2 cups golden brown sugar
- 1 egg, beaten to blend (for glaze)

Direction

- For Dough: Mix yeast and 3 tbsp. flour to blend in small bowl. Add 3 tbsp. warm water; whisk till smooth. Allow mixture to stand for 12 minutes till puffed.
- Beat yeast mixture, salt, vanilla, egg yolks, sugar, sour cream and 2 1/4 cups of flour in a heavy-duty mixer's big bowl with paddle attachment fitted in it on medium speed for 5 minutes till dough is sticky; it it's too dry, add 1-2 tbsp. water. Add butter; beat for 5 minutes till dough is soft and smooth; by tablespoonfuls, add extra flour till dough pulls away from bowl's sides and is slightly firmer. Use plastic wrap to cover dough; allow the dough to rise for 2 hours till at least doubled in volume in a draft-free warm area.
- Meanwhile, prep filling: Preheat an oven to 400°F. Toss oil and pecans to coat on rimmed baking sheet; bake for 5 minutes till aromatic. Sprinkle 1/8 tsp. sea salt on nuts; cool on sheet. Chop pecans coarsely.
- Onto floured surface, scrape out dough; toss dough to coat with flour. Gently press to deflate. Line long parchment paper sheet on work surface; sprinkle flour on paper. Roll dough out to 16x14-in. rectangle on prepped parchment; spread butter lengthwise in 5-in. wide strip down middle of dough using offset spatula. Sprinkle sugar on butter; sprinkle nuts. On either filling's side, cut unfilled dough to 3/4-in. wide diagonal strips. Fold alternating strips on filling on slight diagonal, making lattice tops. Under bread's bottom edge, fold loose ends. Slide parchment with bread onto the large rimmed baking sheet. Use a plastic wrap to cover and allow it to rise for 1 1/2 hours till very puffy in draft-free warm area.
- Put rack in oven's top third; preheat it to 350°F. Brush egg glaze on bread; bake for a total of 25 minutes till golden, turning the sheet after 15 minutes. Slide parchment with bread onto rack; cool for at least 1 hour. Serve at room temperature/warm. (You can make it 1 day ahead. Fully cool; wrap in foil. Keep at room temperature.)

Nutrition Information

- Calories: 312
- Protein: 4 g(8%)
- Total Fat: 19 g(29%)
- Saturated Fat: 7 g(34%)
- Sodium: 142 mg(6%)
- Fiber: 2 g(7%)
- Total Carbohydrate: 34 g(11%)
- Cholesterol: 69 mg(23%)

267. Pecan Sandies For My Mom

Serving: Makes 1 1/2 dozen cookies | Prep: | Cook: | Ready in:

Ingredients

- 1 3/4 cups + 1 1/2 teaspoons all-purpose flour (250 grams)
- 3/4 cup coarsely chopped pecans (80 grams)
- 6 ounces (170 grams) unsalted butter, at room temperature
- 3/4 cup + 1 3/4 teaspoons powdered sugar (90 grams)
- Additional powdered sugar for dusting (optional)

Direction

- In lower and upper oven thirds, put racks; preheat oven to 350°F standard or 325°F convection. Line parchment paper/Silpats on 2 sheet pans.
- Toss pecans and flour in a medium bowl.
- In a stand mixer's bowl with paddle attachment, put butter. Mix at medium low speed till smooth. Add 3/4 cup and 1 3/4 tsp. /90 grams powdered sugar; mix till fluffy for 2 minutes. Scrape down bottom and sides of bowl. Add flour mixture; mix for 30 seconds on low speed till combined. Scrape bowl's bottom to incorporate dry ingredients that settled there.
- Divide dough to 1 1/2-tbsp./30-gram portions; roll to balls. Put on sheet pans, 1 1/2-in. apart; press cookies to 2-in. disks.
- Bake for 22-25 minutes for standard oven, 15-18 minutes for convection oven, reversing pan positions halfway through till pale golden brown. These won't spread as much or have an even color if baked in the convection oven.
- Put pans onto cooling rack; cool for 5-10 minutes. Put cookies onto rack using metal spatula; fully cool.
- Dust powdered sugar (optional).
- You can keep cookies for up to 3 days in a covered container.

Nutrition Information

- Calories: 168
- Protein: 2 g(4%)
- Total Fat: 11 g(17%)
- Saturated Fat: 5 g(26%)
- Sodium: 1 mg(0%)
- Fiber: 1 g(3%)
- Total Carbohydrate: 16 g(5%)
- Cholesterol: 20 mg(7%)

268. Pecan Spice Layer Cake With Cream Cheese Frosting

Serving: Makes 10 servings | Prep: 1hours | Cook: 2.5hours |Ready in:

Ingredients

- 1 1/2 sticks (3/4 cup) unsalted butter, cut into 1-inch pieces and softened, plus additional for buttering pans
- 2 3/4 cups cake flour (not self-rising)
- 2 teaspoons baking powder
- 1 teaspoon baking soda
- 3/4 teaspoon salt
- 1 tablespoon ground cinnamon
- 1 1/4 teaspoons freshly grated nutmeg
- 1 teaspoon ground ginger
- 1/2 teaspoon ground allspice
- 1/4 teaspoon ground cloves
- 1 1/2 cups packed light brown sugar
- 3 large eggs at room temperature 30 minutes
- 1 1/2 teaspoons pure vanilla extract
- 1 1/2 cups sour cream
- 3/4 cup pecans (3 ounces), toasted, cooled, and finely chopped
- 3 (8-ounce) packages cream cheese, softened
- 1 1/2 sticks (3/4 cup) unsalted butter, softened
- 1 tablespoon finely grated fresh lemon zest
- 3 3/4 cups confectioners sugar (from a 1-pound package)
- 1 tablespoon fresh lemon juice
- 1 1/3 cups pecans (5 ounces), toasted, cooled, and finely chopped
- 2 (9-inch) round cake pans (2 inches deep)

Direction

- Make Cake: In center position of the oven, put oven rack; preheat an oven to 350°F. Butter then flour cake pans; knock extra flour out.
- Sift spices, salt, baking soda, baking powder and cake flour into a big bowl.
- Beat brown sugar and 1 1/2 sticks butter using an electric mixer (fitted with a paddle attachment if using stand mixer) on medium high speed for 3-5 minutes till fluffy and pale

in another bowl. One by one, beat in eggs; beat well after each addition. Beat in vanilla. Lower speed to low. Working alternately and in batches, add sour cream and flour mixture, starting and finishing with flour mixture, mixing just till batter is smooth. Stir in pecans just till combined.

- Evenly spoon batters in pans; smooth tops. Rap pans 1-2 times to remove air bubbles. Bake for 30-35 minutes till inserted wooden pick in middle of cake exits clean and pale golden; cool in pans on racks for 10 minutes. Around pan's edges, run a thin knife. Invert racks on pans; reinvert cakes onto racks. Fully cool.
- For Frosting: Beat zest, butter and cream cheese using clean beaters on medium high speed for 1-2 minutes till fluffy in a bowl. Sift in confectioners' sugar; mix using a wooden spoon just till combined. Add lemon juice; beat till frosting is smooth on medium high speed.
- Assemble the frost cake: Slice each cake layer in half horizontally using long-serrated knife in a gently sawing motion. Put 1 layer on a big plate/cake stand, cut side up; spread with 3/4 cup frosting. Stack leftover cake layers, spreading 3/4 cup frosting onto each layer and finishing with top cake layer with cut side down. Spread side and top of cake with leftover 3 1/2 cups frosting; coat cake's side with 1 1/3 cups pecans, pressing gently to adhere.
- You can keep cake layers, not split, for 1 day, chilled, individually wrapped in plastic wrap then put into big sealed plastic bags or frozen for 1 week. Thaw in bags for 2 hours at room temperature if frozen.
- You can make frosting 1 day ahead, covered, chilled. Bring to room temperature; mix before using till smooth.
- You can assemble and frost cake 8 hours ahead; keep at room temperature, covered with plastic wrap loosely.

Nutrition Information

- Calories: 1166
- Total Fat: 76 g(117%)
- Saturated Fat: 37 g(183%)
- Sodium: 674 mg(28%)
- Fiber: 3 g(14%)
- Total Carbohydrate: 115 g(38%)
- Cholesterol: 222 mg(74%)
- Protein: 12 g(24%)

269. Peppermint Meringue Cake With Chocolate Buttercream

Serving: Makes 10 to 12 servings | Prep: | Cook: | Ready in:

Ingredients

- 1 cup powdered sugar
- 1/3 cup superfine sugar
- Pinch of salt
- 3 large egg whites, room temperature
- 1/2 teaspoon cream of tartar
- 1/2 teaspoon vanilla extract
- 1/4 teaspoon peppermint extract
- 1/2 cup water
- 1/2 cup sugar
- 1 tablespoon peppermint schnapps
- 1/2 cup all purpose flour
- 1/4 cup natural unsweetened cocoa powder
- 1/2 teaspoon baking powder
- Pinch of salt
- 2 large eggs
- 2 large egg yolks
- 1/2 cup sugar
- 1/2 teaspoon vanilla extracts
- 1 3/4 cups heavy whipping cream
- 1 cup (2 sticks) unsalted butter, cut into 8 pieces
- 3 tablespoons light corn syrup
- 1 1/2 pounds bittersweet chocolate (do not exceed 61% cacao), chopped
- 1 teaspoon vanilla extract
- Pinch of salt

- Thin chocolate-covered mint wafers, cut into small triangles (for garnish)
- Fresh raspberries (for garnish)
- Fresh mint leaves (for garnish)
- Heavy-duty stand mixer
- 13 x 9 x 1-inch baking sheet
- Small offset spatula
- Pastry bag
- Medium star tip (for decorating)

Direction

- Meringue layers: Put rack in middle of oven; preheat it to 175°F. Trace 2 12x4-in. rectangles on parchment paper sheet using pencil. Flip parchment; rectangles should show through. Put onto big rimmed baking sheet. On 2nd parchment paper sheet, trace 1 12x4-in. rectangle. Flip parchment; put onto 2nd rimmed baking sheet.
- Sift salt, superfine sugar and powdered sugar into medium bowl. Beat cream of tartar and egg whites till frothy on medium low speed in heavy-duty stand mixer's bowl with wire whisk. Put speed on medium high; beat till soft peaks form. Put speed on high. Add sugar mixture slowly; beat for 3 minutes till glossy and stiff peaks form. Beat in peppermint and vanilla extracts; evenly divide meringue to prepped rectangles on parchment, 1 1/3 cups for each then evenly spread meringue within traced line.
- Bake the meringues for 3 hours till crisp and dry yet not brown; turn off oven. Fully cool in oven.
- From parchment, remove meringue rectangles carefully. You can make meringues 1 week ahead; keep in 1 layer in room temperature in airtight container.
- Peppermint syrup: Mix sugar and 1/2 cup water in a small saucepan on medium heat till it boils and sugar dissolves. Take off heat; mix in peppermint schnapps. Put into a bowl; cover. Chill till cold. You can make it 3 days ahead, kept chilled.
- Cake: Put rack in middle of oven; preheat it to 350°F. Butter sides and bottom of 13x9x1-in. baking sheet lightly; line parchment paper on bottom of baking sheet. Dust sheet sides using flour lightly. Sift salt, baking powder, cocoa powder and 1/2 cup flour into medium bowl. Beat egg yolks and eggs with electric mixer for 2 minutes till foamy and pale in another medium bowl. Add vanilla and sugar, beat for 3 minutes till thick and mixture forms a ribbon when you lift the beater. Sift flour mixture on egg mixture; fold in gently till just incorporated with rubber spatula.
- Put batter on baking sheet; evenly spread to edges. Bake for 15 minutes till inserted tester in middle exits clean and tops spring back when touched gently. Put baking sheet on rack; cool for 20 minutes. Run a small knife around cake's sides to loosen then invert cake on parchment-lined work surface. Peel off parchment gently; fully cool. Lengthwise halve cake with serrated knife; trim every half to 12x4-in. rectangle.
- Buttercream: Simmer corn syrup, butter and cream in medium saucepan; take off heat. Add chocolate; whisk till smooth. Whisk in salt and vanilla; stand for 1-1 1/2 hours till thick enough to spread in room temperature. You can make it 4 hours ahead, standing in room temperature.
- Put 1/2 cup buttercream in pastry bag with medium star tip; put aside to pipe rosettes. Brush any crumbs off from cake layers and meringue layers. Put several small buttercream dabs down middle of 15-in. long rectangular serving platter. Put 1 meringue layer on buttercream on platter, top side up, anchoring to platter. To protect platter while spreading buttercream on meringue, put foil strips around meringue layer. Spread over meringue with 2/3 cup buttercream with small offset spatula. Put 1 cake layer over, gently pressing to adhere, top side down. Brush 1/3 cup peppermint syrup on cake layer; it'll be very moist. Spread over with 2/3 cup buttercream; put, top side up, 2nd meringue layer over then spread 2/3 cup buttercream. Top side down, cover using 2nd cake layer; brush 1/3 cup peppermint syrup.

It'll be very moist. Spread 2/3 cup buttercream then, top side up, put 3rd meringue layer over. Spread thin buttercream layer on sides and top of cake; chill for 15 minutes.
- Spread leftover buttercream on sides and top of cake; in 2 rows, pipe small buttercream rosettes over middle of cake. In each rosette, stand 1-2 mint wafer triangles; chill cake for no less than 6 hours. You can make it 2 days ahead, loosely cover; chill. Stand cake for 1 1/2 hours in room temperature before serving.
- Use mint leaves and fresh raspberries to garnish top of cake; serve.

270. Peppermint Patties

Serving: 28 | Prep: 45mins | Cook: 10mins | Ready in:

Ingredients

- 3/4 cup sweetened condensed milk
- 1 1/2 teaspoons peppermint extract
- 4 cups confectioners' sugar
- 3 cups semisweet chocolate chips
- 2 teaspoons shortening

Direction

- Mix together the peppermint extract and condensed milk in a big mixing bowl. Beat in enough confectioner's sugar, a little at a time, to create a stiff dough that is not sticky anymore. Shape it into 1-inch balls, then put it on the waxed paper and use your fingers to flatten it to form the patties. Allow the patties to dry for 2 hours at room temperature, flipping once.
- Melt the chocolate with the shortening in a medium saucepan on low heat, mixing frequently. Take it out of the heat. Dunk the patties into the chocolate, one at a time, by placing them on the tines of a fork and lower the fork on the liquid. Allow to cool on the waxed paper until it becomes set.

Nutrition Information

- Calories: 183 calories;
- Cholesterol: 3
- Protein: 1.4
- Total Fat: 6.5
- Sodium: 13
- Total Carbohydrate: 32.9

271. Peppermint Profiteroles With Chocolate Sauce

Serving: Serves 8 | Prep: | Cook: | Ready in:

Ingredients

- 2 pints vanilla ice cream, softened
- 23 hard red-and-white-striped peppermint candies, crushed
- 1 1/2 teaspoons peppermint extract
- 3/4 cup water
- 6 tablespoons (3/4 stick) unsalted butter, cut into 1/2-inch pieces
- 1 1/2 teaspoons sugar
- 1/8 teaspoon salt
- 3/4 cup unbleached all purpose flour
- 4 large eggs
- 1 cup whipping cream
- 9 ounces semisweet chocolate, chopped
- Additional red-and-white-striped peppermint candies, crushed
- Fresh mint sprigs

Direction

- Ice cream: In big bowl, put ice cream; fold in peppermint extract and candies. Cover; freeze for 4 hours minimum till ice cream is firm.
- Cream puff pastry: Preheat an oven to 400°F. Line parchment on big heavy baking sheet. Boil salt, sugar, butter and 3/4 cup water in medium heavy saucepan, mixing till butter melts. Add flour; mix for 2 minutes on medium till dough makes ball and pulls away from pan sides; cool for 10 minutes.

- One by one, beat 3 eggs into the dough with electric mixer; put dough in pastry bag with 1/2-in. plain tip. Pipe 16 1 1/2-in. dough mounds on sheet, 2-in. apart. In small bowl, beat 1 egg; brush on dough mounds but don't let egg drip onto sheet.
- Bake pastries for 20 minutes. Lower oven temperature to 350°F; bake the pastries for 10 minutes till golden brown. Pierce side of every pastry with skewer to let steam escape. Bake pastries for 5 minutes; put onto racks. Fully cool. You can make pastries and ice cream 1 week ahead; keep the ice cream frozen. In resealable plastic bag, enclose pastries; freeze. Before continuing, thaw pastries.
- Chocolate sauce: Simmer cream in medium heavy saucepan; take off heat. Add chocolate; stand for 5 minutes till chocolate softens. Whisk till smooth. You can make it 2 days ahead. Cover; chill. Rewarm on low heat.
- Crosswise halve pastries; on bottom of each pastry, put 1 scoop ice cream. Use pastry tops to cover. Put some warm chocolate sauce in 8 bowls; in each bowl, put 2 profiteroles on sauce. Put sauce on profiteroles; sprinkle extra crushed peppermints. Use mint sprigs to garnish.

Nutrition Information

- Calories: 604
- Cholesterol: 178 mg(59%)
- Protein: 9 g(19%)
- Total Fat: 42 g(64%)
- Saturated Fat: 25 g(124%)
- Sodium: 142 mg(6%)
- Fiber: 4 g(14%)
- Total Carbohydrate: 56 g(19%)

272. Pie Crust

Serving: Makes 2 pie crusts (enough dough for 1 double-crust pie, 1 lattice-topped pie, or 2 single-crust pies) | Prep: 20mins | Cook: 50mins | Ready in:

Ingredients

- 2 1/2 cups unbleached all purpose flour
- 1 1/2 teaspoons sugar
- 1 teaspoon salt
- 1/2 cup (1 stick) chilled unsalted butter, cut into 1/2-inch cubes
- 1/2 cup frozen non-hydrogenated solid vegetable shortening, cut into pieces
- 5 tablespoons (or more) ice water

Direction

- In processor, blend salt, sugar and flour. Add shortening and butter; process with on/off turns till it looks like coarse meal. Put it into big bowl. Add 5 tbsp. ice water; mix with fork, adding more ice water if dry by teaspoonfuls, till moist crumbs form. Gather dough together; divide to 2 even pieces. Shape each piece to ball and flatten to disks; wrap in plastic. Chill for 30 minutes minimum. You can make it 3 days ahead, kept chilled; before rolling, slightly soften.

Nutrition Information

- Calories: 1441
- Total Fat: 99 g(152%)
- Saturated Fat: 42 g(211%)
- Sodium: 708 mg(29%)
- Fiber: 4 g(17%)
- Total Carbohydrate: 122 g(41%)
- Cholesterol: 122 mg(41%)
- Protein: 17 g(33%)

273. Pierogies

Serving: 16 | Prep: 1hours | Cook: 1hours | Ready in:

Ingredients

- 1 (16 ounce) container sour cream
- 3 cups all-purpose flour
- 2 cups cold mashed potatoes

- 1/2 cup butter
- 2 large onions, chopped

Direction

- In large bowl, put sour cream. Create a dough by mixing in the flour. On floured surface, roll dough out about 1/16-inch thickness. Using a glass or cookie cutter, cut rounds about 3 1/2-inch across. Create more rounds by rerolling unused dough up to four times. After that, the dough will be hard to work with.
- In middle of each dough round, put about one teaspoon mashed potatoes. Fold over into the half-moon shape, use a fork to press and seal edges. Put filled pierogies aside under the towel to avoid drying.
- In a large skillet, melt butter over medium-low heat. Cook while stirring onions for 4-5 mins until translucent. Discard cooked onions. Put aside, retaining the butter in skillet.
- Boil water in a large saucepan. Drop a few filled pierogies carefully at a time into boiling water. After floating on surface, let pierogies gently boil for about 4 mins.
- In the skillet, reheat the butter over medium heat. Scoop pierogies gently out of water (they are easily broken). Put them into skillet for about 3 mins to brown on the bottom. On the buttered baking sheet, place fried pierogies. Sprinkle cooked onions over. Keep them warm on low setting in oven till served.

Nutrition Information

- Calories: 226 calories;
- Protein: 4.1
- Total Fat: 12.1
- Sodium: 136
- Total Carbohydrate: 25.5
- Cholesterol: 28

274. Pineapple Apricot Upside Down Cake

Serving: | Prep: | Cook: | Ready in:

Ingredients

- 3 tablespoons unsalted butter, melted
- 1/2 cup firmly packed brown sugar
- four 1/4-inch-thick fresh pineapple rings plus 2 tablespoons finely chopped fresh pineapple
- 6 dried whole apricots plus 2 tablespoons finely chopped
- 1 cup all-purpose flour
- 1 1/4 teaspoons double-acting baking powder
- 1/4 teaspoon salt
- 1/3 cup vegetable shortening
- 1/2 cup granulated sugar
- 1 large egg
- 1 teaspoon vanilla extract
- whipped cream as an accompaniment

Direction

- Mix brown sugar and butter well in a buttered 9x1 1/2-in. round cake pan; evenly press mixture on bottom of pan. Halve pineapple rings; put them, patted using paper towels, and whole apricots with smooth sides down on sugar mixture decoratively.
- Sift salt, baking powder and flour into a small bowl. Beat granulated sugar and shortening using electric mixer till fluffy and light in a bowl; beat in vanilla and egg. Alternately with 1/3 cup of water, add flour mixture, beating after each; mix in chopped apricots and chopped pineapple, patted dry. Turn batter into pan, evenly spreading; bake cake for 40-45 minutes in center of preheated 350°F till tester exits clean. Cool cake for 5 minutes in pan; invert onto a serving plate. Serve with whipped cream in room temperature/warm.

Nutrition Information

- Calories: 347
- Protein: 4 g(7%)

- Total Fat: 10 g(15%)
- Saturated Fat: 3 g(17%)
- Sodium: 99 mg(4%)
- Fiber: 5 g(19%)
- Total Carbohydrate: 67 g(22%)
- Cholesterol: 23 mg(8%)

275. Pineapple Upside Down Cake With Dried Cherries

Serving: Serves 8 | Prep: | Cook: | Ready in:

Ingredients

- 1 20-ounce can unsweetened whole pineapple slices in juice
- 2 1/2 tablespoons unsalted butter
- 1/4 cup (packed) dark brown sugar
- 1/4 cup dried tart cherries
- 3/4 cup all purpose flour
- 1 teaspoon baking powder
- 3 large egg whites
- 1/8 teaspoon salt
- 1/2 cup sugar
- 2 large egg yolks
- 1/3 cup low-fat (1%) milk
- 1 teaspoon vanilla extract

Direction

- Preheat an oven to 350°F. Drain the pineapple; keep 5 tbsp. juice. Put 1 whole pineapple slice aside; halve 4 slices. Keep leftovers for another time.
- Melt butter on low heat in 9-in. diameter cake pan that has 2-in. high sides. Put 1 1/2 tbsp. butter in small bowl; put aside. Leave leftover butter in pan. Put 3 tbsp. pineapple juice and brown sugar in pan; mix on medium heat till it slightly thickens and boils for 45 seconds. Take off heat. Put whole pineapple slice in middle of pan on sugar mixture; surround using halved pineapple slices with rounded side facing pan edge. Sprinkle hollows of pineapple slices with cherries.
- Mix baking powder and flour in small bowl. Beat salt and egg whites using electric mixer till soft peaks form in big bowl. Add 1/4 cup sugar slowly; beat till stiff peaks form. Beat 1/4 cup sugar and yolks with same beaters till well blended in another big bowl; mix in reserved 1 1/2 tbsp. butter, vanilla and milk. Beat in flour mixture till just blended. Fold whites in 3 additions into batter; spread batter on pineapple slices in the pan.
- Bake cake for 30 minutes till inserted tester in middle exits clean and golden; cool for 5 minutes in pan. Put platter on cake; invert cake on platter. Remove pan; rearrange fruit that might be dislodged. Cool the cake for 30 minutes on platter. Brush 2 tbsp. pineapple juice on pineapple; fully cool.

Nutrition Information

- Calories: 249
- Total Carbohydrate: 47 g(16%)
- Cholesterol: 57 mg(19%)
- Protein: 4 g(8%)
- Total Fat: 5 g(8%)
- Saturated Fat: 3 g(15%)
- Sodium: 113 mg(5%)
- Fiber: 1 g(4%)

276. Pistachio Buttercream Frosting

Serving: Makes About 3 Cups | Prep: | Cook: | Ready in:

Ingredients

- 1 1/4 cups half and half
- 3/4 cup unsalted pistachio nuts
- 1/2 cup sugar
- 4 large egg yolks
- 2 tablespoons all purpose flour
- 1 teaspoon vanilla extract
- 1 cup (2 sticks) unsalted butter, room temperature

Direction

- Boil pistachios and half and half in small heavy saucepan; remove from heat. Cover; allow to stand for 1 hour. Whisk flour, yolks and sugar to blend in medium bowl. Simmer half and half mixture; whisk into yolk mixture slowly. Return into same saucepan; mix on medium heat for 5 minutes till it thickly bubbles. Mix in vanilla. Transfer into processor; blend till nuts are chopped very finely. Transfer pistachio pastry cream in bowl; cover. Cool for 2 hours to room temperature.
- Beat unsalted butter using electric mixer till fluffy in big bowl. By 1/4 cupfuls, add pastry cream; beat well after each addition. (You can make it 2 days ahead; cover. Refrigerate. Before using, bring to room temperature.)

Nutrition Information

- Calories: 268
- Sodium: 15 mg(1%)
- Fiber: 1 g(3%)
- Total Carbohydrate: 13 g(4%)
- Cholesterol: 111 mg(37%)
- Protein: 3 g(7%)
- Total Fat: 23 g(36%)
- Saturated Fat: 12 g(62%)

277. Pistachio Ice Cream

Serving: Makes about 5 cups | Prep: | Cook: | Ready in:

Ingredients

- 4 large egg yolks
- 1/4 cup sugar
- 1 1/2 tablespoons water
- 2 tablespoons well-blended pistachio paste
- 1 cup chilled heavy cream
- an instant-read thermometer

Direction

- Use a hand-held electric mixer on high speed to beat water, sugar and yolks in metal bowl set above saucepan with simmering water till thermometer reads 140°F, and the mixture is pale and thick. Keep on beating over simmering water for additional 3 minutes, maintaining 140°F.
- Take bowl off heat; add pistachio paste gradually, beating till incorporated. Chill for 15 minutes till cold.
- Use cleaned beaters to beat cream till it just holds stiff peaks. Mix 1/3 cream into pistachio base to lighten; gently yet thoroughly fold leftover cream in. Scrape into airtight container; freeze for 4 hours till firm.

278. Plain Bagels

Serving: Makes 12 bagels | Prep: | Cook: | Ready in:

Ingredients

- 1 envelope active dry yeast (1/4 ounce)
- 1 1/2 tablespoons plus 1/4 cup honey, divided
- 1 tablespoon non-diasatic malt powder (such as King Arthur brand)
- 3 tablespoons neutral oil, plus more for greasing
- 9 cups high gluten flour such as bread flour
- 2 teaspoons kosher salt

Direction

- Whisk 1 1/2 tbsp. honey, yeast and 2 2/3 cups water in a stand mixer's bowl; stand it for 5 minutes.
- Add salt, flour, oil and malt; mix for 10 minutes till dough is able to "pull a window" with dough hook attachment on low speed. Pinch off small dough ball to test; pull into see-through thin membrane without tearing. Mix for 1-2 minutes if it tears.

- Oil a baking sheet lightly. Portion dough to 5 1/2-oz. balls; put on sheet. Loosely cover with plastic wrap; refrigerate overnight.
- Pull dough out for 30 minutes to warm up. Line parchment paper on 2 baking sheets. Preheat an oven to 460°F. Boil 1/4 cup honey and 4-qt. water in a big wide pot.
- Roll each ball to 9-in. long strands on a clean countertop. By the ends, take strand; overlap together to make an O. To join, pinch seams together; rest bagels for 5 minutes.
- Lower boiling water to simmer. Drop bagels in boiling honey water, 3-4 at a time, for 2 minutes per side. Use slotted spoon to lift out; if desired, sprinkle toppings. Put 6 onto each baking sheet; 1 sheet at 1 time, bake for 10-12 minutes in middle of oven till firm, shiny and slightly browned, flipping after 6 minutes. Transfer to cooling rack; cool.

279. Plain Genoise

Serving: Makes one 9-inch round layer | Prep: | Cook: | Ready in:

Ingredients

- 3 large eggs
- 3 large egg yolks
- Pinch of salt
- 3/4 cup sugar
- 1/2 cup cake flour (spoon flour into dry-measure cup and level off)
- 1/4 cup cornstarch
- One 9-inch round cake pan or 9-inch springform pan, buttered and bottom lined with buttered parchment or wax paper; a strainer or sifter

Direction

- Put rack in center level of oven; preheat to 350°.
- Boil medium saucepan half-full of water on high heat. Lower heat so water simmers.
- Whisk sugar, salt, yolks and eggs in a heavy-duty mixer's bowl. Put pan above simmering water; gently whisk till just lukewarm, test with your finger, 100°. Attach bowl to mixer with whisk attachment; whip at medium high speed till tripled in volume and egg mixture cools (to know, touch outside of bowl). Egg foam will make slowly dissolving ribbon falling back in bowl with whipped eggs when you lift beaters and is thick.
- Mix cornstarch and flour as eggs whip.
- Sift 1/3 flour mixture above beaten eggs; fold in flour mixture using rubber spatula, scraping all the way to bowl's bottom on every pass through batter to avoid accumulating flour there and creating lumps. Repeat using 1/3 flour mixture then leftover.
- Scrape batter into prepped pan; smooth top.
- Bake genoise till firm to touch, deep gold and well risen for 25 minutes.
- Loosen cake from pan sides immediately using a small paring knife; invert cake onto rack. Reinvert onto another rack; cool on paper, right side up. When cake is cool, remove paper.
- Chocolate genoise: Reduce bake flour to 1/3 cup and increase cornstarch to 1/3 cup. Add 1/4 cup Dutch-process alkalized cocoa powder in cornstarch and flour mixture; sift.
- Genoise sheet: Bake chocolate/plain batter on buttered and parchment-lined 10x15-in. jellyroll pan for 10-12 minutes at 400°. Be sure cake doesn't overbake; it'll be dry, especially in case you want to roll it. Creates 10x15-in. layer.
- Wrap in plastic wrap; refrigerate for a few days. Or, double wrap then freeze for a maximum of 1 month.

280. Plum Hazelnut Torte

Serving: Makes one 9-inch torte | Prep: | Cook: | Ready in:

Ingredients

- 1 1/2 pounds Italian prune plums
- 1 cup sugar
- 3/4 cup hazelnuts
- 1 1/4 cups all-purpose flour
- 1 1/2 teaspoons baking powder
- 1/4 teaspoon salt
- 1/2 teaspoon ground allspice
- 1 1/2 sticks (3/4 cup) unsalted butter, softened
- 3 large eggs
- 1 teaspoon vanilla

Direction

- Preheat an oven to 350°F. Butter then flour 9-in. springform pan.
- Quarter plums; pit. Chop 1/2 plums coarsely; toss with 2 tbsp. sugar in a bowl. Mix 2 tbsp. sugar and leftover plums in another bowl. Lightly toast hazelnuts for 10-15 minutes till insides are golden and fragrant in center of oven on baking sheet; cool nuts. In a food processor, grind finely.
- Whisk allspice, salt, baking powder, flour and hazelnuts in a bowl. Beat leftover 3/4 cup sugar and butter using an electric mixer till fluffy and light in a bowl. One by one, add eggs; beat after each addition. Beat in flour mixture and vanilla till batter just combined.
- In a sieve, drain chopped plums, pressing on fruit; use paper towels to pat dry. Mix plums into batter; evenly spread in pan.
- In sieve, drain quartered plums, pressing on fruit; put on batter, skin sides up. Bake torte for 1 hour 20 minutes till tester exits clean and golden brown in center of oven; cool torte for 30 minutes in pan on rack. Remove pan sides; fully cool.

Nutrition Information

- Calories: 5064
- Total Carbohydrate: 775 g(258%)
- Cholesterol: 924 mg(308%)
- Protein: 66 g(133%)
- Total Fat: 218 g(335%)
- Saturated Fat: 98 g(488%)
- Sodium: 1378 mg(57%)
- Fiber: 63 g(250%)

281. Plum Küchen

Serving: Serves 12 | Prep: | Cook: | Ready in:

Ingredients

- 1 1/2 cups all purpose flour
- 1 1/2 teaspoons baking powder
- 1 1/2 teaspoons ground cinnamon
- 1/4 teaspoon salt
- 8 tablespoons (1 stick) unsalted butter, room temperature
- 2/3 cup plus 1/4 cup sugar
- 2 large eggs
- 2 teaspoons vanilla extract
- 1/2 teaspoon almond extract
- 1/2 cup sour cream
- 5 large plums, halved, pitted, each cut into 8 wedges

Direction

- Preheat an oven to 350°F. Butter a baking pan, 13x9x2-inch in size. Into a small bowl, sift salt, a teaspoon of cinnamon, baking powder and flour. In a big bowl, beat 2/3 cup of sugar and 6 tablespoons of butter with an electric mixer till well incorporates. Beat in the eggs, one by one, then the extracts. Working in 3 additions, beat in the dry ingredients alternating with in 2 additions of sour cream. In the pan, spread the batter.
- On top of batter, set wedges of plum in 4 long rows, on their sides. In small bowl, mix quarter cup sugar and half teaspoon cinnamon. Scatter on top of plums. Melt 2 tablespoons of butter. Sprinkle on top of kuchen.
- Let kuchen bake for 40 minutes till tester pricked into middle of cake gets out clean. Put pan onto rack. Cool for half an hour or to room

temperature or till just warm. Slice to make 4 lengthwise strips. Cut every strip widthwise into 3 pieces.

Nutrition Information

- Calories: 234
- Total Fat: 11 g(16%)
- Saturated Fat: 6 g(31%)
- Sodium: 112 mg(5%)
- Fiber: 1 g(4%)
- Total Carbohydrate: 32 g(11%)
- Cholesterol: 56 mg(19%)
- Protein: 3 g(6%)

282. Polish Rugelach

Serving: Makes 64 | Prep: | Cook: | Ready in:

Ingredients

- 1 cup (2 sticks) unsalted butter, room temperature
- 1 8-ounce package Neufchâtel cheese*, room temperature
- 1/2 cup sugar
- 2 3/4 cups all purpose flour
- 1 teaspoon salt
- 3/4 cup sugar
- 2/3 cup (3 1/2 ounces) dried cranberries, finely chopped
- 2/3 cup (2 3/4 ounces) finely chopped toasted walnuts
- 1/2 cup (1 stick) unsalted butter, melted
- 2 teaspoons ground cinnamon
- 1 teaspoon ground allspice
- 1 large egg, beaten to blend
- Additional sugar
- *A light style of cream cheese available at most supermarkets.

Direction

- Prepare the dough: In a large bowl, beat cheese and butter using an electric mixer until light. Put in sugar and beat until fluffy. Stir in salt and flour. Form the dough into a ball, then knead gently until smooth. Subdivide the dough into eight equal pieces. Shape each into ball and flatten to form disks. Enclose in plastic and refrigerate for an hour. (You can make this one day ahead then store in refrigerator. Allow to soften a bit prior to rolling.)
- For the filling: In a small bowl, combine allspice, cinnamon, butter, walnuts, cranberries and 3/4 cup of sugar to blend. Put aside.
- Set the rack in the middle of oven then preheat to 350°F. Transfer one dough disk onto a floured work surface (chill the remaining seven dough disks). Roll out the dough to eight-inch round. Smear three tablespoons of filling atop round and leave 1/2-inch border. Slice round into eight wedges. Beginning at the wide end of every wedge, tightly and completely roll up to tip. Put the cookies with the tip pointing down onto ungreased baking sheet, then shape into crescents. Repeat this process with three more dough disks and filling. Rub the cookies with egg. Drizzle more sugar on top. Bake for about 20 minutes until turning golden. Place the cookies onto racks to cool. Repeat the process with the remaining sugar, egg, filling and four disks. (You can make this ahead. Keep in an airtight container at lukewarm for up to one week, or freeze for up to one month.)

Nutrition Information

- Calories: 103
- Sodium: 55 mg(2%)
- Fiber: 0 g(1%)
- Total Carbohydrate: 10 g(3%)
- Cholesterol: 19 mg(6%)
- Protein: 1 g(3%)
- Total Fat: 7 g(10%)
- Saturated Fat: 4 g(18%)

283. Pomegranate Sheet Cake With Lime Glaze

Serving: Makes 12 servings | Prep: | Cook: | Ready in:

Ingredients

- 1 1/2 cups all purpose flour
- 1 1/2 teaspoons baking powder
- 1/2 teaspoon salt
- 1 cup sugar
- 1/2 cup unsalted butter, room temperature
- 2 large eggs
- 3/4 cup pomegranate juice, divided
- 4 teaspoons grated lime peel, divided
- 1/2 cup plain Greek-style yogurt*
- 1 1/2 cups powdered sugar
- 1 teaspoon vanilla extract
- 2/3 cup pomegranate seeds
- 2 tablespoons thinly sliced mint leaves

Direction

- Set the oven to 350 degrees F to preheat. Coat a 13"x9"x2" cake pan with butter and flour. In a medium bowl, sift together salt, baking powder and flour. In a big bowl, beat together butter and sugar for a minute, until well combined. Put in 1 egg at a time while beating well with an electric mixer between additions. Beat in 2 tsp. of lime peel and 1/2 cup of pomegranate juice; the mixture may be curdled. Beat into batter with flour mixture until just combined, then stir in yogurt.
- Spread the batter in pan and bake for 25 minutes, until a tester exits clean after being inserted into the center. Allow to cool about 15 minutes. In the meantime, sift into a medium bowl with powdered sugar, then whisk in 1 tsp. of lime peel, vanilla and 1/4 cup of pomegranate juice. Poke holes in the top of warm cake with a fork, spaced 1 inch apart. Add over cake with glaze and spread evenly. Allow to cool thoroughly, then sprinkle over cake with 1 tsp. of lime peel, mint and pomegranate seeds prior to serving.
- You can find a thick yogurt at Greek markets, specialty food stores and some supermarkets.

Nutrition Information

- Calories: 288
- Saturated Fat: 6 g(28%)
- Sodium: 164 mg(7%)
- Fiber: 1 g(4%)
- Total Carbohydrate: 48 g(16%)
- Cholesterol: 53 mg(18%)
- Protein: 4 g(8%)
- Total Fat: 9 g(14%)

284. Poppy Seed Sweet Bread

Serving: Makes 2 (12-inch) loaves | Prep: 1hours | Cook: 5.5hours | Ready in:

Ingredients

- 1/4 cup warm water (105-115°F)
- 1/2 cup plus 1 teaspoon sugar
- 1 (1/4-oz) package active dry yeast (2 1/2 teaspoons)
- 1/2 stick (1/4 cup) unsalted butter, softened
- 2 large egg yolks
- 1 teaspoon vanilla
- 1/4 teaspoon salt
- 1 teaspoon finely grated fresh lemon zest
- 2 1/2 cups plus 2 tablespoons all-purpose flour (plus additional for dusting and rolling)
- 1/2 cup warm milk (105-115°F)
- 3/4 cup golden raisins, coarsely chopped
- 1/2 cup heavy cream
- 1 teaspoon finely grated fresh lemon zest
- 2 teaspoons fresh lemon juice
- 1 1/4 cups canned poppy-seed filling (12 oz)
- 1 large egg yolk
- 1 tablespoon heavy cream
- Accompaniment: vanilla sauce

- a stand mixer fitted with paddle attachment; parchment paper; an offset spatula

Direction

- Dough: Mix 1 tsp. sugar and water in a small bowl then sprinkle yeast; stand for 5 minutes till foamy. Discard then start over using new yeast if yeast doesn't foam.
- Beat leftover 1/2 cup sugar and butter in mixer on medium speed till fluffy and pale. Add zest, salt, yolks and vanilla; beat till combined. Add yeast mixture. Put speed on low. Alternating in 2 batches, add milk and 2 1/2 cups flour, mixing till combined. Put speed on medium; beat for 4-6 minutes till dough is elastic and shiny. It'll be sticky and very soft.
- Scrape bowl's side down; use plastic wrap to cover bowl then a kitchen towel. Use 2 tbsp. flour to dust dough; rise for 1 1/2-2 hours till doubled in bulk in a draft-free, warm area.
- As dough rises, make filling: Simmer juice, zest, cream and raisins in 1-qt. heavy saucepan on medium heat, occasionally mixing; take off heat. Stand for 20 minutes till most cream gets absorbed.
- Stir mixture into the poppy-seed filling in bowl.
- Make loaves: Line parchment paper on 17x12-in. baking sheet.
- Use lightly oiled spatula to punch dough down; divide to 2 even pieces. Roll 1 piece out to 12x9-in. 1/4-in. thick rectangle with floured rolling pin on well-floured surface, long side nearer you.
- Evenly spread 1/2 filling on dough using offset spatula; leave 1/2-in. border all around the edge. Beat cream and yolk for egg wash; brush on the long border near you.
- Roll dough towards you to a snug log, starting with long side furthest from you, firmly pinching to seal along egg-washed edge. Pinch loaf ends together; put on baking sheet lengthwise, seam side down, off center. Slightly tuck ends under. In same manner, make 2nd loaf, spacing loaves 4-in. apart. To use later, chill leftover egg wash. Cover loosely with buttered plastic wrap; rise for 1 hour till loaves double in bulk in a draft-free, warm place.
- In center position, put oven rack; preheat the oven to 350°F.
- In each loaf, cut 3 steam vents with a sharp knife, 3-4-in. apart; brush leftover egg wash on loaves. Bake for 45 minutes till bottoms sound hollow when its tapped and crusts become deep golden brown. Put on rack; cool it to room temperature.
- You can bake loaves 3 days ahead, kept in room temperature, wrapped in foil.

Nutrition Information

- Calories: 2434
- Fiber: 41 g(165%)
- Total Carbohydrate: 277 g(92%)
- Cholesterol: 436 mg(145%)
- Protein: 59 g(118%)
- Total Fat: 130 g(199%)
- Saturated Fat: 42 g(208%)
- Sodium: 416 mg(17%)

285. Potato Ghosts

Serving: Makes 8 servings | Prep: 30mins | Cook: 1.75hours | Ready in:

Ingredients

- 4 pounds large boiling potatoes (preferably white-fleshed)
- 3/4 stick unsalted butter, cut into pieces
- 1 1/4 cups whole milk
- 3 large egg yolks
- Nigella seeds (sometimes mislabeled "black onion seeds") or caraway seeds for garnish
- Equipment: a potato ricer or a food mill fitted with medium disk; a pastry bag with 3/4-inch plain tip

Direction

- Peel then quarter potatoes; cover with water in 4-quart pot. Season with salt well. Simmer for 15-20 minutes till tender, partially covered.
- As potatoes simmer, heat milk and butter in a small saucepan till butter melts. Take off heat; cover. Keep warm.
- Preheat an oven to 400°F. Put rack in the middle.
- Drain potatoes; force through rice into a big bowl/mixer bowl if you have a stand mixer. Beat 1/2 teaspoon each of pepper and salt, yolks and milk mixture in using an electric mixture on low speed till combined.
- Spread 1/3 of the potatoes in a buttered 1 1/2-quart shallow ovenproof dish. Put leftover potatoes in a pastry bag; pipe potatoes to 2 1/2-3-in. high pointed mounds, close together, to make ghosts. Use 2 seeds to garnish each mound for eyes.
- Bake for 20-25 minutes till potatoes are firm and tips of ghosts become golden.
- You can pipe potatoes into dish a day ahead, chilled and covered loosely with plastic wrap.

Nutrition Information

- Calories: 294
- Saturated Fat: 7 g(34%)
- Sodium: 34 mg(1%)
- Fiber: 5 g(20%)
- Total Carbohydrate: 42 g(14%)
- Cholesterol: 96 mg(32%)
- Protein: 7 g(14%)
- Total Fat: 12 g(18%)

286. Prune Souffles

Serving: Makes 4 servings | Prep: | Cook: |Ready in:

Ingredients

- vegetable-oil cooking spray
- 5 1/2 ounces pitted prunes (as soft as possible; about 3/4 cup)
- 1/2 cup hot, freshly brewed Earl Grey tea
- 1 teaspoon fresh lemon juice
- 1/4 teaspoon finely grated fresh orange zest
- 2 large egg whites
- 1/4 teaspoon cream of tartar
- 2 tablespoons granulated sugar
- confectioners' sugar for dusting
- 1/4 cup vanilla frozen yogurt

Direction

- To prepare: Spray four 6-ounce or (2/3-cup) of either soufflé molds or ramekins with vegetable-oil cooking spray.
- Put in together prunes, lemon juice with zest and hot tea in a small bowl. Stir and then cover for 15 minutes. Reserve 3 prunes from mixture and chop coarsely. Put the remaining prune mixture with the liquid juice in a food processor and blend until smooth and pureed. Transfer to a large bowl and add the chopped prunes. This purée can also be prepare 2 days ahead, just keep it chilled. (Note: Make sure it is at room temperature before proceeding.)
- Preheat the oven to 350 deg F.
- In large bowl beat the egg whites with a little salt. Use electric mixer and beat until foamy. Add cream of tartar. Continue beating until soft peaks appear; gradually add sugar and beating until the meringue holds stiff peaks. Slowly add one fourth of the meringue to purée to lighten and then add the remaining mixture gradually. Scoop the mixture into soufflé molds or ramekins and arrange on baking sheet. Bake for about 16 minutes until golden brown and puffed.
- Sprinkle with confectioner's sugar on top of soufflé and serve right away. When eating, use 2 forks to open top and put 1 spoonful of yogurt inside.

Nutrition Information

- Calories: 159
- Saturated Fat: 0 g(2%)

- Sodium: 36 mg(2%)
- Fiber: 3 g(11%)
- Total Carbohydrate: 35 g(12%)
- Cholesterol: 1 mg(0%)
- Protein: 3 g(6%)
- Total Fat: 2 g(3%)

287. Pumpkin Bread Pudding

Serving: 8 | Prep: 15mins | Cook: 1hours | Ready in:

Ingredients

- 6 cups cubed French bread
- 1 cup heavy cream
- 1 cup vanilla soy milk
- 3 eggs
- 1 (16 ounce) can pumpkin puree
- 1 cup brown sugar
- 1 teaspoon ground cinnamon
- 1 teaspoon vanilla extract
- 1 pinch salt
- 1/2 cup raisins

Direction

- Preheat oven to 175°C/350°F.
- Toss soy milk, cream and bread cubes in big bowl till liquid is absorbed; put aside.
- Beat eggs in another bowl; whisk salt, vanilla, cinnamon, brown sugar and pumpkin puree in; put raisins and pumpkin mixture on bread cubes. Gently toss till combined evenly; refrigerate for 30-60 minutes.
- Divide mixture to eight 6-oz. ramekins; in preheated oven, bake for 1 hour till top is golden brown and pudding is firm. Take out from oven; stand for 30 minutes then serve.

Nutrition Information

- Calories: 376 calories;
- Cholesterol: 111
- Protein: 7.9

- Total Fat: 14
- Sodium: 367
- Total Carbohydrate: 57.3

288. Pumpkin Muffins

Serving: 18 | Prep: 20mins | Cook: 15mins | Ready in:

Ingredients

- cooking spray
- 1 (18 ounce) package yellow cake mix
- 1 (7.5 ounce) package corn bread mix (such as Jiffy®)
- 1 (15 ounce) can pumpkin puree
- 1/3 cup milk
- 1 egg
- 1 pinch ground cinnamon
- 1 (8 ounce) can crushed pineapple, drained (optional)
- 1 cup golden raisins (optional)
- 3 tablespoons white sugar, divided

Direction

- Preheat the oven to 175°C or 350°Fahrenheit. Use a cooking spray to grease 18 muffin cups.
- In a bowl, mix cinnamon, yellow cake mix, egg, cornbread mix, milk, and pumpkin together until the batter is well blended; stir in raisins and pineapple. Spoon batter in the greased muffin cups until 2/3 full. Add half teaspoon of sugar on top of each muffin to make crunchy tops.
- Bake muffins for 15min in the 350°Fahrenheit oven until an inserted skewer in the middle comes out without residue or with moist crumbs.

Nutrition Information

- Calories: 226 calories;
- Total Fat: 4.9
- Sodium: 441

- Total Carbohydrate: 43.6
- Cholesterol: 12
- Protein: 3.3

289. Quick Pear Napoleans

Serving: Makes 4 servings | Prep: 30mins | Cook: 45mins | Ready in:

Ingredients

- 1/2 package (1 pound) frozen all-butter puff pastry in 1 piece, thawed
- 1/2 cup chilled heavy cream
- 1/2 cup sour cream
- 1 cup sugar
- 2 (14-ounce) cans pear halves in light syrup, drained, reserving syrup
- 2 tablespoon unsalted butter
- Garnish: confectioners sugar for dusting

Direction

- Preheat an oven with rack on upper third to 400°F.
- Roll pastry out to 16-in. square with floured rolling pin on lightly floured surface; trim edges. Put onto parchment-lined baking sheet; put another baking sheet over. Bake for 15-18 minutes till cooked through and golden. From pastry, remove top baking sheet. Put pastry onto rack; fully cool.
- Beat heavy cream to form soft peaks using an electric mixer as pastry cools; gently yet thoroughly fold in sour cream.
- Meanwhile, cook sugar till it starts to melt in a big heavy dry skillet on medium heat; cook till golden and fully melted, mixing with a fork. Mix in reserved pear syrup; boil for 3-5 minutes till thick, mixing. Mix in pears; take off heat. Swirl in butter till combined.
- Use a big knife to cut pastry to 8 rectangles; on 4 serving plates, put 1/2 rectangles. Spread cream mixture on pastry; put caramel with pears over. Put leftover pastry rectangles over.

Nutrition Information

- Calories: 1543
- Fiber: 2 g(7%)
- Total Carbohydrate: 236 g(79%)
- Cholesterol: 71 mg(24%)
- Protein: 10 g(19%)
- Total Fat: 66 g(101%)
- Saturated Fat: 25 g(124%)
- Sodium: 332 mg(14%)

290. Raspberry Fool

Serving: Serves 12 | Prep: | Cook: |Ready in:

Ingredients

- 3 12-ounce packages frozen unsweetened raspberries, thawed
- 1/2 cup Grand Marnier or other orange liqueur
- 4 1/4 cups chilled whipping cream
- 1 1/3 cups sugar
- 1/2 cup slivered blanched almonds, toasted

Direction

- In a processor, purée 1/2 cup of liqueur and 1/2 of raspberries till smooth. In a large bowl, strain the mixture and use a rubber spatula to press on the solids. Remove seeds. Add the leftover raspberries into purée and stir gently. Let chill, covered.
- In a separate large bowl, use an electric mixer to beat sugar and cream till it forms stiff peaks. Fold 1/2 of whipped cream into the raspberry mixture. Fold in the leftover cream gently.
- Transfer the mixture into 12 goblets. Store for at least 2 hours or no more than 8 hours in the fridge. Sprinkle nuts over and serve.

Nutrition Information

- Calories: 449
- Cholesterol: 94 mg(31%)
- Protein: 4 g(8%)
- Total Fat: 30 g(46%)
- Saturated Fat: 17 g(83%)
- Sodium: 32 mg(1%)
- Fiber: 6 g(25%)
- Total Carbohydrate: 40 g(13%)

291. Raspberry And Peach Parfait Cake

Serving: Makes 12 servings | Prep: | Cook: | Ready in:

Ingredients

- Nonstick vegetable oil spray
- 1 13-ounce package soft coconut macaroons
- 1/2 cup sliced almonds, toasted
- 1 1/2 teaspoons grated lemon peel
- 3 large peaches (about 20 ounces), peeled, pitted, diced
- 3 1/2-pint containers raspberries
- 2 1/2 cups chilled heavy whipping cream
- 9 large egg yolks
- 3/4 cup sugar
- 1/3 cup light corn syrup
- 2 tablespoons (1/4 stick) unsalted butter, room temperature
- 2 tablespoons peach schnapps
- 5 ounces imported white chocolate, finely chopped
- 6 large peaches (about 2 1/2 pounds), peeled, pitted, thinly sliced
- 1/2 cup sugar
- 1/3 cup peach schnapps
- 2 teaspoons fresh lemon juice
- 3 1/2-pint containers raspberries (for topping)

Direction

- Parfait cake: Spray nonstick spray on 9-in. springform pan that has 3-in. high sides. Finely grind lemon peel, almonds and macaroons in processor; press 1/2 mixture on bottom of prepped pan.
- In processor, puree peaches. Put puree in deep-sided, heavy saucepan; simmer on medium heat. Cook for 10 minutes till reduced to 1 cup and color slightly darkens, mixing often. Put into bowl; chill for 15 minutes till cool.
- In processor, puree raspberries. Through sieve, strain into medium bowl; press to extract fruit as much as you can. Chill puree.
- Whisk butter, corn syrup, sugar, egg yolks and 1/4 cup cream to combine in big metal bowl; put bowl above saucepan of simmering water without touching water. Constantly whisk for 8 minutes till inserted thermometer into base reads 160°F and parfait base thickens.
- Take bowl from above water; beat parfait base using electric mixer for 8 minutes till fully cool and billowy. Divide, 1 cup parfait base into each bowl, to 2 medium bowls. Beat leftover 2 1/4 cups cream till medium peaks form in big bowl. Fold schnapps and cold peach puree into 1 parfait base; fold in 1/2 whipped cream. In prepped pan, spread peach parfait; sprinkle with leftover macaroon mixture. Put into freezer.
- Fold 1 cup, keep leftover puree for another time, raspberry puree into parfait base in the 2nd bowl; fold in leftover whipped cream. Spread on macaroon mixture in pan with parfait; cover. Freeze for minimum of 8 hours – maximum of 2 days.
- Decoration: Lengthwise fold 30x7-in. aluminum foil strip in half to make 30x3 1/2-in. strip.
- In glass bowl, microwave white chocolate till chocolate just starts to melt in 10-sec intervals; mix till smooth. Put into resealable small plastic bag; cut 1 bag corner's tip off. In lacy design, pipe white chocolate on foil strips; stand for 10 minute still chocolate sets.
- To loosen, cut around parfait cake using heated knife; remove pan sides. Holding the foil strip parallel to cake's bottom and upright, put 1 end, white chocolate side in, against cake; press strip gently and fully around cake

like a fence. Leave overhang. Freeze for 10 minutes. Peel off foil carefully, beginning at overhang. Trim chocolate overhang off; cover. Put cake in freezer for 12 hours maximum.
- Compote and topping: Mix all ingredients but raspberries in big bowl; stand compote for minimum of 15 minutes – maximum of 1 hour, occasionally mixing. Put raspberries over cake. Cut cake to wedges; serve it with compote.

Nutrition Information

- Calories: 972
- Saturated Fat: 35 g(175%)
- Sodium: 132 mg(6%)
- Fiber: 16 g(64%)
- Total Carbohydrate: 94 g(31%)
- Cholesterol: 296 mg(99%)
- Protein: 11 g(23%)
- Total Fat: 67 g(102%)

292. Raspberry Yogurt Cake

Serving: Makes 10 to 12 servings | Prep: | Cook: | Ready in:

Ingredients

- 3 cups unbleached all purpose flour, divided
- 1 1/2 teaspoons baking powder
- 1/4 teaspoon salt
- 1 cup (2 sticks) unsalted butter, room temperature
- 1 3/4 cups sugar
- 2 tablespoons fresh orange juice
- 1 1/2 teaspoons almond extract, divided
- 1 teaspoon finely grated orange peel
- 3 large eggs, room temperature
- 1 cup plain low-fat yogurt
- 2 1/2 cups fresh raspberries (two 6-ounce containers)
- 1 cup powdered sugar
- 1 tablespoon (or more) water

Direction

- Preheat an oven to 350°F then butter a 12-cup Bundt pan. In medium bowl, whisk 1/4 tsp. salt, baking powder and 2 1/2 cups flour.
- Beat sugar and butter using electric mixer till creamy in big bowl; beat in orange peel, 1 tsp. almond extract and orange juice. One by one, add eggs; beat after each. Stir in yogurt.
- Put dry ingredients in batter; beat till just blended.
- In big bowl, toss raspberries and 1/2 cup flour; fold berry mixture into the batter. Put batter in prepped pan; smooth top.
- Bake cake for 1 hour 10 minutes till inserted wooden skewer near middle exits clean; cool for 30 minutes.
- Invert cake onto a plate; cool.
- You can make it 1 day ahead. Cover; stand in room temperature.
- In medium bowl, whisk 1/2 tsp. almond extract, 1 tbsp. water and powdered sugar; as needed, add 1/2 tsp. full more water for thick glaze. Drizzle on cake; stand till glaze sets.

Nutrition Information

- Calories: 540
- Fiber: 3 g(13%)
- Total Carbohydrate: 82 g(27%)
- Cholesterol: 106 mg(35%)
- Protein: 8 g(15%)
- Total Fat: 21 g(32%)
- Saturated Fat: 12 g(62%)
- Sodium: 155 mg(6%)

293. Red Velvet Cake With Raspberries And Blueberries

Serving: Makes 12 servings | Prep: | Cook: | Ready in:

Ingredients

- 2 1/4 cups sifted cake flour (sifted, then measured)
- 2 tablespoons unsweetened cocoa powder
- 1 teaspoon baking powder
- 1 teaspoon baking soda
- 1/2 teaspoon salt
- 1 cup buttermilk
- 1 tablespoon red food coloring
- 1 teaspoon distilled white vinegar
- 1 teaspoon vanilla extract
- 1 1/2 cups sugar
- 1/2 cup (1 stick) unsalted butter, room temperature
- 2 large eggs
- 2 8-ounce packages cream cheese, room temperature
- 1/2 cup (1 stick) unsalted butter, room temperature
- 1 tablespoon vanilla extract
- 2 1/2 cups powdered sugar
- 3 1/2-pint baskets fresh raspberries
- 3 1/2-pint baskets fresh blueberries

Direction

- Cake: Preheat an oven to 350°F. Butter then flour 2 9-in. diameter cake pans that have 1 1/2-in. high sides. Sift salt, baking soda, baking powder, cocoa powder and sifted flour into medium bowl. Whisk vanilla, vinegar, food coloring and buttermilk to blend in small bowl. Beat butter and sugar using electric mixer till well blended in big bowl. Add eggs, one by one; beat after every addition till well blended. Alternately with the buttermilk mixture in 3 batches, beat in dry ingredients in 4 batches.
- Divide batter to prepped pans; bake cakes for 27 minutes till inserted tester in middle exits clean. Cool for 10 minutes in pans on racks. Turn out cakes on racks; fully cool.
- Frosting: Beat butter and cream cheese till smooth in big bowl; beat in vanilla. Add the powdered sugar; beat till smooth.
- Put 1 cake layer on platter, flat side up; spread top of cake with 1 cup frosting. Put 1/2 basket blueberries and 1 basket raspberries on frosting; lightly press to adhere. Put, flat side down, 2nd cake layer over; spread leftover frosting on sides and top of cake. Decoratively put leftover berries on cake's top. You can make it 1 day ahead; cover. Refrigerate. 1 hour before serving, stand in room temperature.

Nutrition Information

- Calories: 675
- Sodium: 426 mg(18%)
- Fiber: 9 g(35%)
- Total Carbohydrate: 97 g(32%)
- Cholesterol: 114 mg(38%)
- Protein: 8 g(16%)
- Total Fat: 30 g(47%)
- Saturated Fat: 18 g(88%)

294. Rhubarb Fool

Serving: 8 | Prep: 15mins | Cook: 10mins | Ready in:

Ingredients

- 2 1/4 pounds rhubarb
- 1/3 cup orange juice
- 1 cup white sugar
- 1 pinch salt
- 2 cups cold heavy whipping cream
- 2 tablespoons white sugar

Direction

- Trim the ends from the rhubarb and cut into 6 inches in length. In a big bowl filled with cold water, soak the sliced rhubarbs for 20 minutes. Remove the water and pat dry, then cut into 1/2-inch slices crosswise.
- In a pot, combine 1 cup sugar, orange juice and salt. Stir together then bring mixture to a boil. Toss in the rhubarb slices then bring back to a boil. Set heat to medium-low and continue to simmer, stirring only 2 or 3 times, for 7-10 minutes until the rhubarb is tender. Stirring

often will cause the rhubarb to break down. Pour rhubarb mixture to a ceramic or glass bowl then top with plastic wrap to cover. Store in the refrigerator for at least 1 hour until cold.
- In a big bowl, beat the heavy cream and the remaining sugar together using an electric mixer until soft peaks are formed.
- Assemble dessert into 8 small glasses. Scoop 1/4 cup of the rhubarb mixture into each glass then top with whipped cream, with the same amount. Repeat layering until you reach the top of the glasses. Cover and chill in the fridge for a minimum of 1 hour to a maximum of 6 hours.

Nutrition Information

- Calories: 346 calories;
- Total Fat: 22.3
- Sodium: 28
- Total Carbohydrate: 36.7
- Cholesterol: 82
- Protein: 2.4

295. Rhubarb Sponge Pudding

Serving: Makes 8 servings | Prep: | Cook: |Ready in:

Ingredients

- 1 1/3 pounds rhubarb, cut into 1-inch lengths (about 5 cups)
- 1/3 cup (packed) golden brown sugar
- 2 tablespoons water
- 1 cup plus 2 tablespoons all purpose flour
- 1 1/2 teaspoons baking powder
- 1/2 cup sugar
- 7 tablespoons butter, room temperature
- 2 large eggs
- 6 1/2 tablespoons whole milk
- Softly whipped cream

Direction

- Preheat an oven to 375°F. Butter the 11x7x2-in. baking dish. In an even layer, put rhubarb pieces into baking dish. Scatter brown sugar on top; sprinkle 2 tbsp. water.
- Whisk baking powder and flour to blend in small bowl. Beat butter and sugar using electric mixer for 3 minutes till fluffy and pale in big bowl. One by one, add eggs; beat well between additions. Alternately with milk in 2 batches, fold in flour mixture in 3 batches; mix to just blend after every addition. Put batter on rhubarb; smooth the top to cover.
- Bake the dessert for 40 minutes till inserted toothpick in middle exits clean and top is golden brown; cool for a minimum of 30 minutes to the maximum of 60 minutes. Serve warm with some softly whipped cream.

Nutrition Information

- Calories: 294
- Cholesterol: 81 mg(27%)
- Protein: 5 g(9%)
- Total Fat: 14 g(21%)
- Saturated Fat: 8 g(41%)
- Sodium: 100 mg(4%)
- Fiber: 2 g(7%)
- Total Carbohydrate: 39 g(13%)

296. Rhubarb Gingersnap Parfaits

Serving: Makes 4 servings | Prep: | Cook: |Ready in:

Ingredients

- 1 pound fresh or 3/4 pound frozen rhubarb (do not thaw)
- 1/2 cup granulated sugar
- 3/4 cup chilled heavy cream
- 3 tablespoons confectioners sugar
- 1/3 cup sour cream
- 1 tablespoon Sherry
- 8 gingersnaps, finely ground (6 tablespoons)

Direction

- Trim and chop the fresh rhubarb finely, if using.
- In a wide 3-4-quart heavy saucepan, cook the granulated sugar and rhubarb over moderately high heat, stirring the mixture often until the rhubarb starts to release juices. Lower the heat. Let it simmer for 20 minutes, stirring constantly until the rhubarb is reduced to 1 1/2 cups and falls apart.
- Place the rhubarb in a metal bowl that is set in a larger bowl filled with ice and cold water. Let it chill for 5 minutes, stirring occasionally until cold.
- In a bowl, whisk confectioners' sugar and heavy cream using an electric mixer until the mixture holds stiff peaks. Add the sherry and sour cream. Whisk until the mixture returns to a stiff-peak stage.
- In each of the four 6-ounce stemmed glasses, layer a 1/3 cup of rhubarb, a 1/2 cup of whipped cream, and 1 1/2 tablespoon of gingersnap crumbs. Take note that there's going to be little leftovers of rhubarb. Let it chill until ready to serve.

Nutrition Information

- Calories: 824
- Sodium: 494 mg(21%)
- Fiber: 3 g(13%)
- Total Carbohydrate: 125 g(42%)
- Cholesterol: 72 mg(24%)
- Protein: 8 g(15%)
- Total Fat: 33 g(51%)
- Saturated Fat: 16 g(78%)

297. Rich Chocolate Cake With Salty Dulce De Leche & Hazelnut Brittle

Serving: Makes one 10-inch cake | Prep: | Cook: | Ready in:

Ingredients

- 1 cup freshly brewed hot coffee
- 1/2 cup Dutch-processed cocoa powder
- 3/4 cup packed light brown sugar
- 1/2 cup plain whole-milk yogurt
- 2 teaspoons vanilla extract
- 8 tablespoons (1 stick) unsalted butter, at room temperature
- 1 1/4 cups granulated sugar
- 2 eggs
- 1 1/4 cups all-purpose flour
- 3/4 teaspoon baking soda
- 1 teaspoon table salt
- Hazelnut Brittle
- 1/2 cup dulce de leche
- 1 1/2 teaspoons kosher salt

Direction

- Preheat an oven to 350°F. Grease 10-in. round cake pan with cooking spray to prep; line parchment paper on bottom.
- Cake: Mix cocoa powder into hot coffee till it is dissolved in a medium bowl; mix in brown sugar then vanilla and yogurt. Thoroughly mix so all ingredients get incorporated.
- Beat granulated sugar and butter at medium speed for 3 minutes till fluffy and light-yellow in electric mixer's bowl with paddle attachment; scrape down bowl's sides. Add eggs; stir for 2 minutes, scraping bowl down if needed.
- Whisk salt, baking soda and flour in medium bowl. Mix in 1/2 coffee mixture and 1/3 flour mixture as mixer runs on low speed; scrape bowl down. Add leftover coffee mixture and 1/3 flour mixture; take bowl from mixer. Fold in leftover flour mixture using rubber spatula

till all ingredients are incorporated fully. Put batter in prepped cake pan.
- Bake for 25 minutes then rotate pan in oven; bake till inserted cake tester in middle of cake exits clean for 20 minutes. Take pan from oven; cool cake for 20 minutes in pan. Turn out cake onto clean plate; remove parchment. Flip cake onto wire rack; fully cool cake.
- Pulse brittle pieces 3-4 times till brittle is powdery in a food processor.
- Put cooled cake on serving dish. Heat dulce de leche in microwave-safe dish for 30 seconds till just liquid on high power. Put dulce de leche on cake; sprinkle kosher salt on dulce de leche. Sprinkle 1/2 cup ground brittle around cake's outer edge to decorate.

Nutrition Information

- Calories: 3775
- Saturated Fat: 74 g(370%)
- Sodium: 3110 mg(130%)
- Fiber: 17 g(68%)
- Total Carbohydrate: 648 g(216%)
- Cholesterol: 624 mg(208%)
- Protein: 51 g(102%)
- Total Fat: 123 g(189%)

298. Ricotta Pancakes With Brown Sugar Cherry Sauce

Serving: Makes about 16 | Prep: | Cook: | Ready in:

Ingredients

- 1/2 cup (or more) water, divided
- 2 teaspoons cornstarch
- 1 tablespoon unsalted butter
- 2 cups halved pitted fresh Bing cherries or other dark sweet cherries (about 14 ounces unpitted cherries)
- 2 tablespoons (packed) golden brown sugar
- 1 tablespoon fresh lemon juice
- 3/4 cup unbleached all purpose flour
- 2 tablespoons sugar
- 1/2 teaspoon baking powder
- 1/4 teaspoon salt
- 1 1/3 cups whole-milk ricotta cheese
- 4 large egg yolks
- 1/2 cup whole milk
- 3 large egg whites
- Vegetable oil (for brushing)
- Plain Greek-style yogurt or plain regular yogurt (optional)

Direction

- Sauce: In small bowl, whisk cornstarch and 1/4 cup water. Melt butter on medium heat in medium nonstick skillet. Add brown sugar, 1/4 cup water and cherries; mix till sugar is dissolved. Put heat on medium high then add cornstarch mixture; mix for 1 minute till it thickens and boils. If sauce gets very thick, add water by tablespoonfuls. Take off heat; mix in lemon juice.
- Pancakes: Whisk salt, baking powder, sugar and flour in small bowl. Beat egg yolks and ricotta cheese using electric mixer on medium high speed for 1 minute till fluffy and light in big bowl. Put mixer speed on low. Alternately with milk, add flour mixture, in 2 batches each, beating till just blended, scraping bowl's sides down if needed.
- Beat egg whites using electric mixer with clean beaters till stiff yet not dry in medium bowl. Fold 1/4 whites to lighten into ricotta mixture; fold in leftover whites in 3 extra additions.
- Heat big nonstick skillet/griddle on medium heat; lightly brush oil on griddle. By generous 1/4 cupfuls, drop batter on griddle; spread each pancake to make 3 1/2-in. round with offset spatula. Cook for 3 minutes till bottoms are golden and bubbles appear over pancakes. Flip pancakes; cook for 2 minutes till bottoms are golden brown.
- Put pancakes on plates; put yogurt, optional, and cherry sauce over. Serve.

Nutrition Information

- Calories: 131
- Saturated Fat: 3 g(14%)
- Sodium: 83 mg(3%)
- Fiber: 1 g(3%)
- Total Carbohydrate: 15 g(5%)
- Cholesterol: 59 mg(20%)
- Protein: 5 g(9%)
- Total Fat: 6 g(9%)

299. Ricotta And Cherry Strudel

Serving: | Prep: | Cook: |Ready in:

Ingredients

- 1 1/4 cups all purpose flour
- 1/4 teaspoon (generous) salt
- 1 tablespoon plus 2 teaspoons olive oil
- 6 tablespoons (or more) water
- 3 tablespoons unsalted butter
- 1 1/2 cups unflavored dry breadcrumbs
- 6 tablespoons sugar
- Cheesecloth
- 2 pounds fresh whole-milk ricotta cheese (preferably large-curd)
- 1 3/4 cups sugar
- 3 tablespoons unsalted butter, room temperature
- 3 large eggs
- 1 tablespoon finely grated lemon peel
- 2 teaspoons finely grated orange peel
- 1 teaspoon vanilla extract
- 2 1/2 pounds fresh cherries, pitted, drained, juices reserved, or two (12-ounce) packages frozen dark sweet pitted cherries (about 3 cups), thawed, drained, juices reserved
- 1 cup sugar
- 2 tablespoons fresh lemon juice
- 2 tablespoons maraschino liqueur or Cointreau (orange-flavored liqueur)
- 4 tablespoons (1/2 stick) unsalted butter
- Powdered sugar

- • cheese Use fresh ricotta cheese with a dry texture, preferably one with large curds. It's sold at some supermarkets and at specialty foods stores and Italian markets.
- • cherries If using fresh cherries, add enough purchased cherry juice to the drained juices to measure 1 1/2 cups total — the fresh cherries won't release as much juice as frozen ones.

Direction

- For the Dough: In medium bowl, whisk salt and flour. Drizzle with olive oil; toss with flour. Sprinkle with 6 tbsp. water, 1 tbsp. at a time; mix in using fork. There will be small clumps. Knead mixture till dough is pliable and comes together in bowl; if dough is dry, add extra water by teaspoonfuls. Turn dough on work surface; knead till elastic and smooth for 6 minutes. If dough is sticky, add flour on work surface only. Flatten to disk. Wrap in plastic; chill overnight. (You can make dough 2 days ahead, kept chilled. Just 1 hour before rolling, allow it to stand in room temperature.)
- For Filling: Sprinkle breadcrumb mixture over the strudel dough. Top it with drained cherries and drained ricotta cheese. The leftover cherries and juices are turned into a cherry sauce.
- For Breadcrumb mixture: In big skillet, melt 3 tbsp. butter on medium heat then add breadcrumbs; constantly mix for 5 minutes till light golden. Remove from heat. Mix in 6 tbsp. sugar; cool.
- For Ricotta filling: Line double layer of cheesecloth on a big strainer; put above deep bowl. In strainer, put ricotta cheese; use plastic wrap to cover. Refrigerate overnight. The liquid will drain from cheese; discard liquid. Put cheese on a clean kitchen towel; squeeze out as much liquid as you can.
- Beat 3 tbsp. butter and 1 3/4 cups sugar using electric mixer in medium bowl. Add eggs, one at a time; beat for 4 minutes till pale yellow and smooth. Add vanilla, orange peel, lemon peel and drained ricotta; beat till just blended.

- Refrigerate filling as you roll out dough and prep cherries.
- For Cherries: Mix liqueur, lemon juice, 1 cup sugar, 1 1/2 cups reserved juices and drained cherries in medium bowl; put aside for at least 1 hour and up to 1 day.
- Drain cherry mixture; keep liquid. On paper towel layers, arrange 2 cups cherries; for sauce, keep leftover 1 cup cherries.
- Transfer reserved cherry liquid in small saucepan; boil, mixing till sugar dissolves. Boil for 4 minutes till slightly thick. Mix in the reserved 1 cup cherries; fully cool sauce.
- Assembly: Preheat an oven to 450°F. Brush olive oil on 18x12-in. rimmed baking sheet. Melt 4 tbsp. butter in small saucepan; put aside. Flour big work surface lightly; roll dough to 22x17-in. thin rectangle, starting from center to edges using long rolling pin, with 1 long side being parallel to work surface. It'll slightly retract and resist.
- Pull then stretch: As dough gets thinner, pull and stretch dough very gently to 22x17-in. rectangle. (Dough might slightly tear in spots and doesn't have to be a perfect rectangle. Slide long kitchen towel 4-inches under the long edge of dough farthest from you so you can easily put strudel on baking sheet when filled.
- Brush 2 tbsp. melted butter on dough. Sprinkle breadcrumbs on dough; leave all sides with 1 1/2-in. border. Starting at long side nearest you, 2-in. from dough edge, spoon ricotta mixture lengthwise in 3-in. wide log, leaving short sides with 3-in. plain border. Lightly press 2 cups of drained cherries over ricotta mixture, evenly spacing.
- Roll up: Fold dough over the filling, beginning on long side nearest you. Roll up strudel slowly, fully enclosing filling. Fold dough's short ends under; to seal, pinch.
- Put strudel, seam side down, bending into horseshoe/crescent shape to fit sheet, onto prepped baking sheet using towel as aid. Brush strudel with 2 tbsp. melted butter; along top, cut a few 1/8-in. deep, 1-in. long slits.
- Put strudel in oven; lower temperature to 375°F. Bake for 1 hour 10 minutes till light golden and firm; juices might spill onto sheet and strudel might crack. To loosen, run a thin knife under strudel; on sheet, cool. (You can make it 1 day ahead; cover then chill. Before serving, bring to room temperature.)
- Strudel shortcut: Use purchased thawed frozen phyllo sheets instead of strudel dough and follow recipe as directed. You'll need 32 thawed 14x9-in. frozen phyllo sheets from 1 16-oz. package along with 14 tbsp. melted unsalted butter. On work surface, put big kitchen towel. Overlap 4 14x9-in. phyllo sheets slightly, making 22x17-in. rectangle atop towel. Brush with butter. Repeat 7 times with leftover butter and phyllo, making 8 layers in total. Assemble as mentioned with prepped breadcrumb mixture, ricotta filling, and cherries. Roll up strudel; brush with batter. Bake for 1 hour at 375°F till phyllo is golden.

Nutrition Information

- Calories: 348
- Saturated Fat: 7 g(36%)
- Sodium: 126 mg(5%)
- Fiber: 2 g(7%)
- Total Carbohydrate: 51 g(17%)
- Cholesterol: 60 mg(20%)
- Protein: 8 g(16%)
- Total Fat: 13 g(20%)

300. Roasted Pear And Amaretto Trifle

Serving: Makes 8 servings | Prep: | Cook: | Ready in:

Ingredients

- 1 1/2 cups heavy whipping cream
- 1 1/4 cups whole milk
- 1 1/4 cups sugar
- 4 large egg yolks

- 1/2 cup all purpose flour
- 2 tablespoons amaretto or other almond liqueur
- 2 teaspoons vanilla extract
- Pinch of salt
- 8 firm but ripe Bosc pears (about 3 1/4 pounds), peeled, halved lengthwise, cored
- 1/3 cup sugar
- 2 tablespoons fresh lemon juice
- 56 (about) day-old soft ladyfingers (from about three 3-ounce packages)
- 1 1/2 cups coarsely crushed amaretti cookies (Italian macaroons)* or almond macaroons (about 4 ounces)
- 3/4 cup apricot fruit spread (100% spreadable fruit) or apricot preserves
- 4 tablespoons brandy
- 4 tablespoons amaretto or other almond liqueur
- 2 cups chilled whipping cream
- 1/4 cup powdered sugar
- 1 tablespoon vanilla extract
- 1/4 cup sliced almonds, toasted
- Fresh mint sprigs (optional)

Direction

- Pastry cream: Simmer milk and cream in medium saucepan; take off heat. Whisk salt, vanilla, amaretto, flour, egg yolks and sugar till smooth, pasty and thick in big bowl. Whisk hot cream mixture slowly into yolk mixture; put mixture in saucepan. Whisk on medium heat for 6 minutes till it is smooth, thickens and boils. Put pastry cream in bowl. Directly press plastic wrap on pastry cream's surface; refrigerate overnight.
- Pears: Put rack in middle of oven; preheat it to 400°F. Toss lemon juice, 1/3 cup sugar and pear halves in big bowl; put pears on big heavy rimmed baking sheet, cut side down. Put sugar mixture from bowl on pears; roast pears for 40 minutes till golden brown in spots and tender, occasionally turning. Cool. Cut pears to 1/2-in. pieces; put into bowl with juices from baking sheet. You can make it 1 day ahead, chilled, covered.
- Put 13-14 ladyfingers on bottom of 3-qt. 8-in. diameter trifle bowl; to tightly fit, trim. Sprinkle over 1/2 cup of crushed amaretti cookies. Use 1/4 cup fruit spread to dot; put 1 cup roasted pears over. Drizzle 1 tbsp. amaretto and 1 tbsp. brandy; spread over 1 cup pastry cream. Repeat layers twice with pastry cream, amaretto, brandy, pears, fruit spread, amaretti cookies and ladyfingers. Put 13-14 ladyfingers over; sprinkle leftover amaretto and brandy. Spread leftover pastry cream over; cover. Refrigerate for 4 hours till cold.
- Beat vanilla, powdered sugar and cream till peaks form in big bowl; spread top of trifle with 1 1/2 cups of whipped cream. Put leftover whipped cream in pastry bag with a medium star tip; around trifle's top, pipe whipped-cream rosettes. Garnish with mint sprigs, optional, and sliced almonds; refrigerate for a maximum of 6 hours.

Nutrition Information

- Calories: 1435
- Total Carbohydrate: 174 g(58%)
- Cholesterol: 468 mg(156%)
- Protein: 18 g(36%)
- Total Fat: 74 g(113%)
- Saturated Fat: 43 g(213%)
- Sodium: 308 mg(13%)
- Fiber: 8 g(32%)

301. Roquefort Dip With Apple, Endive, And Celery Hearts

Serving: Serves 8 as an hors d'oeuvre | Prep: | Cook: | Ready in:

Ingredients

- 4 ounces fromage blanc or softened cream cheese (about 1/2 cup)

- 3 tablespoons milk
- 2 teaspoons medium-dry Sherry
- 4 ounces Roquefort (about 1 cup crumbled)
- 2 Belgian endives
- 12 inner celery ribs with leaves
- 1 medium head white radicchio* (optional)
- 1 crisp red apple such as Gala or Fuji
- *available at some specialty produce shops

Direction

- Mix sherry and milk with fromage blanc, if using, till smooth in a bowl. Beat sherry and milk with cream cheese, if using, till smooth using an electric mixer. Crumble Roquefort; mix into mixture carefully without breaking up lumps. You can make dip 1 day ahead, covered, chilled.
- Prep a big bowl of cold water and ice. From endives, trim root ends; separate leaves. Trim celery to 4-6-in. lengths. From radicchio, remove discolored outer leaves; slightly trim root end so the radicchio stands upright. Put veggies into bowl of ice water to crisp and so radicchio leaves open. Allow veggies to stand for at least 15 minutes and up to 2 hours.
- Drain radicchio in a colander; to remove water, shake. Twist then pull center leaves out to make a bowl for the dip. Put dip into a small bowl/radicchio.
- Drain celery and endive in colander; pat dry. Quarter apple; remove core. Slice quarters to thin wedges. In each of the 2 wine glasses, put few ice cubes; stand apple, celery and endive on rice.
- Serve dip with celery, endive and apple.

Nutrition Information

- Calories: 101
- Fiber: 2 g(8%)
- Total Carbohydrate: 7 g(2%)
- Cholesterol: 16 mg(5%)
- Protein: 5 g(10%)
- Total Fat: 6 g(9%)
- Saturated Fat: 3 g(17%)
- Sodium: 316 mg(13%)

302. Royal Icing

Serving: 12 | Prep: | Cook: | Ready in:

Ingredients

- 2 egg whites
- 4 cups confectioners' sugar
- 2 tablespoons lemon juice

Direction

- Lightly beat egg whites. Add enough sugar to create icing that holds shape. To get desired consistency, blend in lemon juice. Spread almond paste on cake; let harden. Decorate.

Nutrition Information

- Calories: 159 calories;
- Protein: 0.6
- Total Fat: 0
- Sodium: 10
- Total Carbohydrate: 40.1
- Cholesterol: 0

303. Salvadorian "Quesadilla" Cake

Serving: Makes 8 to 12 servings | Prep: 20mins | Cook: 1.25hours | Ready in:

Ingredients

- 1 3/4 cups sifted cake flour (not self-rising; sift before measuring)
- 1 teaspoon baking powder
- 1/4 teaspoon salt
- 1 stick unsalted butter, softened
- 3/4 cup sugar

- 2 large eggs at room temperature 30 minutes
- 3 tablespoons sour cream
- 1/2 ounces finely grated parmesan
- 1/2 cup whole milk
- 1 teaspoon sesame seeds (optional), not toasted
- Equipment: a 9- by 5-inch loaf pan

Direction

- Preheat an oven with rack in center to 400°F. Line parchment paper on sides and bottom of pan.
- Whisk salt, baking powder and flour. Beat sugar and butter using an electric mixer on medium high speed for 1 minute till pale in another bowl; beat in cheese, sour cream and eggs.
- Lower speed to low, blend in milk. Add the flour mixture; mix just till combined.
- Put batter in pan; smooth top. If using, sprinkle sesame seeds; bake for 30-40 minutes till inserted skewer/wooden pick in middle of cake exits clean.
- Cool for 20-30 minutes to warm in pan; turn out cake on rack. Serve cake in room temperature/slightly warm.
- Cake keeps for 3 days in room temperature in airtight container.

Nutrition Information

- Calories: 262
- Sodium: 137 mg(6%)
- Fiber: 0 g(2%)
- Total Carbohydrate: 35 g(12%)
- Cholesterol: 66 mg(22%)
- Protein: 4 g(9%)
- Total Fat: 12 g(18%)
- Saturated Fat: 7 g(35%)

304. Savory Mascarpone Cheesecake With Sun Dried Tomato Pesto

Serving: | Prep: | Cook: |Ready in:

Ingredients

- 1 cup finely ground Wheat Thins or other wheat crackers
- 1/2 cup finely chopped walnuts
- 1 tablespoon unsalted butter, melted and cooled
- 1 1/2 cups packed fresh basil leaves
- 6 ounces sun-dried tomatoes in oil, drained, reserving 2 tablespoons of the oil
- 1 garlic clove, minced
- 1/4 cup freshly grated Parmesan
- 3 tablespoons pine nuts
- 1 pound mascarpone (available at specialty foods shops and cheese shops)
- 8 ounces cream cheese, cut into bits and softened
- 3 large eggs, beaten lightly
- 1 tablespoon all-purpose flour
- 8 ounces sour cream
- 1 teaspoon all-purpose flour
- sun-dried tomato slices for garnish
- basil sprigs for garnish
- assorted greens with vinaigrette

Direction

- Crust: Mix pepper and salt to taste, butter, walnuts and cracker crumbs in a bowl; press onto bottom of 10-in. buttered springform pan. Bake curst for 10 minutes in center of preheated 325°F oven.
- Pesto: Puree pine nuts, Parmesan, garlic, sun-dried tomatoes with reserved oil, basil and pepper and salt to taste till smooth in a food processor.
- Filling: Blend flour, eggs, cream cheese and mascarpone till very smooth in an electric mixer's bowl.
- Put 1/2 filling into crust; put pesto over, carefully spreading pesto with a spoon's back.

Spread leftover filling on pesto; bake cheesecake for 1 hour in center of preheated 325°F oven.
- Blend flour and sour cream in a bowl; spread sour cream topping over cheesecake. Bake cheesecake till set for 5-10 minutes; cool in pan on rack. Chill for at least 3 hours – overnight, loosely covered. Remove pan sides then use basil and sun-dried tomato slices to garnish; serve with greens.

Nutrition Information

- Calories: 331
- Protein: 10 g(20%)
- Total Fat: 30 g(47%)
- Saturated Fat: 11 g(54%)
- Sodium: 280 mg(12%)
- Fiber: 1 g(3%)
- Total Carbohydrate: 6 g(2%)
- Cholesterol: 80 mg(27%)

305. Scrambled Egg Pasta

Serving: Makes 4 servings | Prep: | Cook: 20mins | Ready in:

Ingredients

- 4 eggs
- 1/2 cup grated Parmesan
- 8 slices thick bacon, chopped
- 1 onion, chopped
- 4 cups al-dente cooked pasta
- Salt and pepper to taste

Direction

- Beat cheese and eggs in a small bowl; put aside.
- Fry onion and bacon till onion starts to caramelize and meat is crispy and brown in a big skillet.
- Add pasta. Cook till warmed through for 1 minute if using day-old cold pasta.
- Put cheese-and-egg mixture in skillet; lower heat to low. Continuously mix till pasta is coated in eggs and they start to solidify.
- Season with pepper and salt; immediately serve with more grated parmesan alongside.

Nutrition Information

- Calories: 586
- Fiber: 3 g(13%)
- Total Carbohydrate: 48 g(16%)
- Cholesterol: 207 mg(69%)
- Protein: 26 g(52%)
- Total Fat: 31 g(48%)
- Saturated Fat: 11 g(57%)
- Sodium: 663 mg(28%)

306. Sefrou Apricot (Galettes Sucrees)

Serving: Makes about 30 cookies | Prep: | Cook: | Ready in:

Ingredients

- 4 large eggs
- 3/4 cup sugar
- 1/2 cup vegetable oil
- 3 cups unbleached all-purpose flour
- 2 teaspoons baking powder
- 1/2 teaspoon salt
- 1/2 teaspoon cinnamon
- 1/2 cup chopped almonds
- 1/2 cup chopped walnuts
- 1/2 cup chopped dried apricots
- 1/2 cup chopped pitted dates
- 1 tablespoon sesame seeds

Direction

- Heat an oven to 350 degrees; oil cookie sheet.

- Whip sugar and 3 of eggs in an electric mixer's bowl. Put in cinnamon, salt, baking powder, flour and oil, then fold in fruit and chopped nuts.
- Transfer dough on a board dusted with flour. Split dough to two portions; shape every portion to 14-inch long and 1 1/2- to 2-inch wide roll. Arrange rolls on cookie sheet, spacing 1-inch away.
- Whip the rest of egg and brush whipped eggs on dough. Scatter sesame seeds over.
- Bake on center rack for 20 minutes. Cool rolls about 5 minutes. Cut every roll making 3/4-inch slices with serrated knife. Lace slices on cookie sheet, cut side facing up, and place back to oven for an additional of 15 minutes, or till cookies turn golden brown.

Nutrition Information

- Calories: 147
- Sodium: 74 mg(3%)
- Fiber: 1 g(5%)
- Total Carbohydrate: 20 g(7%)
- Cholesterol: 25 mg(8%)
- Protein: 3 g(6%)
- Total Fat: 6 g(9%)
- Saturated Fat: 1 g(4%)

307. Self Stomped Thick White Noodles

Serving: Makes 4 servings | Prep: | Cook: | Ready in:

Ingredients

- 3 1/2 cups udon flour (see Tips, below) or other high-gluten white wheat flour
- 1 tablespoon salt, dissolved in 3/4 cups warm water

Direction

- Prepare the noodles: In a bowl, stir three cups of flour then steadily and slowly pour in half of the saltwater as a stream; mix gently to combine. Pour in more salted water gradually while mixing until it forms in a slightly crumbly mass. Exert a bit pressure to shape the dough into a ball; put in a sealable plastic bag for around half an hour at room temperature for a chill for a few hours or overnight.
- Place the rested of the noodle dough in the middle of heavy-duty plastic layers. You can use a 6ft plastic, vinyl tablecloth, or oilcloth that is folded in half. Put the noodle dough that is enclosed in plastic on the floor then stand on top while barefoot to press down with both of your whole feet, not only heels. Turn in a circular fashion with stomping, small steps to stretch and flatten out the dough while applying your body weight. Stop from time to time to fold and remove the dough using your hands then place it again in the middle of plastic cloth layers; do the procedure of pressing again. Dust with extra flour if needed to avoid the noodle dough sticking to the plastic.
- Once the dough is elastic and acquires a satiny sheen after 4 or 5 mins, make the last round of stomping to flatten the dough into a quarter-inch thick, more or less oval form.
- Move the dough to a big and lightly floured board. Stretch the dough with a lightly floured rolling pin into a big, around 1/8-in thick oval, a foot wide and about 1 1/2ft long, alternating with horizontal and vertical strokes. Halve the dough if needed to make 2 smaller ovals.
- Liberally dust flour on the rolled-out dough, fold for 4 or 5 times back on itself like folding a paper fan but avoid creasing or pressing on the folded dough. Slice the dough into a quarter-inch thick ribbons, 1 1/2 ft. long using a long and sharp knife. Dust noodles lightly with flour then lift from the board.
- Cook the noodles. Boil a big pot of water to reach a rolling boil. Shake off the excess flour gently from the noodles then lower into the pot. Mix the noodles to ensure separate the

noodles into individual strands; boil for 7-8mins steadily while mixing from time to time. To test, pull a noodle out of the pot then plunge into cold water; the noodle should be still firm and translucent with no hard core. Boil further if needed then check the procedure for every 45secs or so.

- If serving it hot for later, lift the noodles out of the pot then set aside the boiling water. You can use a colander under the noodles, or spoon a strainer, or a pasta insert.
- If serving it cold; drain the noodles.
- Whether you want to serve it cold or hot, rinse the noodles well under cold running water to get rid of the starch on the surface that can make the noodles gummy.
- Set the noodles aside until ready to serve. It can stay for a few hours or chill if holding for longer than 20 mins. Rinse in boiling hot water once ready to use then serve in hot soup or rinse in cold water to serve in salad.
- You can find high-gluten udon flour or udon ko in Asian groceries, you can also use high-gluten bread flour. You can substitute high-gluten bread flour. You can stomp the noodles on an American linoleum-covered floor but tatami-matted floor works the best. If you have a flagstone or hard wood floor in the kitchen, put a big bath towel beneath the plastic cloth to provide some cushion. You can also use mechanical kneading equipment like a food processor with a dough hook or pasta machine with the lasagna attachment if you don't want the food-stomping style.

308. Semolina Pudding With Fresh Berries

Serving: Makes 8 servings | Prep: | Cook: | Ready in:

Ingredients

- 4 cups whole milk
- 1 1/2 tablespoons finely grated orange zest (from 1/2 medium orange)
- 1 teaspoon finely grated lemon zest (from 1/2 medium lemon)
- 1 vanilla bean, split lengthwise
- 1 cup semolina flour (pasta flour), plus additional for dusting baking dish
- 5 large egg yolks, room temperature
- 1/2 cup (1 stick) unsalted butter, cut into 1-inch cubes
- 5 large egg whites, room temperature
- 1 cup sugar
- 4 cups (from about 1 1/2 to 2 pounds, picked over) strawberries, hulled and thinly sliced lengthwise

Direction

- Preheat an oven to 325°F. In freezer, chill big metal mixing bowl. Butter 9x13-in. baking dish; dust using semolina flour.
- Mix lemon zest, orange zest and milk in a big heavy saucepan on medium high heat; from vanilla bean, scrape in seeds. Boil; lower heat to low immediately. In slow, steady stream, add semolina flour, constantly whisking; cook for 1 minute till it thickens, constantly whisking. Add butter and egg yolks; whisk for 2 minutes till butter is fully incorporated and melts. Put mixture into a big bowl; put aside.
- Beat egg whites using electric mixer with whisk attachment for 1-1 1/2 minutes till soft peaks just start to firm in a chilled big metal bowl. Add sugar; beat for 30 seconds till soft peaks fully form. Fold 1/3 egg whites to lighten into semolina batter; fold in leftover whites gently till just incorporated. Put batter into prepped pan; smooth top.
- Bake pudding for 35-45 minutes till edges just start to brown, golden on top and fully set in center. Put onto rack; cool before serving to room temperature. Serve: Cut to 8 portions; put strawberries over.
- Best served, unrefrigerated, within a few hours. Or, refrigerate for a few hours – overnight; before serving, bring to room temperature.

Nutrition Information

- Calories: 422
- Saturated Fat: 11 g(53%)
- Sodium: 95 mg(4%)
- Fiber: 3 g(10%)
- Total Carbohydrate: 53 g(18%)
- Cholesterol: 158 mg(53%)
- Protein: 11 g(22%)
- Total Fat: 19 g(29%)

309. Sesame Citrus Crackers

Serving: Makes about 32 | Prep: | Cook: 45mins | Ready in:

Ingredients

- 1 large egg
- 1 tablespoon orange juice
- 1/2 tablespoon fresh lemon juice
- 1 1/2 cups all purpose flour
- 1/2 cup sugar
- 1/2 teaspoon salt
- 1/2 teaspoon baking powder
- 1/2 cup (1 stick) chilled unsalted butter, diced
- 2 teaspoons sesame seeds
- 1 teaspoon (packed) finely grated orange peel
- 1/2 teaspoon (packed) finely grated lemon peel
- Whipping cream

Direction

- Preheat an oven to 350°F. Line parchment paper on 2 rimmed baking sheets. Whisk lemon juice, orange juice and egg to blend in small bowl. Whisk baking powder, salt, sugar and flour to blend in big bowl; add butter. With fingertips, rub in till coarse meal forms. Stir in lemon peel, orange peel and sesame seeds. Add egg mixture; toss till moist clumps form. If dough is dry, add cream by tablespoonfuls. Turn out dough on floured work surface; gently knead till dough comes together for several turns.
- Roll out dough to 1/4-in. thick on floured surface; cut dough rounds using 2-in. round cutter. Gather dough scraps; reroll then cut more rounds out. Put on prepped sheets; bake for 15 minutes till cooked through yet pale and firm to touch.

Nutrition Information

- Calories: 63
- Sodium: 35 mg(1%)
- Fiber: 0 g(1%)
- Total Carbohydrate: 8 g(3%)
- Cholesterol: 13 mg(4%)
- Protein: 1 g(2%)
- Total Fat: 3 g(5%)
- Saturated Fat: 2 g(9%)

310. Smoked Trout Soufflé In A Phyllo Crust

Serving: Serves 6 as a main course | Prep: | Cook: | Ready in:

Ingredients

- eight 17- by 12-inch phyllo sheets
- 5 1/2 tablespoons unsalted butter
- 1 1/2 tablespoons all-purpose flour
- 1/2 cup whole milk
- 1/2 cup heavy cream
- 2 smoked trout fillets* (about 1/2 pound total)
- 6 large eggs
- 1 1/2 teaspoons drained bottled horseradish
- 2 tablespoons fresh dill leaves
- *available at fish markets, the deli counter of many supermarkets

Direction

- With overlapping plastic wrap sheets, cover phyllo stack then with a damp kitchen towel.
- Melt 4 tbsp. butter. On a work surface, put 1 phyllo sheet. Brush some melted butter on. Put an extra sheet to overlap the original one. Make a 17-in. square. Brush butter on it. Keep layering with butter and remaining 6 sheets. Over a 10-in. tart pan that has a removable bottom, drape phyllo stack and fit phyllo in the pan. Crumple the overhang against the rim's inside edges to make a ragged edge that is 1-in. above the rim. Chill shell for at least 3 hours until firm while loosely covered.
- Preheat the oven to 375 degrees F.
- Use a fork to prick the shell's bottom all over. Bake for 15 minutes in the center of the oven until it's golden. On a rack, cool shell in pan. You can make this 1 day in advance, covered in cool room temperature.
- Melt remaining 1 1/2 tbsp. butter in a saucepan on medium low heat. Whisk flour in. Cook roux for 3 minutes, stirring, and mix in cream and milk. Boil mixture, constantly whisking, then simmer for 3 minutes, occasionally whisking. Season pepper and salt into mixture. Cool.
- Throw trout bones and skin. Break fish to small pieces. Separate the eggs. Pulse dill, horseradish, yolks, trout and milk mixture in a food processor until smooth. Put in a big bowl.
- Use an electric mixer to beat a pinch of salt and whites in another big bowl just until they hold stiff peaks. Mix 1/4 whites in the trout mixture to lighten. Fold remaining whites thoroughly but gently.
- Put soufflé mixture in the shell. Run a knife's tip around the souffle's edge to aid in rising. Bake soufflé for 25 minutes on a baking sheet on the lower third of the oven until golden brown and puffed. Immediately serve soufflé.

Nutrition Information

- Calories: 395
- Total Carbohydrate: 17 g(6%)
- Cholesterol: 271 mg(90%)
- Protein: 19 g(38%)
- Total Fat: 28 g(43%)
- Saturated Fat: 14 g(71%)
- Sodium: 241 mg(10%)
- Fiber: 1 g(2%)

311. Soft Chocolate Cookies With Grapefruit And Star Anise

Serving: Makes about 40 | Prep: | Cook: | Ready in:

Ingredients

- 8 ounces bittersweet chocolate, finely chopped
- 1/4 cup (1/2 stick) unsalted butter, diced
- 1 teaspoon plus 1/4 cup sugar
- 3 whole star anise*
- 1/4 cup all purpose flour
- 1 tablespoon unsweetened cocoa powder
- 1/2 teaspoon coarse kosher salt
- 1/4 teaspoon baking powder
- 2 large eggs
- 2 tablespoons honey
- 2 teaspoons finely grated grapefruit peel

Direction

- In a medium microwave-safe bowl, mix butter and chocolate. Place in the microwave with intervals of 10 seconds until chocolate is just melted; take out and whisk until smooth and melted. In a small coffee grinder or spice mill, grind 3-star anise and 1 teaspoon sugar finely. Place into a small bowl; mix in baking powder, coarse salt, cocoa, and flour.
- In a large bowl, whisk grapefruit peel, honey, eggs, and the rest 1/4 cup sugar until smooth and thick. Add chocolate and fold, and then the dry ingredients. Cover the bowl; let the batter chill for at least 45 minutes and up to 1 day until firm and cold.
- Prepare the oven by preheating to 375 degrees F. Use parchment paper to line 3 large baking sheets. Place batter by tablespoonfuls onto prepared sheets, keeping mounds 2-inch apart.

- Bake the cookies for about 10 minutes, 1 sheet at a time, until a tester comes out with moist crumbs remain attached and dry-looking. Cool for 3 minutes on sheets then place onto racks and cool fully. DO AHEAD: You can prepare 1 day in advance. Keep in an airtight between sheets of waxed paper.
- A brown and star-shaped seedpod is called star anise. You can find it at specialty food stores and spice section of some supermarkets.

Nutrition Information

- Calories: 53
- Fiber: 0 g(2%)
- Total Carbohydrate: 7 g(2%)
- Cholesterol: 12 mg(4%)
- Protein: 1 g(1%)
- Total Fat: 3 g(5%)
- Saturated Fat: 2 g(9%)
- Sodium: 30 mg(1%)

312. Sour Cream Chocolate Cake

Serving: 18 | Prep: | Cook: | Ready in:

Ingredients

- 2 eggs
- 1 1/2 cups sour cream
- 2 tablespoons shortening
- 1 1/4 cups white sugar
- 2 cups all-purpose flour
- 4 tablespoons unsweetened cocoa powder
- 1/4 teaspoon salt
- 1 teaspoon vanilla extract
- 2 teaspoons baking soda
- 1/4 cup hot water
- 2 cups white sugar
- 1/4 cup light corn syrup
- 1/2 cup milk
- 1/2 cup shortening
- 2 (1 ounce) squares unsweetened chocolate
- 1/4 teaspoon salt
- 1 teaspoon vanilla extract

Direction

- In a big mixing bowl, whip the eggs. Dissolve 2 tablespoons shortening. Add it and sour cream to eggs.
- Strain in a separate bowl the 1/4 teaspoon salt, cocoa, flour, and 1 1/4 cup sugar. Put these dry ingredients to egg mixture. Mix the batter until it is smooth. Mix in the vanilla. P put soda melted in the hot water. Mix.
- Transfer batter into a 9x13-inch pan that's greased and floured. Place in the oven and bake for 35 minutes at 350°F (175°C) or until it's cooked. Let cool.
- For frosting: In a small saucepan, mix 1/4 teaspoon salt, unsweetened chocolate, 1/2 cup shortening, milk, corn syrup, and 2 cups sugar. Stir on low heat until chocolate dissolves. Put on a rolling boil and simmer for a minute, whisking constantly. Take pan off heat. Put 1 teaspoon vanilla and whisk the frosting mixture until it has a spreading consistency that's smooth.
- Then frost cake once it has fully cooled.

Nutrition Information

- Calories: 338 calories;
- Protein: 3.6
- Total Fat: 13.7
- Sodium: 229
- Total Carbohydrate: 53
- Cholesterol: 30

313. Sour Cream Chocolate Chip Cake

Serving: Makes 12 servings | Prep: | Cook: | Ready in:

Ingredients

- 1 cup finely chopped pecans
- 1/4 cup whole pecans
- 1 12-ounce package of chocolate chips
- 1/4 cup packed brown sugar
- 2 teaspoons cinnamon
- 2 cups flour
- 1 cup sugar
- 1/2 cup (1 stick) butter
- 2 eggs
- 1 cup sour cream
- 2 teaspoons vanilla
- 1 1/2 teaspoons baking powder
- 1 teaspoon baking soda
- 1 teaspoon cinnamon
- 1/4 cup powdered sugar (optional)

Direction

- Preheat an oven to 350°F. Butter the 10- to 12-cup Bundt pan and dust with flour.
- Topping: Mix cinnamon, chopped pecans, chocolate chips and brown sugar in medium bowl; put aside.
- Batter: Sift baking soda, baking powder and flour into a medium bowl; put aside.
- Cream sugar and butter using an electric mixer till blended fully. Beat in eggs then sour cream till smooth and creamy; add sifted dry ingredients slowly, being sure to scrape bowl's sides into mixture. Mix in vanilla and cinnamon; mix till batter is blended well.
- Sprinkle bottom of prepped pan with whole pecans; distribute 1/4 cup topping evenly in pan. Fold leftover topping into batter till well mixed. Put batter into pan; evenly spread. Bake for 35-40 minutes. Insert tester, like a toothpick, into middle to test cake; if done, it should exit clean without batter sticking on it.
- Cool cake in pan for minimum of 20 minutes. Put a serving piece/plate upside down over top of cake pan when cake is cool so plate's face covers open portion of cake pan fully. Invert pan and plate at the same time; put onto flat surface. Raise pan slowly using pot holders so cake stands upright on serving plate. To decorate, sprinkle powdered sugar.
- Cake freezes well; you can make it maximum of 2 days ahead.

Nutrition Information

- Calories: 503
- Protein: 6 g(12%)
- Total Fat: 28 g(43%)
- Saturated Fat: 12 g(61%)
- Sodium: 192 mg(8%)
- Fiber: 3 g(11%)
- Total Carbohydrate: 59 g(20%)
- Cholesterol: 61 mg(20%)

314. Sour Cream Layer Cake With Pecan Brittle

Serving: Makes 10 to 12 servings | Prep: | Cook: | Ready in:

Ingredients

- Nonstick vegetable oil spray
- 3/4 cup sugar
- 1/4 cup water
- 1/8 teaspoon cream of tartar
- 3/4 cup pecan halves, toastedcoarsely chopped
- Nonstick vegetable oil spray
- 1 18.25-ounce box yellow cake mix
- 4 large eggs
- 1 cup sour cream
- 1/3 cup vegetable oil
- 1/2 teaspoon vanilla extract
- 1/2 teaspoon almond extract
- 2 ounces bittersweet (not unsweetened) or semisweet chocolate, coarsely grated
- 1/2 cup (packed) dark brown sugar
- 3 tablespoons water
- 1/4 cup whipping cream
- 6 cups (about) powdered sugar
- 1 cup (2 sticks) unsalted butter, room temperature

Direction

- Pecan brittle: Spray nonstick spray on baking sheet. Mix cream of tartar, 1/4 cup water and sugar in small heavy saucepan on medium low heat till sugar dissolves. Increase heat; boil without mixing, brushing down pan sides with a wet pastry brush occasionally, for 9 minutes till syrup gets deep amber color. Add chopped pecans; swirl to blend. Put onto prepped baking sheet; evenly spread. Fully cool brittle. Cut 3 big brittle pieces, each around 1 1/2-in. Cut leftover brittle to 1/3-in. pieces. You can make it 1 week ahead; keep in room temperature, airtight.
- Cake: Preheat an oven to 350°F. Spray nonstick spray on 2 9-in. diameter cake pans that have 1 1/2-in. high sides; line waxed paper on bottom of pans. Beat almond extract, vanilla extract, oil, sour cream, eggs and cake mix with electric mixer for 3 minutes till well blended in a big bowl; fold in the grated bittersweet chocolate. Evenly divide batter to prepped pans.
- Bake cakes for 30 minutes till inserted tester in middle exits clean and brown on top; cool cakes for 10 minutes in pans on racks. To loosen, cut around cakes; turn onto racks. Peel paper off; fully cool cakes.
- Frosting: Mix 3 tbsp. water and 1/2 cup brown sugar in small heavy saucepan on medium low heat till sugar dissolves. Increase heat; boil for 3 minutes till slightly thick. Take off heat; cool for 5 minutes. Stir in cream. Beat butter and 3 cups powdered sugar till well blended in big bowl; beat in the brown sugar mixture. To make a frosting that gets thick enough to spread, beat in enough leftover powdered sugar.
- Put 1 cake layer on platter, flat side up; spread 1 cup frosting. Sprinkle 1/2 cup of small brittle pieces then press into frosting. Put 2nd cake layer over, flat side down; spread leftover frosting on sides and top of cake. Put big brittle pieces in middle of cake. Put smaller brittle pieces in 1-in. wide border around cake's top edge. You can make it 1 day ahead. Use a cake dome to cover; refrigerate. Stand 1 hour before serving at room temperature.

Nutrition Information

- Calories: 980
- Total Fat: 44 g(68%)
- Saturated Fat: 19 g(94%)
- Sodium: 426 mg(18%)
- Fiber: 1 g(4%)
- Total Carbohydrate: 145 g(48%)
- Cholesterol: 142 mg(47%)
- Protein: 5 g(11%)

315. Sour Cream Raisin Pie

Serving: Makes 1 pie | Prep: | Cook: |Ready in:

Ingredients

- 1 cup raisins
- Pastry dough
- Pie weights or raw rice for weighting shell
- 2 large eggs
- 1 cup sour cream
- 3/4 cup sugar
- 1 tablespoon all-purpose flour
- 1 teaspoon vanilla extract
- 1/4 teaspoon ground cloves
- 1/4 teaspoon freshly grated nutmeg
- 1/8 teaspoon salt

Direction

- In water, submerge raisins in bowl to soak by 2-inch for a minimum of 8 hours to 24 hours. Let raisins drain in sieve.
- Using a rolling pin dusted with flour, unroll dough on a slightly floured area making a 14-inch circle, approximately 1/8-inch thick and suit into a 1-quart glass 9-inches pie plate. Clip the dough, keeping a half-inch overhang, and decoratively flute edge. Refrigerate shell for half an hour, till firm.

- Preheat the oven to 425° F.
- Slightly puncture the entire shell bottom using fork and line foil on shell. Fill the foil with rice or pie weights and let shell bake for 15 minutes in center of oven. Cautiously take rice or weights and foil off and bake shell for an additional of 8 minutes till golden. Let shell cool in pan on rack.
- Lower heat to 400° F.
- Separate the eggs. Refrigerate whites till set to use. Whip sour cream and yolks together in bowl and whip in raisins, salt, nutmeg, cloves, vanilla, flour and half-cup sugar. Into the shell, put the filling and bake for 10 minutes in the center of oven. Lower heat to 350° F. and bake pie till filling is firm for an additional of 30 to 40 minutes.
- Take pie out of oven however keep heat at 350° F. Whip whites in a separate bowl using electric mixer till they barely hold soft peaks. Slowly put in leftover quarter cup of sugar, whipping till meringue barely holds firm peaks. Scatter meringue on warm pie, fully coating the filling and ensuring meringue reaches shell all way around.
- In center of the oven, let pie bake for 10 minutes till meringue turn golden. Let pie cool on rack and serve at room temperature.

316. Spiced Cranberry Bundt Cake

Serving: Makes 12 to 14 servings | Prep: | Cook: |Ready in:

Ingredients

- 2 cups all purpose flour
- 3/4 cup almond flour or almond meal* (about 2 1/2 ounces)
- 2 1/2 teaspoons Chinese five-spice powder**
- 1 teaspoon baking powder
- 1/2 teaspoon baking soda
- 1/2 teaspoon salt
- 1/2 teaspoon ground cinnamon
- 1/2 teaspoon ground ginger
- 1 cup (2 sticks) unsalted butter, room temperature
- 1 cup sugar
- 1 cup (packed) golden brown sugar
- 3 large eggs
- 1 1/2 teaspoons vanilla extract
- 1 cup plain reduced-fat (2%) Greek-style yogurt
- 1 cup chopped toasted almonds
- 1 cup halved fresh or frozen cranberries (do not thaw)
- 1/2 cup dried sweetened cranberries
- 2/3 cup powdered sugar
- 4 teaspoons (about) orange juice

Direction

- Cake: Preheat an oven to 350°F. Butter then flour a 12-cup Bundt pan. Whisk initial 8 ingredients to blend in medium bowl. Beat butter using electric mixer till smooth in big bowl. Add both sugars; beat for 3 minutes till fluffy. One by one, add eggs; beat for 1 minute after every addition. Beat in the vanilla extract; beta in Greek-style yogurt. Add the dry ingredients; beat till just blended. Fold in all cranberries and almonds; put batter in prepped Bundt pan.
- Bake cake for 1 hour 10 minutes till inserted tester in middle exits clean; cool cake for 10 minutes in pan. Turn cake onto rack; fully cool.
- Icing: Mix 2 tsp. orange juice and powdered sugar till sugar is dissolved in small bowl; by 1/2 tbsp., mix in extra juice to get heavy cream consistency. Put icing on cake, letting it drip down sides; stand for a minimum of 30 minutes till icing sets. You can make it 3 days ahead; use cake dome to cover. Keep in room temperature.

Nutrition Information

- Calories: 524
- Sodium: 217 mg(9%)

- Fiber: 3 g(14%)
- Total Carbohydrate: 64 g(21%)
- Cholesterol: 90 mg(30%)
- Protein: 10 g(19%)
- Total Fat: 27 g(41%)
- Saturated Fat: 12 g(58%)

317. Spiced Crumble Cake With Chocolate Frosting

Serving: Serves 8 | Prep: | Cook: | Ready in:

Ingredients

- 1 cup pecans (about 4 ounces)
- 1/3 cup (packed) golden brown sugar
- 2 tablespoons (1/4 stick) chilled unsalted butter, diced
- 1 tablespoon unsweetened cocoa powder
- 2 1/3 cups unbleached all purpose flour
- 1 tablespoon cornstarch
- 1 teaspoon baking soda
- 1 teaspoon ground cinnamon
- 3/4 teaspoon salt
- 1/4 teaspoon ground cloves
- 1/4 teaspoon ground allspice
- 3/4 cup sour cream
- 1/4 cup whole milk
- 1 teaspoon vanilla extract
- 1 cup (2 sticks) unsalted butter, room temperature
- 1 cup sugar
- 3/4 cup (packed) golden brown sugar
- 5 large eggs
- 6 ounces semisweet chocolate, finely chopped
- 1 8-ounce package cream cheese, room temperature
- 1/4 cup (1/2 stick) unsalted butter, room temperature
- 1 teaspoon vanilla extract
- 2 1/2 cups powdered sugar
- 2 tablespoons unsweetened cocoa powder

Direction

- Crumble: Blend all ingredients till nuts are chopped finely in processor.
- Cake: Preheat an oven to 350°F. Butter then flour 13x9x2-in. baking pan. Whisk initial 7 ingredients to blend in medium bowl. Whisk vanilla, milk and sour cream to blend in small bowl.
- Beat butter using electric mixer till fluffy in big bowl; beat in both sugars slowly. One by one, beat in 3 eggs. Beat in 1/2 cup of dry ingredients. One by one, beat in 2 eggs. Alternately with the sour cream mixture in 2 batches, beat in leftover dry ingredients in 3 batches.
- Spread 3 cups of batter in prepped pan. Sprinkle crumble; lightly press in batter. Spread leftover batter to cover crumble; bake cake for 35 minutes till inserted tester in middle exits clean. Cool cake in the pan on the rack.
- Frosting: Melt chocolate on top of double boiler above simmering water, mixing till smooth and melted. Cool to room temperature. Beat vanilla, butter and cream cheese using electric mixer to blend in big bowl. In 3 additions, beat in powdered sugar then cocoa and cooled chocolate.
- Spread frosting on top of cake; you can make it 1 day ahead. Chill till frosting sets; cover. Keep chilled. Stand before serving for 1 hour in room temperature.

Nutrition Information

- Calories: 1169
- Total Fat: 66 g(102%)
- Saturated Fat: 34 g(170%)
- Sodium: 554 mg(23%)
- Fiber: 5 g(18%)
- Total Carbohydrate: 140 g(47%)
- Cholesterol: 243 mg(81%)
- Protein: 13 g(26%)

318. Spiced Pumpkin Layer Cake With Cream Cheese Frosting

Serving: Serves 12 | Prep: | Cook: | Ready in:

Ingredients

- Butter for coating cake pans, at room temperature
- 2 cups all-purpose flour, plus extra for dusting the pan
- 2 cups granulated sugar
- 2 teaspoons baking soda
- 2 teaspoons ground cinnamon
- 1 teaspoon kosher or sea salt
- 1/2 teaspoon freshly grated nutmeg
- 1/4 teaspoon ground cloves
- 3 large eggs, beaten
- 1 cup canola or vegetable oil
- 2 teaspoons pure vanilla extract
- 1 1/4 cups canned unsweetened pumpkin purée
- 1 cup lightly packed sweetened flaked coconut
- 3/4 cup canned crushed pineapple (do not drain)
- 1/3 cup dried currants
- 2 packages (8 ounces each) cream cheese, at room temperature
- 1 cup (2 sticks) unsalted butter, at room temperature
- 2 tablespoons canned unsweetened pumpkin purée
- 1 1/2 cups confectioners' sugar, sifted
- 1 teaspoon pure vanilla extract

Direction

- Put a rack in middle of oven; preheat it to 350°F. Butter the 2 9-in. diameter cake pans that have 1 1/2-in. sides. Line parchment paper circle on bottom of every pan; butter parchment paper. Sprinkle flour on pans; tap pans to distribute flour evenly. Shake excess flour off; put aside.
- Cake: sift cloves, nutmeg, salt, cinnamon, baking soda, granulated sugar and 2 cups flour in a big bowl. Mix vanilla, oil and eggs in a medium bowl. Mix currants, crushed pineapple, coconut and pumpkin puree in another medium bowl.
- Put egg mixture in flour mixture; mix till just combined with a wooden spoon. Add pumpkin mixture; mix till just combined. Divide batter to prepped pans; evenly spread it. Bake till inserted toothpick in middle of cake exits clean for 35-40 minutes. Put on wire racks; cool for 15 minutes in pan. To loosen cakes, run table knife around pan's edges; invert cakes onto racks. Peel off parchment paper. Fully cool then frost cakes.
- Frosting: Beat cheese for 3 minutes till smooth on medium speed in an electric mixer's bowl with paddle attachment. Add butter; beat till combined for 2 minutes. Add pumpkin puree; beat for 1 minute till incorporated. Add vanilla and confectioners' sugar; beat till fluffy for 3 minutes.
- Put 1 cake layer on platter/cake plate. Spread 1/2 frosting over 1st cake layer using an offset spatula. Spread frosting right up to top edge without frosting cake's sides. Put 2nd cake over carefully, lining up edges. Spread leftover frosting on cake's top without frosting sides. To decorate top, swirl frosting. Refrigerate cake to set frosting. 30-40 minutes before serving, remove from fridge.
- You can make cake 2 days ahead; refrigerate till cold. Cover with plastic wrap carefully. You can also wrap cake tightly then freeze for maximum of 1 month. Thaw for 12 hours in the fridge.

Nutrition Information

- Calories: 792
- Protein: 7 g(14%)
- Total Fat: 53 g(81%)
- Saturated Fat: 22 g(110%)
- Sodium: 500 mg(21%)
- Fiber: 3 g(11%)
- Total Carbohydrate: 76 g(25%)
- Cholesterol: 135 mg(45%)

319. Spiced Snowflakes

Serving: Makes about 2 dozen | Prep: | Cook: | Ready in:

Ingredients

- 1 1/2 cups sifted all purpose flour
- 1 1/2 teaspoons baking powder
- 1 1/4 teaspoons ground cinnamon
- 1 teaspoon ground ginger
- 1/2 teaspoon ground nutmeg
- 1/4 teaspoon ground cloves
- 1/4 teaspoon salt
- 1/2 cup (1 stick) unsalted butter, room temperature
- 3/4 cup sugar
- 1 large egg
- 2 teaspoons vanilla extract
- Powdered sugar

Direction

- Sift salt, spices, baking powder and flour into medium bowl. Beat butter using electric mixer till light in big bowl. Beat in 3/4 cup of sugar slowly; beat in vanilla extract and egg. Beat in dry ingredients slowly; refrigerate till firm enough if dough becomes too soft to mold.
- Put dough onto big plastic wrap sheet; roll to 2 1/4-in. diameter 7-in. long log; tightly wrap. Cover; refrigerate overnight.
- Preheat an oven to 350°F and grease 2 big baking sheets. Unwrap dough; cut to 1/4-in. thick slices. Put on baking sheets, 1-in. apart; bake for 12 minutes, till light golden brown. Put cookies on rack; cool. You can make it 1 week ahead; keep in room temperature in airtight container.
- Put stencils/doilies over cookies; sift powdered sugar. Remove stencils/doilies carefully; serve.

Nutrition Information

- Calories: 222
- Total Carbohydrate: 31 g(10%)
- Cholesterol: 43 mg(14%)
- Protein: 3 g(5%)
- Total Fat: 10 g(15%)
- Saturated Fat: 6 g(30%)
- Sodium: 122 mg(5%)
- Fiber: 1 g(3%)

320. Spinach Soufflé With Shallots And Smoked Gouda Cheese

Serving: Serves 8 | Prep: | Cook: | Ready in:

Ingredients

- 2 1/2 cups whole milk
- 5 tablespoon butter
- 1/4 cup all purpose flour
- 4 large eggs, separated
- 1 cup shopped shallots (about 6 ounces)
- 1 10-ounce package frozen chopped spinach, thawed, drained, squeezed dry
- 2 cups (packed) grated smoked Gouda cheese (about 7 ounces)
- 3/4 teaspoon salt
- 1/2 teaspoon ground black pepper
- 1/2 teaspoon ground nutmeg

Direction

- Preheat an oven to 350°F. Butter the 11x7x2-in. glass baking dish. Boil milk in medium saucepan; take off heat. Melt 4 tbsp. butter on low heat in medium heavy saucepan. Add flour; mix for 3 minutes. Whisk in warm milk slowly. Put heat on medium; constantly whisk for 4 minutes till it is smooth and thick. Take off heat; whisk in the yolks. Slightly cool.
- Melt 1 tbsp. butter on medium heat in a big skillet. Add shallots; sauté for 3 minutes till tender. Put into a big bowl. Mix in nutmeg, pepper, salt, 1 1/3 cups cheese, spinach and

sauce. You can make it 2 hours ahead; cover. Stand in room temperature. Before continuing, mix on low heat just till lukewarm.
- Beat egg whites using electric mixer till stiff yet not dry in big bowl. In 2 additions, fold whites into the spinach mixture; put in prepped baking dish. Sprinkle leftover 2/3 cup cheese; bake for 45 minutes till set and puffed.

Nutrition Information

- Calories: 273
- Total Fat: 19 g(29%)
- Saturated Fat: 11 g(56%)
- Sodium: 455 mg(19%)
- Fiber: 2 g(7%)
- Total Carbohydrate: 12 g(4%)
- Cholesterol: 148 mg(49%)
- Protein: 14 g(28%)

321. Spinach Parmesan Soufflés

Serving: Makes 8 | Prep: 45mins | Cook: 1hours15mins | Ready in:

Ingredients

- 1/4 cup (1/2 stick) unsalted butter
- 6 tablespoons all purpose flour
- 1 1/4 cups buttermilk
- 1 9-to 10-ounce package frozen chopped spinach, thawed, squeezed dry
- 1 1/2 cups grated parmesan cheese
- 6 large egg yolks
- 2 teaspoons coarse kosher salt
- 3/4 teaspoon freshly ground black pepper
- 8 large egg whites
- 8 1-cup soufflé dishes or custard cups

Direction

- Preheat an oven to 375°F and butter 8 custard cups/1-cup soufflé dish; put onto big rimmed baking sheet. In big saucepan, melt 1/4 cup butter on medium heat. Add the flour; whisk for 1 minute. Add buttermilk; whisk for 1 minute. Mix in spinach and following 4 ingredients; put aside.
- Beat egg whites using electric mixer till firm peaks form in big bowl. Fold egg whites, in 3 additions, into spinach mixture; evenly divide to prepped dishes.
- Bake soufflés for 30 minutes till browned on top and puffed; immediately serve.

Nutrition Information

- Calories: 274
- Total Carbohydrate: 13 g(4%)
- Cholesterol: 199 mg(66%)
- Protein: 18 g(36%)
- Total Fat: 17 g(26%)
- Saturated Fat: 9 g(47%)
- Sodium: 476 mg(20%)
- Fiber: 1 g(4%)

322. Stained Glass Lemon Cookies

Serving: Makes about 30 | Prep: | Cook: | Ready in:

Ingredients

- 1 cup (2 sticks) unsalted butter, room temperature
- 3/4 cup sugar
- 1 large egg yolk
- 2 teaspoons grated lemon peel
- 1 teaspoon vanilla extract
- 2 1/4 cups all purpose flour
- 1/2 teaspoon salt
- 6 ounces (about) red and/or green hard candies
- Additional sugar

Direction

- Beat 3/4 cup sugar and butter using electric mixer till well blended in a big bowl; beat in vanilla extract, lemon peel and egg yolk. Add salt and all-purpose flour; beat till it starts to clump together. Divide the dough to 3 even pieces; flatten every piece to disk. In plastic, wrap each; refrigerate for 2 hours. You can make it 2 days ahead; slightly soften dough before rolling out in room temperature.
- Separately grind green and/or red hard candies finely in processor. Put each candy color in different small bowls; cover candies. Put aside.
- Put 1 rack in top third and 1 rack in middle of oven; preheat the oven to 375°F. Line parchment paper on 2 big baking sheets. Roll 1 dough disk out to 1/4-in. thick on lightly floured surface. Cut out cookies with 2 1/2-2 3/4-in. diameter biscuit/cookie cutter. Create cutouts in middle of each cookie using 1-in. diameter small cookie cutter.
- Put cookies on prepped baking sheets. Put ground hard candies in cookie cutouts, fully filling cutouts, same as cookie's thickness. Lightly sprinkle extra sugar on cookies; repeat using extra sugar, leftover ground hard candies and dough disks. Reroll dough scraps; cut out extra cookies. Put on baking sheets; use hard candies to fill. Sprinkle extra sugar.
- Bake cookies for 8 minutes till ground candies look translucent and cookies are light golden and firm. Fully cool cookies on baking sheets. You can prep ahead; keep for maximum of 1 week in room temperature in airtight container/freeze for maximum of 1 month.

Nutrition Information

- Calories: 134
- Sodium: 42 mg(2%)
- Fiber: 0 g(1%)
- Total Carbohydrate: 18 g(6%)
- Cholesterol: 22 mg(7%)
- Protein: 1 g(2%)
- Total Fat: 6 g(10%)
- Saturated Fat: 4 g(20%)

323. Sticky Toffee Banana Pudding

Serving: Makes 9 to 12 servings | Prep: 45mins | Cook: 2hours | Ready in:

Ingredients

- 1 1/4 cups plus 3 tablespoons (or more) heavy whipping cream
- 1/2 cup (packed) golden brown sugar
- 1/2 cup dark corn syrup
- 1/4 cup (1/2 stick) unsalted butter
- 2 cups unbleached all purpose flour
- 1 1/2 teaspoons baking powder
- 3/4 cup (1 1/2 sticks) unsalted butter, room temperature
- 2/3 cup (packed) dark brown sugar
- 2 large eggs
- 1 cup mashed very ripe bananas (2 to 3)
- 1 tablespoon dark rum
- 1 1/2 teaspoons vanilla extract
- Sliced bananas (optional)
- 8 x 8 x 2-inch nonstick metal baking pan

Direction

- Make toffee sauce: In a heavy small saucepan over medium heat, bring 1/8 teaspoon salt, butter, corn syrup, brown sugar, and 1 1/4 cup cream to a boil, stirring until sugar dissolved. Lower the heat to medium-low and cook at a gentle boil for about 15 minutes, stirring occasionally, until the sauce is reduced to 1 1/2 cups and coats spoon thickly. Take away from the heat and cool. Stir in 3 tablespoons or more cream to thin the sauce to the consistency desired. DO AHEAD: prepare 2 days in advance. Chill it covered. Slightly rewarm before using.
- Make the banana cake: Prepare the oven by preheating to 350 degrees F. Prepare buttered nonstick metal baking pan (8x8x2-inch).

- Sprinkle flour on the baking pan, knocking out excess.
- In a medium bowl, combine 1/2 teaspoon salt, baking powder, and flour. In a large bowl, whisk sugar and butter with an electric mixer until well combined. Whisk in 1 egg at a time. Whisk in vanilla, rum, and mashed bananas (batter may appear curdled). Put in the dry ingredients in 4 additions, whisking just to mix after each addition. Transfer the batter to the prepared baking pan and spread evenly.
- Bake the cake for 35-38 minutes until a tester poked into the center comes out clean. Pour 1/2 cup toffee sauce over the cake and spread evenly. Place the cake back to the oven and bake for about 6 minutes until sauce is bubbling thickly. Cool the cake for 30 minutes in the pan on a rack. Cut surrounding the cake in pan, then slice it into twelve rectangles or nine squares. Serve cake at room temperature or slightly warm with toffee sauce and put sliced bananas on top, if wished.

Nutrition Information

- Calories: 674
- Total Carbohydrate: 65 g(22%)
- Cholesterol: 183 mg(61%)
- Protein: 6 g(13%)
- Total Fat: 45 g(70%)
- Saturated Fat: 27 g(135%)
- Sodium: 126 mg(5%)
- Fiber: 1 g(5%)

324. Strawberry Cream Puffs With Strawberry Sauce

Serving: Makes about 18 | Prep: | Cook: | Ready in:

Ingredients

- 3/4 cups water
- 3 tablespoons unsalted butter, cut into pieces
- 1/4 teaspoon salt
- 1/4 teaspoon sugar
- 3/4 cup all purpose flour
- 3 large eggs
- 1 cup chilled whipping cream
- 1 teaspoon plus 2 tablespoons sugar
- 1/4 teaspoon kirsch (clear cherry brandy)
- 1/8 teaspoon vanilla extract
- 6 large strawberries, hulled
- 2 1-pint strawberries, hulled
- 3 tablespoons sugar
- Powdered sugar

Direction

- Cream puffs: Preheat an oven to 375°F; line parchment paper on baking sheet. Boil sugar, salt, butter and water in medium heavy saucepan, mixing to melt butter. Add the flour; vigorously mix using wooden spoon till mixture clumps together, making ball. Mix for 1 minute; take off heat. Put dough in medium bowl. One by one, add eggs, beating using electric mixer till dough is shiny, slightly soft and smooth after every addition.
- Put dough, 1 rounded tbsp. dough for every cream puff, on prepped baking sheet, making mounds 1 1/4-in. diameter, 3/4-1-in. high, 2-in. apart. Press cream puff's tops gently with moist fingertips; flatten peaks. Bake for 37 minutes till golden brown. Put baking sheet on rack; cool. You can make it 4 hours ahead, standing in room temperature.
- Filling: Beat vanilla, kirsch, 1 tsp. sugar and cream till stiff peaks form in medium bowl. Mix 2 tbsp. sugar and 6 strawberries in small bowl; crush berries using fork. Fold crush strawberry mixture in the cream.
- Off each cream puff, cut top third. Put cream puff bottoms on plates, cut side up. Put filling on bottoms, slightly mounding. Put sauce over; let sauce spill onto plates. Put cream puff tops over; dust powdered sugar.
- Sauce: In processor, puree 1 basket strawberries; put into bowl. Mix in sugar. Quarter leftover strawberries; put into sauce.
- Creates 2 1/3 cups.

Nutrition Information

- Calories: 120
- Saturated Fat: 4 g(20%)
- Sodium: 50 mg(2%)
- Fiber: 1 g(4%)
- Total Carbohydrate: 13 g(4%)
- Cholesterol: 51 mg(17%)
- Protein: 2 g(4%)
- Total Fat: 7 g(11%)

325. Sugar Cookies

Serving: | Prep: | Cook: | Ready in:

Ingredients

- 2 Dozen bag
- 1 1/2 cups butter, softened
- 2 cups white sugar
- 4 eggs
- 1 teaspoon vanilla extract
- 5 cups all-purpose flour
- 2 teaspoons baking powder
- 1 teaspoon salt

Direction

- Preparation
- Cream sugar and butter till smooth in a big bowl; beat in vanilla and eggs. Mix in salt, baking powder and flour; cover. Chill dough for a minimum of 1 hour – overnight. Preheat an oven to 200°C/400°F. Roll dough out to 1/4-1/2-in. thick on floured surface; use any cookie cutter to cut into shapes. Put cookies on ungreased cookie sheets, 1-in. apart. In preheated oven, bake for 6-8 minutes; fully cool.

326. Sugarplum Orange And Apricot Earl Grey Jam Tarts

Serving: Makes 2 tarts | Prep: | Cook: | Ready in:

Ingredients

- 1 1/2 cups hazelnuts with skins
- 4 1/2 cups all-purpose flour, divided, plus more for surface
- 2 1/4 teaspoons kosher salt
- 1 1/2 teaspoons baking powder
- 2 teaspoons freshly grated nutmeg, divided
- 1 1/2 cups sugar
- 1 1/2 cups (3 sticks) unsalted butter, room temperature
- 7 tablespoons heavy cream, divided
- 4 large egg yolks, divided
- 1 teaspoon (or 1 bag) Earl Grey tea
- 1 1/2 cups apricot jam
- 1 1/2 cups plum jam
- 2 teaspoons finely grated orange zest
- 1/4 cup raw sugar
- Two tart pans with removable bottoms, either 11"-diameter or 11x8" rectangle; decorative cookie cutters in 2 sizes

Direction

- In food processor, put 1 1/2 cups of flour and nuts. Blend to finely ground the nuts. Put 1 1/2 teaspoons of nutmeg, baking powder, salt and leftover 3 cups of flour; blend to combine.
- In a big bowl, beat butter and sugar with electric mixer for 2 minutes, till creamy. Put three egg yolks and 6 tablespoons of cream; beat for a minute, to thoroughly incorporate. Add 1/2 mixture of flour; beat barely to incorporate. Add leftover mixture off flour and beat to form moist, big clumps. Split dough evenly to 3 portions. Shape a portion to a ball; flatten, making a disk. Wrap in plastic and refrigerate while prepping tarts.
- Force the two leftover portions of dough smoothly on bottom and up the tart pan sides using your slightly floured hands. May be

done a day in advance. Keep in refrigerator with cover.

- Heat the oven to 375°F. In small bowl, combine quarter cup of boiling water and tea; put aside and let steep, about 15 minutes. In one medium sized bowl, mix strained tea and apricot jam to incorporate. Mix orange zest and plum jam in a separate medium bowl to incorporate.
- On a slightly floured counter, unroll the reserved dough disk with a rolling pin slightly dusted with flour into 1/8-inch-thick. Cut out shapes with decorative cookie cutter. Collect dough to a ball, unroll, and redo till sufficient cutouts are done to place on tarts tops. Put any leftover dough in freezer for other use.
- Spread mixture of apricot jam in an even layer on top of crust in a tart pan. Spread mixture of plum jam in an even layer on top of crust in another pan. Put the cutouts of dough on top of jam in decorative manner. In one small bowl, whip leftover 1 tablespoon of cream and leftover egg yolk. Brush cream mixture on cutouts. Stir raw sugar and leftover half teaspoon of nutmeg; scatter on top of tarts.
- Let tarts bake for 45 to 50 minutes, turning pans halfway through and cover the edges of crust in case it browns very fast, till the top turns golden brown and jam becomes bubbly. Turn onto wire racks and cool down, jam sets as tarts cool down. May be done a day in advance. Keep at room temperature airtight.

Nutrition Information

- Calories: 5190
- Cholesterol: 818 mg(273%)
- Protein: 56 g(111%)
- Total Fat: 237 g(364%)
- Saturated Fat: 111 g(553%)
- Sodium: 2679 mg(112%)
- Fiber: 21 g(86%)
- Total Carbohydrate: 741 g(247%)

327. Super Quick Mocha Yule Log

Serving: Makes 10 servings | Prep: | Cook: | Ready in:

Ingredients

- 1/2 cup powdered sugar plus additional for garnish
- 1/4 cup natural unsweetened cocoa powder
- 2 teaspoons instant espresso powder
- 2 cups chilled heavy whipping cream
- 1 teaspoon vanilla extract
- 1 9-ounce package chocolate wafer cookies
- 8 purchased vanilla meringue cookies

Direction

- Sift espresso powder, cocoa powder and 1/2 cup powdered sugar in small bowl. Beat vanilla and cream with electric mixer till soft peaks form in big bowl. Add cocoa mixture; beat till stiff peaks form.
- Spread 1 rounded tsp. mocha cream on 1 side of a chocolate wafer; put another wafer over. Keep layering mocha cream and wafers for stack with 5 cookies. Put stack on long platter on its side. Repeat creating stacks with some mocha cream and leftover wafers; shape log on platters by using mocha crema to attach stacks. Spread leftover mocha cream on log's outside to coat using rubber/offset spatula. Cover; chill for 2 hours. You can make it 1 day ahead, kept chilled.
- On work surface, put platter with yule log; pull fork tines gently using fork along frosting's length on log to make design that looks like tree bark. Sift powdered sugar on log to imitate snow. Put meringue mushrooms/meringue cookies along log's sides. On diagonal, cut logs to thick slices; immediately serve.

328. Sweet Breakfast Bread

Serving: Makes 1 loaf | Prep: | Cook: | Ready in:

Ingredients

- 1 cup sugar
- 2 large eggs
- 3 tablespoons unsalted butter, room temperature
- 1 cup milk
- 1 1/2 cups all purpose flour
- 2 teaspoons baking powder
- 1 teaspoon ground cinnamon
- 1 teaspoon salt

Direction

- Prepare the oven by preheating to 350 degrees F. Prepare buttered and floured loaf pan (9x5-inch). In a large bowl, whisk butter, eggs, and sugar with an electric mixer until well combined. Whisk in milk. In a medium bowl, combine salt, cinnamon, baking powder, and flour. Place to the butter mixture and whisk just until combined.
- Transfer the batter into the prepared pan. Bake for about 1 hour until a tester poked into the center of the bread comes out clean and golden brown. Remove pan to a rack and cool for 10 minutes. Cut around sides of pan to loosen bread with a small knife. Turn out the bread onto a rack and cool fully. (You can prepare 1 day in advance. Use foil to wrap it and keep at room temperature.)

Nutrition Information

- Calories: 258
- Saturated Fat: 4 g(19%)
- Sodium: 228 mg(10%)
- Fiber: 1 g(3%)
- Total Carbohydrate: 45 g(15%)
- Cholesterol: 61 mg(20%)
- Protein: 5 g(10%)
- Total Fat: 7 g(10%)

329. Sweet Lemon Thyme Crisps

Serving: Makes 2 logs; each log makes 60 crisps | Prep: | Cook: | Ready in:

Ingredients

- 3 1/4 cups all-purpose flour
- 2 teaspoons baking soda
- 1/2 teaspoon salt
- 4 teaspoons finely chopped fresh lemon thyme or regular thyme leaves
- 2 sticks (1 cup) unsalted butter, softened
- 1 1/2 cups granulated sugar
- 2 1/2 tablespoons finely grated fresh lemon zest
- 1 large egg
- 3 tablespoons fresh lemon juice
- 1 tablespoon finely grated peeled fresh gingerroot
- confectioners' sugar for dusting

Direction

- Sift together salt, baking soda and flour into a bowl, stir in thyme. In a big bowl, beat together zest, granulated sugar and butter with an electric mixer until fluffy and light. Put in egg, beating until well blended, and beat in gingerroot and lemon juice. Put in flour mixture, beating until just blended.
- Halve the dough and using wax paper as a guide to form each half into a 14- by 1 1/2-inch log on separate sheets of wax paper. Freeze the logs, wrapped in wax paper and foil until firm, or about 20 minutes, and up to 3 weeks. If frozen solid, bring to room temperature to make it easier to slice.
- Set oven to 350 degrees F and start preheating.
- Cut diagonally 1 log into 1/4-inch-thick ovals and halve diagonally each slice. Place the cookies about 1 inch apart on an ungreased baking sheets and bake in batches in upper and lower thirds of the oven, switching the position of the sheets halfway through baking

until golden, about 12 minutes total. Using a spatula to transfer crisps immediately to racks to cool. Make more cookies with the remaining log if you wish. Lightly dust cookies with confectioners' sugar.

Nutrition Information

- Calories: 276
- Fiber: 1 g(3%)
- Total Carbohydrate: 39 g(13%)
- Cholesterol: 42 mg(14%)
- Protein: 3 g(6%)
- Total Fat: 12 g(19%)
- Saturated Fat: 7 g(37%)
- Sodium: 164 mg(7%)

330. Swiss Sandwich Cookies (spitzbuben)

Serving: Makes about 5 dozen | Prep: 1hours | Cook: 2.5hours | Ready in:

Ingredients

- 3 cups all-purpose flour
- 1 1/4 cups confectioners sugar
- 1 tablespoon vanilla powder
- 3/4 teaspoon salt
- 2 1/2 sticks (1 1/4 cups) unsalted butter, softened
- 2 teaspoons powdered egg whites
- 2 tablespoons warm water
- 1/4 cup sanding or granulated sugar
- 1/2 cup seedless raspberry jam
- 1/2 cup apricot preserves, strained

Direction

- Cookies: Sift salt, vanilla powder, confectioners' sugar and flour together.
- Heat butter till creamy with an electric mixer; mix in flour mixture till just blended on low speed. Shape dough to a disk; chill for 1 hour till firm, wrapped in plastic wrap.
- Preheat an oven to 300°F.
- Roll dough out slightly less than 1/4-in. thick on lightly floured surface; cut out 1 1/2-in. rounds.
- Put on greased baking sheets, 1-in. apart. Reroll scraps once; it'll be tough if dough gets worked too much. Whisk water and powdered egg whites; brush egg whites on cookies. Sprinkle sanding sugar.
- In batches, bake cookies for 10-15 minutes till pale golden in center of oven. Put on rack; cool.
- Fill cookies: Sandwich preserves and jam between unsugared cookie sides, filling half with apricot and half with raspberry.

Nutrition Information

- Calories: 316
- Fiber: 1 g(3%)
- Total Carbohydrate: 44 g(15%)
- Cholesterol: 38 mg(13%)
- Protein: 3 g(5%)
- Total Fat: 15 g(23%)
- Saturated Fat: 9 g(46%)
- Sodium: 120 mg(5%)

331. Tangerine Semifreddo With Salted Almond Brittle

Serving: Makes 8 servings | Prep: | Cook: | Ready in:

Ingredients

- 2 tablespoons (1/4 stick) unsalted butter, divided
- 2 cups sugar
- 1 cup light corn syrup
- 1 cup water
- 1/4 teaspoon salt
- 2 cups blanched whole almonds, toasted , coarsely chopped

- 1/2 teaspoon baking soda
- 1 teaspoon flaked sea salt (such as Maldon)
- 5 large eggs, separated
- 1 cup sugar, divided
- 1/4 cup fresh tangerine juice or tangelo juice
- 2 tablespoons finely grated tangerine peel or tangelo peel
- 2 cups chilled heavy whipping cream
- 1 cup fresh tangerine juice or tangelo juice
- 2 tablespoons honey
- 4 tangerines or 3 tangelos, peeled, separated into segments

Direction

- Brittle: Use 1 tbsp. butter to coat big rimmed baking sheet. Mix 1/4 tsp. salt, 1 cup water, corn syrup and sugar in big heavy saucepan; mix on medium heat till sugar melts. To pan's side, attach candy thermometer. Upper heat on medium high; boil without mixing for 10 minutes till thermometer reads 330-340°F and mixture is amber. Take off heat; mix in leftover 1 tbsp. butter immediately then baking soda and almonds. It'll bubble. Put mixture onto prepped baking sheet quickly; spread mixture to irregular 15x10-in. rectangle quickly using offset metal spatula. Evenly sprinkle 1 tsp. sea salt on brittle; fully cool brittle for 2 hours till firm in room temperature. You can make it 1 week ahead. Break the brittle to irregular pieces; keep in airtight container.
- Chop brittle coarsely to get 1 1/2 cups; while making semifreddo mixture, keep in airtight container.
- Semifreddo: Line 2 plastic wrap layers on 9x5x3-in. metal loaf pan; on all sides, leave generous overhang and fill big bowl with water and ice cubes. Whisk tangerine peel, tangerine juice, 1/2 cup sugar and egg yolks in metal medium bowl. Put bowl with yolk mixture above saucepan of simmering water; constantly whisk for 3 minutes till inserted instant-read thermometer into it reads 160°F and thickens. Take bowl from above hot water; put above bowl with ice water. Beat mixture using electric mixer for 3 minutes till cool and thick. Take bowl from above ice water.
- Beat cream till peaks form in another big bowl; put aside. Beat egg whites using dry clean beaters till soft peaks form in another big bowl. 1 tbsp. at a time, add 1/2 cup sugar slowly; beat till stiff yet not dry. Fold 1/3 egg whites to lighten into yolk mixture; in 2 batches, fold in leftover whites. In 2 additions, fold in whipped cream just till incorporated.
- Spread 1/3, 3 cups, semifreddo mixture in loaf pan evenly; evenly sprinkle 3/4 cup of chopped brittle. Repeat layers with leftover 1/2 semifreddo mixture; sprinkle leftover 3/4 cup brittle. Spread leftover semifreddo mixture over; it'll slightly extend over top of pan and loaf pan will get very full. To cover, fold plastic wrap overhang on semifreddo; freeze overnight. You can make it 2 days ahead, kept frozen.
- Sauce: Boil honey and tangerine juice in small heavy saucepan on medium high heat, occasionally mixing and boil for 10 minutes till reduces to generous 1/3 cup and syrupy, mixing often. Put in bowl; fully cool. Mix in tangerine segments. You can make it 8 hours ahead, chilled, covered.
- Onto platter, invert semifreddo; remove plastic wrap. Into hot water, dip big knife; wipe dry. Crosswise cut semifreddo to 1-in. thick slices, dipping the knife into water then wiping dry as needed. On each plate, put 1 slice; put tangerine sauce next to semifreddo. Serve.
- Don't make this more than 2 days ahead for best results.

Nutrition Information

- Calories: 1187
- Cholesterol: 304 mg(101%)
- Protein: 16 g(32%)
- Total Fat: 72 g(111%)
- Saturated Fat: 32 g(161%)
- Sodium: 502 mg(21%)
- Fiber: 6 g(22%)

- Total Carbohydrate: 135 g(45%)

332. Tea Cake Sandwich Cookies

Serving: Makes about 32 | Prep: | Cook: |Ready in:

Ingredients

- 3 cups all purpose flour
- 1/2 teaspoon salt
- 1 1/4 cups (21/2 sticks) unsalted butter, room temperature
- 2/3 cup sugar
- 2 1/2 tablespoons whole milk
- 1 tablespoon grated lemon peel
- 2 teaspoons vanilla extract
- Nonstick vegetable oil spray
- Assorted decorations (such as powdered sugar, icing, colored sugar crystals, and edible glitter)
- 2/3 cup preserves (such as apricot, seedless raspberry, or seedless blackberry)

Direction

- Whisk salt and flour to blend well in medium bowl. Beat 2/3 cup sugar and butter using electric mixer till fluffy in big bowl; beat in vanilla extract, lemon peel and milk. Add flour mixture; beat till blended. Bring dough to ball; halve. Flatten to disks. In plastic, wrap; chill for at least 2 hours. You can make it 2 days ahead, kept chilled; before rolling out, slightly soften.
- Roll each dough disk out to 14x11-in. rectangle between waxed paper sheets, lifting wax paper occasionally to smooth out wrinkles. On baking sheets, refrigerate dough, still between waxed paper sheets, for 30 minutes till firm and cold. On work surface, put 1 dough piece; peel off top waxed paper sheet. Gently press same waxed paper onto dough again. Flip dough, still between the waxed paper sheets then peel off top waxed paper sheet; discard. Cut out cookies with dough on waxed paper bottom using 1-1 1/4-in. scalloped round cutter. Cut out middle from 1/2 cookies using 1-1 1/4-in. scalloped round cutter. Gather excess dough around cutouts and dough centers; form excess dough to dish and chill. Slide the wax paper onto baking sheet with cutouts; chill. Repeat with leftover dough disk, cutting rounds out, cutting middles from 1/2 rounds to create top rings, gathering then chilling extra dough. Roll extra dough out between waxed paper sheets, creating more top rings and cookie bottoms. Repeat rolling them cutting till you use all the dough.
- Put rack into middle of oven; preheat it to 350°F. Spray nonstick spray on 2 big baking sheets. Lift cutouts using metal spatula from waxed paper; put top rings on 1 prepped sheet then cookie bottoms on second sheet, slightly spacing apart. They spread a little. Sprinkle colored sugar crystals (or not to decorate later (over some top rings). 1 sheet at 1 time, bake cookies for 8 minutes till pale golden; cool for 5 minutes on baking sheets. Put cookies on racks; fully cool.
- On work surface, put cookie bottoms; spread 1 tsp. preserves on each. Sift powdered sugar/decorate with sugar crystals/edible glitter and icing as desired on plain cookie rings. Onto each prepped cookie bottom, press 1 top ring. You can make cookies 3 days ahead; keep airtight between waxed paper sheets in the fridge.

Nutrition Information

- Calories: 148
- Saturated Fat: 5 g(23%)
- Sodium: 40 mg(2%)
- Fiber: 0 g(2%)
- Total Carbohydrate: 18 g(6%)
- Cholesterol: 19 mg(6%)
- Protein: 1 g(3%)
- Total Fat: 8 g(12%)

333. The Ultimate Valentine Cake

Serving: Serves 12 | Prep: | Cook: |Ready in:

Ingredients

- 3 ounces imported white chocolate (such as Lindt or Tobler), chopped
- 3 ounces bittersweet (not unsweetened) or semisweet chocolate, chopped
- 9 ounces imported white chocolate (such as Lindt or Tobler), chopped
- 5 large eggs, separated, room temperature
- 1/2 cup plus 1 tablespoon sugar
- 1tablespoon framboise liqueur or Grand Marnier
- 1 teaspoon vanilla extract
- 6 tablespoons (3/4 stick) unsalted butter, melted, warm
- 3/4 cup cake flour
- 12 ounces bittersweet (not unsweetened) or semisweet chocolate, chopped
- 1 1/4 cups (2 1/2 sticks) unsalted butter
- 3 tablespoon light corn syrup
- 3 tablespoons framboise liqueur or Grand Marnier
- 1 1-pint basket strawberries, hulled and halved
- 1 1/2-pint basket raspberries
- 1 1-pint basket strawberries with stems, halved through stem end (stems left intact)
- 2 1-pint baskets strawberries, hulled and sliced
- 3 tablespoons sugar
- 2 tablespoons framboise liqueur or Grand Marnier
- 2 1/2-pint baskets raspberries

Direction

- For heart lid: Cut heart-shaped waxed paper pieces about 4 inches larger than an 8x2-in. bottomless cake pan with the heart shape. Put on a cookie sheet. Use vegetable oil to lightly oil the inside of the heart pan and spread butter on the outside of the pan. Put the heart pan on top of the paper on cookie sheet. Prevent the chocolate from leaking out by pressing the waxed paper up onto the outside of the pan that has been buttered to adhere. Add white chocolate in a bowl then set it over a saucepan filled with simmering water, stir till smooth. Take out from over the water. Add bittersweet in a separate bowl then set it over a saucepan filled with simmering water, stir till smooth. Take out from over the water.
- Drop spoonfuls of white chocolate inside of the heart, spacing apart and let some touch the pan on the inner edge. Drop spoonfuls of bittersweet chocolate into the spaces. Gently move the heart pan from side to side till the chocolate is distributed evenly and the heart is completely filled. Use the tip of a knife to swirl the mixture together. Use your hands to hold the cake pan to cookie sheet then flatten the chocolate by firmly tap the sheet on counter. Let freeze for 20 minutes till firm.
- Use a small sharp knife to run around the outer side of the pan till the chocolate is loosened. Discard the pan and store the chocolate lid in the fridge till ready to use. You can prepare this 1 week ahead and use plastic wrap to cover.
- For cake: Preheat the oven to 350°F. Butter and spread flour onto an 8x2-in. bottomless cake pan with heart shape. Cut heavy-duty foil into heart-shaped pieces with 4 inches larger the heart-shaped cake pan. Butter and spread flour on the foil. Place on double-stacked cookie sheets or a heavy large cookie sheet. Place the heart pan on the middle of the foil. Wrap around the outer sides of the pan with foil and prevent the batter from leaking out by folding, pressing and firmly crimping to adhere. Put the white chocolate in a bowl then set it over a saucepan filled with simmering water; stir till smooth. Take out from over the water.
- In a large bowl, beat 1/2 cup of sugar and yolks with an electric mixer for 3 minutes till pale yellow in color and it forms a ribbon that is dissolving slowly when you lift the beaters.

Beat in vanilla and framboise then butter. Beat in melted chocolate to combine.

- In a large bowl, use an electric mixer with clean dry beaters fitted to beat whites till soft peaks form. Slowly beat in the leftover 1 tbsp. of sugar till stiff. Place flour into the chocolate mixture; mix to have a very thick batter. Add in 1/4 of whites and stir till lightened. Slowly fold in the leftover whites. Transfer the batter into the prepped pan and let bake for 45 minutes. Use foil to cover the top then bake for 20 minutes till the tip of a small knife comes out clean after being inserted in the middle of the cake and the cake should be much browned. Let cool in pan on rack.
- For icing: In a heavy medium saucepan, melt corn syrup, butter and chocolate over low heat and stir till smooth. Add in framboise and stir. Let the icing cool for 2 hours till firm enough to spread.
- Use a small sharp knife to run around the sides of the cake pan till loosened. Use a serrated knife to halve the cake into layers. On a platter, place the bottom of the cake with the cut side facing up. Spread over with 2/3 cup of icing then place the top layer of the cake on top, cut side facing down. Spread over the sides and top of the cake with all but 1/2 cup of icing. Store the cake for 1 hour to set the icing. You can prepare this 1 day ahead. Cover and store the leftover icing and the cake separately. Over very low heat, rewarm the icing till just spreadable then continuing with the recipe.
- For assembly: On the right half of the cake, mound some raspberries and hulled strawberries. Top the berries with lid positioned at angle, move the berries around to let the left edge of the lid rest on the left edge of the cake. Tuck stems in half of the strawberries between lid and cake with the stems facing out. Spread over the cake sides with the leftover icing where the lid is attached, use a spatula to smooth and make a boxlike appearance. Reserve the leftover raspberries and strawberries to garnish. Store for 1 hour in the fridge to set the icing. You can assemble it for 12 hours in advance.
- For Berry Compote: In a large bowl, toss framboise and sugar with two 1-pint basket of strawberries. Let chill for at least 1 hour and no more than 6 hours. Place in raspberries and gently toss.
- Place on platter around the cake with the reserved berries. Spoon compote over each cake piece to serve.

Nutrition Information

- Calories: 773
- Saturated Fat: 28 g(141%)
- Sodium: 68 mg(3%)
- Fiber: 11 g(45%)
- Total Carbohydrate: 84 g(28%)
- Cholesterol: 150 mg(50%)
- Protein: 9 g(17%)
- Total Fat: 48 g(73%)

334. Three Berry Butter Cake

Serving: Makes 12 servings | Prep: 30mins | Cook: 2hours | Ready in:

Ingredients

- 1 stick (1/2 cup) unsalted butter
- 1/4 cup heavy cream
- 3 large eggs at room temperature
- 1 1/4 cups granulated sugar
- 1/2 teaspoon salt
- 2 teaspoons finely grated fresh lemon zest
- 2 teaspoons baking powder
- 1 teaspoon vanilla
- 2 1/2 cups cake flour (not self-rising)
- 6 cups mixed berries (1 3/4 ponds) such as raspberries, blackberries, and blueberries
- 2 tablespoons confectioners sugar

Direction

- Preheat an oven to 350°F. Grease 13x9x2-in. metal baking pan; line grease paper/wax paper on bottom.
- Heat cream and butter till melted in a small saucepan on low heat; cool.
- Beat salt, granulated sugar and eggs using an electric mixer at high speed for 12 minutes if using a handheld or for 5 minutes if using the standing mixer, till makes a ribbon when you lift beaters, pale and thick. Add vanilla, baking powder and zest; mix till blended on low speed.
- Add 1/2 butter mixture and 1 1/4 cups flour; mix till blended on low speed. Mix in 1 1/4 cups flour and leftover butter the same way. Adjust speed on medium; beat till batter is sticky and thick, about 2 minutes with handheld or 1 minute with standing mixer. Add berries; fold in carefully using a rubber spatula till barely combines. Batter will get slightly pink and raspberries will start to fall apart. Spoon batter in baking pan; smooth top gently. Bake in center of oven for 45-50 minutes till inserted tester in middle exits clean and springy to the touch; fully cool in pan on rack.
- Around cake's edge, run a knife; invert rack over cake. Flip cake onto it. Remove the wax paper; reinvert onto platter.
- Dust with confectioners' sugar before serving.

Nutrition Information

- Calories: 336
- Protein: 5 g(9%)
- Total Fat: 11 g(17%)
- Saturated Fat: 6 g(32%)
- Sodium: 180 mg(7%)
- Fiber: 2 g(9%)
- Total Carbohydrate: 56 g(19%)
- Cholesterol: 74 mg(25%)

335. Tomato Focaccia

Serving: Makes 8 (as part of antipasti) servings | Prep: 45mins | Cook: 5.5hours | Ready in:

Ingredients

- 1 (1/2-pound) Yukon Gold potato, peeled and quartered
- 1 cup warm water (105-115°F)
- 1/2 teaspoon sugar
- 3 teaspoons active dry yeast (from two 1/4-ounce packages)
- 1/2 cup extra-virgin olive oil, divided
- 4 1/4 cups "00" flour, divided
- 1 tablespoon plus 1/4 teaspoon fine sea salt, divided
- 1/2 pound plum tomatoes, thinly sliced crosswise
- 1/4 teaspoon dried oregano
- Equipment: a stand mixer with paddle and dough-hook attachments

Direction

- In a small heavy pot, generously cover potato with cold and salted water (3 cups water for 1 teaspoon salt), then simmer, uncovered, about 10-15 minutes, until just tender. Drain and lightly cool, mash until smooth.
- In bowl of mixer, mix sugar and warm water together. Sprinkle the mixture with yeast, let it sit until foamy, in 5 minutes (start over with new yeast if the mixture doesn't foam).
- Add 1/4 cup oil and potato to yeast. On medium speed, whisk with paddle attachment for 2 minutes, until combined. Take out paddle attachment then attach dough hook. On medium-high speed, mix in 1 tablespoon sea salt and 4 cups flour for 3 minutes, until thoroughly combined (the dough will be very sticky and soft).
- Place into a well-floured surface; flour hands lightly and use hands to knead in the remaining 1/4 cup flour until elastic and smooth, about 8-10 minutes (the dough will still be very sticky and soft).

- Lightly grease a big bowl with oil, scape the dough in, then use oiled plastic wrap to cover the bowl. Put the dough in a draft-free place at warm room temperature, allow to rise for 2 – 2 1/2 hours, until doubled in size. Generously grease a 15- by 10- by 1-inch baking pan with oil.
- Punch dough down but do not knead. Place into a baking pan, stretch gently to cover the bottom as much as possible. (Dough may not completely fit).
- Use a kitchen towel and oiled plastic wrap to cover dough, put in a draft-free place at warm room temperature, allow to rise in 1 - 1 1/2 hours, until doubled in size.
- Set oven to 425 degrees F and start preheating, positioning rack in the lower third.
- Spread tomatoes (do not overlap) on focaccia. Sprinkle oregano and the remaining 1/4 teaspoon sea salt on top, drizzle the remaining 1/4 cup oil over the surface.
- Bake for 20-25 minutes, until underside turns golden (lift to check), top turns pale golden, and the center is firm.
- Use a spatula to loosen focaccia from the pan, slide onto a rack to let it cool slightly. Cut into pieces. Serve at room temperature or serve warm.
- Cooks' note: Focaccia should be eaten during the day of making it. However, you can bake it in the previous day, use foil to wrap, then put it in a sealed bag and keep at room temperature. You can also uncover it and reheat for 10 minutes in oven at 350 degrees F until just heated through.

Nutrition Information

- Calories: 389
- Total Fat: 14 g(22%)
- Saturated Fat: 2 g(10%)
- Sodium: 391 mg(16%)
- Fiber: 3 g(12%)
- Total Carbohydrate: 56 g(19%)
- Protein: 8 g(16%)

336. Triple Chocolate Biscotti

Serving: Makes about 30 | Prep: | Cook: |Ready in:

Ingredients

- 1 3/4 cups all purpose flour
- 1/3 cup unsweetened cocoa powder
- 2 teaspoons baking powder
- 1/2 teaspoon salt
- 1 cup sugar
- 6 tablespoons (3/4 stick) unsalted butter, room temperature
- 3 large eggs
- 1 1/2 teaspoons vanilla extract
- 8 ounces semisweet chocolate chips
- 1/2 cup white chocolate baking chips

Direction

- Line double foil thickness on big baking sheet. Sift salt, baking powder, cocoa and flour into medium bowl. Beat butter and sugar using electric mixer to blend in big bowl. One by one, beat in eggs then vanilla; beat in the flour mixture. Mix in white chips and semisweet. By heaping tablespoonfuls, drop dough in 2 10-11-in. long strips on prepped sheet, 3-in. apart. Shape strips to 11x2 1/2-in. logs using wet fingertips/metal spatula; refrigerate for 30 minutes.
- Preheat an oven to 350°F. Bake the logs for 25 minutes till inserted tester in middle exits clean and tops are dry and cracked; cool for 10 minutes.
- Lower oven temperature to 300°F. Lift logs on work surface using foil as aid. Line clean foil on baking sheets. Crosswise cut warm logs gently to 3/4-in. thick slices using serrated knife; put 1/2 slices on each prepped baking sheet, cut side down. Bake biscotti for 8 minutes till just dry to touch. Flip biscotti; bake for 8 minutes till top is dry to the touch. Cool on sheets.

Nutrition Information

- Calories: 119
- Sodium: 72 mg(3%)
- Fiber: 1 g(4%)
- Total Carbohydrate: 18 g(6%)
- Cholesterol: 25 mg(8%)
- Protein: 2 g(4%)
- Total Fat: 5 g(8%)
- Saturated Fat: 3 g(15%)

337. Triple Ginger Layer Cake

Serving: Makes 8 to 10 servings | Prep: | Cook: | Ready in:

Ingredients

- Nonstick vegetable oil spray
- 3 cups cake flour, sifted
- 1 cup finely chopped crystallized ginger
- 2 teaspoons ground ginger
- 1 teaspoon ground cinnamon
- 1 teaspoon baking soda
- 1/4 teaspoon salt
- 3/4 cup (1 1/2 sticks) unsalted butter, room temperature
- 3/4 cup (packed) golden brown sugar
- 2 large eggs
- 1 cup plus 2 tablespoons buttermilk
- 2 8-ounce packages cream cheese, room temperature
- 1/2 cup (1 stick) unsalted butter, room temperature
- 3/4 cup (packed) golden brown sugar
- 2/3 cup powdered sugar
- 1/2 teaspoon ground cinnamon
- 1/4 teaspoon ground ginger
- 1/4 teaspoon vanilla extract
- 1/2 cup minced crystallized ginger

Direction

- Cake: Preheat an oven to 350°F. Spray nonstick spray on 2 8-in. round cake pans that have 2-in. high sides. Line parchment on bottoms. In medium bowl, mix salt, baking soda, cinnamon, ground ginger, crystallized ginger and flour. Beat sugar and butter using electric mixer till fluffy and light in big bowl. One by one, add eggs; beat after each addition till well blended. Alternately with buttermilk, mix in dry ingredients in 3 batches each, scraping down bowl's sides; beat till batter is just smooth. Divide batter to prepped pans.
- Bake cakes for 30 minutes till inserted tester in middle exits clean; cool cakes for 10 minutes in pans on racks. To loosen cakes, run small knife around sides of pan. Turn cakes onto racks; fully cool. Peel parchment off.
- Frosting: Beat butter and cream cheese with electric mixer till fluffy in big bowl. Add vanilla, ground ginger, cinnamon, powdered sugar and brown sugar; beat till blended well. Mix in 1/4 cup of crystallized ginger.
- On platter, put 1 cake layer; spread over with 1 cup frosting. Put 2nd cake layer over; spread leftover frosting on sides and top of cake. Decoratively sprinkle leftover 1/4 cup crystallized ginger on cake. You can make it 1 day ahead. Use cake dome to cover; refrigerate. Stand at room temperature before serving for 2 hours.

Nutrition Information

- Calories: 1035
- Total Carbohydrate: 130 g(43%)
- Cholesterol: 187 mg(62%)
- Protein: 11 g(22%)
- Total Fat: 54 g(83%)
- Saturated Fat: 30 g(150%)
- Sodium: 578 mg(24%)
- Fiber: 2 g(8%)

338. Tropical Lime Torte With Mango Compote

Serving: Makes 12 servings | Prep: | Cook: | Ready in:

Ingredients

- 4 large eggs
- 3/4 cup plus 2 tablespoons sugar
- 1/2 cup fresh lime juice
- 1 tablespoon grated lime peel
- 1/2 cup dark rum
- 1 16-ounce frozen all-butter pound cake, thawed
- 2 8-ounce packages cream cheese, room temperature
- 1/2 cup water
- 1/2 cup sugar
- 1/2 cup fresh lime juice
- 1/2 teaspoon grated lime peel
- 4 large ripe mangoes (5 to 6 pounds), peeled, pitted, diced
- Lime slices

Direction

- Torte: Whisk lime peel, lime juice, 3/4 cup sugar and eggs to blend in medium heavy saucepan; whisk on medium high heat for 6 minutes till it just boils and thickens. Put lime curd in small bowl; directly press plastic wrap on surface. Chill for a minimum of 3 hours - maximum of 3 days till very cold.
- Line 2 plastic wrap layers on 9 1/4x5 1/4x2 3/4-in. loaf pan; leave long overhang. Mix leftover 2 tbsp. sugar and rum till sugar is dissolved in small bowl. From outside of cake, trim brown layer. Horizontally cut cake to 3 even layers. Beat cream cheese till fluffy in big bowl; fold in the cold lime curd gently.
- To fit pan bottom, trim bottom cake layer; keep cake trimmings. Brush 1/3 rum syrup on both sides of layer. Put in pan; spread top with 1 1/2 cups of lime curd mixture. Brush 1/3 rum syrup on both sides of 2nd cake layer. Put in pan; spread leftover lime curd mixture on top. Brush leftover rum syrup on 3rd cake layer, on both sides; put on lime curd mixture. To adhere, press. Around sides, press reserved cake trimmings. Use plastic overhang to cover torte; refrigerate torte for a minimum of 1- maximum of 2 days.
- Compote: Mix initial 4 ingredients till sugar is dissolved in big bowl; stir in mangoes.
- Cover; chill for a maximum of 1 day.
- Lift torte from pan using plastic as aid; unwrap. Crosswise cut to 12 slices; put slices on plates. Put compote over; garnish using lime slices.

Nutrition Information

- Calories: 491
- Total Fat: 20 g(31%)
- Saturated Fat: 10 g(49%)
- Sodium: 307 mg(13%)
- Fiber: 3 g(11%)
- Total Carbohydrate: 69 g(23%)
- Cholesterol: 129 mg(43%)
- Protein: 8 g(15%)

339. Trout Dale Oatmeal Raisin Cookies

Serving: Makes 55 to 60 cookies (2-inch diameter) | Prep: | Cook: | Ready in:

Ingredients

- 1 1/2 cups all-purpose flour
- 1/2 teaspoon baking soda
- 1 teaspoon salt
- 1/2 teaspoon ground cinnamon
- 1/2 pound (2 sticks) unsalted butter, at room temperature
- 1 cup granulated sugar
- 1/2 cup dark brown sugar, packed
- 2 large eggs at room temperature
- 1 teaspoon vanilla extract
- 3 cups old-fashioned rolled oats
- 1 cup (6 ounces) raisins

- Pan Preparation: Line the cookie sheets with baking parchment or nonstick mats or coat with butter or nonstick vegetable spray.
- Cookie sheets (not insulated); baking parchment or Silpat or other nonstick baking mats (optional); flat paddle aattachment for electric mixer (optional)

Direction

- Divide oven to thirds; preheat it to 350°F. Bake for 12-16 minutes. As directed, prep cookie sheets.
- Whisk cinnamon, salt, baking soda and flour in a medium bowl.
- Beat butter till creamy and soft using a sturdy spoon in a large bowl or in a bowl of an electric mixer with a paddle attachment; beat in both sugars then scrape bowl and beater, if using, down. Beat till smooth. Beat in vanilla and eggs; scrape bowl down again.
- Slowly mixing, or with mixer on lowest speed, work in flour mixture slowly, then raisins and oats. It'll feel very stiff. (You may make dough ahead; cover. Refrigerate for a few hours.)
- By heaping tablespoons, drop dough onto prepped cookie sheets, 2-in. apart; bake according to time indicated for altitude in the card or for 12-16 minutes till cookies are golden brown. They get crisper as they bake longer.
- On a wire rack, cool cookies. Slide it off cookie sheet onto wire rack and cool if you baked cookies on a baking mat/parchment. Keep them in an airtight container when cookies are fully cool.

Nutrition Information

- Calories: 88
- Protein: 1 g(3%)
- Total Fat: 4 g(6%)
- Saturated Fat: 2 g(11%)
- Sodium: 50 mg(2%)
- Fiber: 1 g(2%)
- Total Carbohydrate: 13 g(4%)
- Cholesterol: 15 mg(5%)

---

340. Turkish Water Borek (Suborgei)

Serving: Makes 4 to 6 servings | Prep: | Cook: | Ready in:

Ingredients

- 3 1/2 cups all-purpose flour, plus more for dusting
- 2/3 cup wheat starch
- 5 large eggs
- 1 tablespoon lemon juice
- 1/2 teaspoon salt
- Olive oil
- 1/2 cup plus 1 tablespoon olive oil, plus more for greasing
- 4 cups spinach, cleaned
- 4 large eggs
- 1 cup milk
- 12 ounces Feta cheese, crumbled
- 2 tablespoons fresh dill, chopped
- 2 tablespoons flat-leaf parsley, chopped

Direction

- Dough preparation: 1. Combine the flour, lemon juice, wheat starch, eggs, and salt in a mixing bowl. Knead the dough for about 10 minutes on a lightly floured surface until elastic and soft, or use a stand mixer equipped with an attachment for kneading the dough on medium speed until dough becomes elastic and soft for 6 to 7 minutes. Cover the mixing bowl with the kitchen towel and let the dough rest for 30 minutes.
- 2. Place a large pot of water on the stove and let it boil. Prepare a separate large bowl of ice water and set aside. Cut the dough into 4 equal pieces. Cover each portion with a damp kitchen towel while working in batches. Roll each piece of the dough using a pasta machine or a rolling pin to about 1/8-inch thick circles. After you roll each dough piece, lightly

sprinkle with flour, to prevent the dough pieces from sticking together.

- 3. One by one, cook and boil each piece of dough for 3 to 4 minutes until tender. Immediately after removing from the boiling water, cool each piece of the cooked dough placing it in the bowl of ice water. Then take the dough from the ice water, pat dry, and gently brush each piece with some olive oil, keeping the dough rolls from sticking together. Set them aside.
- Filling preparation: 1. Add 1 tablespoon of oil to a large skillet and heat it over medium heat. Toss the spinach in the skillet and cover the skillet with a lid. Sauté the spinach for 3 to 4 minutes, stirring occasionally, until wilted. Set it aside and allow to cool.
- 2. Whisk milk, eggs, and remaining 1/2 cup oil in a large mixing bowl and set aside.
- Assemble the borek: 1. Preheat oven to 375 degrees F. Grease the inside of a large baking dish with some olive oil.
- 2. Start layering borek by laying the first layer of cooked dough, spreading wilted spinach, herbs, and Feta on top of the dough. Drizzle with the milk-egg mixture over top. Repeat with the next layer in following the same order. Ending layer should contain herbs and cheese.
- 3. Bake for about 35 minutes until the top is golden brown and the egg is done. Let it cool for 10 minutes and serve.

Nutrition Information

- Calories: 1247
- Total Fat: 69 g(106%)
- Saturated Fat: 23 g(114%)
- Sodium: 1092 mg(45%)
- Fiber: 7 g(29%)
- Total Carbohydrate: 113 g(38%)
- Cholesterol: 500 mg(167%)
- Protein: 43 g(87%)

341. Two Layer Cake

Serving: Makes a 9-inch round cake | Prep: | Cook: | Ready in:

Ingredients

- 1/4 cup unsalted butter (1/2 stick), at room temperature
- 1/2 cup granulated sugar
- 1 egg
- 1/2 teaspoon pure vanilla extract
- 1 teaspoon baking powder
- 1/2 teaspoon salt
- 1 cup cake flour or bleached flour
- 1/3 cup whole milk
- 1 cup unsalted butter (2 sticks), at room temperature
- 2 tablespoons vanilla extract
- 1/2 cup whole milk
- 32 ounces confectioners' sugar
- 1 1/2 cups unsalted butter (3 sticks), at room temperature
- 1 tablespoon pure vanilla extract
- 1/2 cup plus 1 tablespoon whole milk
- 48 ounces confectioners' sugar
- 4 (or more) different shades of food coloring

Direction

- For Cake layers: Preheat an oven to 375°F. Mix sugar and butter till well combined in a big bowl.
- Add vanilla and egg; thoroughly mix. Put aside.
- Mix flour, salt and baking powder in another bowl.
- Sift dry ingredients into butter mixture; mix.
- Add milk slowly; mix till batter becomes smooth.
- Grease then flour two 9-in. baking pans. Pour batter in; bake for 20 minutes till an inserted toothpick in middle exits clean. Remove.
- For Vanilla buttercream icing: Beat butter till fluffy and light on high. Add milk and vanilla; beat while adding sugar slowly. Cover;

refrigerate. Before frosting cake, bring to room temperature.
- For Colored flower frosting: Beat butter till fluffy and light on high. Add milk and vanilla; beat while slowly adding sugar. Beat again. Divide it to 4 bowls; mix a few food coloring drops into each. Cut off tips of disposable pastry bags; insert metal flower tips. Use colored frosting to fill each bag; use rubber bands to cinch open ends. Squeeze rosettes to 9-in. parchment round to decorate; allow frosting to set for several minutes. Transfer flowers from parchment onto frosted cake using a metal, thin spatula.
- Tip: You can give a lesson on color mixing through frosting while you and your guests are waiting for the cake to finish baking. You can use clear glasses or beakers with a few drops of food coloring. Green = Blue + Yellow Pink = Tiny dab of red in white frosting Violet = Blue + Red Orange = Red + Yellow

342. Ultimate Mud Pie

Serving: Makes 8 servings | Prep: | Cook: | Ready in:

Ingredients

- 1 1/2 cups chocolate wafer cookie crumbs
- 3 tablespoons unsalted butter, melted, plus more for the pie pan
- 1 tablespoon sugar
- 3 cups half-and-half
- 2/3 cup sugar
- 1/8 teaspoon salt
- 1/4 cup cornstarch
- 4 large egg yolks
- 5 ounces high-quality bittersweet or semisweet chocolate, finely chopped
- 2 tablespoons unsalted butter
- 1/2 teaspoon vanilla extract
- 1 cup heavy cream
- 2 tablespoons confectioners' sugar
- 1/2 teaspoon vanilla extract
- 2 tablespoons chocolate wafer crumbs, for garnish

Direction

- Put rack in middle of oven; preheat an oven to 350°F. Butter 9-in. pie pan lightly.
- Crust: Mix sugar, melted butter and crumbs till moist in a medium bowl; evenly and firmly press into pie pan. Bake for 12 minutes till crust smells like warm cookies and is set; fully cool.
- Filling: Heat salt, sugar and 2 1/2 cups half and half in a medium saucepan on medium heat till simmering, mixing often to dissolve sugar. Put into heatproof bowl then rinse out saucepan.
- Sprinkle cornstarch on leftover 1/2 cup of half and half in a small bowl; whisk till dissolved. In a medium bowl, whisk yolks; whisk in cornstarch mixture slowly. Whisk in hot half and half mixture slowly; put into rinsed-out saucepan. Cook on medium heat till it boils, constantly mixing using flat wooden spatula to avoid scorching. Put heat on medium low; bubbly mixture for 1 minute, constantly mixing. Take off heat. Add vanilla, butter and chocolate; whisk till chocolate fully melts. Through wire sieve, strain into a clean bowl.
- Put filling into cooled crust; directly on filling, press plastic wrap to avoid forming a skin. Fully cool. Refrigerate for at least 2 hours till filling is set and chilled.
- Topping: Use an electric mixer to whip cream, vanilla and confectioners' sugar on high speed till stiff in chilled medium bowl. Uncover pie; spread then swirl topping on filling. Put whipped cream into pastry bag with a star tip then pipe cream onto pie, if desired. Sprinkle cookie crumbs on pie; slice. Serve chilled.

Nutrition Information

- Calories: 693
- Protein: 8 g(15%)
- Total Fat: 45 g(70%)
- Saturated Fat: 24 g(118%)

- Sodium: 316 mg(13%)
- Fiber: 2 g(10%)
- Total Carbohydrate: 70 g(23%)
- Cholesterol: 186 mg(62%)

343. Upside Down Pear Chocolate Cake

Serving: Serves 12 to 15 | Prep: | Cook: |Ready in:

Ingredients

- 1 tablespoon unsalted butter, at room temperature, for pan
- 1 cup (7 ounces) granulated sugar
- 1/4 cup water
- 3 firm but ripe pears, peeled, cored, and each cut into 12 slices (1 pound prepped)
- 1/4 cup (2 ounces) unsalted butter
- 4 ounces dark chocolate, chopped
- 1 cup (5 ounces) all-purpose flour
- 1/3 cup (1 ounce) unsweetened Dutch-processed cocoa powder
- 3/4 teaspoon baking soda
- 1/2 teaspoon fine sea salt
- 3/4 cup (5 1/4 ounces) granulated sugar
- 2 eggs
- 1 teaspoon pure vanilla extract
- 1/2 cup whole milk
- Chantilly cream or Vanilla Bean Ice Cream, for serving (optional)

Direction

- Butter 9-in. round baking pan.
- Fruit topping: Mix water and sugar in a heavy saucepan with a tight fitting lid till sugar is dissolved; boil on medium heat. Cover; cook for 2 minutes. Steam washes down pan's sides to avoid forming sugar crystals, which happens when you cover that way. Uncover saucepan; boil sugar till it is dark amber color, slowly and gently swirling pan to evenly cook caramel as needed. Use a pastry brush submerged in cold water to wash down the pan's sides sometimes. Put caramel in prepped pan carefully; let harden. Being careful are you move the pan as it'll be very hot from sugar. Fan pear slices over caramel in a circle around perimeter, filling in middle with leftover slices.
- Preheat an oven to 350°F.
- Cake: Melt chocolate and butter in a small saucepan on low heat, occasionally mixing. Sift salt, baking soda, cocoa and flour in a bowl. Put melted chocolate into a stand mixer's bowl/mixing bowl; add sugar. Beat for 3 minutes at medium speed till fluffy and light with a stand mixer with paddle attachment or handheld mixer with beaters. One by one, add eggs, scraping down bowl's sides after every addition. Mix in vanilla. In 3 batches, mix in flour mixture, alternating with milk in 2 batches, starting and ending with flour, occasionally scraping bowl's sides down.
- Put batter in prepped pan; bake in center of oven till cake slightly bounces back when touched for 40-45 minutes. Cool for 15 minutes on wire rack. Invert cake onto plate; leave pan over cake for 5 minutes before removing it. Serve cake warm with vanilla bean ice cream scoop/small Chantilly cream dollop over.
- Keeps for a maximum of 3 days in room temperature, wrapped in plastic wrap.

Nutrition Information

- Calories: 292
- Fiber: 3 g(12%)
- Total Carbohydrate: 53 g(18%)
- Cholesterol: 40 mg(13%)
- Protein: 3 g(7%)
- Total Fat: 9 g(14%)
- Saturated Fat: 5 g(27%)
- Sodium: 193 mg(8%)

344. Valrhona Chocolate Cherry Cake

Serving: Makes 1 cake | Prep: | Cook: |Ready in:

Ingredients

- 1 cup dried sour cherries (about 5 ounces)
- 1/4 cup brandy
- 12 ounces fine-quality semisweet chocolate (preferable Valrhona), chopped
- 1 stick (1/2 cup) unsalted butter
- 6 large eggs, separated
- 3/4 cup plus 2 tablespoons sugar
- 1/4 cup plus 2 tablespoons fine-quality unsweetened cocoa powder, sifted

Direction

- Macerate cherries in brandy for 2 hours till brandy is nearly absorbed in a bowl, occasionally mixing.
- Preheat an oven to 350°F. Line parchment/wax paper on 10x2-in. buttered round cake pan's bottom; butter paper.
- Melt butter and chocolate in a double boiler/metal bowl above saucepan with barely simmering water, occasionally mixing. Take bowl/top of double boiler off heat; cool it.
- Beat 1/2 cup sugar and yolks till fluffy and light using electric mixer in a bowl. Add chocolate mixture; mix till combined. Fold in the cocoa powder till well combined; don't overmix.
- Beat whites till they hold soft peaks using cleaned beaters in another bowl. In a slow stream, beat in leftover sugar till meringue holds stiff peaks. Mix 1/4 meringue to lighten into chocolate mixture; gently yet thoroughly fold in leftover meringue. Fold in cherries.
- Put batter in pan; smooth top. Bake cake in center of oven till center is set for 40 minutes; cool cake for 15 minutes in pan on rack. Around pan's edge, run a thin knife; invert cake onto rack. Fully cool.

Nutrition Information

- Calories: 3826
- Saturated Fat: 131 g(654%)
- Sodium: 489 mg(20%)
- Fiber: 34 g(137%)
- Total Carbohydrate: 431 g(144%)
- Cholesterol: 1360 mg(453%)
- Protein: 61 g(121%)
- Total Fat: 227 g(350%)

345. Vanilla Buttercream

Serving: Makes enough for one 8-inch cake | Prep: 45mins | Cook: 45mins |Ready in:

Ingredients

- 1 1/3 cups (9.5 oz / 266 g) sugar
- 1/3 cup (2.9 oz / 80 g) water
- 7 large egg whites (7.4 oz / 210 g), at room temperature
- 1/2 teaspoon cream of tartar
- 2 cups (16 oz / 454 g) unsalted butter, cut into 1 tablespoon pieces, at room temperature
- 2 tablespoons vanilla extract

Direction

- You need to have egg whites and sugar syrup ready at nearly the same time; prep will need some coordination. Simmer water and sugar in a small saucepan on medium low heat, occasionally swirling; cook till sugar melts. Simmer without mixing for 5 minutes till digital thermometer reads 248°F in syrup.
- Meanwhile, whip cream of tartar and egg whites on medium speed for 8-10 minutes till whites hold soft peaks in a stand mixer's bowl with whisk attachment.
- Put sugar syrup into heatproof liquid measuring cup immediately. In a steady, thin stream, put hot sugar syrup in whites as mixer runs at medium high speed; try to put it into small space between whisk and mixer bowl.

Whip for 10 minutes till outside of bowl feels cool to touch and is shiny and thick.
- Lower speed to medium. One piece at 1 time, add butter as mixer runs; it won't look like perfect buttercream till you add last of butter. Be sure butter is in room temperature then slow down additions, adding next piece once the last one is incorporated fully if it looks broken, wet or delated while mixing. Add vanilla; beat at medium speed for 1 minute till it has a mayonnaise-like texture and well combined.
- When taking sugar syrup's temperature, you need an accurate thermometer. Instant-read thermometer is a great choice. Check calibration before using; boil a small pot with water to check if it reads 212°F, at sea level, when you put it into water. Fill measuring cup/pan will warm water to easily clean if it is sticky with sugar syrup remnants; stand for 30 minutes till sugar melts.
- You can keep buttercream for up to 1 week in the fridge in an airtight container/4 months in freezer.
- Variations: Thiebaud Pink Cake. Replace vanilla extract with Strawberry Concentrate; slowly add as mixing runs.
- Buttercream:
- The buttercream should be spreadable and perfectly smooth. You have to warm then rewhip it whether you use a refrigerated or just-made batch:
- Heat 292-g/10.4-oz/2 cups buttercream in microwaveable container at full powder 5-sec at a time till not at all melted and starts to look slightly glossy. Should have a sheen from softened exterior and be solid, similar to ice cream that starts to melt and drip on a cone. Warm a few cups at 1 time then use short bursts in microwave, it's very easy to melt and overheat buttercream. Beat warmed buttercream for 30 seconds till it looks like mayonnaise in a stand mixer's bowl with paddle attachment; repeat as needed.

Nutrition Information

- Calories: 4482
- Saturated Fat: 233 g(1165%)
- Sodium: 407 mg(17%)
- Fiber: 0 g(0%)
- Total Carbohydrate: 275 g(92%)
- Cholesterol: 975 mg(325%)
- Protein: 27 g(53%)
- Total Fat: 368 g(567%)

346. Vanilla Crumb

Serving: Makes 2 cups | Prep: | Cook: | Ready in:

Ingredients

- 1 cup (5 ounces) all-purpose flour
- 3/4 cup (5 1/4 ounces) granulated sugar
- 1/4 cup packed (1⅞ ounces) light brown sugar
- 1/4 teaspoon fine sea salt
- 1/2 cup (4 ounces) cold unsalted butter, cut into 1/4-inch cubes
- 1 tablespoon pure vanilla extract

Direction

- In a stand mixer with paddle attachment/food processor's bowl, mix butter, salt, sugars and flour. Pulse till it has coarse crumbs texture if using food processor. Mix on low speed till it has coarse crumbs texture if using stand mixer. Drizzle vanilla on mixture; briefly mix/pulse to distribute vanilla.

347. Vanilla Ice Cream And Ginger Molasses Cookie Sandwiches

Serving: Makes 6 Sandwiches | Prep: | Cook: | Ready in:

Ingredients

- 2 cups all purpose flour

- 2 teaspoons baking soda
- 2 1/2 teaspoons ground ginger
- 1 teaspoon ground cinnamon
- 1 teaspoon ground cloves
- 1 teaspoon salt
- 1/2 cup (1 stick) unsalted butter, room temperature
- 1/4 cup vegetable shortening, room temperature
- 1 cup (packed) dark brown sugar
- 1 egg
- 1/4 cup unsulfured (light) molasses
- 1 tablespoon grated orange peel
- Sugar
- 1 pint vanilla ice cream, softened slightly
- 1/2 cup chopped drained stem ginger in syrup
- Fresh strawberries, hulled, sliced

Direction

- To make cookies: into medium bowl, sift the initial 6 ingredients. In a big bowl, mix brown sugar, shortening and butter. Whisk the butter mixture with electric mixer till fluffy. Put the peel, molasses and egg; whisk till incorporated. Put in the dry ingredients; stir just till blended. Place a cover; refrigerate for an hour.
- Preheat the oven to 350°F. Grease 2 baking sheets with butter. Put the sugar in a small bowl. Shape dough into a dozen even portions with damp hands; form portions into balls. Roll in sugar to cover. Turn onto prepped sheets, set 2 1/2-inch away. Allow to bake for 15 minutes till cookies are light golden and cracked on surface yet remain soft. Let cool on sheets for a minute. Turn onto racks; cool fully.
- To make sandwiches: in a medium bowl, put the ice cream. Mix in the ginger. Put to freezer for half an hour till nearly firm.
- On a work area, put 6 cookies flat side facing up. Place 1/3 cup of ice cream on top of each. From edge of the cookies, scatter to quarter-inch. Put another cookie on top of each. Push to adhere. Put in the freezer. Freeze for a minimum of 2 hours till firm. Can be done a day in advance. Wrap securely; retain frozen.
- On plates, set the sandwiches. Jazz up with berries, serve.

Nutrition Information

- Calories: 665
- Cholesterol: 87 mg(29%)
- Protein: 7 g(14%)
- Total Fat: 30 g(46%)
- Saturated Fat: 15 g(76%)
- Sodium: 486 mg(20%)
- Fiber: 2 g(9%)
- Total Carbohydrate: 94 g(31%)

348. Vanilla Whipped Buttercream

Serving: Makes 3 1/2 c cups frosting, enough to frost and fill one 8-inch Layer cake or to frost 24 cupcakes | Prep: | Cook: | Ready in:

Ingredients

- 2 sticks (1 cup) organic unsalted butter, softened
- 1 cup organic cane sugar
- 1 cup organic whole milk
- 1/4 cup sifted organic all-purpose flour
- 1 1/2 tablespoons organic vanilla extract

Direction

- Cream butter at medium speed in a standing mixer for 3-5 minutes or with a hand mixer for 30 seconds till soft. Add sugar; beat on high speed for 5-7 minutes till fluffy and light.
- Whisk vanilla extract, flour and 1/4 cup milk till there are no lumps in a small saucepan. Add leftover 3/4 cup milk on medium heat, constantly whisking; cook till it reaches a low boil. Lower heat to low; whisk for several minutes till it begins to thicken.

- Remove from heat immediately; keep mixing. It'll cook for 1-2 minutes on its own after taking the pan off heat. Vigorously whisk to remove small lumps/pass it through fine-mesh sieve if you overheat it and get small lumps. Put pan over a bowl with ice water to sop cooking process and cool it if needed.
- Put aside when milk mixture is thick; cool to room temperature. To rush cooling, put into a freezer.
- Pour milk mixture slowly into butter-sugar mixture with mixer on low speed. Increase speed to medium; beat for 3-5 minutes till frosting is fluffy and light. Add vanilla to mix.
- Espresso whipped buttercream: Dissolve 1 heaping tsp. instant espresso powder in the 1 tbsp. boiling water; mix with butter-sugar mixture.
- Chocolate whipped buttercream: Melt 4-oz. dark/unsweetened chocolate as milk mixture cools on top of double boiler that is set over simmering water or in a microwave in 30-sec bursts. Cool to room temperature. Mix chocolate with butter-sugar mixture with mixer on low speed.

Nutrition Information

- Calories: 272
- Saturated Fat: 12 g(61%)
- Sodium: 13 mg(1%)
- Fiber: 0 g(0%)
- Total Carbohydrate: 24 g(8%)
- Cholesterol: 51 mg(17%)
- Protein: 1 g(3%)
- Total Fat: 19 g(30%)

349. Virginia Eggnog

Serving: 24 | Prep: 10mins | Cook: | Ready in:

Ingredients

- 1 cup white sugar, or more to taste
- 10 eggs, divided
- 1 quart milk
- 1 quart heavy whipping cream
- 1/4 cup rum
- 1/4 cup whisky

Direction

- Using an electric mixer, whisk the egg yolks and sugar in a bowl until the color turns very light. Pour the cream and milk into the mixture.
- In another bowl, with the electric mixer, whisk the egg whites to form stiff peaks. You can add more sugar if wanted. Add by folding the egg whites into the milk mixture and stir until it smoothens. Pour in the whiskey and rum. Chill for 1 or more hours.

Nutrition Information

- Calories: 230 calories;
- Cholesterol: 135
- Protein: 4.8
- Total Fat: 17.5
- Sodium: 61
- Total Carbohydrate: 11.5

350. Walnut Cake With Sauteed Pears And Cinnamon Cream

Serving: Serves 6 to 8 | Prep: | Cook: | Ready in:

Ingredients

- 1 1/4 cups unbleached all-purpose flour
- 1 teaspoon baking powder
- pinch of salt
- 1/2 cup (1 stick) unsalted butter, at room temperature, cut into pieces
- 1 cup sugar
- 2 large eggs, at room temperature, separated
- 1/2 cup milk

- 1 cup chopped walnuts
- 1 teaspoon pure vanilla extract
- 2 tablespoons unsalted butter
- 6 small Bosc pears, cored, peeled and cut into 1/4-inch pieces
- 2 tablespoons brown sugar
- 1 tablespoon ground cinnamon
- 1 teaspoon ground nutmeg
- 2 tablespoons fresh lemon juice
- 1 cup heavy cream
- 1 tablespoon sugar
- 1 teaspoon ground cinnamon

Direction

- Preheat an oven to 350°F and lightly butter then flour 9-in. round cake pan; tap out extra flour.
- Prep cake: Whisk salt, baking powder and flour 8-10 times till well mixed in a bowl.
- Cream sugar and butter using an electric mixer at medium high speed. Add egg yolks; beat till smooth. In 3-4 batches, add dry ingredients, alternating with milk; end with dry ingredients. Mix well. Fold in vanilla and nuts.
- Beat egg whites till it holds stiff peaks using electric mixer at medium high speed. Fold whites into batter till just mixed; spread batter in cake pan. Bake in middle of oven till inserted toothpick in middle exits clean for 35-40 minutes. Turn onto wire rack; cool.
- Prep pears: Melt butter in a sauté pan/skillet on medium high heat; cook pears till for 5 minutes till soft, mixing. Sprinkle sugar. Add lemon juice, nutmeg and cinnamon; stir well. To keep warm, cover.
- Cream: Whip sugar and cream using electric mixer at medium high speed till cream is thick yet not dry. Add cinnamon; whip till cream reaches preferred consistency. Put pears and cream on cake; serve.

Nutrition Information

- Calories: 830
- Fiber: 8 g(32%)
- Total Carbohydrate: 91 g(30%)
- Cholesterol: 169 mg(56%)
- Protein: 10 g(20%)
- Total Fat: 49 g(76%)
- Saturated Fat: 24 g(118%)
- Sodium: 163 mg(7%)

351. Walnut Cigarette Cookies

Serving: Makes about 28 cookies | Prep: | Cook: | Ready in:

Ingredients

- 1/4 cup unsalted butter, softened
- 1/2 cup sugar
- 2 large egg whites
- 1/4 teaspoon salt
- 1/4 cup cake flour (not self-rising)
- 1/3 cup walnuts, toasted lightly and minced

Direction

- Cream sugar and butter till fluffy and light using an electric mixer in a bowl. Add salt and egg whites; beat till well combined yet not frothy for 10 seconds. Sift flour above mixture; fold in walnuts. Drop level teaspoons batter onto buttered baking sheets, 4-in. apart; spread batter to 2-in. rounds. In batches, bake cookies for 6-8 minutes just till firm enough to remove from baking sheet in center of preheated 375°F oven. Loosen cookies from sheet using a metal spatula, quickly working with 1 cookie at 1 time; quickly roll them around a chopstick/wooden spoon's handle, rough side out, to make a thin cylinder, transferring as rolled onto rack. Cool. Put cookies into oven to soften for 30 seconds if cookies are too brittle. Cookies keep for 3 days in an airtight container.

Nutrition Information

- Calories: 36

- Cholesterol: 4 mg(1%)
- Protein: 0 g(1%)
- Total Fat: 2 g(3%)
- Saturated Fat: 1 g(5%)
- Sodium: 22 mg(1%)
- Fiber: 0 g(0%)
- Total Carbohydrate: 5 g(2%)

352. Walnut And Almond Cake With Orange Pomegranate Compote

Serving: Makes 10 to 12 servings | Prep: | Cook: |Ready in:

Ingredients

- Vegetable oil
- 1 3/4 cups walnuts
- 1 cup whole almonds
- 1/4 cup matzo cake meal
- 8 large eggs, separated
- 1 tablespoon grated lemon peel
- 1 tablespoon grated orange peel
- 1 teaspoon ground cinnamon
- 1/4 teaspoon salt
- 1 cup sugar, divided
- 2 tablespoons orange juice
- 4 large oranges, peel of 1 orange removed in strips and reserved
- 1 cup pure unsweetened pomegranate juice
- 1 cup sugar
- 1 tablespoon fresh lemon juice

Direction

- Cake: Preheat an oven to 350°F. Brush oil on a 13x9x2-in. metal baking pan. Mix cake meal, almonds and walnuts in processor; finely grind nuts.
- Beat salt, cinnamon, orange peel, lemon peel and egg yolks using electric mixer for 3 minutes till it starts to thicken in a big bowl. Add 1/2 cup sugar slowly, beating for 2 minutes till light in color and very thick. Beat in orange juice and fold in nut mixture. Beat egg whites using clean dry beaters till soft peaks form in another big bowl. Add leftover 1/2 cup sugar slowly, beating till stiff yet not dry. In 3 additions, fold egg whites into the yolk mixture.
- Put batter in prepped pan; bake cake for 35 minutes till inserted tester in middle exits clean and cake is deep golden and puffed; cool cake in the pan on the rack. Middle of cake will fall.
- Syrup and compote: Put big sieve above a bowl. Cut all pith and peel from oranges. Cut oranges between membranes, working above sieve, to release segments into the sieve. Squeeze over juice from membranes; while prepping syrup, let oranges drain.
- Boil reserved orange peel, lemon juice, sugar and pomegranate juice in medium saucepan on medium high heat, mixing till thin syrup forms and sugar is dissolved; take off heat.
- Put 3/4 cup syrup in small bowl, holding back orange peel with spoon. Put on cake; stand for a minimum of 1 hour.
- Put drained orange juice in leftover syrup in pan; boil peel and syrup for 8 minutes till reduced enough to coat a spoon. Discard peel. You can make it 1 day ahead; cover. Stand in room temperature. In bowl, put orange segments; cover. Refrigerate syrup and orange segments separately.
- Put syrup in orange segments; stand compote for 15 minutes. Trim cake edges. Lengthwise cut cake to 2 1/2-in. wide strips. On diagonal, cut strips to diamonds; put on plates. Put compote over; serve.

Nutrition Information

- Calories: 408
- Total Carbohydrate: 58 g(19%)
- Cholesterol: 149 mg(50%)
- Protein: 10 g(19%)
- Total Fat: 17 g(26%)
- Saturated Fat: 2 g(12%)

- Sodium: 118 mg(5%)
- Fiber: 4 g(17%)

353. Walnut Date Torte

Serving: Makes 8 servings | Prep: 30mins | Cook: 1.5hours | Ready in:

Ingredients

- 1/4 cup boiling-hot water
- 1 1/2 cups pitted dates (1/2 pound), finely chopped
- 1 1/2 cups walnuts (5 ounces), toasted and cooled
- 3/4 cup sugar, divided
- 2/3 cup matzo meal
- 1 tablespoon grated orange zest
- 1/2 teaspoon ground cardamom
- 1/4 teaspoon salt
- 4 large eggs, separated, at room temperature 30 minutes
- Accompaniment: unsweetened whipped cream
- Garnish: Passover powdered sugar

Direction

- Preheat an oven with rack in the center to 350°F. Use vegetable oil/softened butter to grease 9x2-in. round cake pan generously. Dust some matzo meal; knock excess out.
- Put hot water on dates in a big bowl; stand to soften for 15 minutes.
- Pulse walnuts till chopped in a food processor. Add 1/4 cup sugar; pulse till nuts are ground finely. Add salt, cardamom, zest and 2/3 cup matzo meal; pulse till combined.
- Using an electric mixer on medium high speed, beat pinch of salt and egg whites till they hold soft peaks in a bowl. In a slow stream, add leftover 1/2 cup sugar; beat till whites hold glossy, stiff peaks.
- Whisk yolks into the date mixture. Fold 1/3 of yolk mixture into whites; thoroughly yet gently fold in leftover yolk mixture. Fold all of the nut mixture into the batter.
- Put batter into the cake pan; bake for 35-40 minutes till cake starts to pull away from pan's sides, springy to the touch and golden; cool for 30 minutes in pan on a rack. Invert onto the rack; fully cool.
- You can make the cake 2 days ahead; keep in room temperature, tightly wrapped in plastic wrap or in sealed bag.

Nutrition Information

- Calories: 322
- Cholesterol: 93 mg(31%)
- Protein: 7 g(14%)
- Total Fat: 14 g(22%)
- Saturated Fat: 2 g(9%)
- Sodium: 109 mg(5%)
- Fiber: 3 g(13%)
- Total Carbohydrate: 47 g(16%)

354. Warm Lemon Chiboust With Lemon Thyme Infused Milk Chocolate Velouté

Serving: Makes 12 servings | Prep: | Cook: | Ready in:

Ingredients

- 3/4 cup milk
- 3/4 cup heavy cream
- 4 large eggs, separated
- 3 tablespoons cornstarch
- 3/4 cup (12 tablespoons) sugar
- 1/4 cup fresh Meyer lemon juice* (from 1 medium lemon)
- 2 teaspoons powdered gelatin (from 1 -1/4-ounce envelope)
- 1 tablespoon finely grated Meyer lemon zest* (from 2 medium lemons)
- 1/8 teaspoon salt
- 1 1/2 cups all-purpose flour

- 1/2 cup sugar
- 1/2 teaspoon salt
- 7 tablespoons cold, unsalted butter, cut into 1/2-inch cubes
- 4 large egg yolks
- 1/2 teaspoon pure vanilla extract
- 1/2 cup confectioners' sugar
- 1 cup heavy cream
- 1 1/2 cups (9 ounces) high-quality milk chocolate such as Valrhona, coarsely chopped
- 4 1/2 teaspoons sugar
- 2 teaspoons fresh Meyer lemon juice* (from 1/2 lemon)
- 1/2 teaspoon fresh lemon thyme** leaves, minced
- *If Meyer lemons are unavailable, regular lemons can be substituted. **If lemon thyme is unavailable, regular thyme can be substituted
- 12-cup silicone muffin pan; small blowtorch

Direction

- Chiboust: boil cream and milk in 3-qt. pot on medium heat. Whisk 1 tbsp. sugar, cornstarch and egg yolks in medium bowl; whisk cream and hot milk mixture into egg-yolk mixture slowly; put into pot. Lower heat to low; cook for 2 minutes till it's smooth and thick, constantly whisking. Strain custard through fine-mesh strainer in a big bowl, pressing on solids.
- In small bowl, put lemon juice. Sprinkle gelatin on juice; stand to soften for 1 minute. Mix for 1 minute till dissolved. Mix lemon zest and lemon juice mixture into custard then press plastic wrap on custard's surface; cool in room temperature.
- Mix leftover 11 tbsp. sugar and 3/4 cup water in small saucepan; clamp on candy thermometer. Put on medium heat; simmer for 10-12 minutes, undisturbed, uncovered, till thermometer reads 235°F. Use an electric mixer to beat salt and egg whites for 3-4 minutes till soft peaks start to form in a big bowl as syrup simmers. Carefully and slowly put hot syrup into the egg whites as mixer runs; whip for 6-8 minutest till meringue holds soft peaks, is glossy and thickens.
- Fold in meringue gently when custard is cool; evenly divide Chiboust to 12 silicone muffin cups. Freeze for 4-24 hours till firm.
- Dough: Whisk salt, sugar and flour in a big bowl. Blend in butter till it looks like coarse meal with some roughly pea-size small butter lumps using fingertips/pastry blender. Whisk 1 tbsp. ice water and yolks in small bowl. Drizzle on flour mixture; mix till just combined with fork. Knead mixture gently till dough forms with floured hands. Turn out dough on lightly floured surface; knead gently 4-5 times till smooth. Shape dough to ball; flatten to 5-in. disk. Tightly wrap in plastic; chill for 30-60 minutes till firm.
- Roll dough on 13x18-in. parchment piece dusted with flour lightly to 12-13-in. diameter 1/4-in. thick round. Put dough and parchment on sheet pan; cover in plastic. Chill for 30 minutes in fridge.
- Bake Chiboust: Preheat an oven to 350°F.
- Take dough from fridge. Cut 12 rounds out using 3-in. round cookie cutter; put onto big baking sheet. Take Chibousts from freezer then unmold; put 1 on every dough and sift confectioners' sugar over. Bake for 20 minutes till thin crust forms on top and Chibousts are puffy.
- Make chocolate velouté as Chibousts bake: Boil cream in a big saucepan on medium heat; take off heat. Add chocolate; whisk till smooth and chocolate melts.
- Heat 1 1/2 tbsp. water and sugar for 2-3 minutes till sugar dissolves in 1-qt. pot on medium heat, constantly whisking. Put syrup on chocolate; whisk for 2-3 minutes till smooth. Whisk in thyme and lemon juice; keep warm.
- Assembly: Take Chibousts from oven. Brown top of each using blowtorch by evenly moving flame back and forth on top for 1-2 minutes till golden brown. Drizzle 2 tbsp. chocolate velouté on each Chiboust; serve warm.

- You can brown chibousts in shallow baking pan in broiler 5-in. from heat for 1-2 minutes till golden brown.

355. Warm Sour Apple And Buttermilk Torte

Serving: Makes 8 servings | Prep: | Cook: | Ready in:

Ingredients

- Canola-oil cooking spray
- 2/3 cup flour plus extra for dusting
- 3 tbsp unsalted butter, softened
- 2/3 cup plus 1 tbsp raw cane sugar
- 1/4 cup lowfat buttermilk
- 2 egg whites
- 1/3 cup polenta (or cornmeal)
- 3/4 tsp baking powder
- 3/4 tsp vanilla extract
- 4 Granny Smith apples, peeled, cored and thinly sliced

Direction

- Heat an oven to 350°F. Use cooking spray to coat 9-in. cake pan; dust in flour. Beat 1/3 cup sugar and butter using electric mixer till fluffy in a bowl; beat in 1/3 cup more sugar. Add buttermilk then, one by one, egg whites, beating well. Mix baking powder, polenta and flour in another bowl. Add together with vanilla to butter mixture; stir. Put into pan; put apples over. Sprinkle leftover 1 tbsp. sugar; bake for 45-55 minutes.

356. Whipped Parsnips With Roasted Garlic

Serving: Makes 4 servings | Prep: | Cook: | Ready in:

Ingredients

- 1 medium head of garlic
- 1 pound parsnips, peeled, coarsely chopped (about 3 cups)
- 1/4 cup whipping cream
- 2 tablespoons (1/4 stick) butter
- 1/4 teaspoon ground nutmeg

Direction

- Preheat an oven to 350°F; cut 1/4-in. off top of garlic. Discard top. Tightly wrap head in foil, putting on rack in the oven. Roast for 1 hour till garlic is tender, then cool. To release from skin, press garlic. Put garlic in small bowl; mash.
- Cook the parsnips in pot with boiling salted water for 25 minutes till very tender. Drain well and keep 1/2 cup of cooking liquid for later. Put parsnips back in pot. Add mashed garlic, nutmeg, butter and cream; beat using handheld electric mixer till smooth. If it is too thick, thin with some reserved cooking liquid. Season with pepper and salt to taste.

Nutrition Information

- Calories: 189
- Total Fat: 11 g(17%)
- Saturated Fat: 7 g(33%)
- Sodium: 18 mg(1%)
- Fiber: 5 g(21%)
- Total Carbohydrate: 23 g(8%)
- Cholesterol: 32 mg(11%)
- Protein: 2 g(5%)

357. White Chocolate Tartlets With Strawberries And Bananas

Serving: Makes 6 servings | Prep: | Cook: | Ready in:

Ingredients

- 1 1/4 cups all purpose flour
- 1/2 cup hazelnuts, toasted, husked

- 1/4 cup sugar
- 1/4 teaspoon salt
- 1/2 cup (1 stick) chilled unsalted butter, cut into 1/2-inch pieces
- 2 tablespoons (or more) ice water
- 1 teaspoon vanilla extract
- 2 ounces bittersweet (not unsweetened) or semisweet chocolate, finely chopped
- 6 ounces good-quality white chocolate (such as Lindt or Baker's), finely chopped
- 3/4 cup chilled whipping cream
- 2 tablespoons Grand Marnier or other orange liqueur
- 2 medium bananas, peeled, thinly sliced
- 1/4 cup orange juice
- 1 1-pint basket strawberries

Direction

- Crust: Blend initial 4 ingredients till nuts are ground finely in processor. Add butter; use on/off turns to cut in till it looks like coarse meal. Add vanilla and 2 tbsp. ice water; process till moist clumps form. If dough is dry, add extra ice water by teaspoonfuls. Gather dough to ball; divide to 6 even pieces then flatten each to disk. In plastic, wrap each; chill for 2 hours. You can make it 2 days ahead, kept chilled. Slightly soften dough before continuing.
- Preheat an oven to 375°F. Evenly press 1 dough disk up sides and on bottom of 4 1/2-in. diameter tartlet pan that has removable bottom. Use fork to pierce crust all over; repeat with leftover 5 dough disks. Freeze the crusts for 20 minutes till firm.
- Bake crusts for 25 minutes till baked through and golden; remove from oven. Sprinkle bottom of hot crusts with bittersweet chocolate immediately, evenly dividing. Stand for 5 minutes till chocolate melts. Spread chocolate on bottom of crusts with back of spoon; chill for 10 minutes till chocolate sets.
- Filling: Mix white chocolate till smooth and melted on top of double boiler above barely simmering water; take top of double boiler off above water. Cool the white chocolate down to room temperature. Beat liqueur and cream till soft peaks form in medium bowl; fold cream mixture in 3 additions into melted white chocolate. Divide filling to tartlet crusts; smooth the tops. Chill for 4 hours till filling is set; you can make it 1 day ahead, kept chilled, loosely covered with foil.
- Toss orange juice and banana slices gently in bowl. On paper towels, put banana slices; pat try. In circle, alternate strawberry and banana slices on tartlets, overlapping. You can make it 2 hours ahead, chilled.

Nutrition Information

- Calories: 696
- Saturated Fat: 23 g(116%)
- Sodium: 138 mg(6%)
- Fiber: 5 g(18%)
- Total Carbohydrate: 70 g(23%)
- Cholesterol: 80 mg(27%)
- Protein: 8 g(16%)
- Total Fat: 44 g(68%)

358. White Chocolate And Lemon Wedding Cake

Serving: Makes 50 servings | Prep: | Cook: | Ready in:

Ingredients

- 6 cups sugar
- 9 teaspoons cornstarch
- 3 cups fresh lemon juice
- 36 large egg yolks
- 3 cups (6 sticks) chilled unsalted butter, cut into 1/2-inch cubes
- 16 ounces imported white chocolate (such as Lindt or Perugina), finely chopped (do not use chips)
- 6 8-ounce packages Philadelphia-brand cream cheese, room temperature
- 5 cups (packed) powdered sugar (about 1 1/4 pounds)

- 4 cups chilled heavy whipping cream
- 4 cups lemon curd (see above)
- 14 ounces imported white chocolate (such as Lindt or Perugina), finely chopped (do not use chips)
- 1 1/3 cups chilled heavy whipping cream
- 11 cups sifted cake flour
- 11 teaspoons baking powder
- 2 1/2 teaspoons salt
- 3 cups buttermilk
- 6 tablespoons thawed frozen orange juice concentrate
- 5 tablespoons vanilla extract
- 1 1/2 cups (3 sticks) unsalted butter, room temperature
- 6 1/2 cups sugar
- 1 1/2 cups vegetable oil
- 2 1/2 cups egg whites (about 20 large)
- 1/2 teaspoon cream of tartar
- 2 11-inch-diameter tart-pan bottoms or cardboard rounds
- 1 8-inch-diameter tart-pan bottom or cardboard round (cut from 9-inch round)
- 1 5-inch-diameter tart-pan bottom or cardboard round (cut from 6-inch round)
- 14 12-inch-long, 1/4-inch-diameter wooden dowels
- Mix of large and tiny white roses and fresias (about 5 dozen)
- 8 1-pint containers fresh strawberries, hulled, halved
- 2 1/2-pint containers fresh blackberries
- 2 1/2-pint containers fresh raspberries
- 2 1/2-pint containers fresh blueberries
- 1 cup sugar

Direction

- Lemon curd: In 2 separate batches, make curd to fill between cake layers and to use in mousse.
- Whisk 4 1/2 tsp. cornstarch and 3 cups sugar to blend in medium heavy saucepan; whisk in 1 1/2 cups of lemon juice slowly then 18 yolks then add 1 1/2 cups of butter. Cook on medium heat, constantly whisking, for 18 minutes till curd boils and thickens. Put curd in medium bowl. Directly on curd's surface, press plastic wrap. Create 2nd curd batch, using same amount of every ingredient; refrigerate for 1 day minimum. You can make it 1 week ahead, kept chilled.
- Frosting: In 2 different batches, make frosting minimum of 1 day ahead. 1 batch will be for 12-in. cake and the other for other 2 cakes. You'll use cream for butter in this cream cheese frosting; it'll spreadable straight from fridge. For best results, use heavy whipping cream.
- Put 8-oz. chocolate on top of double boiler above barely simmering water; mix till chocolate is just warm, smooth and melted; don't overheat. Take from above water. Beat 3 cream cheese packages using electric mixer till fluffy in a big bowl. Beat in 1 1/4 cups sugar; beat in warm chocolate. Beat 1 1/4 cups sugar and 2 cups cream till medium firm peaks form in medium bowl. Fold in 3 additions into cream cheese mixture. Cover; chill. Create 2nd frosting batch, using same amount of every ingredient; refrigerate frosting for 1 day minimum - 4 days maximum.
- The lemon-white chocolate mousse: Put lemon curd in a big bowl; refrigerate. Put white chocolate on top of double boiler above barely simmering water; mix till chocolate is just warm, smooth and melted; don't overheat. Take from above water. Beat whipping cream till medium firm peaks form in another big bowl; fold in the warm white chocolate. In 3 additions, fold it into lemon curd. Cover bowl; chill mousse for minimum of 1 day - maximum of 4 days till set and cold.
- Orange buttermilk cake: To make 12-in. cake, use 1/2 the ingredients then 1/2 to make both 6-in. and 9-in. cakes. Sift flour first; measure it.
- Put rack right under middle of oven; preheat to 350°F. Butter then flour 12-in. diameter cake pan with 3-in. high sides and removable bottom. Butter then flour 9-in. diameter cake pan with 3-in. high sides and removable bottom. Butter then flour 6-in. diameter cake pan with 3-in. high sides and removable bottom. Into big bowl, sift 1/4 tsp. salt, 5 1/2

tsp. baking powder and 5 1/2 cups of sifted cake flour thrice. In small bowl, mix 2 1/2 tbsp. vanilla, 3 tbsp. orange juice concentrate and 1 1/2 cups buttermilk.

- Beat 1 1/2 sticks/3/4 cup butter till fluffy and smooth using electric mixer in big bowl. Beat in 1 1/4 cups of sugar slowly then 3/4 cup oil; beat in 1 cup sugar more. In 4 additions and alternately with buttermilk mixture in 3 batches, beat in flour mixture, scraping bowl's sides down often. Beat 1/4 tsp. cream of tartar and 1 1/4 cups/10 egg whites till soft peaks form using clean dry beaters in another big bowl. Add 1 cup sugar slowly, beating for 4 minutes till whites fall in puffy, thick not stiff ribbon from beaters. Fold whites in 4 additions into batter. Put batter in prepped 12-in. pan; bake cake for 1 hour 25 minutes till inserted tester in middle exits clean and brown. Cool cake for 30 minutes in pan on rack. To loosen, cut around cake; remove pan sides then maintain the oven temperature.
- Follow same technique for 1st cake and same amount of every ingredient to make 2nd cake batter batch. Put 8 1/2 cups batter in prepped 9-in. pan; put 4 cups batter in prepped 6-in. pan. Bake cakes for 1 hour 18 minutes for 9-in. cake, 1 hour 10 minutes for 6-in. cake, till inserted tester in middle exits clean and brown. Cool cakes for 30 minutes in pans on racks. To loosen, cut around cakes; remove pan sides. Fully cool all cakes. You can make it 1 day before filling then frosting cakes. Put cakes in pan. Use foil to cover; keep in room temperature.
- Fill and frost cakes: Get cardboard rounds from candy and cake supply store or use tart-pan bottoms to fill and frost cakes easily.
- To release from pan, push 12-in. cake up. Cut enough top crust off to make cake 2 1/2-in. high using a big serrated knife. Horizontally cut cake to 3 3/4-in. thick layers. Put top layer on work surface using 11-in. cardboard round/tart-pan bottom; cover. Put center layer on work surface; cover. From pan bottom, cut bottom layer; put onto cardboard round/tart-pan bottom. Spread with generous 1 3/4 cups of mousse. By tablespoonfuls, drop 1 3/4 cups of curd over; spread in even layer to cover mousse. Refrigerate for 1 hour till curd and mousse are firm. Put center layer on bottom layer using tart-pan bottom. Spread same amounts of curd and mousse. Put top layer on cake using tart-pan bottom; lightly press. Refrigerate the assembled cake.
- To release from pan, push 9-in. cake up; cut enough top crust off so cake is 2 1/2-in. high. Horizontally cut cake to 3 3/4-in. thick layers. Put top layer onto work surface using cardboard round/tart-pan bottom; cover. Repeat with center layer. From pan bottom, cut bottom layer; put on cardboard round/8-in. tart-pan bottom. Spread with 1 1/4 cups of mousse. By tablespoonfuls, drop generous 2/3 cup of curd; spread in even layer to cover mousse. Refrigerate for 1 hour till curd and mouse are firm. Put center layer on bottom layer using tart-pan bottom. Spread same amount of curd and mousse. Put top layer on cake using tart-pan bottom; lightly press. Refrigerate the assembled cake.
- To release from pan, push 6-in. cake up. Cut enough top crust off so cake is 2 1/2-in. high. Horizontally cut cake to 3 3/4-in. thick layers. Put top layer on work surface; cover. Repeat with center layer. From pan bottom, cut bottom layer; put on cardboard round/5-in. tart-pan bottom. Spread with generous 1/2 cup of mousse. By tablespoonfuls, drop 6 tbsp. curd; spread in even layer to cover mousse. Refrigerate for 1 hour till curd and mousse are firm. Put center layer on bottom layer using big spatula. Spread with same amount of curd and mousse. Put top layer on cake using big spatula; lightly press. Refrigerate the assembled cake.
- As first coat, thinly spread 2 1/4 cups of frosting on sides and top of 12-in. assembled cake. Thinly spread 1 1/2 cups of frosting on sides and top of 9-in. assembled cake; thinly spread 3/4 cup of frosting on sides and top of 6-in. assembled cake then chill all cakes for 1 hour.

- Spread 12-in. cake with 5 cups frosting. Spread 9-in. cake with 3 2/3 cups frosting. Spread 6-in. cake with 2 cups frosting; refrigerate 6-in. cake.
- On platter, put 12-in. cake. Press a dowel straight down in middle then through cake's bottom. Mark dowel 1 1/4-in. over frosting's level. Remove dowel; at marked point, cut with serrated knife. To same length, cut 7 more dowels. Press a dowel back in middle of cake. Press leftover 7 dowels in cake, 3-3 1/4-in. from middle dowel, evenly spaced apart; chill cake with the dowels.
- Press a dowel straight down in middle of 9-in. cake. Mark the dowel 1 1/4-in. over frosting's level. Remove dowel; cut at marked point with serrated knife. To same length, cut 5 more dowels. Press a dowel back in middle of cake; press leftover dowels in cake, 2-in. from center, evenly spaced apart. Chill with the dowels. You can make it 2 days ahead. Cover cakes using cake domes or with foil loosely when frosting is firm; keep chilled.
- Decoration and assembly: Mix of small and big freesias and white roses, around 5 dozen.
- Put 9-in. cake on dowels in 12-in. cake; put 6-in. cake on dowels in 9-in. cake. Put big roses between middle and bottom tiers, fitting in small freesias and roses to fill space. Use mix of flowers to fill space between top and middle tiers.
- Berry compote: Toss all ingredients to coat in big bowl. Cover; chill for minimum of 1 hour – maximum of 6 hours till juices form.
- Serving: Put middle and top cake tiers onto work surface. Take dowels and flowers from cakes. Cut the top cake to 8 slices. Cut center cake to 16 slices. 3-in. from edge and straight down, insert knife into 12-in. cake; cut around cake 3-in. from edge, creating 6-in. diameter circle in middle. Cut outer ring to 18 slices. Cut 6-in. middle to 8 slices. Put cake slices onto plates; put compote alongside each.

| 359. | Winter Raspberry Souffles |

Serving: Serves 6 | Prep: | Cook: | Ready in:

Ingredients

- 1/2 cup sugar plus additional for coating ramekins
- two 10-ounce packages frozen raspberries in syrup, thawed
- 1 tablespoon cornstarch
- 1 teaspoon balsamic vinegar
- 4 large eggs
- 1/4 teaspoon cream of tartar

Direction

- Preheat an oven to 375°F. Butter 6 4x2-in. 1-cup ramekins. Coat in sugar; knock extra sugar out.
- Remove 30 raspberries; on paper towels, drain. Simmer vinegar, cornstarch, syrup and leftover raspberries in 3-qt. saucepan for 3 minutes, mixing. Through fine sieve, put into bowl; press on solids hard. Mix in drained raspberries; cool. You can make raspberry mixture 1 day ahead, covered, chilled.
- Separate eggs; beat 6 tbsp. sugar and yolks using electric mixer for 5 minutes till mixture makes ribbon when you lift beater in a big bowl, pale and thick. Fold raspberry mixture into the yolk mixture just till combined. Beat cream of tartar, pinch salt and whites using cleaned beaters till it holds soft peaks in another big bowl. Add leftover 2 tbsp. sugar slowly; beat till whites hold stiff peaks. Mix 1/4 whites to lighten into raspberry mixture; gently yet thoroughly fold in leftover whites.
- Divide soufflé mixture to ramekins; use knife to smooth tops. To help rising, run knife's tip around souffle's edges. Bake soufflés on baking sheet in lower oven third for 18-20 minutes till golden brown and puffed; immediately serve.

Nutrition Information

- Calories: 167
- Total Carbohydrate: 30 g(10%)
- Cholesterol: 124 mg(41%)
- Protein: 5 g(11%)
- Total Fat: 4 g(6%)
- Saturated Fat: 1 g(5%)
- Sodium: 49 mg(2%)
- Fiber: 6 g(25%)

360. World Peace Cookies

Serving: Makes about 36 | Prep: 25mins | Cook: 1hours | Ready in:

Ingredients

- 1 1/4 cups all purpose flour
- 1/3 cup natural unsweetened cocoa powder
- 1/2 teaspoon baking soda
- 11 tablespoons (1 stick plus 3 tablespoons) unsalted butter, room temperature
- 2/3 cup (packed) golden brown sugar
- 1/4 cup sugar
- 1 teaspoon vanilla extract
- 1/4 teaspoon fine sea salt
- 5 ounces extra-bittersweet chocolate (do not exceed 85% cacao), chopped (no pieces bigger than 1/3 inch)

Direction

- Into medium bowl, sift baking soda, cocoa and flour. Beat butter using electric mixer till smooth yet not fluffy in big bowl. Add sea salt, vanilla and both sugars; beat for 2 minutes till fluffy. Add flour mixture; beat till just blended (it might be crumbly). Add the chopped chocolate; mix to just distribute. Lightly knead in bowl to make ball if dough won't come together. Halve dough. On plastic wrap sheet, put each half. Shape each to 1 1/2-in. diameter log; in plastic, wrap each. Chill for 3 hours till firm. You can make it 3 days ahead, kept chilled.
- Preheat an oven to 325°F. Line parchment paper on 2 baking sheets. Crosswise cut logs to 1/2-in. thick rounds using thin sharp knife. Put on prepped sheets, 1-in. apart; bake 1 sheet at 1 time for 11-12 minutes till cookies look dry (won't be golden at edges or firm). Put on rack; cool. You can make it 1 day ahead; keep airtight in room temperature.

Nutrition Information

- Calories: 89
- Sodium: 36 mg(1%)
- Fiber: 1 g(3%)
- Total Carbohydrate: 12 g(4%)
- Cholesterol: 9 mg(3%)
- Protein: 1 g(2%)
- Total Fat: 5 g(7%)
- Saturated Fat: 3 g(15%)

361. Yellow Cake

Serving: 12 | Prep: 15mins | Cook: 45mins | Ready in:

Ingredients

- 1 1/2 cups all-purpose flour
- 2 cups white sugar
- 2 teaspoons baking powder
- 4 eggs
- 1 cup vegetable oil
- 3/4 cup orange juice
- 2 teaspoons vanilla extract

Direction

- Preheat an oven to 175°C/350°F. Grease then flour 9x13-in. pan.
- Mix baking powder, sugar and flour in big bowl. Create a well in middle; add vanilla, orange juice, oil and eggs. Mix well; put into prepped pans.

- In the preheated oven, bake till inserted toothpick in middle of cake exits clean for 45 minutes; cool.

Nutrition Information

- Calories: 380 calories;
- Total Fat: 20
- Sodium: 84
- Total Carbohydrate: 47.2
- Cholesterol: 62
- Protein: 3.8

362. Yogurt Cake With Currant Raspberry Sauce

Serving: Makes 8 to 12 servings | Prep: 1hours | Cook: 2.75hours | Ready in:

Ingredients

- 3 cups sifted cake flour (not self-rising; sift before measuring)
- 2 teaspoons baking powder
- 1 teaspoons baking soda
- 1/2 teaspoon salt
- 2 sticks unsalted butter, softened
- 2 cups granulated sugar
- 2 teaspoons pure vanilla extract
- 3 large eggs, warmed in shell in warm water 10 minutes
- 2 cups well-stirred plain whole-milk yogurt (not Greek-style) atroom temperature 30 minutes
- 2 cups fresh red currants (1/2 pound), stemmed
- 4 cups fresh raspberries (16 ounces), divided
- 2/3 cup granulated sugar room temperature 30 minutes
- 3 cups confectioners sugar
- 3 tablespoons light corn syrup
- 1/2 cup heavy cream
- Scant 1/2 teaspoon pure vanilla extract
- Equipment: a 13- by 9-inch cake pan

Direction

- Cake: Preheat an oven with rack in center to 350°F. Butter a cake pan; line parchment paper rectangle on bottom. Butter parchment. Use flour to dust; knock excess out.
- Sift salt, baking soda, baking powder and cake flour together.
- Beat vanilla, sugar and butter with an electric mixer on high speed for 3-5 minutes till fluffy and pale. One by one, beat in eggs on medium speed; in 3 batches, mix in flour mixture together with yogurt, alternately, on low speed, starting and ending with flour mixture, mixing just till combined. Evenly spread batter in pan; rap pan on counter a few times to remove air bubbles.
- Bake for 35-45 minutes till inserted wooden pick in middle exits clean and cake pulls away from pan's sides; cool for 10 minutes in pan. Around edge, run a knife. Invert onto rack; discard parchment. Fully cool for 1 hour.
- As cake bakes, make sauce: Mix 1/8 tsp. salt, sugar, 2 cups raspberries and currants in medium saucepan then stand for 15 minutes till juicy; simmer for 8 minutes till fruit breaks down, occasionally mixing. Through fine-mesh sieve, force into bowl; discard solids. Cool the sauce.
- Icing and assemble cake: Mix vanilla, cream, corn syrup and confectioners' sugar till smooth.
- On a platter, put cake; in a thick layer, spread icing on top, letting it run down the sides. Set icing for a minimum of 15 minutes; serve with leftover 2 cups raspberries alongside and sauce.
- You can use 2 extra cups raspberries for red currants, if they are not available.
- Sauce keeps for 2 days, chilled.
- You can bake and ice cake 1 day ahead; keep in cake keeper/covered with inverted roasting pan without touching icing in room temperature.

Nutrition Information

- Calories: 808
- Sodium: 373 mg(16%)
- Fiber: 5 g(18%)
- Total Carbohydrate: 138 g(46%)
- Cholesterol: 127 mg(42%)
- Protein: 8 g(17%)
- Total Fat: 26 g(41%)
- Saturated Fat: 16 g(80%)

363. Zeppole

Serving: 35 | Prep: 15mins | Cook: 25mins | Ready in:

Ingredients

- 2 quarts vegetable oil for frying
- 1 cup all-purpose flour
- 2 teaspoons baking powder
- 1 pinch salt
- 1 1/2 teaspoons white sugar
- 2 eggs, beaten
- 1 cup ricotta cheese
- 1/4 teaspoon vanilla extract
- 1/2 cup confectioners' sugar for dusting

Direction

- In a deep-fryer, heat oil to 190 degrees C or 375 degrees F.
- Mix sugar, salt, baking powder, and flour in a medium saucepan. Mix in vanilla, ricotta cheese, and eggs. Gently mix on low heat until incorporated. Batter should be sticky.
- Drop by tablespoons in the hot oil, several at one time. The Zeppole should turn over on their own. Fry for 3 or 4 minutes until golden brown. Drain inside a paper sack then dust with confectioners' sugar. Serve while warm.

Nutrition Information

- Calories: 69 calories;
- Total Fat: 5.4
- Sodium: 24
- Total Carbohydrate: 4.7
- Cholesterol: 12
- Protein: 0.7

364. Zucchini Ginger Cupcakes

Serving: Makes 12 cupcakes | Prep: 15mins | Cook: 1hours | Ready in:

Ingredients

- 1/3 cup crystallized ginger (1 3/4 oz), coarsely chopped
- 2 cups all-purpose flour
- 1 teaspoon ground ginger
- 1 teaspoon ground cinnamon
- 1 teaspoon finely grated fresh orange zest
- 1 teaspoon salt
- 1 teaspoon baking soda
- 1/2 teaspoon baking powder
- 2 cups coarsely grated zucchini (2 medium)
- 3/4 cup mild olive oil
- 3/4 cup mild honey
- 2 large eggs, lightly beaten
- 1 teaspoon vanilla
- 8 oz cream cheese, softened
- 2 tablespoons unsalted butter, softened
- 1/2 cup confectioners sugar
- 1 teaspoon vanilla
- 1/2 teaspoon ground ginger
- 1/2 teaspoon ground cinnamon
- 1/2 teaspoon finely grated fresh orange zest
- a muffin pan with 12 (1/2-cup) cups; 12 paper liners

Direction

- Bake cupcakes: In the middle position, put oven rack; preheat the oven to 350°F. Line liners on muffin cups.
- Pulse crystallized ginger till finely ground in a food processor. Add baking powder, baking soda, salt, zest, cinnamon, ground ginger and flour; pulse till combined.

- Whisk vanilla, eggs, honey, oil and zucchini in medium bowl. Mix in flour mixture just till combined.
- Divide batter to muffin cups; bake for 20-24 minutes till inserted skewer/wooden pick in the middle of cupcake exits clean and cupcakes are golden.
- Cool for 10 minutes in pan on a rack. Take cupcakes out of the pan; fully cool for 1 hour.
- Frosting: Use an electric mixer on high speed to beat frosting ingredients for 3-5 minutes till fluffy and well combined.
- Frost cooled cupcake's tops.

Nutrition Information

- Calories: 393
- Saturated Fat: 7 g(35%)
- Sodium: 272 mg(11%)
- Fiber: 1 g(4%)
- Total Carbohydrate: 44 g(15%)
- Cholesterol: 57 mg(19%)
- Protein: 5 g(9%)
- Total Fat: 23 g(35%)

365. Zucchini Pecan Cake With Cream Cheese Frosting

Serving: Makes 10 servings | Prep: 50mins | Cook: 2hours35mins | Ready in:

Ingredients

- Nonstick vegetable oil spray
- 1 1/2 cups all purpose flour
- 1 1/2 teaspoons baking powder
- 1 teaspoon coarse kosher salt
- 1 teaspoon ground cinnamon
- 1/2 teaspoon ground ginger
- 1/4 teaspoon ground nutmeg
- 3/4 cup olive oil (not extra-virgin)
- 1 cup (packed) golden brown sugar
- 3 large eggs
- 1 teaspoon vanilla extract
- 1 1/2 cups coarsely grated zucchini (about 8 ounces)
- 3/4 cup chopped pecans
- 1/2 8-ounce package Philadelphia brand cream cheese (do not use reduced-fat or fat-free), room temperature
- 3 tablespoons unsalted butter, room temperature
- 3/4 cup powdered sugar
- 1/2 teaspoon vanilla extract
- 1/2 teaspoon ground cinnamon

Direction

- Cake: Put rack in middle of oven; preheat it to 350°F. Line parchment paper on 9-in. diameter cake pan that has 2-in. high sides. Use nonstick spray to coat parchment paper.
- Whisk nutmeg, ginger, cinnamon, coarse salt, baking powder and flour to blend well in medium bowl. Whisk vanilla, eggs, sugar and oil to blend well in big bowl; fold into flour mixture then pecans and grated zucchini. Put cake batter in prepped pan.
- Bake cake for 45 minutes till inserted tester in middle exits clean; fully cool cake for 1 hour in pan on rack. To loosen, cut around pan's sides. Turn out cake on platter; peel parchment off.
- Frosting: Beat butter and cream cheese using electric mixer till blended in medium bowl; beat in vanilla, cinnamon and sugar. Thickly spread frosting on cake's top. You can make it 1 day ahead, chilled, covered.
- Cut cake to wedges. Serve.

Nutrition Information

- Calories: 501
- Fiber: 2 g(7%)
- Total Carbohydrate: 48 g(16%)
- Cholesterol: 77 mg(26%)
- Protein: 6 g(11%)
- Total Fat: 33 g(51%)
- Saturated Fat: 8 g(39%)
- Sodium: 305 mg(13%)

Index

A

Almond 3,4,6,7,8,9,10,26,31,47,52,102,109,183,184,242,260

Amaretti 6,188

Anise 3,5,7,12,13,125,228

Apple 3,4,5,7,14,103,119,221,263

Apricot 3,6,7,10,14,15,16,202,224,239

B

Bacon 3,17

Bagel 6,98,204

Baking 141

Banana 3,4,5,7,17,20,21,69,84,153,237,263

Basil 5,146

Berry 7,246,267

Biscotti 3,7,25,248

Black sesame seeds 26

Blackberry 3,4,14,111

Blini 3,4,26,27,89

Blueberry 3,27,28

Bran 3,38,39

Bread 3,4,5,6,7,30,77,84,88,105,153,208,211,219,241

Brie 152,180

Brioche 3,30

Butter 3,4,5,6,7,8,14,16,18,19,23,26,27,29,31,32,35,36,37,43,52,56,62,66,67,72,74,77,83,86,88,90,91,94,96,97,98,100,102,107,113,114,116,118,119,125,130,135,142,143,147,148,149,154,155,158,159,162,163,164,166,167,170,174,177,178,180,182,183,184,186,190,191,192,193,197,198,199,203,206,215,216,226,230,232,233,234,235,245,246,253,254,255,256,257,263,265,267,269

C

Cake 3,4,5,6,7,9,20,21,22,25,27,28,29,33,34,35,40,49,52,53,58,59,60,61,66,68,71,72,77,78,79,80,81,82,83,84,86,89,90,91,96,97,98,99,100,101,103,107,108,109,110,114,115,121,128,133,134,135,137,138,145,148,149,154,156,157,163,167,171,174,177,178,180,183,184,197,198,199,202,203,208,213,214,215,217,222,223,229,230,231,232,233,234,244,245,246,249,252,254,255,256,258,260,264,268,269,271

Calvados 42

Caramel 3,4,6,40,41,42,43,52,54,67,75,77,180,192,193,195

Cardamom 3,4,43,44,88

Carrot 4,5,71,137

Cashew 3,44

Caviar 3,26

Celery 7,221

Champ 162

Chantilly cream 254

Chard 128

Cheddar 3,45

Cheese 3,4,5,6,7,33,39,45,46,50,63,92,93,98,108,126,138,143,153,162,186,189,195,197,219,223,234,235,271

Cherry 3,4,5,6,7,31,47,48,49,70,102,163,218,219,255

Chestnut 3,50

Chicken 3,5,51,125

Chicory 3,58

Chipotle 3,57

Chips 98

Chocolate 3,4,5,6,7,20,22,23,39,40,48,52,53,54,55,56,57,58,59,60,61,62,63,64,65,66,67,68,69,70,71,72,73,74,75,81,85,96,98,100,101,107,112,114,121,130,149,155,159,163,167,168,169,17

0,179,181,183,193,198,200,201,205,217,228,229,233,248,254,255,258,261,263,264

Chutney 5,138

Cinnamon 3,4,7,18,29,38,57,77,258

Coconut 3,4,5,18,52,79,80,81,82,83,84,85,86,138

Coffee 3,4,5,27,58,88,107,158

Cognac 128,174

Crab 6,171

Crackers 4,7,106,227

Cranberry 4,7,91,103,232

Cream 3,4,5,6,7,15,20,28,29,33,36,37,45,55,57,62,63,65,66,67,81,88,92,93,95,108,110,111,116,117,130,133,134,143,155,158,159,161,173,176,184,188,191,192,197,200,204,229,230,231,234,238,239,254,256,257,258,259,271

Crisps 3,5,7,8,144,241

Crostini 98

Crumble 6,7,110,187,222,233

Curd 5,6,164,187

Curry 5,125

Custard 3,4,5,24,42,43,94,146

D

Dal 7,250

Dark chocolate 100

Date 3,4,5,7,13,98,131,261

E

Egg 3,4,5,7,10,30,99,104,122,146,205,224,258

F

Fat 5,8,9,10,11,12,13,14,15,16,17,18,19,20,21,22,23,24,25,26,27,28,30,31,32,35,36,37,38,39,40,42,44,45,46,48,49,50,51,52,53,55,56,57,58,59,61,63,64,65,66,67,68,69,71,72,73,74,75,77,78,79,80,81,82,83,84,85,86,87,89,90,91,92,93,94,95,96,99,100,101,102,103,104,105,106,107,108,110,111,112,113,114,115,116,117,118,119,120,121,124,125,126,127,129,130,131,132,133,134,136,137,138,139,141,142,143,144,145,146,147,148,150,151,152,153,154,155,157,158,159,160,161,162,163,164,166,168,171,172,173,175,176,177,178,179,180,181,182,183,185,186,187,188,189,190,191,192,193,194,195,196,197,198,200,201,202,203,204,206,207,208,209,210,211,212,213,214,215,216,217,218,219,220,221,222,223,224,225,227,228,229,230,231,233,234,235,236,237,238,239,240,241,242,243,244,246,247,248,249,250,251,252,253,254,255,256,257,258,259,260,261,263,264,268,269,270,271

Fennel 4,6,105,179

Feta 251,252

Fig 3,4,13,105,106

Flatbread 5,6,127,179

Flour 4,107,220

Focaccia 7,247,248

French bread 211

Fruit 3,4,5,6,26,42,70,73,138,173,180,185,254

Fudge 40

G

Garlic 7,263

Gin 3,5,6,7,24,33,51,115,116,117,118,119,120,155,216,249,256,270

Gouda 7,235

Grapefruit 5,7,124,228

Grapes 5,124,162

Gratin 3,8

Green tea 127

H

Ham 5,128

Hazelnut 3,4,5,6,59,61,62,128,130,205,217

Heart 7,221

Honey 5,116,125,128,131,132,141,154,156

I

Ice cream 119,200

Icing 6,7,44,183,222,232,269

J

Jam 7,239

Jus 128,219

K

Kumquat 5,128

L

Lemon 3,4,5,6,7,28,29,33,110,111,136,142,143,144,145,146,147,148,149,150,151,153,164,165,173,236,241,261,264,265

Lime 5,6,7,138,139,151,208,250

Liqueur 4,107

M

Macadamia 3,4,40,84,86

Mace 5,87,154,255

Madeleines 5,132,147,154

Mango 7,250

Marmalade 165

Marshmallow 5,150

Marzipan 70

Mascarpone 6,7,152,189,223

Meringue 3,4,5,6,14,109,110,113,120,156,173,190,198,199

Milk 5,6,7,29,133,168,169,261

Mince 6,114,158,170

Mint 4,5,6,63,72,126,172,173

Molasses 6,7,176,256

Muffins 4,6,88,102,211

N

Nectarine 6,177,178

Noodles 7,225

Nougat 6,169,170

Nut 3,4,8,9,10,11,12,13,14,15,16,17,18,19,20,21,22,23,24,25,26,27,28,30,31,32,35,36,37,38,39,40,41,42,44,45,46,48,49,50,51,52,53,55,56,57,58,59,60,61,63,64,65,66,67,68,69,71,72,73,74,75,76,77,78,79,80,81,82,83,84,85,86,87,89,90,91,92,93,94,95,96,99,100,101,102,103,104,105,106,107,108,110,111,112,113,114,115,116,117,118,119,120,121,124,125,126,127,129,130,131,132,133,134,136,137,138,139,141,142,143,144,145,146,148,150,151,153,154,155,157,158,159,160,161,162,163,164,166,168,171,172,173,175,176,177,178,179,180,181,182,183,185,186,187,188,189,190,191,192,193,194,195,196,197,198,200,201,202,203,204,206,207,208,209,210,211,212,214,215,216,217,218,220,221,222,223,224,225,227,228,229,230,231,232,233,234,235,236,237,238,239,240,241,242,243,244,246,247,248,249,250,251,252,253,254,255,256,257,258,259,260,261,263,264,267,268,269,270,271

O

Oatmeal 3,4,7,48,94,250

Oil 10,31,36,41,78,153,176,187,205

Olive 5,161,251

Onion 5,6,123,179

Orange 3,4,5,6,7,34,53,63,65,71,72,73,96,97,108,114,118,132,180,181,182,183,184,239,253,260,265

P

Pancakes 6,218

Panettone 6,185

Parfait 3,6,54,213,216

Parmesan 7,223,224,236

Parsnip 7,263

Pasta 7,224

Pastry 95,199,221,231

Peach 4,5,6,86,120,188,189,190,213

Peanuts 4,74

Pear 3,4,6,7,25,91,212,220,221,254,258

Pecan 3,4,5,6,7,26,37,73,131,195,196,197,230,231,271

275

Peel 8,29,33,58,79,99,114,122,199,210,214,231,234,249

Pepper 3,4,6,25,64,99,100,198,199,200

Pesto 7,223

Pie 3,4,5,6,7,20,22,24,28,57,81,123,124,141,188,191,201,231,253

Pineapple 4,6,83,84,202,203

Pistachio 6,203,204

Plum 3,6,10,46,205,206

Pomegranate 6,7,208,260

Port 6,47,169,205

Potato 3,4,5,6,17,78,93,137,161,209

Praline 3,4,6,10,59,60,62,195

Prune 6,210

Puff pastry 19

Pulse 10,24,61,62,63,95,145,151,218,228,256,261,270

Pumpkin 4,6,7,108,211,234

Q

Quark 3,15

R

Raisins 5,155

Raspberry 4,5,6,7,66,70,112,126,150,174,212,213,214,267,269

Rhubarb 6,215,216

Ricotta 5,6,7,153,218,219

Roquefort 7,221,222

Rosemary 4,89,90,91

Rum 3,6,16,20,46,84,174

S

Salsa 4,89

Salt 6,7,134,217,224,242

Sausage 3,51

Savory 7,223

Semolina 7,226

Sesame seeds 125

Shallot 7,235

Sherry 128,216,222

Shortbread 3,5,47,57,159

Spinach 7,235,236

Strawberry 4,7,71,238,256

Sugar 3,4,5,6,7,22,25,32,33,55,74,75,103,116,133,151,159,218,239,257

Syrup 4,5,6,89,90,91,114,147,175,184,189,260

T

Tangerine 4,7,63,242

Tapioca 3,6,26,182

Tea 3,5,7,25,54,126,244

Terrine 4,74,75

Thyme 5,7,147,241,261

Toffee 7,237

Tomato 4,7,89,223,247

Trout 7,227,250

Truffle 4,75

V

Vegetable oil 26,46,157,218,260

Vodka 5,147

W

Walnut 3,4,5,7,20,21,106,112,158,159,258,259,260,261

Whipping cream 227

White chocolate 100

Y

Yam 3,18

L

lasagna 226

Conclusion

Thank you again for downloading this book!

I hope you enjoyed reading about my book!

If you enjoyed this book, please take the time to share your thoughts and post a review on Amazon. It'd be greatly appreciated!

Write me an honest review about the book – I truly value your opinion and thoughts and I will incorporate them into my next book, which is already underway.

Thank you!

If you have any questions, **feel free to contact at:** *publishing@crumblerecipes.com*

Mary Traylor

crumblerecipes.com

Printed in Great Britain
by Amazon